A World of Homeowners

HISTORICAL STUDIES OF URBAN AMERICA

Edited by Lilia Fernández, Timothy J. Gilfoyle, Becky M. Nicolaides, and Amanda Seligman

James R. Grossman, editor emeritus

ADDITIONAL SERIES TITLES FOLLOW THE INDEX.

A World of Homeowners

*American Power and
the Politics of Housing Aid*

NANCY H. KWAK

The University of Chicago Press   Chicago and London

PUBLICATION OF THIS BOOK HAS BEEN AIDED BY A GRANT
FROM THE BEVINGTON FUND.

The University of Chicago Press, Chicago 60637
The University of Chicago Press, Ltd., London
Published 2015
Paperback edition 2018
Printed in the United States of America

27 26 25 24 23 22 21 20 19 18   1 2 3 4 5

ISBN-13: 978-0-226-28235-0 (cloth)
ISBN-13: 978-0-226-59825-3 (paper)
ISBN-13: 978-0-226-28249-7 (e-book)
DOI: https://doi.org/10.7208/chicago/9780226282497.001.0001

Library of Congress Cataloging-in-Publication Data
Kwak, Nancy H., 1973– author.
   A world of homeowners : American power and the politics of housing
aid / Nancy H. Kwak.
      pages ; cm
   Includes bibliographical references and index.
   ISBN 978-0-226-28235-0 (cloth : alk. paper)—ISBN 978-0-226-28249-7
(ebook) 1. Home ownership—United States—History—20th century.
2. Home ownership—Political aspects—United States. 3. Housing
policy—United States. 4. Federal aid to housing—United States—
History—20th century. 5. Federal aid to housing—Political aspects—
United States. I. Title.
      HD7287.82.U6K93 2015
      363.5'820973—dc23   2015001693

♾ This paper meets the requirements of ANSI/NISO Z39.48–1992
(Permanence of Paper).

Contents

Introduction

We have built up in the minds of our people—and of the world—the belief that the American system makes it possible for all to live at least at the American minimum standard of decency. RAYMOND M. FOLEY, ADMINISTRATOR OF THE US HOUSING AND HOME FINANCE AGENCY (1950)[1]

At the end of World War II, American advisors began urging countries around the world to embrace the ideal of mass homeownership. More accessible, mortgage-driven home-ownership could simultaneously strengthen democratic governments and capitalism, they argued. The war had decimated some cities and left others with an excess of newcomers and a shortage of building materials. More housing, better housing, was needed everywhere. With large-scale national reconstruction plans in the works, what better time was there to rethink housing policy at the highest levels?

US dominance in the postwar global economy led traveling American advisors and experts to believe they could exert greater influence over the architecture of nascent housing industries around the world. In building a new international language of homeownership, however, these men and women did not—indeed, could not—impose their own ideas wholesale. Newly independent or transitional states hardly welcomed another imperial power, and American experts themselves did not concur on all points. Rather, local implementation reflected processes of negotiation. At times, participants in this negotiation were highly unequal, as in cases where US aid money outmuscled local or national considerations; other times, Americans proved surprisingly

WWII ↓ need for homes ↓ new housing policy

1

powerless to implement their ideas on foreign soil. National prejudices could shape policy, but ideas also flowed readily across state lines, with actors observing best practices and learning from each other without regard for national origin. Misinformation and individual caprice played equally important roles in shaping the evolution of global housing finance. The commodification of homes, the legitimization of some forms of ownership over others, the transformation of housing into investment vehicles, and the expansion of global management of housing credit and debt were not inevitable steps in the evolution of capitalism, but rather the products of specific actors and institutions yielding highly variable outcomes.

If housing and financing programs varied greatly from place to place in actual implementation, Americans were nonetheless highly successful in one important regard: they persuaded many governments to push local, undocumented land uses to the margins and to consider formal homeownership as a long-term goal for the masses. In urging mass homeownership, American advisors often pushed at an open door. Given the practical limits of land and money, many governments willingly accepted that increased access to bank-based, state-regulated homeownership could build up a middle class which would, in turn, stabilize politics while nurturing local building trades and strengthening labor markets. This interconnected set of ideals and practical needs brought together ideas about democracy—whether through widespread access to a consumer economy, a more diffuse sense of equality, or specifically anticommunist dogma—with a very specific, "modern" version of debt-driven, state-regulated ownership that gave at least the illusion of growing affluence and security. This was mass ownership of housing, but it was also something more: it had positive implications for the character of the state facilitating this sort of consumption. Citizens would surely applaud a government that installed a more modern, homeowning society.

Mass homeownership also proved a critical building block for a larger, more pervasive American model of capitalism that connected open markets to democratic institutions by the early twenty-first century.[2] It fueled the expansion of global capitalism by standardizing local processes of housing and land valuation, use, and tenure into a uniform system facilitating national and international investment. As more people participated in a globalizing property and credit system, more of the urban landscape included infrastructure friendly to corporate investment, which in turn resulted in more policymakers accepting massive urban resettlement, relocation, and modernization schemes as

The U.S. tried to bring their influence internationally, but it was only adopted piecemeal

Motives for formalization

a desirable corollary to the goal of "decent homes in wholesome surroundings for low-income families now living in the squalor of the
slums"—to broaden president Harry Truman's words to an international
context.[3] Implicit and reinforced in this system was the belief that the
middle class served as a critical anchor for political stability, and that
homeownership not only anchored the middle class but actually created
it. By giving families the "ontological security" found through control
over their physical space, homeownership proponents argued, participants would have strengthened commitment to property rights and to
greater civic engagement.[4]

Vastly different constituencies found this formula compelling, not
because American housing experts and advisors single-mindedly forced
this ideal upon others, or because capitalist markets followed an inexorable logic, but rather because the homeownership formula had the
potential to satisfy wide-ranging political needs.[5] It appealed to US government officials by nurturing a global middle class and protecting geopolitical Cold War interests, while also opening up potential investment
opportunities for American businesses. Policymakers and politicians in
postcolonial or transitional governments leapt at the potential mobilization of savings and the generation of development capital. Some hoped
US capital assistance would accompany technical advice. Others simply
craved the potential political calm and "buy in" from a greater number of citizens. From the point of view of everyday citizens, modern
homeownership tapped into longstanding desires for landownership,
and housing and human rights advocates around the world welcomed
what they hoped would become greater access for lower-income families with all the benefits of tenure security implicit in property ownership. Recovering European nations looked to American bilateral aid
programs for assistance rebuilding—or in some cases, building for the
first time—modern infrastructure in devastated urban landscapes. In a
more bizarre twist, European imperial officers also took advantage of US
and intergovernmental training programs in order to gather planning
and housing ideas that might be applied toward winning back colonial
authority. From a variety of perspectives, then, mass homeownership
had mass appeal.

What were the mechanisms by which Americans directed their attention to overseas housing programs? During the immediate postwar
decades, most efforts flowed through two administrative branches: first,
there was the International Housing Service within the Office of the
Administrator of the Housing and Home Finance Agency (HHFA, 1947–
65), replaced in 1966 by the Office of International Affairs in the new

Why adopted

How?
HHFA/HUD and Dept. of State agencies

Department of Housing and Urban Development (HUD, 1965–); and second, there were the Economic Cooperation Administration (1948–51), the Technical Cooperation Administration (TCA, 1950–53), the Mutual Security Administration (MSA, 1951–53), the Institute of Inter-American Affairs, (1942–53), the Foreign Operations Administration (FOA, 1953–55), the International Cooperation Administration (ICA, 1955–61), and the US Agency for International Development (USAID, 1961–) within the Department of State. The first cluster—namely, the HHFA and HUD—dealt exclusively with housing issues. The HHFA and HUD managed subordinate branches including the Federal Housing Administration (FHA, 1934–), the Public Housing Administration, the Federal National Mortgage Association (FNMA, or Fannie Mae, 1938–), and the Urban Renewal Administration; for these organizations, international housing was a subset of all housing matters. The second cluster, meanwhile, dealt with all bilateral aid programs not under the purview of the Department of Defense. For the second group, housing was one of many areas within the category of development assistance. New housing programs emerged from the bilateral Marshall Plan, Point Four, Development Loan Fund, the Export-Import Bank of the US, and Public Law 480 (later renamed Food for Peace). Housing aid was incorporated into a wide array of missions, from the planning and construction of entire communities to more dispersed technical assistance and training programs.

Whether through institutional frameworks or personal contacts, Americans exulted at the possibility of teaching the world. In a letter to friend and fellow planner Catherine Bauer, housing expert Charles Abrams observed, "I find myself talking more and more about the international scene which should offer as piquant a frontier to the Bauer pioneers as housing did in 1933. In fact it is very odd that we got into federal housing on the basis of what foreign countries were doing, and now foreign countries are looking to America to find out how they should do things."[6] HHFA administrator Raymond Foley concurred with this perspective on international exchange: "Since the end of the war," Foley wrote in 1950, "the United States has become, in a large sense, a major laboratory in housing development, and has drawn a total of almost five hundred missions—experts and officials engaged in housing and urban redevelopment—to its shores."[7] Americans like Charles Abrams, Jacob Crane, Henry S. Churchill, Catherine Bauer, William Wurster, and Elizabeth Wood traveled, observed, and advised on such diverse topics as town planning, housing, transportation, savings-and-loan programs, and estate management in Singapore, India, Ireland, Taiwan, South Korea,

Syria, Kenya, Nigeria, and Jamaica. As they traveled and worked in the field, they became correspondingly more self-confident in their advisory capacities. Working alongside Frederic Osborn, Otto Koenigsberger, Jacqueline Tyrwhitt, John F. C. Turner, Anatole Solow, Constantinos Doxiadis, Susume Kobe, Antonio Kayanan, and other architects and planners from around the world, these Americans saw themselves as part of a small elite capable of educating, advising, and otherwise guiding the way out of an international housing crisis. If the emphasis on homeownership was American, the interest in housing was global.

The fact that prominent figures *believed* they led the way did not actually make it so, of course. In reality, countless low- and high-ranking government officials, investors, savings-and-loan experts, former military personnel, scientists, secretaries, laborers, and more played equal— sometimes greater—parts in deciding the character of exchange. Even at the highest levels of intergovernmental organization, the list of contributing bodies indicates some of the breadth of actors involved: the Economic and Social Council, Bureau of Social Affairs, Secretariat, and Educational, Scientific, and Cultural Organization (all within the UN), the International Labour Office, the Food and Agriculture Organization, the World Health Organization, and the International Federation for Housing and Town Planning (among others) brought ideas and money to bear on the universal problem of decent shelter. American participants cooperated with other international experts in these organizations, and exerted varying degrees of influence within them. Here, details matter: in certain projects and places, American advisors exhibited greater interest and wielded more influence than in others. These intricate relationships constitute a critical part of this history.

Funding trails tell a complex story as well. American dollars disproportionately paid for work in the field, sometimes with direct impacts. When the Philippines requested advice, for instance, the National Housing Agency in Washington, DC, and the US Navy paid for US experts N. J. Demerath and Richard N. Kuhlman to research and write two influential reports in 1945 and 1946.[8] The latter publication recommended that the Philippine government "undertake steps to lower the costs of home financing to borrowers acquiring home properties through the use of long-term, high-ratio, amortized loans at low interest rates to approved borrowers"—a recommendation subsequently incorporated into the Philippines Republic Act 580 (1950).[9] In another effort, USAID provided approximately $10 million to fund an experimental Investment Guaranty Program for Latin American pilot demonstration programs of homeownership in the early 1960s, and by the end of that same decade, total "seed" loans had risen to approximately $550 million. (They were called "seed" loans because they were meant to jumpstart and eventually be replaced by domestic savings.)[10]

Dollars did not always translate into direct policy results, however. In South and Southeast Asia in the 1950s and '60s, for instance, colonial, transitional, and then independent governments may have courted American technical and capital assistance, but they also had to contend with preexisting patterns of European colonial housing. Competing internal factions and intense debate over future government action often pushed external influences to the margins. Newly independent countries faced the daunting prospect of modernizing an entire economy and not merely the housing sector; many governments balked at pouring limited resources into long-term financial commitments for extensive housing improvement, and leading economists supported the view of housing as a pure social expenditure and an unproductive investment.[11] Political and economic incentives for mass homeownership required local tuning, then. Bolstering mass homeownership in the US meant something entirely different from attempting the same in the developing world. It also meant something different from site to site and group to group *within* the developing world. Given the wide array of participants in international housing and US aid programs, and given the diversity of conditions on the ground, it is all the more remarkable that the idea of mass homeownership spread globally.

In the US, the homeownership ideal had begun forming from at least the mid-nineteenth century. Tracts on pastoral-republican suburbanization, Calvin Coolidge's call for a "Nation of Home-Owners," the Better Homes in America Movement, the Architects' Small House Service Bureau, and the Home Modernizing Bureau all helped build an ideology that connected national identity with single-family owner occupancy.[12] For increasing numbers of white Americans, homeownership grew from aspiration to reality as Depression-era institutions like the FHA and Fannie Mae worked alongside the GI Bill of 1944 to open up participation in ostensibly private, heavily government-supported "market" housing. By the postwar years, American experiences with FHA and Veterans Administration (VA) mortgage guarantees along with the expanded federal role in the secondary mortgage market via Fannie Mae became critical institutional benchmarks by which policymakers outside the US might chart their course. Even in countries with minuscule middle classes or overwhelming housing shortages, even in nations with unmitigated urban poverty, the idea of wider access to homeownership gained ground. In the US, critics like Abrams, sociologist John P. Dean,

National Identity

Buhl Foundation director Charles Lewis, sociologist Robert Lynd, and former administrator of the USHA Nathan Straus all sounded cautionary notes, but few heard them in domestic housing debates, as Americans marched ever forward toward mass homeownership.[13]

The World Bank played a particularly important role in normalizing an American version of mass homeownership at the end of the twentieth century. In its sites-and-services, slum upgrading, market enabling, and finally, sector-wide initiatives from the 1970s to the 2000s, the Bank urged techniques and institutions specific to the American experience. While its programs did not always progress in predictable ways, traveling advisors nonetheless helped spread awareness of American models.

By the twenty-first century, elements of the American homeownership ideal had become commonly accepted wisdom across the world. Even the UN took for granted the value of low-income homeownership, with secretary general Kofi Annan praising innovative techniques like shelter microfinance in 2005, describing it as one step toward less government-subsidized, more "effective shelter financing systems."[14] Peruvian economist Hernando de Soto's widely embraced polemic *The Mystery of Capital* built upon the homeownership ideal, arguing that the formalization of land titles in the developing world would provide badly needed collateral for entrepreneurial credit. If "the single most important source of funds for new business in the United States is a mortgage on the entrepreneur's house," de Soto argued, homeownership could just as easily open access to capital in third world and former communist cities.[15] World Bank housing experts concurred, declaring de Soto's observations "almost certainly correct," if oversimplified in their emphasis on titling. Broadly, clarified property rights could confer "enormous benefits on many poor families."[16]

It was the form of that property right, then, that remained contentious, and public intellectuals and scholars sounded early, persistent warnings about mass homeownership.[17] Still, the World Bank believed developing countries were marching inexorably toward housing finance systems that encouraged private ownership, with Chile, China, India, Jordan, Kazakhstan, South Korea, Malaysia, Mexico, Poland, Singapore, and the Baltic states all boasting their own "functioning housing finance system" by 2001—up from just one (Colombia) in the 1980s.[18] Ultimately, it took an American subprime mortgage meltdown followed by a global financial crisis to raise serious questions about the value of mass homeownership as a general ideal. Only in 2008 did UN special rapporteur Raquel Rolnik's two-part criticism of the "transfer of responsibility for provision of housing to the private market" and the accepted wisdom that "homeownership was the best option for all" at long last mark an era of serious debate about the more pointedly undemocratic, ineffective, and at times destructive aspects of the current homeowner-ship system.[19] Looking back, it is clear that there was nothing natural or inevitable about each man wanting to own his own house. Rather, current iterations of the homeownership ideal were the products of countless negotiations, and inextricably tied to gendered, racialized ideas about citizenship. The fact that housing systems overseas at times resembled those of the US likewise indicated a history of exchange and interaction rather than a rational progression.

Not inevitable + gendered + racialized

It remains to be seen whether the most recent housing crisis will mark the beginning of a new era of thinking about mass homeownership. At the very least, the crisis does seem to have opened up a more frank dis-cussion of class mobility and housing access. Hopefully, the long-term effect will be lively public debates about real costs and benefits rather than a return to uncritical, indiscriminate praise for the American dream of homeownership. This books ends with the start of the US housing crisis—not because the homeownership ideal disappeared in the late 2000s—but rather because it remains to be seen what will happen in the coming decades and what the most recent crisis will mean for home-ownership in the long run.

This book charts the story of mass homeownership from the American housing landscape and booming economy of the 1940s, its evolution as a tool of foreign policy and as a vehicle for international investment during the 1950s, '60s, and '70s, the application of lessons learned to lower-income homeownership programs in the US, especially in the first two formative decades of the 1960s and 1970s, and finally, the diffusion of ideas about homeownership as seen in the strategies of international agencies like the World Bank from the 1980s to early 2000s. While the scope of research is global, this story centers on American engagements with the world vis-à-vis housing.

This is not a comprehensive history of either American foreign aid or of international housing. Local, national, and regional housing ex-periences deserve separate telling, and concurrent stories of American foreign policy, global development, modernization campaigns, human rights efforts, and the like are vast topics outside the scope of this single volume. Rather, this book focuses on the complicated role of American housing aid specifically with regard to tenure type. Countries did not consider mass homeownership programs by pure happenstance. Single-country or even regional studies can omit the ways in which mass homeownership evolved at the transnational, international, or global levels. Yet houses were without doubt transnational objects built by ideas and ideals flowing across borders, international symbols serving as focal points for competing national identities and state-to-state relations, and sophisticated global commodities brought about by globalizing markets and methods.

Chapter 1 begins by explaining the transformation of single-family homeownership in the US from dream to right for middle-class white American families. This transformation had international dimensions: up to the early 1940s, reformers, housing activists, and some politicians actively engaged European counterparts in crafting domestic housing policies that engaged the state, as a regulatory, and for a brief moment, as a progressive force. During and after World War II, however, the federal government shied away from "socialistic" government housing programs such as those developed in Britain, and congressional representatives embraced exceptionalist narratives about the US's system of housing vis-à-vis cooperative programs such as those developed in Denmark, Norway, Sweden, the Netherlands, France, and Switzerland. US business interests actively rejected any attempt to experiment with European housing ideas that might push private builders to the sidelines. Instead, they subsumed an unprecedentedly large federal government role in postwar housing construction and mortgage issuance under a language of free-market rights. As older bonds of transatlantic social politics loosened and fell apart, builders, banks, and realtors gained the upper hand in shaping a uniquely American social and spatial order based on mass homeownership.

This seeming contraction of American global housing interests did not result in isolationism. Instead, a new confidence in American housing successes inspired countless individuals from all walks of the political and social spectrum to interact with (in their words, to "educate") the rest of the world. These international ambitions took on a much more urgent tone as Cold War concerns gave Americans immediate reasons for caring about overseas living standards. Chapter 2 scrutinizes the US government's Cold War motives in funding overseas housing assistance specifically in China, Taiwan, Burma, and South Korea from the late 1940s to the 1950s and '60s. Other countries and regions certainly played vital roles in American Cold War diplomacy, but Taiwan and South Korea were seminal for the first stage of American housing aid. In an effort to combat communism and establish market-based housing systems, American experts endorsed heavy-handed, sustained state involvement in these countries' housing production, distribution, and

CH 1:
Dream→
Right

Non-isolation

CH 2:
Cold War

management. Paradoxically, Cold War imperatives drove US advisors to set up self-help programs that depended heavily on state funding and management, and that were subsequently praised for showcasing capitalist housing at its best. Put simply, the success of aided self-help programs depended on the strength of the state. This approach to national housing policy also left American advisors unaware of local needs and customs, leading in turn to inaccurate assessments of policy success or failure. Despite these flaws, aided self-help techniques tested in East Asia were then exported to other parts of the world. (By contrast, American housing aid monies sent to places like Israel in the mid-1950s paid for "literally hundreds of communities and new settlements" but had less impact on American housing aid elsewhere, given that the assistance was "short-lived" and "primarily financial rather than technical.")[20]

CH 3: "tropical" decolonizing

Chapter 3 turns to the next wave of experimentation in the late 1950s and '60s, particularly in what was referred to as the "tropical" region. Through this seemingly neutral category, Americans joined conversations and attempted to exert indirect influence in politically sensitive, decolonizing areas of the world. Shelter in hot, humid climes could be best improved through government-aided self-construction, according to American HHFA officials. Aided self-help, in turn, only worked if builders owned their homes. At first, the US did not directly engage in areas just emerging from colonial rule (for instance, sub-Saharan Africa, India, and much of the Caribbean), but instead experimented with "tropical" aided self-help in the territory of Puerto Rico. Only after practices were proven effective did American experts urge organizations like the Caribbean Commission to emulate the Puerto Rican model. Americans could not ultimately control their influence, however. "Tropical" territories and nations like the Philippines responded to American advisors and aid with housing programs that included elements of mass homeownership, but in ways that were uniquely shaped by local and domestic politics. On close inspection, even the Puerto Rican model included a large public housing program that openly contradicted the much-praised emphasis on private market solutions.

CH 4: Latin America and businessmen investors

The East Asian and tropical housing cases underscore the importance of Cold War geopolitics in determining aid recipients. When issues of regional American security claimed State Department interest in the 1960s, housing programs followed. Chapter 4 tracks US housing aid to Latin America from the 1960s to the 1990s, but approaches questions of housing aid from the point of view of investors and businessmen. US private interests played a large role in moving housing aid away from support for improved low-*income* housing, to an emphasis on low-*cost* housing.

By looking at issues of production and finance instead of distribution, American builders and bankers successfully refocused foreign aid programs on homeownership support for small middle classes in countries like Peru, Bolivia, and Mexico. In so doing, investors—with the sanction of host governments and the praise of prospective homeowners—helped construct a global middle-class pattern of housing that resembled American counterparts in form. Single-family, owner-occupied homes appeared in large tracts of tidy clusters with cul-de-sacs and curvilinear roads. These new communities were deliberately single-use, residential spaces usually set apart physically from dense urban neighborhoods and often protected by gates and guards. Such housing provision more strikingly divided those who could afford to live in formal housing from those who had to make do in the informal sector.

Chapter 5 brings the story back to the United States from the late 1960s to the early 2000s, when overseas lessons about mass homeownership came to be reapplied in the domestic context. International disgust and dismay with American racial inequality reached a climax by the late 1960s, when many foreign governments summarily rejected US housing systems as a visible example of the deeply unjust treatment of minorities within the US. Beginning in the late 1960s and persisting through the late 1990s and 2000s, presidents and congressional members agreed that the federal government needed to address obvious racial inequalities by boosting minority homeownership rates with publicly funded incentives and creative business tactics. Techniques from abroad, including self-help incentives and housing investment guaranties, were reapplied to Indian reservations, inner-city communities of color, migrant worker camps, and poor rural areas, with sometimes positive, other times profoundly problematic, outcomes.

By the late twentieth century, mass homeownership had become unremarkable as an ideal, even if it was poorly understood in its various manifestations. The last chapter, chapter 6, looks at the way in which mass homeownership played out as accepted wisdom in the policies of the World Bank from the 1970s on. Up until that decade, the Bank had not exhibited much interest in directly addressing urban poverty, and its workers thought of housing primarily as welfare provision rather than generative investment. It was only in an era of explosive urban poverty and declining congressional support for American bilateral aid programs—in the words of USAID administrator John A. Hannah, a desire "to lower the US profile around the world"[21]—that the Bank took a more active role, beginning in Senegal, then moving to Tanzania, Zambia, Indonesia, the Philippines, and more. Bank officials shared

[handwritten margin notes: CH5: Domestic racial housing; CH6: World Bank]

common goals of privatization, strengthened mortgage institutions, and owner-occupied homeownership, but like those managing earlier US aid programs, they bumped up against innumerable practical difficulties as well as objections from residents. Tensions between homeownership-as-ideology and homeownership-as-practice would again dominate the story of housing aid, this time for the World Bank, and well into the twenty-first century.

In the end, this tension forms the core of this history: mass home-ownership was on the one hand, a normative vision of the good life all citizens deserved, and on the other, a practice that could perpetuate or even deepen undemocratic patterns of settlement. It is a complicated story, but surely one that deserves telling.

ONE

Building a New American Model of Homeownership

Certainly the precedent of Britain drives us to the conclusion that if we go into the public ownership of houses and apartments, we shall strike dangerously at the American tradition of home and farm ownership, thrift, and the incentives to individual effort and to saving. . . . Must we drink from the same bitter cup as Britain? MORTON BODFISH, UNITED STATES SAVINGS AND LOAN LEAGUE, 1949[1]

There is nothing particularly American about owning a house. For most of this country's history, the majority of citizens did not own their own abode, nor is it clear they uniformly aspired to do so given the financial risks and limitations. If Americans (like many others around the world) longed for security of tenure and for the peculiar freedoms that came with such tenure, they did not envision urban or suburban ownership in the specific form of a mass, government-backed, mortgage-based system until the twentieth century.[2] It was only in the cataclysm of the Great Depression that the federal government birthed institutions powerful enough to generate this form of modern homeownership for a wide swath of American society. The government did so primarily to assure bank stability and to rejuvenate the construction industry, but newly accessible long-term mortgages and an enlarged federal assumption of risk also opened up for the first time ideas about a *right* to homeownership that breathed life into idealized discourses of previous decades.

The 1930s saw a wave of new federal policies putting into action homeownership aspirations articulated since at least the late nineteenth century. The idea of a right to homeownership would quickly be repackaged as a staple of the "American dream," a longstanding reward for those Americans willing to work hard and do right. As a compelling symbol of "America, the Land of Freedom and the Home of peoples from all the earth, who have and seek the comforts derived from the pursuit of free enterprise," the homeownership ideology spread quickly across national boundaries.[3] American housing experts, itinerant planners, and aid givers exhorted others to adopt similar programs and institutions and to benefit from the comforts of free enterprise. Mass homeownership represented all that was best about American capitalism: more accessible, mortgage-driven homeownership could simultaneously strengthen democratic governments and global capitalism, fueling domestic savings and buy-in on the part of the populace while granting all citizens equal access to the good life. This chapter outlines the transition from progressive collaborations with European counterparts to a broader assertion of American leadership in the world, beginning with the transatlantic crossings of the late nineteenth and early twentieth centuries, and moving toward a new American model and explicit rejection of "socialistic" housing experiments particularly in Britain in the 1940s and '50s.

Background

From the mid-nineteenth century to the 1930s, housing advocates had carefully considered the shelter policies of their European counterparts, borrowing and learning from what they often perceived as more "advanced" international standards. Transatlantic crossings had flowed more freely westward: philanthropic and voluntary organizations like the American Octavia Hill Society emerged as an offshoot of English institutions, for instance, emphasizing housing reform as a function of moral and social "uplift" for residents.[4] Subsequent settlement house workers-turned-reformers like Lawrence Veiller exerted social control over slum dwellers in the late nineteenth century through housing codes and stringent regulations, and the 1901 Tenement House Law of New York served as a groundbreaking and prototypical product of this effort.[5] Veiller himself made a point of keeping abreast of cutting-edge European experiments and using this knowledge to inform the American housing scene. Although he ultimately rejected any large-scale public housing as "socialistic and undesirable class legislation" that was "foreign to the genius of the American people," Veiller nonetheless argued that European housing reforms set a "precedent" for Americans like himself, an example that would need to be regularly visited and observed.[6] Likewise, those who challenged Veiller's vision for housing reform relied on European examples to bolster their positions. Edith Elmer Wood, for example, probed the economic dimensions of working-class housing and for the first time advocated direct public housing provision for the poorest third of the nation by researching and comparing American housing with European examples. Wood praised Britain's achievements above all, noting that country had "set the highest standard for her working classes, and done the most to realize it, of any nation in the world."[7]

In the American housing scene, two different focuses emerged by the 1920s with respect to the urban slum problem, both fully engaged in transnational debates about how to improve housing in dense urban centers.[8] The first—the Progressive reformers—included such outspoken and well-known members as Mary Simkhovitch and Helen Alfred. This group focused more on the protection of slum dwellers through careful regulation and, by the early 1930s, direct federal construction of public housing on cleared urban slum sites. By contrast, the second group sought an end to disorderly cities and burgeoning slums through a regional, community-centered approach to urban planning. Wood joined forces with other likeminded intellectuals like Charles Harris Whitaker, Lewis Mumford, Clarence Stein, Henry Wright, Frederick L. Ackerman, Benton MacKaye, and Catherine Bauer, eventually forming a small but very influential group called the Regional Plan Association of America (RPAA, 1923). RPAA members drew upon their extensive European studies to urge regional solutions to American housing problems as well as to encourage alternate forms of tenure type such as cooperative housing.[9] Wood and Bauer were particularly enthusiastic and effective in their use of European research to reconceptualize American programs, although they were hardly alone in their embrace of modernist architecture, "garden city" experiments, or regional planning.[10] Core members of the RPAA brought different aspects of American urban planning into closer conversation with European counterparts: Whitaker, for instance, published reports on British war workers' housing in the journal of the American Institute of Architects beginning in 1917, and he sent New York City architect Frederick Ackerman to report back on further developments in British munitions towns.[11] (Wood would later claim that Ackerman's reports "prevented our war housing from taking the form of temporary wooden barracks.")[12] Mumford and Stein drew heavily from British garden city principles as well as German experiences to reconceptualize future design around principles of region-oriented development.

Bauer, meanwhile, adeptly applied European lessons to the fight for public housing in the US. According to US Housing Authority administrator Nathan Straus, American housing laws could be directly tied to European examples, for the 1937 US Housing Act launching federal support for public housing was "modeled on the most successful public housing experience in the world, that of England."[13] Whether reformers emphasized stringent city government enforcement of housing regulations, or RPAA "housers" argued for good shelter developed along the periphery or outside city limits in entirely separate new towns, perhaps with alternate tenure types such as cooperative housing and with full property taxation, both groups nonetheless depended upon and responded to debates that were unmistakably transatlantic.[14]

There were at least two reasons why this transatlantic progressivism dissolved by the end of World War II and the beginning of the Cold War. First, the rise of American economic power and the devastation of European cities created a new national hubris that reframed European cities as needy aid recipients rather than as laboratories for cutting-edge housing development. To many congressional representatives, Europeans did not look like they were in any position to teach others. Worse, openly subsidized housing programs looked alarmingly anti-American in the context of increasing Cold War tensions. Second, the public housing movement that had stimulated so much transatlantic research in the 1920s and '30s had largely lost the fierce political battle by World War II, even as FHA- and VA-supported homeownership campaigns became more powerful and omnipresent in the US. Although the Housing Act of 1937 officially created the federal United States Housing Authority (USHA) and established deep government subsidies with federally managed local implementation, the successful legal installation of these "core elements" resulted, not in "European-style communitarian Bauhaus developments," as some public housing advocates had hoped, but rather in angry debates over purported government extravagances, housing quality standards, and appropriate resident selection—debates that yielded austere, "generic, uninspired [public] housing blocks" by the mid-1950s, in the words of historian D. Bradford Hunt.[15] Unfortunately, no new generation took up these issues, and even fiery urban critic Lewis Mumford ruefully noted the absence of "fresh ideas and objectives" within his own cohort by the late 1940s and early 1950s.[16]

While public housing faltered, the real estate lobby and business interests whittled away at existing programs and the USHA and its successor organization, the Housing and Home Finance Agency (HHFA, 1947–

65) shifted to monumental projects that broke dramatically with preexisting neighborhoods and that set the groundwork for a host of new difficulties for public housing residents. From the beginning, motives for this sort of architecture were problematic: housing officials gravitated toward such forms in the hopes that new projects would "'dominate the neighborhood and discourage regression' to slum life" through sheer size.[17] Catherine Bauer wrote a particularly stinging critique of these programs in May 1957, decrying a public housing that "drags along in a kind of limbo, continuously controversial, not dead but never more than half alive."[18] While Bauer's words cut too close for beleaguered public housing advocates, she did make the astute observation that public housing was unnaturally separated from FHA-financed, suburban single-family housing, creating a bifurcated housing system—what scholar Gail Radford would later call a dual housing market. Planners should not have unquestioningly implemented British garden city plans and Bauhaus principles without adequate local adaptation, Bauer observed in hindsight.[19]

Homeownership programs suffered none of the malaise permeating public housing campaigns by the 1950s, as more families adopted middle-class values and habits, including "a life style based on family housing with gardens, in a good general environment fairly near to the open countryside . . . involv[ing] a massive move towards the suburbs and the exurbs" with a heavy emphasis on family life and the rearing of children, as well as on the pursuit of consumption and the apparent comforts found therein.[20] Riding on the federal legislative supports put into place by real estate interests, private developers like William Levitt helped transform the US into a suburban nation, converting a long-standing homeownership ideal from its nineteenth- and early twentieth-century forms to a very specific postwar reality. Perhaps one of the first nations to be directly influenced by US national homeownership efforts was Canada: one year after the creation of the FHA and the Federal Savings and Loan Insurance Corporation, the Dominion Housing Act of 1935 promoted long-term amortization and mortgage insurance as well as modeling the Canadian Home Insurance Plan on section 1 of the US Housing Act of 1934.[21]

The wane of transatlantic progressive exchange did not signal the end of American internationalism, however. Rather, market liberals and proponents of government-supported private housing envisioned a new role for themselves where housers and reformers had once flourished. In place of Edith Elmer Wood, Catherine Bauer, Lewis Mumford, Clarence Stein, and other progressive planners and experts came increasing numbers of American private industry representatives keen on exploring new markets for American housing products, members of Congress eager to witness the gratifying effects of American housing aid, and real estate men intent on proselytizing a new American "tradition" of government-backed private housing. This rising wave of international interactions was marked by bolder assertions of American leadership and an active promulgation of homeownership with a downplayed government role, as opposed to forthright public provision. Government assistance needed to be framed as a temporary measure, as tax "relief" rather than government "provision." Those progressives still active in international housing programs slipped into the language of this new American model: Jacob Crane, for instance, wrote extensive reports on urban land policies in German, Hungarian, French, and Italian cities, among others, but he also agreed with National Association of Real Estate Boards (NAREB) executive vice president Herbert Nelson that "it is a mistake to assume that land policies in European countries derive out of circumstances comparable to ours in this country."[22] Indeed, as Crane argued in a separate postwar housing plan written with Hugh R. Pomeroy, executive director of National Association of Housing Officials (NAHO), "We, as a people, set this objective of adequate housing for all families, not because . . . England is committed to such a program for her people and, therefore, it must be good for us [but because] it is what we, in the United States, want for our people and know that we can have."[23] Future policy needed to respect "a deep desire on the part of most families to own their own home," for "in this, rather than in slogans, lies the reality of our faith in democratic processes."[24]

An American model thus took shape, one that elicited resistance and, at times, passionate opposition by European counterparts. This was not a moment of isolationism or retreat, but rather an era of heightened international exchanges and observation distinct from the transatlantic progressivism that preceded it. Assertions of national identity would be threaded throughout debates about best housing designs and layouts, and the American side of the debate would come to be dominated by proponents of single-family, mortgage-driven, government-supported private housing. Those Americans still promoting public housing or suggesting alternate housing schemes would find their voices drowned out by the chorus of realtors, bankers, investors, and free-market congressional representatives. Even supporters of cooperative apartments like John D. Rockefeller, Jr. and Abraham Kazan in the 1920s and Herbert Nelson in the 1940s eventually lost the debate to the National Association of Home Builders (NAHB), which very effectively pointed out the high cost of direct loans for coop production in the midst of a Cold War—clearly "another excursion into Government-subsidized social-ism," from NAHB's point of view.[25]

Reversing the Anglo-American Special Relationship

These changes did not come abruptly in 1945, but rather evolved slowly through the war years. The shift in perceived leadership can most clearly be seen in Anglo-American interactions in the early to mid-1940s. If the US and Britain had a historic "special relationship," as Winston Churchill proposed in 1946, that relationship was increasingly based upon shared economic and security interests rather than a reflexive American deference for British progressive reform. To be sure, occasional flashes of progressive transatlantic exchange did still occur between planners like Mumford, Stein, Frederic J. Osborn, Patrick Abercrombie, and George Pepler. Even these limited progressive exchanges reflected shifting power dynamics, however, with Americans more eager to shape British urban planning practices than to borrow and learn from them.

British planners and government officials, for their part, found do-mestic needs urgent and pervasive during and after World War II. Plan-ning problems at home took center stage over any potential intellectual exchange with an ally. The postwar years presented a unique opportu-nity to remake the landscape—a chance to correct housing woes that were years in the making. The war had merely aggravated a preexist-ing malady, not created a new one: according to member of Parliament (MP) and minister of health Aneurin Bevan, "the housing problem for the lower income groups in this country [had] not been solved since the industrial revolution," and conditions certainly had not improved with two wars.[26] In the capital, the London County Council (LCC, 1889–1965) had begun to rectify the sorry state of affairs after World War I by building "homes fit for heroes."[27] Even the remarkable Housing, Town Planning Act of 1919 (Addison Act) resulted in only roughly 170,000 of the half million new units promised by July 1921, however.[28] The National Exchequer promised to subsidize local authority construction, but lack of funds prematurely aborted that program, and subsequent laws of the 1920s and early 1930s served more as stopgap measures than radical overhauls. During the worldwide depression of the 1930s, the al-ready sluggish pace of construction slowed further. Winston Churchill's promise of a great house-building machine succeeded only insofar as private middle-class housing construction was concerned, and that solely through unnaturally depressed interest rates, cheap labor, and low-cost building materials. Indeed, Churchill's plan "was never designed to serve the whole nation" or even the majority of the working class.[29]

World War II brought the shortage of affordable housing to calamitous conditions. Hitler's Luftwaffe leveled entire neighborhoods of the 117-square-mile Administrative County of London during the Battle of Britain (1940), and while planners rejoiced that German bombs had been "an active agent in slum clearance," a "fresh start" from the old "zoo paddocks," segregated spaces, and "appalling monotony" of uncontrolled urban growth, homeless Londoners probably felt less cheerful after three waves of air raids (September 1940–May 1941, June 1944–August 1944, September 1944–March 1945).[30] The capital bore the brunt of the attacks, with some neighborhoods suffering more than others. By 1941, the LCC had marked Bermondsey, Poplar, Stepney, Islington, and Shoreditch for new housing programs due to "considerable air raid damage."[31] The East End's docks and industries were particularly hard-hit. Scholar Michael Hebbert vividly describes the uneven nature of the devastation: "In the East End, Poplar High Street was almost intact but behind it stretched one of the most extensive areas of devastation in London. In the City of London, the main financial district around the Bank of England sustained only slight damage, but the warehousing districts west of Aldermanbury were obliterated."[32] Of London's two million houses (roughly one-sixth of the nation's housing stock), 90% suffered some form of damage, and in Bermondsey, "only four houses in every hundred came through the war unscathed."[33] An astounding 89,000 of the LCC's 98,000 homes would require repairs, and 2,500 would be completely destroyed by the end of war. Besides houses, the government and the LCC had to worry about infrastructural reconstruction issues like roads, sewage, water, and the general ordering of the city. A tangle of outdated legislation further complicated matters.

It was in this beleaguered state that British MPs and politicians began to exhibit greater curiosity about the housing techniques of their ally. Wartime exchanges with American planners were hardly organized: one New York architectural professor complained in 1940 that waves of eager European visitors were "shunted from pillar to post, from individual to individual, with a regular round robin of introductory letters, with a constant series of hopeful procrastinations."[34] Despite the lack of preparedness on the part of many American hosts, the flood continued unabated. While it might seem odd in retrospect that planners worked so avidly, some even risking travel across the Atlantic during wartime, British planners were convinced they needed to prepare well before the end of war. If they did not research and have plans ready by ceasefire, ad hoc reconstruction would destroy the possibility of large-scale reorganization.

The US played standard-bearer when it came to questions of modernization. In the fall of 1943, the Ministry of Works and Planning sent a mission of MPs and experts to complete a nationwide survey of American housing. In an interview held shortly before the trip, former LCC architect and MP Alfred Bossom predicted that the British would use more electricity, that they would "try to take as much drudgery as possible out of women's working day," and that they would "streamlin[e] on American lines . . . where practical."[35] He promised his constituents that Conservatives would build between four and five million new homes in the decade following war, and that modernization—presumably along American lines—would occur "chiefly in the interior," with "efforts . . . made to keep the exterior of buildings in harmony with their surroundings."[36] Like the Swiss architect Le Corbusier, Bossom imagined the US to be a forerunner in modern home technologies and a critical exemplar for any country seeking to modernize.[37] While the cultural and historical flavor of British homes deserved preservation, Bossom argued the actual operative machinery badly needed an American-style upgrade.

For those who could not or would not travel, ideas flowed across the Atlantic through a time-tested medium—the simple pamphlet. The writers of these humble booklets justified their publications despite wartime paper shortages by arguing the pamphlets served two mutually reinforcing functions: they transmitted ideas from one democratic country to another, and they put forward a positive image of democratic planning practices to the world. Architects and urban planners believed they waged a battle of ideas that was "psychologically bound up with our war effort."[38] Series like Francis Williams's "Democratic Order" or Frederic J. Osborn's "Rebuilding Britain" promoted the work of planners as a showcase of British preparedness and efficiency, and they touted the virtues of a democratic government ready to begin a reconstruction after Hitler's inevitable demise. In a democratically planned society, the "fundamental needs of the plain man" dominated planning, and to architect Patrick Abercrombie, resulting plans were "an affair upon which every man and woman has a right to express an opinion, and is, broadly speaking, as likely to be right as the expert!"[39]

Osborn proved particularly important in forming a personal bridge between the two continents. He argued British reconstruction depended heavily on international cooperation and aid, and he pointed to Lewis

Mumford's writings as a prime example of what might be learned from abroad. Although Mumford's proposals might be too "idealistic" or "impracticable" in their totality, Osborn endorsed "a qualified form" as a "most attractive aim"; for instance, Mumford's "poly-nucleated" (multicentered—in effect, decentered) city meshed well with Ebenezer Howard's "elemental truths."[40] (Howard was a British planner most noted for his advocacy of garden cities.) In 1942, Osborn requisitioned and received an essay from Mumford for his pamphlet series, a piece that Osborn praised as "another form of American aid to Britain, on generous lease-lend terms."[41] Avowing that Mumford's revelations about cities delved into fundamentals "transcend[ing] national boundaries and local variations," Osborn argued Mumford "disclose[d] and evaluate[d] facts and trends that [were] common to cities in America and Britain, if not in all parts of the world."[42] The eager editor added that Mumford's *The Culture of Cities* (1938) and *Faith for Living* (1940) had been widely read and that Britain herself was following the same basic principles of thought, for "though the texture of Mr. Mumford's presentation is very different from that of a Royal Commission, it is significant that in principle his conclusions are those of the *Barlow Report* [which argued for planned decentralization]. And the great objectives to which he gives priority are practicable objectives for Britain with the instruments we now have, or can have, in our hands."[43] Osborn nurtured American connections because he was convinced that the two countries were on the same track—Mumford's "conclusions are those of the Barlow Report"—and because he believed Americans could help modernize British town planning with "practicable objectives" and specific "instruments."[44]

This interest in American models reflected not only a lingering Anglo-American connection, but also a new and growing ambition among some British planners. Sir George Pepler (1882–1959) played a particularly key role in urging fellow British planners to develop a greater understanding of international developments, contending that only by studying other countries' housing problems and accomplishments could Britain stay globally competitive. Worldwide solutions to unregulated urban growth and indecent shelter had to be researched if the British intended to maintain at minimum comparable, and preferably superior, living standards. In arguing for systematic national planning with a more thorough study of international examples and standards, Pepler served as what biographer Myles Wright termed a sort of "John the Baptist" for post–World War II planning: "Pepler must have been conscious that the country was becoming ready for real planning and that a lot of the preparation had been his."[45]

Pepler's cosmopolitanism did not extend equally across the globe. He placed disproportionate emphasis on American examples, and as early as the Barlow Commission (1937–40), Pepler compared the "national menace" of unregulated British urbanization most closely with American and German experiences. Pepler also included more general summaries of Italian, Swedish, Dutch, Japanese, Polish, Indian, and Singaporean developments, but it was clear that the US—and New York in particular—stood out. If experts and national government worked together and were led by a visionary like New York City parks commissioner Robert Moses, much might be accomplished. Despite his attempts to maintain a neutral tone, the British planner's enthusiasm for Gotham could not be contained: Moses had achieved a "remarkable achievement" in the city, acquiring federal funds and drawing upon a New York regional plan in order to establish "a complete system of parks, playgrounds, pleasure beaches, swimming pools, parkways and bridges all tied together radially, circumferentially and comprehensively into a unified and linked pattern."[46] Roads, with their interlocking "clover-leaf patterns" and flyovers, were "astounding in their ingenuity and one is staggered both at the engineering skill that is displayed and at the cost that must have been incurred." Although expensive, in Pepler's estimation Moses had correctly assessed the need for these public works, for "in all cases the response of the public has been so great that the widest parkways and the largest of parks have been quickly used to capacity."[47] Pepler's internationalizing urban planning efforts would be slowed by the exigencies of World War II, but the seeds of British interest in American urban planning had been planted.

How did Americans respond to these overtures? From across the Atlantic, British interest elicited mixed reactions. To those opposing Moses's vision of the modern American city, for instance, Pepler's and other international experts' admiration was inexplicable or ill-informed. Long-time New Yorker Mumford despaired in a letter to Osborn,

I fear that people like Clarence Stein and myself and the group we worked with in the twenties have not been feeding the housing movement with fresh ideas and objectives. . . . So far backward have we gone in the meanwhile, thanks to the leadership of reactionary opportunists like Robert Moses, that New York City's municipal housing is the most prison-like and congested that can be shown anywhere, and has become worse during the last seven years.[48]

Mumford would eventually go even farther to describe New York City's housing debacles as Moses's "unrelieved nightmare," the "architecture of the Police State."[49] Moses, for his part, made a loud show of dismissing professional planners from both sides of the Atlantic as "people who make pretty pictures" and who "draw things": "many of them are entirely satisfied when they finish the plan; when they've announced the plan that's the end of it."[50] Downplaying his own Oxford education, Robert Moses cultivated an image of himself as a pragmatic American with little time for European socialist experiments; Moses had only the most disdainful words for Pepler's former student and now famed planner Patrick Abercrombie, and he described Abercrombie and James Paton-Watson's 1944 celebrated plan for Plymouth, UK, in the most biting tones:

It appears that two well known British town planners, Professor Abercrombie and Mr. Watson, or is it Sherlock Holmes and Dr. Watson, have thought up a completely new Plymouth which will cost one hundred million dollars based on pre-war figures. . . . Assuming for the sake of argument that it is desirable for any central government to attempt such drastic and expensive improvements, how could funds be found? . . .

Don't let the planning revolutionaries spoof you. There is much to be done, but in the end hard-working people with common sense will have to do it.[51]

Despite this seeming rejection of British efforts, however, Moses quietly followed overseas developments through the postwar decades, for—in his words—"nothing approaching the amount of slum clearance in New York has ever been thought of in any city except the bombed areas abroad."[52] Even Moses could not resist transatlantic observation, albeit as secretly as possible.

Wurster, Mumford, Stein, and likeminded experts John Gaus, Frederick Clark, and Jacob Crane, for their part, approached Pepler and Abercrombie's work with more enthusiasm, closely reading the latter's famed *County of London Plan* (1943) and *Greater London Plan* (1944) and offering critical feedback. According to historian Kermit Carlyle Parsons, it was at this moment that Stein and Mumford "developed an intense interest in British planning for the London Region and played a part in its evolution," for Osborn, Abercrombie, and others read American critiques and refined their plans in response to them.[53] There were also echoes of an older progressive exchange still evident in the 1940s: Abercrombie's neighborhood units, for instance, drew inspiration from American architect William Drummond's neighborhood unit, as appropriated by American town planner Clarence Perry in *The Neighborhood Unit: A Scheme of Arrangement for the Family-Life Community* (1929).[54] The idea of the neighborhood unit hearkened back to Ebenezer Howard's principles by putting all basic amenities within walking distance and separating pedestrian and car traffic. These points were then reabsorbed into British debates over Abercrombie's London plan, the 1944 Design of Dwellings Report (Dudley Report), and the 1945 Ministry of Town and Country Planning's Residential Neighbourhood Manual.[55] Unlike the intellectual traffic of the 1930s, however, the exchanges of the war years reflected a newfound confidence among American housing experts and an eagerness to advise as much as to be advised.

Resisting the USA House

At the same time that the Anglo-American special relationship shifted among elite planners, another more concrete exchange exposed discontent with changing power dynamics and concerns over transnational housing—this time, by the broader British and American populace. In 1944, the US government conducted an experiment with a literal housing export, initiating what it believed would be a welcome demonstration of American magnanimity. To American officials' surprise and dismay, the furor on both sides of the Atlantic quickly dispensed with the idea that the American way of life could be so easily packaged and sold. Housing represented more than shelter; it connoted hearth and home, and on a practical level, it delineated the physical boundaries of daily life. Ironically, this 1944 experiment with the USA House would teach the limitations and compromises inherent in any export of an American ideal, rather than showcasing American leadership vis-à-vis housing.

The program began promisingly enough. In November 1944, president Franklin D. Roosevelt's 1941 Lend-Lease program expanded generously to include housing—specifically, $50 million for over 30,000 American temporary homes built on a Tennessee Valley Authority (TVA) model to be packed up and shipped to Britain.[56] From the point of view of the US government, something had to be done to aid the Allies; parts of London had been bombed nearly to oblivion, and entire blocks of the East End were in shambles. Britons needed housing, and Americans had the financial wherewithal to give it to them. The US government momentarily suspended interest in tenure type to promote a somewhat shoddier version of an American suburban tract home as rentals to needy British families. Single-family, single-story bungalows were promoted in Britain for the same practical reasons that such housing took

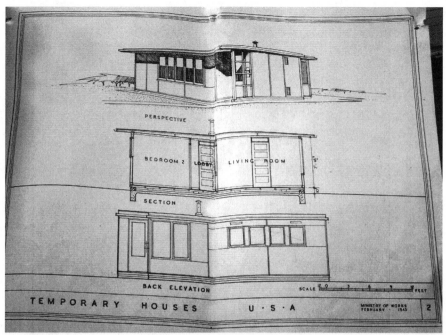

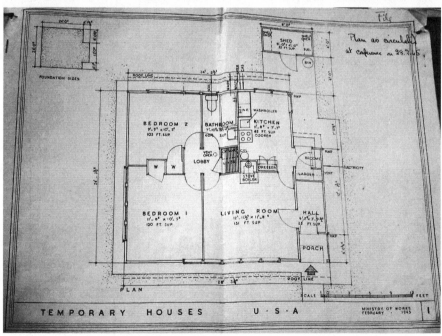

1 and 2 The USA House with British alterations, February 1945. Source: Ministry of Works, CO-537-5130, National Archives (UK).

hold in the American landscape: the units would provide an affordable, quickly erected option for overcrowded families.

To American aid-givers' great surprise, however, the housing lend-lease program proved more difficult than expected. The American public presented the first hurdle to the USA House program. Given the dire housing shortage in the US, many needy families felt less than charitable. A 30,000-house donation seemed absurdly generous, and the extension of wartime production aid to everyday Britons, unjustifiable. One American lend-lease official noted "political difficulties in America" and "a good deal of feeling over the sending of houses to Britain before American needs had been more fully met."[57] He made a twofold request that the British henceforth target war workers and discontinue the current policy of refurbishing bombed districts in London. Alas, British lend-lease staff politely refused to comply with either request. John Maynard Keynes had brokered the agreement and had explicitly stipulated American units should go to bombed areas. The British official concluded snippily that although "nothing had been done in America for returning soldiers . . . [i]n this country [UK] the serving man was regarded as being at the top of the list of war workers. As a result of enemy bombing, which had not occurred in the States, many families of serving men were now living under deplorable conditions with an adverse effect on the morale of the Services, particularly in the Far East."[58]

The looming public relations disaster only grew as the British media began raising hue and cry about the incompatibility of "shoddy" American houses and foreign design with London neighborhoods. Initially, the British Ministry of Works staff took a pragmatic approach, welcoming the infusion of foreign homes and acknowledging the dearth of local raw materials and skilled labor. Even with foreign aid, the Ministry of Works staff noted that labor shortages in site preparation delayed the effective use of American imports, and with a cold winter fast approaching, they urged greater cooperation with and acceptance of American aid givers. From this point of view, the British had no choice but to cope with cultural disjunctions, since the basic TVA design was non-negotiable. The US had already made it clear that they wanted to showcase the "best design that America has produced" rather than using an "American copy" of a British design.[59]

Minister of Works Duncan Sandys disagreed with his staff's conciliatory approach. Sandys pointed out problematic design conflicts in placing the imports in urban areas: the USA House did not fit the same slab as the British temporary houses. Foundation-laying would be greatly delayed by this incompatibility. Furthermore, timber usage posed a fire risk, and the proposed bungalows would unsatisfactorily lower densities in the very areas requiring the most high-density new housing.[60] Sandys's vociferous protests stoked the fears of many Londoners, triggering a new surge of governmental efforts to find a workable compromise. American architects cooperated with Ministry of Works officials to widen windows for better escape and access by firefighting units. They prioritized the rights of private homeowners adjacent to the new bungalows, for "the Government have felt justified in taking greater risks as regards the spread of fire between the bungalows themselves, which are Government property, than between the bungalows and neighbouring property in private ownership."[61]

Such measures still did not assuage the concerns of a sensitive public, and the British government testily observed an upsurge of negative press from "ill-informed or irresponsible persons."[62] When the *News Chronicle* castigated the houses for being of inferior design, three London authorities immediately delayed their allocated shipments until they had an opportunity to view the units themselves. (London had been slated to receive 4,000 of these homes, with most going to those areas farthest from the central city.)[63] Models of the prefabricated units were displayed at the Building Research Station in Garston, after which the *Chronicle* followed up with the damning assessment, "Bungalows from US are poorly finished." The architectural correspondent described the samples erected in Garston as "a packing-case building," with workmanship and finish being "very poor." Construction was different from "our own temporary houses" since timber was "used freely and the walls are covered externally with a painted wallboard of a type not yet tried in positions exposed to British weather." In addition, "the bath will probably surprise most people, as it is a shallow American type 4 ft. 10 in. long overall."[64]

Local authorities shared the press' distaste for American dwellings. The USA House was intended to last "for a few years" but was being "dovetailed into the general temporary housing scheme based on a ten years' life," one anonymous government memo explained. "Local authorities allege (probably with reason) that owing to the much lighter construction of the American house the cost of maintenance will be greater than in the case of British types."[65] In a spate of bad luck, the very first shipment of American houses arrived damaged, feeding local consternation. And, to add insult to injury from the point of view of the local authorities, the national exchequer demanded local authorities supply the site (using section 6 of the Housing Temporary

Accommodation Act) and pay rates (taxes) of at least £4 per year per house for these substandard units.

Ultimately, the disconnections between local, national, and international needs compromised the lend-lease of American housing, and only 8,244 of the slated 30,000 homes actually made it across the Atlantic.[66] International aid failed because it clashed with local visions for future development. Serious structural flaws like heavy preparation and maintenance costs and potential fire hazard played a critical role, as did the shorter lifespan and foreign internal fixtures, but the widespread emotional reaction and the wholesale rejection of the USA House in the midst of an unparalleled housing shortage hinted at the real affront: international housing diplomacy required popular consent, and the USA House had not earned it.

Americans learned a lesson, also: from the US, New York City Parks Commissioner Robert Moses read memos about the failed attempt of these American exports, one of which stated, "Demonstrations of so-called prefabricated houses have, to say the least, been very unimpressive so that it is not surprising to find publicity in the *Washington Post* under date of July 30, 1945, headed 'Britons "disgusted" with "premade" US Type Houses.'"[67] Based upon this report and others decrying prefabricated experiments in the US, Moses decided temporary housing "would make the worst slums in New York City that the city has ever had" and that "My definite recommendation . . . would be to stay away from the proposed temporary housing developments."[68] While the US had unquestionably superior economic power by the end of the war, Americans would still need to navigate local building traditions and meet standards for new construction if they intended to provide housing and export American ideas of decent shelter.

Rejecting "Socialistic" Housing

The USA House incident gave a glimpse of the unequal power relations between aid donor and recipient as well as the power of popular opinion when it came to control over housing. On the domestic front, the British populace reacted to their poor material circumstances in late 1945 by voting in a government promising greater public provision—a move watched with increasing alarm by the Republican-dominated American legislature of 1946. A British socialist government intent on expanding council (public) housing went against the basic principles of a Congress intent on curtailing New Deal social programs and reinstating private industry as the engine of growth.

In retrospect, it is not so surprising that postwar American housing debates should center on debates over the inherent "socialism" of any given policy. This concern with socialist policies had already been on display during congressional hearings over the 1937 Housing Act when public housing advocates Bauer, Edith Elmer Wood, Helen Alfred, Mary Simkhovitch, and others fielded repeated accusations by NAREB, the US Chamber of Commerce, the Apartment House Owners' Association, the National Association of Home Builders, the American Savings and Loan League, the Mortgage Bankers Association, and the American Bankers Association.[69] The Taft-Ellender-Wagner bill of 1948 met a similar fate: first drafted in 1945 by Bauer and other housing reformers seeking a more comprehensive national housing policy, the proposed legislation included a provision for 500,000 new public housing units that rankled anti–public housing Republicans.[70] Even though senators Robert Taft (Rep-OH), Allen Ellender (Dem-LA), and Robert Wagner, Sr. (Dem-NY) worked with a bipartisan coalition including the AFL, CIO, Conference of Mayors, veterans' organizations, and housers to get the bill through the Senate, conservative public housing opponents like Jesse P. Wolcott (Rep-MI) and the real estate lobby successfully blocked the bill in the House. Senator Joseph McCarthy (Rep-WI) promptly added fuel to the anti–public housing fire with a US Senate Joint Committee *Study and Investigation of Housing* (1947–48), essentially putting public provision on trial and giving private housing advocates "a public forum to attack the New Deal's commitment to a comprehensive federal housing policy."[71] McCarthy intended to brand public housing as "a breeding ground for communists," a menace to the virtues of private enterprise, and a threat to the national economy.[72] Only the surprise victory of Harry Truman in 1948 finally overcame the congressional stalemate. Truman proved outspoken in his opposition to the "do-nothing" Republican Congress and the real estate lobby's "shortsighted and utterly selfish . . . [cries of] 'socialism' in a last effort to smother the real facts and real issues which this [TEW] bill is designed to meet."[73]

What is remarkable about US housing debates from 1945 to 1949 is the extent to which conservative congressional members and the real estate lobby relied on European examples as a foil for a uniquely American homeowning "tradition"—this, despite the fact that European home-ownership rates varied dramatically by country (in 1950, Switzerland, the Netherlands, West Germany, Sweden, France, Austria, Italy, and Luxemburg all had lower homeownership rates than the US, while Belgium had comparable, and Finland significantly higher, rates); federal government aids for homeownership were still in the process of being implemented; and some polls like a 1946 *Fortune Magazine* study even showed that Americans preferred rentals over ownership.[74] In much the same way that the real estate lobby and conservative politicians argued homeownership formed a bulwark against potential domestic racial integration in public housing or the infiltration of foreign, usually immigrant renter ideologies, so also did they contend homeownership could protect against dangerous European ideas.

In order to understand what the real estate lobby was rejecting, a brief explanation of British housing programs is required. To be sure, there was much for American conservatives to dislike in events unfolding across the Atlantic. The new British postwar housing program undeniably rested on an increased commitment to substantial new council housing construction. Labor victories in the British elections of July 1945 must have looked alarming indeed, as housing shortages (and the Conservative government's inability to address those shortages) played no small role in prime minister Winston Churchill's electoral demise. In a series of "eve of the poll" visits on July 4, 1945, the war hero was met with "a storm of booing" when he mentioned housing in Norwood.[75] On East Hill in Central Wandsworth, Churchill's query "How . . . are we going to get the houses built, the peace made, the Japanese war finished?" was met with the unwelcome response "By voting Labour."[76] While American housing shortages did not come close to the scale of devastation witnessed in the UK, jubilant Labour Party celebrations a mere three months after VE Day could not have reassured conservative American politicians surveying their own domestic housing troubles. The ascendant Labour Party promised an expansion of the social welfare state that was thoroughly antithetical to the advocacy of mass homeownership in the US.

The party intended to create "a full programme of land planning and drastic action to ensure an efficient building industry," to make the most of "modern methods, modern materials" in construction, to help build "comfortable, labour-saving homes that take full advantage of the resources of modern science and productive industry," and to institute "good town planning."[77] While "five million homes" could not be provided "in quick time," as secretary of state for foreign affairs Ernest Bevin overexcitedly promised in 1945, hefty changes seemed underway with the passage of two new laws in 1946 and 1947.[78] Previously the LCC Housing Committee chairman, Lewis Silkin now occupied the key position of minister of town and country planning; Silkin promptly put

Lord John Reith in charge of a committee to plan for satellite towns, and both men drew from Abercrombie's delineation of new towns outside the greenbelt as well as from the thoroughly researched Pepler Committee memorandum, "Creation of New Towns" (1944), to successfully argue for a national program. No longer would unregulated "central flat-building and a great suburban explosion . . . be repeated," according to Osborn.[79] Again, the New Towns Act of 1946 asserted a role for government that went against the core fiber of the homeownership movement in the US. As geographer Gordon Cherry explains:

The state's primary role in determining where people would live, in what social mix, and in what sort of houses (rented from public authorities) was not seriously questioned. *The building of a new town was simply not a fit subject for private enterprise; on this the major political parties were all agreed.* . . . Wasteful sprawl had characterized the unco-ordinated activities of the building industry pre-war; it was more rational and socially effective for the state to determine the distribution of its population and it was more efficient for the state to organize the huge scale of building development that would be necessary.[80]

Certainly, the US had built its own Ebenezer Howard–inspired garden cities in the early twentieth century. The US Greenbelt Program had begun with high aims, for instance, although it did ultimately yield only three sites in Greenbelt, Maryland, Greendale, Wisconsin, and Greenhills, Ohio. Forest Hills Gardens in Queens, New York (1909) and the garden suburb of Radburn, New Jersey (1929). It attempted to establish self-sufficient towns that incorporated some aspects of the garden city ideal of "short, often curving streets, a clear division between major thoroughfares and secondary streets, an emphasis on open space, and large blocks closed to vehicular traffic."[81] The US was nowhere near ready to follow the path of the Labourites, however, who quickly passed the New Towns Act of 1946 and planned fourteen new towns by 1950, eight in the greater London area.[82] While the Labour program from 1945 to 1950 may have come from a transatlantic progressive heritage, a desire "not to abolish capitalism but to assuage its excesses, extracting from it a few key social goods and setting a common floor under a few of its most acute risks," Americans did not follow the British path in this regard.[83]

Meanwhile, the Labour Party assembled the second and arguably most important piece of planning legislation to be passed during prime minister Clement Attlee's tenure: the Town and Country Planning Act of 1947 helped structure future planning by creating a highly centralized process again quite different from the US system.[84] According to the 1947 act, all exemptions needed to be appealed individually to the council, reviewed, and approved. Ultimate authority rested with a central minister (e.g., in the Department of Environment), rather than with the courts as in the US. Appeals included alternate zoning uses (residential for office and vice versa), the erection of single-family homes or maisonettes on open land, and alternate commercial or industrial uses.[85] The act "nationalised the right to develop land and set up the system of flexible regulation or development control which forms the basis of British planning to this day."[86] Planners would have the power not only to prevent certain types of development, but to actively direct future land use. If a private landowner chose not to comply with the directives of the Central Land Board (an arm of the Ministry of Town and Country Planning), the government could then use the power of compulsory purchase to take away the property. The new law divorced the right to own property ("existing use value") from the right to determine its future use ("improvement value").[87] Any rise in property value would be siphoned off through a "development charge" collected through the Central Land Board; any drop would be compensated for through a £300 million fund set aside for this purpose. (This shared fund, or "global sum," followed the recommendations of the *Uthwatt Report*.)

Under the 1947 act, property owners in London could experience three possible scenarios: first, they could submit a proposal to develop their land, receive approval from the LCC and/or borough council, see a rise in their land value, and essentially hand over that appreciation to the nation through the "development charge"; second, they could submit a proposal to develop their land, receive a denial from the LCC and/or borough council, see a drop in their land value, and receive no compensation; or third, they could make no plan but see a drop in their land value because of the act's restrictions, and consequently qualify for compensation.[88] The remarkable 1947 act left a strong impression on watching Americans and ultimately played a critical role in shaping congressional debates about British "socialistic" housing.

Before returning to the American rejection of these "socialistic" policies, it is important to note that the actual implementation of the 1947 act was shaped in no small way by American macroeconomic policies, and that these dulling effects did not appear in American debates about British housing. It is true that in theory, the 1947 act could radically transform real estate practices and the very meaning of property ownership. In practice, however, American demands for convertible sterling and nondiscriminatory commercial practices (i.e., an opening of Commonwealth markets) resulted in increasingly stringent loan agreement stipulations that neither Keynes nor other British politicians were adequately prepared for.[89] President Truman's decision to abruptly terminate lend-lease in 1946 struck what Prime Minister Attlee would call a "body blow" to Labour, as the limited resources of the party prevented the promised mass construction. From 1945 to 1949, the LCC built a gross total of 21,894 houses (including 2,869 rebuilds). Roughly half (10,816) were in the County of London, and the remaining (11,078) in the outer regions. It also erected 7,865 temporary (ten-year) houses. Metropolitan boroughs, meanwhile, completed 9,581 permanent dwellings and 7,361 temporary ones from 1946 to 1949.[90] These numbers did not come close to resolving the massive housing shortage, nor did they adequately address the needs of current LCC residents. American aid may have saved Europe from potential financial catastrophe, but the Labour Party also found their "radical plans for a new social and economic order" abruptly curtailed by the conditions of that assistance. In the words of sociologist Michael Harloe, "In Britain . . . the connections between economic dependency on America and the containment of reform were . . . clear."[91]

The Labour Party's inability to meet housing targets resulted in widespread discontent among those still waiting for government assistance. Some LCC residents still had to cope with "the rain and snow [coming] through in appreciable quantities" eight years after their first registered complaints, and one fisherman tersely articulated his discontent, "I think I'll be Conservative. Sod the Labour. Never did me any f..g good. . . . Can't get f..g houses."[92] After years of Crippsian austerity (after Attlee's chancellor of the exchequer Stafford Cripps), the postwar British Labour connection with council housing proved to be a political liability.[93] The Conservatives swept the 1951 elections and would stay in power until 1964. Like the Labour Party six years prior, the Conservatives won at least partly on the promise that they would build more and better housing.[94]

Neither the impact of American macroeconomic policies nor the Labour Party's troubles and eventual demise in 1951 made its way into American housing debates, however, and it is clear from this partial use of the British "example" that international study often fueled the fight against domestic public housing programs rather than stimulating a real exploration of alternative housing systems. *Fortune* magazine published a critical article in March 1949 entitled, "Socialism by Default," and a New York organization flooded the city with a pamphlet called "Soft Socialism," asking: "Do you want Congress to set up a housing dictatorship? Do you want Congress to permit Government housing to be used as the machinery for socializing American industry? Do you want your children and your grandchildren to be taxed to provide expensive benefits for the favorites of the public housing lobby?"[95]

British "mistakes" proved particularly useful in the midst of debates infused with Red Scare rhetoric. Real estate interests were keen to point out the dangerous precedent of the LCC. Some, like James P. Bourne, president of the Louisville & Jefferson County Property Owners Association, drew on the "lessons of history, particularly with respect to England's public housing experience" to articulate dramatic assessments of British practices: "In Britain, Parliament began with a well-intended effort to improve housing conditions for low-income families. In the 30 years since these programs began, tenants have revolted against the Government; the cost has assumed staggering proportions; politics, not providence, has become the main qualification for securing better housing, and 80% of the construction is now done by the Government." If Congress passed the proposed Housing Act of 1949 with a stipulation for more public housing, the United States would be easily led "down the same road to ruin" where people would be "sheltered by Government houses instead of by homes of their own." Bourne finished, "Of course, we are just country boys from Kentucky, but let me tell you that down our way we could call this just plain communism. There is not any 'soft socialism' to it. When you read Karl Marx saying 'From each according to his abilities; and to each according to his needs,' you know that is just what public housing is."[96]

Others agreed wholeheartedly. General Dwight D. Eisenhower warned that "soft socialism," a continued centralization of bureaucracy, would eventually lead to "a swarming of bureaucrats all over the land" with "ownership of property . . . gradually drift[ing] into that Central Government." Thomas Holden, president of the Dodge Corporation, emphasized that the world simply could not afford a socialist America. "The United States has a responsibility for world leadership," he argued. "Its position will be weakened if it drives further in the direction of socialism." Calvin K. Snyder, representing NAREB, put it concisely: "Russia confiscated property rights. England has followed suit with its Town and Country Planning Act of 1947. Are we to follow the same pattern?" Douglas Whitlock, chairman of the Building Products Institute, testified along the same lines, protesting mayor W. Dwyer's positive testimony with statistics: according to Whitlock, public housing had provided 8,132 units as opposed to 3,906 private units during the first three months of 1949, "or, gentlemen, 3 to 1. Three public housing units in New York to one built by private industry . . . where they have a public housing program going forward that the mayor says is fine. Does that not smack of the 4 to 1 ratio of Socialist England? Four public housing units to one private unit? We have already got it in New York City. . . . And I think it is time for this Congress to stop and think whether we are going the road of England in socialism."[97]

At times, congressional members became impatient with the constant references to England, as in the case of Oscar Kreutz's testimony. When Kreutz, the executive manager of the National Savings and Loan League, offered his skimpy understanding of British council housing—"Public housing there has become a consistently heavier burden on the higher-income groups, including those just barely above the income groups which are supposed to be eligible for public housing"—Representative Rolla McMillen testily retorted, "You made a brief statement here with regard to what is happening to public housing in England. Are you prepared to elaborate on that situation, and further, as to what has happened to public housing in other countries in Europe, with regard to its merits? Do you know what the facts are? You have made a brief statement about England here, and I wish you would elaborate if you are prepared to, on what, in your opinion, has happened to public housing not only in England but in other countries in Europe over the past 25 years." Kreutz, unfortunately, was unable to satisfy McMillen; he acknowledged that he was "not prepared to say how justifiable that program is," nor was he "sufficiently familiar with conditions in Great Britain. Perhaps they have conditions there which are somewhat different from the conditions we have in this country."[98]

If Kreutz offered many opinions based on little evidence, Morton Bodfish, chairman of the Executive Committee of the United States Savings and Loan League, prepared a much more detailed analysis of British failures and reasons for not passing the US Housing Act of 1949, along with suggested alternative policies. The British government subsidized rentals, thereby penalizing middle-income people who continued to purchase, said Bodfish. By nationalizing "four out of five new homes," the government not only prevented new private house-building, but also left men without jobs and building materials "piling up in yards and warehouses." According to Bodfish, these developments were partly the fault of the Labour government, but the Conservative party also laid the legal foundations for government ownership of residential property, as the government built some 700,000 units between World War I and World War II. Bureaucracy caused inefficiencies; the Town and Country Act of 1947 charged development fees; rent control froze rents of 8.5 million homes; and temporary homes were erected at an exorbitant average per unit fee of $5,512—all to the detriment of widespread homeowner-ship. All of this contributed to the "creeping socialism of the past hun-dred years" in this "great Nation [Britain], the original home of private enterprise and small proprietorship as we know it."

In the US, Bodfish offered five recommendations. First, a select com-mittee of the House should go to England to "see first-hand the results of a prolonged and substantial Government housing program." Sec-ond, the slum land acquisition program ought to be administered by the Federal Works Agency with cleared land going to a local initiative, not to public housing as currently written. Third, housing research (Ti-tle III) should be removed ("A program of the type proposed in the language of the bill would lead, in our judgment, more to propaganda and pressure for Government housing than to a balanced and fair re-search undertaking which would recognize homeownership, the existing supply of housing and various ways and means by which we maintain and produce homes"). Fourth, the declaration of a national housing pol-icy should be removed, the objectives being excessively broad. Fifth and lastly, the clear income limit for public housing ought to be set in law, most likely at $1,500. Although Bodfish failed to persuade the House on all counts, he did succeed in his first and third points.

Study Abroad, but for What Purpose?

Of all recommendations, Republicans and Democrats were perhaps most in agreement with Bodfish's suggestion that they travel abroad to see low-income housing programs "first-hand." Study abroad might indeed illuminate the potential lessons of European housing. Congressman Abraham Multer, obviously enchanted with the idea of a trip to England, queried, "You do not think that if we adopt your suggestion of this select committee going to England—you did not intend to exclude Sweden?" (Bodfish had earlier testified that the reason Swedish, or for that matter, German, Danish, or Norwegian cities, did not have slums was because "they just do not permit people to throw stuff around in their back yards or dump garbage out in the streets. . . . Many of the houses in Sweden are old, a hundred or two hundred years old, and they are kept in immaculate condition.") In response to Multer's suggestions, Bodfish concurred, "I think it would be excellent [to go to Sweden.]" Multer then wondered aloud, "England and Sweden. You do not think the same people who are calling us bureaucrats would then be accusing us of tak-ing a junket at public expense?" Bodfish replied, "Probably, but I think it is a wholesome thing for Members of Congress to study these problems first-hand. I think it has had much to do with our intelligent development of foreign policy in recent years."[99]

Even as savings-and-loan representatives urged senators to take exploratory trips abroad to see European housing problems firsthand, so also did real estate, construction, and other industry heads use international examples to persuade labor leaders to pursue private over public housing. In 1949, for example, Herbert Nelson (executive vice president of the National Association of Real Estate Boards) wrote to Walter Reuther (president of the Automobile Workers of the Congress of Industrial Organizations and chairman of that body's national committee on housing) urging the staunch public housing advocate to consider alternatives: "Recently, in England, I had occasion to see some of the work of what they called the housing societies, which are mutuals or cooperatives and which are making good progress. These are private enterprise in character and now represent about the best housing being built there. The Government housing is not so good, and it is results that I am interested in."[100] Reuther himself was not opposed to learning from European examples, having just published a booklet, *Homes for People, Jobs for Prosperity, Plans for Peace, a Program to Meet the Inner and Outer Threats to Democracy's Survival*, in which he urged greater application of prefabrication techniques from Europe.[101]

Following House representatives and labor leaders, senators in the Banking and Currency Committee decided that before passing "a program of loans and technical assistance to cooperatives as a means of providing homes which families of moderate income could afford" (S. 2246, title III) they needed to know more about experiences "in those countries that have the greatest experience with them." The group thought Norway, Sweden, and Denmark provided the best examples, but it also added the Netherlands, France, Switzerland, and Great Britain to their itinerary for good measure.[102] In their final report of March 1950, the subcommittee waffled between a sense of leadership and exceptionalism vis-à-vis their European counterparts. On the one hand, they rejoiced in the successes of the Economic Cooperation Administration (ECA). The ECA had been established "For European Recovery supplied by the United States of America,"[103] and the senators were delighted to see that

Everywhere we went we were greeted with continuous expressions of appreciation and evident understanding of what we in the United States had done and were doing to help the European people in their recovery efforts. We saw on all sides evidences of the success of the program and operations of the Economic Cooperation Administration.[104]

3   American aid givers felt a newfound confidence after World War II. This image was included
     in a series of ECA photos showcasing the global impact of American aid. The original caption
     read: "Even the daily bottle of wine which belongs to the French dinner table, however sim-
     ple the meal, owes its existence, or at least its quality, to scarce non-ferrous metals and thus
     indirectly to the Marshall Plan." Source: Folder France, box 2 of 8, RG 286, NARA.

On the other hand, the senators displayed little hope that their research
into European housing patterns would yield much for American application; despite their disavowal of any explicit recommendations within
the report, they wrote, "It is generally our belief that our system of housing is sufficiently different that any program of cooperative housing
would probably take a form different from any system we studied in our
European investigation."[105]

Exchanges continued regardless of such reservations. In fact, American visitors came so frequently and in such numbers that they inter-
fered with the daily operation of LCC employees, for "the pressure
on the architectural staff is heavy and time spent in showing visitors
around estates and interviewing them in the office is largely at the

expense of progress on production work," according to internal LCC memos.[106] Unfortunately for the architectural staff, the tide of visitors swelled rather than abating: shortly after the senate subcommittee, yet another round of ECA staff members including William Gausmann and William Morgan arrived, and in the spring of the same year, a group of congressional representatives, this time from the House Committee on Banking and Currency, decided they needed to conduct a European study mission as well.

This second group of congressional representatives observed how a program in between public and private housing might actually work. They perused "published documents," "unpublished materials made available by officials of the countries visited," and "information . . . furnished by United States embassies and delegations," and participated in "discussions in Europe with national and local government officials as well as representatives of private industry."[107] Cooperative housing, or "a project in which a nongovernmental association of voluntary members actually develops new housing on a nonprofit basis," suited these American representatives' interests in a fundamentally important way: it provided better, cheaper housing through economies of scale, efficiencies of joint maintenance, better group credit, and elimination of profit, while not resorting to total government provision (i.e., public housing). Congressmen discovered that most families occupying coops were in the middle or lower-middle income bracket and that the national government frequently provided, directly or indirectly, part or all of the loan at reduced interest rates with long amortization periods. National governments used coops as "one of the three principal elements of their programs for dealing with the housing crisis" (the other two being private and public housing):

In general, cooperative housing in these countries is given as much or more assistance by the governments as is given to private-enterprise housing and public housing. This arrangement applies to the granting of priorities to secure materials and equipment. It applies to government subsidies, which generally are handled separately from the loans, and which are made available in some cases to help equalize high postwar construction costs, in some cases to help reduce the charges for occupancy or "rent," and in a number of cases to make it possible for large families or elderly people to occupy cooperative housing accommodations which otherwise they could not afford.

Despite all the praise for European cooperative housing, however, the Senate and the House both roundly refused to consider implementing such programs at home. The *Wall Street Journal* explained the reasons for such a refusal: "The Senate and House already have turned thumbs down on this idea of putting Federal funds to work subsidizing coopera- tive building of homes. Should such a program ever develop it could chase private builders to the sidelines."[108]

Ultimately, international case studies served as ammunition rather than as learning laboratories. Upon returning home to the White House in 1950, House representatives began hearings on a bill to extend the Housing and Rent Act of 1947 (HR 8276). The 1947 act replaced the first ever national rent control put into place by the 1942 Emergency Price Control Act, since the conclusion of war demanded slightly differ- ent measures; it split the national market into those constructed before February 1, 1947, and still protected by rent control, versus those built after the same date and freed from regulation.[109] Returning congressio- nal representatives needed to decide whether or not to continue such national government control over rents. Interestingly, in their report from Europe, members wrote that "rent-control programs have been re- alistic with the single exception of France," yet in the actual House hear- ings, the only international example cited was that of France.[110] When NAREB presented a negative *Wall Street Journal* article titled "Lessons from France," no member interrupted or interjected, and the NAREB representative was subjected to few questions. The real estate board's argument that in France, "a generation of rent ceilings has encouraged the deterioration of apartment buildings and other for-rent quarters," that rent-control had "discouraged people with money to invest from putting it into new housing," simply went into the *Congressional Record* without debate about other European examples that attending congres- sional members surely knew about.[111]

While legislation was being written at home, Americans continued to fly themselves or help others to make the journey across the Atlantic to see what the LCC had accomplished. Yngve Larsson of Stockholm met the director of the LCC with a personal recommendation from American architect Clarence Stein.[112] American ministers of religion went to London to learn more about "the Welfare State"; chairman of the Bowery Savings Bank Henry Bruère visited in early 1951; and a travel association contacted the LCC for assistance with tours to be arranged for "20 Americans who wish to spend a week in the greater London area studying English housing."[113] For all the continued in- vestment of energy and money into researching European and British housing systems, however, such study abroad became a way of assert- ing distinctly non-European American values. Congressmen and busi- nessmen traveled abroad—not to be inspired or to dramatically rethink

American housing systems—but rather to gain a more cosmopolitan understanding of international experiments and to use these to affirm the superiority of American mass homeownership over other tenure types. Transatlantic exchanges flourished but learning did not, and the American model stood apart from any potentially "socialist" European developments.

Meanwhile, American housing aid to Europe continued apace. In one of many European reconstruction projects, the US provided $25 million to improve housing in the Ruhr region of Germany, although aid remained hidden from view for most Ruhr residents because of the American distaste for openly state-managed housing and community development.[114] American aid monies consistently bolstered European private housing programs instead of supporting open subsidies. In the early 1950s, for instance, HHFA representative Jacob Crane condemned French use of rent control, building restrictions, and taxes, techniques that looked much more like state control of the private sector. Crane believed the French system would deter private investment and make that country, "from the US point of view," one of the worst-off in Western Europe. West Germany, by contrast, adopted what Crane called an aided self-help subsidization formula where residents paid roughly 20% of wage income for housing and the government made up the difference. Italy also garnered praise for considering a wide range of government supports of private-market housing. First-generation Italian American advisor Guido Nadzo, who helped coordinate the United Nations Rehabilitation and Relief Administration (UNRRA) operations and ECA counterpart funds in Italy, would eventually be sent to Korea and Peru to share lessons learned in Europe.

Remarkable changes in the American domestic sphere informed the work of overseas advisors and would-be aid givers. From 1940 to 1950, homeownership rates in the US jumped from 43.6% to 55%, the highest single-decade increase in American history. That number rose again in the successive decade to 61.9%, and then to 62.9% (1970), 64.4% (1980), 64.2% (1990), and 66.2% (2000).[115] This increase went hand-in-hand with a transformation of the American mortgage market, as more and more Americans engaged in debt-driven homeownership. Loan-to-value ratios for single-family homes leapt from 81% to 91.5% from 1948 to 1958 alone.[116] Politicians may have extolled this new, majority-homeowning society as the realization of a longstanding American dream, but postwar mass homeownership policies were connected with many other important factors: Depression-era measures intended to stem financial crisis, wartime concerns with veterans' rights, and advancements in construction technologies, to name a few, all fueled the domestic suburban explosion after 1945.[117] The apparent successes of homeownership in the domestic sphere informed how American officials envisioned effective recovery abroad.

By the 1950s, it had become accepted wisdom in the State Department that housing problems could only be solved through better use of private initiative and accumulated individual savings. The American example had "clearly demonstrate[d] that private savings [were] potentially the most important source of mortgage credit," and that any overseas housing assistance must concentrate on bolstering the self-help, regenerative, market-driven aspects of housing improvement. US-backed housing programs "should be intended primarily for employed workers whose earnings are such that there is a reasonable possibility that they can pay for project costs on long-term, low-interest credit and thereby become homeowners." As seen in the US context, savings and loans and federal home-loan bank systems would transform local accumulated savings into capital for national economic development, even as homeownership provided a "powerful motivation" for family savings and produced "not only . . . low-cost housing" but also "responsible, self-respecting citizens."[118] NAREB's executive vice president Herbert Nelson believed deposit insurance could help smooth out European troubles with home lending by creating a greater pool of domestic savings, which could in turn lead to the creation of a home-loan bank system in which banks insured each other's mortgage portfolios: "Our American system of having one first mortgage to cover the entire indebtedness of the borrower and thus consolidating both the security and the risk, would seem to be a much preferable plan. . . . European countries [might] try out the American method of deposit insurance and internal mortgage insurance, and if we could at the same time offer some of our help in creating such systems, the idea might be well accepted."[119] Indeed, if exchanges rates were tied together more closely, "the economies of the Western powers [might] move into the next stage of closer harmony" and allow the creation of mortgage banking and/or insurance systems across international boundaries.[120]

The State Department embraced government-backed free-market housing in the domestic sphere, but American officials also understood that political pressures could push West European governments to contemplate ambitious, costly housing programs. In fact, HHFA and ICA officials applauded "Europe's recognition that the dramatic improvement of housing conditions is absolutely essential in their economic and political scheme of things," and Congress increased overseas housing aid funds as necessary to subdue simmering political discontent where necessary. If the US were to "play a vital role in the attack on the housing deficiencies as was vividly demonstrated in the Ruhr," Stanley Baruch argued, funds would need to be "sufficiently large scale" to provoke "thousands of women in each country . . . [to] see our professionals working with their professionals in overcoming the problems which their communities and their governments face."[121] Ongoing, serious housing needs in France and Italy, and "explosive" conditions in Spain all demanded substantial, ongoing assistance; the Marshall Plan had already provided the equivalent of $500 million in counterpart funds for new dwellings in French port cities, workers' housing projects in the industrial centers of Germany, Italy, and Austria, prefabricated homes in the Netherlands, and "entire villages for homeless refugees" in Greece from 1947 to 1950—not including the over $120 million in ECA-authorized timber, $700 million in nonferrous metals, $200 million in construction and engineering equipment, and sponsorship of twelve Technical Assistance Teams brought to the US to "investigate building techniques."[122] After the Marshall Plan concluded in 1951, Technical Cooperation Administration, Foreign Operations Administration, and International Cooperation Administration aid continued to direct American resources toward European housing programs. In 1956 alone, Germany was slated to receive roughly $26 million; Italy and France, $12 million each; Spain, $7 million; and Yugoslavia and Austria, $2.5 million each.[123] Aid always came with the familiar refrain: FOA officials encouraged recipients to focus on "efforts to increase savings and develop accumulations for housing finance" and "efforts to develop practices and experience in homeownership loans—[especially] lower interest rates [and] longer amortizations."[124] American connections to European housing programs had strengthened in some regards, then, as political interests and fear of burgeoning communism led to more government-to-government interaction and assistance. These connections in turn helped solidify American self-perceptions of leadership in the realm of housing.

Expanding the American Model

In 1952, Kanji Dwarkadas, a member of the Indian Parliament, astutely observed, "Whilst the US Congress under pressure from the Real Estate Lobby . . . is quarrelling for months over sanctioning 5,000 to 50,000 public houses, the US Government under ECA and other programs is building houses in Brazil, Ecuador, Chile, El Salvador, Antigua, Liberia, France, Germany, Italy, Greece, Turkey, Burma, Indonesia, [and] the Philippines."[125] Indeed, Dwarkadas precisely captured the paradox of postwar American housing policy: on the one hand, Congress and Presidents Truman and Eisenhower spent countless legislative hours debating and whittling away the 1949 Housing Act's already moderate mandate of 135,000 public housing units per year, referring liberally to what they saw as misguided European—and especially British—socialist examples. On the other hand, private investors and government agencies sought an expansion of overseas housing aid.

This seemingly contradictory engagement with international housing efforts had one core value in common: at home and abroad, Americans were laying the foundations for an expansive, ultimately global model of homeownership. Whether by disabling public housing and bolstering government-backed mortgages at home, or by stimulating private investment and government-supported self-help programs abroad, congressional representatives, business leaders, and housing investors were intent on nurturing mass homeownership and thus ensuring vibrant capitalist economies around the world. Harry Truman would take the next decisive step in 1949.

TWO

Combatting Communism with Homeownership

An old miner looked into House No. 5 and spoke to the occupant Hsu Wan-yang: "Ah, such a beautiful house; and it is going to belong to you!" CENTRAL DAILY NEWS, FREE CHINA, APRIL 12, 1955[1]

Harry Truman needed something extraordinary—an electrifying finale, "an exciting and dramatic punch line" to inspire the crowd after the more predictable parts of his 1949 inaugural speech.[2] Points One, Two, and Three would announce ongoing support for the United Nations and Marshall Plan as well as the creation of a new joint defense alliance, the North Atlantic Treaty Organization; Truman still lacked a "fresh and provocative" finish.[3] Through personal initiative and luck, State Department officer Benjamin Hardy managed to get the ear of the president in time to put forward a suggestion: why not have the US declare its support for developing nations, to teach them to "have a *mind* to do for themselves, to raise themselves up by their bootstraps"?[4]

Truman loved it. He termed his fourth point a "bold new program" for overseas assistance, one that included those parts of the world hitherto neglected by the Marshall Plan (1947–51). Although the president was leery of direct capital assistance, stating that "material resources . . . for the assistance of other peoples are limited," he exhibited an unwavering faith that the US's "imponderable resources in technical knowledge"—"constantly growing," perhaps "inexhaustible"—could secure prosperity and peace for the "free peoples" of the world. The US should help build capitalism abroad, "foster[ing] capital investment in areas needing development" and making sure that "guarantees in the interest of the people" balanced "guarantees to the investor."[5]

Overseas housing aid began as part of larger Cold War concerns, and these programs changed in direct response to Cold War fears and geopolitical maneuverings. In the early years of the Marshall Plan and Point Four, US officials imagined a foreign aid program that would be relatively cheap and small in scale. The "loss" of China in 1949 and the Korean hot war from 1950 to 1953 adjusted this vision, however, with American housing aid programs becoming increasingly complex, and homeownership campaigns requiring extensive state management despite rhetoric about self-help and "bootstraps" capitalism. The Cold War was more than a backdrop to housing aid programs of the late 1940s and 1950s. It fundamentally shaped ideology and policy.

National Security through Housing Aid

Point Four marked an important start to American engagement in the developing world, with direct effects on volume and type of international housing aid.[6] Congress cemented Truman's Point Four into law on June 5, 1950, with the passage of Title IV of the Act for International Development; the State Department birthed the Technical Cooperation Administration (1950–53) shortly thereafter. In less than a year, the US government appropriated $34.5 million for technical assistance, with $13 million of that sum to be used by intergovernmental organizations like the United Nations (UN) and the Organization of American States.[7] In the realms of international housing and city planning, the Point Four administrator delegated such aid programs to the Office of International Housing within the Housing and Home Finance Agency (HHFA), led by Roy Burroughs and Jacob Crane. The Office of International Housing had already been founded in 1945 as the National Housing Agency's (1942–47) liaison with public, private, and intergovernmental organizations; it now directly advised the State Department on housing-related technical assistance missions.[8]

Of course Point Four had its precedents, not only in foreign assistance broadly, but in housing and community development specifically. Private investors directed much of this earlier interaction, however, and the US government played but a minor role. For the last century, US experts had exchanged ideas with overseas urban planners and builders

HOUSING AND HOME FINANCE AGENCY

4   This image was used in a document explaining the Housing and Home Finance Agency to other governments around the world. The text below the image was written by Dan R. Hamady, assistant to the administrator for the Office of International Housing: "The home building industry in the United States produces quality housing in vast quantities. It is a highly successful operation carried on by free, vigorous, private enterprise. The role of government is directed to assisting the forces of private enterprise and not to supplanting them. In other words, we have a partnership in which the people themselves, the ultimate consumers, are the beneficiaries." Source: Untitled document, Dan R. Hamady, n.d., folder HHFA, Office of the Administrator-General, 1962, accession 69A5149, box 2, NARA.

primarily through corporate venues. For instance, American companies and engineers had exported the "steel-framed skeletons of American modernity" as part of a late nineteenth and early twentieth-century age of competitive skyscraper production.[9] The multinational American construction firm the Milliken Brothers Company, as well as a host of architects, including Alfred Zucker, Daniel Burnham, Bertram Goodhue, and Kenneth Murchison, all left their mark around the world, with "the Philippines serv[ing] as the first, most visible example of how assiduously US companies, planners, government agencies, architects, and other 'brokers' of American architectural form and space positioned themselves to work in Asia and elsewhere."[10] Foreign trade in US steel and concrete stimulated ongoing exchanges throughout the first half of the twentieth century.

After World War II, exchanges continued, with one important difference: the US government began more actively engaging in questions of housing quality and quantity abroad, funding a housing mission to the Philippines (1946), an HHFA study of Haitian housing (1948), a UN study of housing in South and Southeast Asia (1950–51), and a Pan American Union study of housing in El Salvador, Guatemala, and Costa Rica (1953–54), among others. Point Four added official language to justify this increased public sector involvement, subsuming what had once been disparate housing programs under the twin foreign policy goals of development and anticommunism. Previously scattershot efforts now functioned under a more unified, government-directed agenda, launching ideological warfare through housing assistance.

Federal government efforts reflected economic concerns borne out of the uncertainties of postwar European recovery and the decline of European empires. Officials like Willard Thorp (assistant secretary of state for economic affairs) and C. Tyler Wood (Economic Cooperation Administration) saw Point Four as a supplement to the concurrent Marshall Plan. Point Four could "intensify" the European Recovery Program's efforts, according to Wood.[11] The US needed to "play [the] role of investment banker comparable to that played by Great Britain in the nineteenth century" by resurrecting European production and closing the dollar gap.[12] Thorp believed Point Four would help address trade imbalances in particular by releasing "new sources of supply of necessary raw materials" from Asia, Africa, and Latin America, and by introducing these continents' potential consumers to European and American products, thus "bringing about the kind of healthy economic balance which should work towards bringing an end to our extraordinary financial assistance which we have been giving in the last several years."[13] Wood agreed with Thorp's comments, adding that the Marshall Plan's technical assistance program was "very similar to the Point Four program" and that both had "tremendous possibilities not only for increasing production, but for increasing trade."[14]

In these officials' imaginings, the cost of Point Four would be attractively low compared with the Marshall Plan, since no direct government investment would be made. Instead, "large-scale investment [would] rely upon private capital that in many instances [would] receive a government guarantee. . . . Under this program, the governments of backward areas would provide suitable conditions for the investment of

US private capital to carry out the development."[15] At least in theory, then, the expensive Marshall Plan and the relatively cheap Point Four program would further American economic interests by balancing international trade, raising living standards in ostensibly "backward areas," and opening up new markets for American goods.

Housing aid could also promote international security by addressing the needs of the masses and squelching the appeal of revolutionaries. In part, this sort of housing aid dovetailed with propaganda wars surrounding the good life, first launched in the immediate postwar chaos of Berlin.[16] More practically, it also flowed where geopolitical concerns demanded; in 1947, for instance, the American mission for aid to Greece brought George L. Reed to help with the "extremely difficult and urgent housing problems" facing that country in the midst of civil war (1944–49). Whether in Europe or elsewhere, American advisors hoped homeownership would have an inoculating effect against radical impulses.

While the Truman and Eisenhower administrations doled out housing assistance to a wide variety of countries, one important difference set apart Western European from Latin American, Asian, or African programs: American housing agencies typically classified Western European aid as rehabilitation, even as they labeled non-European nations' problems with housing production and distribution a condition of "underdevelopment."[17] Americans rarely talked about a single global housing crisis despite the fact that slums and shantytowns proliferated just as alarmingly in cities like Paris and Berlin as in Bombay or Seoul.[18] By classifying Western European housing needs separately from East Asian, Southeast Asian, African, Middle Eastern, and Latin American ones, then, American aid givers created an artificial divide between the housing needs of the industrial versus the nonindustrial world, overriding any similarities in housing conditions, limited industrial capacity, or deficiencies in construction materials. This divide would eventually shape circuits of knowledge as much as it determined extent and character of housing aid.

In what would be called the third world, Americans like HHFA official Jacob Crane spoke candidly of the US's primary interest in improved shelter for those nations that were faced with a "temptation to commit aggression against neighbors."[19] Crane and others justified Point Four's cheaper export of "know-how" as a faster way to help more underdeveloped countries overcome their poverty "handicap" through the satisfaction of "solv[ing] their own problems."[20] These nations could shed their "primitive" housing and "achieve our [American] high standard of housing and community environment," thus fending off communist advances, building "democratic ways of life," expanding "mutually beneficial commerce," and developing "an international understanding and good will."[21] In the words of human rights champion and former first lady Eleanor Roosevelt, the US needed to respond to the developing world's "highly emotional" demands that the US do "exactly [for it] what had been done for the children of Europe"—albeit in less expensive ways.[22]

By the late 1940s, anticommunist goals shaped all levels of decision-making in housing aid to the developing world. The rapidly growing number of traveling experts and interested individuals included not only engineers and housers, but also bankers, senators, and State Department workers. These officials favored methods like demonstration housing (prominently located displays of improved shelter), aided self-help (provision of better building materials, more efficient designs for laborers, or experts), and educational training programs (the creation of a domestic professional class of planners and housing experts, or "inperts," as advisor Charles Abrams put it).[23] All of these measures were designed to bolster the formation of capitalist infrastructure and technocratic culture (including the longevity Max Weber observed in bureaucracies), and to inspire capitalist values, most especially by instilling a desire to improve one's own shelter through personal effort rather than through government handouts or foreign, often American, aid. Designed to bring countries into the capitalist fold, these programs also had a politically stabilizing element: families who bought homes had a reason to participate in the political system and to protect their stake in it. As William Levitt put it, "No man who owns his own house and lot can be a communist. He has too much to do."[24]

The idea that the US could help others house themselves—the "aided self-help" principle—emerged from broader applications of self-help vis-à-vis industrialization, agricultural improvement, and other large-scale economic development programs. Self-help techniques gained currency in Europe after World War I "as a pragmatic, untheorised response to severe housing shortages and political unrest," in the words of geographer Richard Harris, and the term "aided self-help" itself was coined by Crane. Post-1945 applications decisively linked such housing programs to national economic development—a connection driven by both expansionary capitalist and Cold War security interests.[25] By 1952, self-help Point Four programs included Puerto Rican training of Antiguan housing personnel, adapted native building materials programs in Egypt, basic housing design for Liberia, study missions in Costa Rica, a new port development plan for Kandla, India, water and sewage systems in Karachi, and a village improvement plan in Iran.[26] In these and successive projects, aid givers emphasized that housing assistance only mattered in the context of broader development. When aided self-help housing programs took off before a "general aided self-help approach covering fuel, water, food, health, et al.," American officials like Ellery Foster worried that "we put the cart before the horse."[27] Underneath these policies lay a firm conviction in a "system of self-effort, which we call capitalism," according to Crane's successor Dan Hamady.[28] "We are selling democracy and buying security at a nominal cost through this [international housing] program," Hamady noted.

Advisors underscored the temporary nature of US-subsidized technical assistance in any demonstration of capitalism, and they emphasized that such temporary assistance must jumpstart larger development processes, not simply provide badly needed houses. This was the US's mission and obligation. According to Henry Luce, the US had thus far failed to play its part as a world power.[29] In the postwar years, anticommunist rhetoric added a missionary-like zeal to those who would amend this failure: as Roy Burroughs (HHFA) wrote to George Reed (Foreign Operations Administration) in 1954, "It is urgent that you get a Housing Generalist out at once . . . 'The fields are white unto harvest.' "[30]

In looking back at this fervent, highly politicized, technical rather than capital aid (advice over cash) approach, it is not so clear whether the Marshall Plan and Point Four actually succeeded at improving housing conditions through the build-up of expertise and short-term incentives for private investors, as Economic Cooperation Administration, Technical Cooperation Administration, and Mutual Security Administration officers claimed. Nor is it self-evident that housing aid promoted capitalism. Government-supported private aid was designed generally to reduce dependence on state aid, and specifically in housing programs, to enable homeowners to invest their own labor and savings in home improvements instead of waiting for handouts. Ideally, these programs should have helped develop "a closer understanding of this country [the US], among less fortunate peoples," according to the HHFA. Hamady explained, "We are helping them to erect a barrier between them and the communistic ideology that proclaims that all that is good flows from the power of the state."[31]

In practice, however, US aid strengthened—not weakened—the role of governments in improved housing. Developing states relied on substantive, sustained capital assistance (not merely technical assistance or advice) from the US, and American investors likewise relied on government incentives to spur speculation in improved shelter overseas. Those programs that did not receive long-lasting, substantial US government aid faltered and generally failed to address mass housing needs. This unexpectedly large government role complicated the rhetorical emphasis on a purely market-driven housing system and had direct consequences on the ground. In addition, the centralized, top-down character of US housing assistance negatively affected implementation of specific aid programs, where local tailoring might have made a difference. Houser Catherine Bauer anticipated these problems in 1946, noting that international aid would "necessarily, and properly, be dominated by . . . professional planners and housers," but that officials needed to understand that

[housing] issues involve profound social decisions, not merely questions of modern technique, efficient administration, good design and progressive legislation. For instance, as an ideal standard, should every family have the opportunity to live in a private house with a garden? Or are there inevitable trends toward more collective living habits? That is a basic question for housers and planners, and *one they cannot answer by themselves.*[32]

American officials did not systematically address Bauer's point about local involvement because they thought of the international housing issue in crisis terms requiring immediate concrete action, not prolonged discussion or deep, substantive community input. For the US, housing assistance was more Cold War diplomacy and international public relations campaign than grassroots reform effort. Consequently, American advisors were often caught off guard and ill prepared to handle troubles with local implementation when they inevitably arose. Compounding these difficulties, American housing experts often glossed over inconsistent details in published findings, applauded "successfully" concluded anticommunist self-help programs, and ultimately yielded inaccurate policy judgments. The need to showcase anticommunist victories left little room for error or for nuanced assessments. In short, Cold War motives had long-lasting impacts on how housing aid was granted, sold, and repackaged to domestic and foreign audiences.

Fighting Chinese Communism, One House at a Time

Up until 1948, Americans felt little urgency in addressing the specific housing needs of China. The global housing crisis was expanding at an alarming pace for at least four basic reasons: the suspension of new construction during the global depression and war, the destruction of housing stock during World War II, the postwar chaos of returning soldiers, refugee flows, and internal migration, and rising birth rates all led to an inadequate supply of housing and severe deprivations for impoverished populations around the world. In this context, China's housing woes hardly seemed extraordinary.

The limited aid that did make its way across the Pacific came in the form of young, inexperienced housing advisors like twenty-five-year-old Navy lieutenant Norman J. Gordon. Originally from Brooklyn, New York, Gordon had been sent by the US military to China in February 1944, where he spent a year training anticommunist guerillas. After World War II ended, the United Nations Relief and Rehabilitation Administration (UNRRA, 1943–49)[33] tapped Gordon for a new post as housing advisor to China. In January 1946, general Chiang Kai-shek himself chose the young New Yorker to advise the Chinese Ministry of the Interior and to join Ha Shiung-wen (Department of Construction within the Ministry of the Interior) in planning a new Shanghai. Eventually, Chiang expected Gordon to devise a "program for rebuilding some of the cities into modern economic entities under a general industrial and business plan for China." According to the *New York Times*, Gordon was a man who "understands the Chinese well."[34]

Gordon was green to be writing housing policy for major Chinese cities, even in an advisory capacity. He had completed his master's degree in city planning at MIT in 1943, served on regional planning boards in Cleveland, Boston, and Montclair, New Jersey, and had been in China since February 1944 completing two housing studies of Nanjing and Hankou.[35] This brief resume hardly gave him the necessary skills to adequately assist Chiang and Ha, but the depth and breadth of the worldwide housing shortage meant weathered experts were in short supply. That the US saw fit to send no other men or women reflected both the low priority of Chinese housing issues in 1946 and 1947, and the overwhelming shortage of able-bodied international advisors.

Despite the weak American response, the Nationalist government's housing problems were far from trivial. General Chiang had to cope with severe shortages in the midst of an ongoing civil war. The recently concluded Sino-Japanese war had devastated major cities, and places like Shanghai and Nanjing suffered some of the worst living conditions in the world. Even before the war, mortgages had been limited in access because of high interest rates and brief amortization periods; after 1945, a shortage of building materials brought construction costs up as well.[36] Not surprisingly, few new houses had been built in any major Chinese

5   The original UNRRA caption from March 10, 1947, read, "A Chinese mother and her children survey the wreckage of what was once home. UNRRA is helping to rehabilitate people like these." Source: UNRRA Visual Information Office, Washington, DC, as catalogued by UN Archives. UNRRA 745.

city from 1937 to 1945. All this led to a brief but on-target assessment from Gordon to Jacob Crane: "Exhibits of what we are doing here in the United States will not be of much practical value to the Chinese . . . [They will come back with] the common Chinese comment on things American, 'Well that's all right in America but we are not as rich as you.'"[37] Given the escalating civil war, Gordon had little recourse but to focus on small, practical measures such as the setting up of technical assistance programs for architects and engineers and the establishment of a reference library for the Department of Construction and Planning. By 1948, postwar US-China relief funding only approached $46 million total.

Congress did not fully comprehend the details of the Chinese civil war, nor did representatives understand what role living standards played in Mao Zedong's movement. It took the dedicated efforts of congressmen like House representative Walter Henry Judd (Rep-MN) to explain the importance of US aid. Formerly a medical missionary in

China (1925–38), Judd repeatedly confronted secretary of state George Marshall's (1947–49) reluctance to help non-European nations and openly disagreed with the secretary's claim that the "character of the emergency" in Europe was quite different from that in China, according to Marshall. The European crisis was "immediate," while "China, under its present importing procedure and its present resources is able to go along to that extent in the way it has been going."[38] In one committee meeting, Judd directly confronted the lackadaisical attitude toward China:

There is grave doubt that the proposed assistance to Europe can really do what we want, or all we want, unless there is a check in the deterioration of conditions in the Far East, and the beginning of recovery. For example, how can European countries like France, Britain, and the Netherlands recover until something like their prewar pattern of trade with the Far East can be restored. China is the key to the Far East.[39]

According to Judd, it was utterly perplexing for "the United States [to take] such a position with respect to European nations which [were] threatened by Communist minorities and . . . [not] with respect to China when it [was] threatened by a Communist minority."[40]

The secretary of state agreed that the situation in China caused "deep concern" and that "we should extend to the Government and its people certain economic aid and assistance," but it was unclear exactly what that aid would look like; at the November 1947 meeting, Marshall hemmed and hawed before refocusing attention on European funding.[41] Ultimately, however, the secretary would put China on the agenda. In February 1948, Marshall came back to the same Committee on Foreign Affairs with a proposal for $570 million in Chinese aid.[42] That same year, legislators created the Economic Cooperation Administration (ECA, 1948–51) to distribute Marshall Plan funds in Europe and to manage aid to China and Korea as nonmember states. (The official sixteen member states were all European.) The US government kept close tabs on housing in China, and Marshall received updates from the American consulate on new construction, especially the "jerry-built" squatter variety.[43]

After the ostensible "loss" of China with Mao Zedong officially declaring the People's Republic of China in October 1949, the ECA turned a much keener eye to housing conditions on Formosa, a 225-mile-long island and new headquarters for General Chiang and the Kuomintang (KMT). For many reasons, American strategists found regional developments alarming, most notably since a successful communist invasion from the mainland would make Formosa a "serious threat to the defense of Japan, Okinawa, and the Philippines, and indirectly, to Southeast Asia."[44] According to the ECA, the island needed to be "economically self-supporting within a few years" and the "political climate" needed to foster public confidence in the KMT.[45] With UNRRA disbanding in 1949, US aid steadily increased, and ECA aid surpassed the $12 million mark in fiscal 1950. US policy toward "Free China" (Taiwan) emphasized the supply of commodities and capital, and technical help through the advisory services of an American private engineering firm, the J. G. White Engineering Corporation, as well as the Joint Commission on Rural Reconstruction (JCRR), an advisory group funded entirely by the International Cooperation Administration and consisting of two Chinese and three American members. In 1951, US aid rose by another $60 million and included a new military component—not surprising, given President Truman's explicit concern over regional security after the outbreak of the Korean War on June 25, 1950.[46]

Meanwhile General Chiang and the Chinese Nationalists focused on what they believed was one of the most important steps in building public confidence: local land reform. Nationalists and Americans agreed land reform would lay the foundations for greater political stability. Secretary of state Dean Acheson and the JCRR understood well the potential ramifications if the Nationalists failed to address massive inequities in landownership. Even before Mao reaped the full benefits of mass rural discontent in October 1949, the JCRR urged the KMT to reduce rents and offer greater tenure security in Taiwan, Szechuan, and Guangxi.[47] Taiwanese governor and future KMT vice president Chen Cheng in fact began a three-stage land reform program in June 1949 with a US$30,000 grant-in-aid from the JCRR, a program that would continue in Taiwan long after Mao assumed control of the mainland.[48] This support may have been modest as a percentage of American investment abroad, but it was significant in that it broke new ground by "put[ting] the United States in the position not only of urging or morally supporting such reform but also of helping to carry it out" and providing a "genuine demonstration of American interest and concern for [Chinese] welfare."[49] Under the terms of Chen's program, the government would go on to reduce farm rent, sell "public farm land to tenant farmers with long-term repayment periods," and enact a "land to the tiller" program by breaking up large holdings and permanently limiting the amount possessed by any single landlord.[50] These policies served related interests: the KMT needed farmers to have a stake in their government, and privatization of public landholdings would create a pool of capital for investment in industry and commerce.

From 1949 to 1953, land reforms produced dramatic results. Over 70% of tenant farmers in the Taiwanese system had their rents reduced. Sale of public grounds increased tillable land by roughly 25%. The ratio of tenants to owners shifted from 44% (1948) to 17% (1953). According to economist Samuel P. S. Ho, "By adopting a policy of redistribution first and growth later, the benefits of government policies introduced to stimulate agricultural growth . . . [were] spread relatively evenly over the entire rural population."[51] The rapid expansion of owner over tenant cultivation also set an important precedent: land reform proved that government-stimulated mass property ownership could serve the interests of the KMT, the general populace, and possibly even the US. More farmers owned their land; more capital went to seedling industries; and the KMT had a more compliant and satisfied populace and therefore more political stability.[52]

It was not entirely clear to the American Congress how involved the US should be in funding Nationalist housing reforms, even with their anxiety over the "loss" of China. Some congressional representatives argued vaguely, "A line must be drawn against communism somewhere,"[53] but Taiwan faced a bevy of political and economic challenges with no clear prioritization of housing needs. American legislators, meanwhile, remained leery of large aid programs for overseas economic development.[54] In a climate of intense American economic and military aid abroad—in retrospect, the peak of US foreign aid spending in the second half of the twentieth century—senators and representatives demanded compelling reasons to add new programs. Overall, development aid spiked upward from 1946 to the early 1950s because of twin concerns with national security and human rights, but of the two, the former mattered more by law: the US Mutual Security Act of 1951 explicitly stated, "No economic or technical assistance shall be supplied to any other nation unless the President finds that the supplying of such assistance will strengthen the security of the United States."[55]

Chinese dockworker housing therefore attracted American attention only because its dire state threatened Formosan ports, the Chinese Nationalist economy, and regional political stability. Put bluntly, impoverished urban residents could only attract US aid if their living conditions jeopardized international security. Workers at key ports received first attention. In the case of Taiwan, the port cities of Keelung (in the north) and Kaohsiung (in the south) mattered most because they served as conduits for Taiwan's export of sugar and rice and import of fertilizer and crude oil, among other items.[56] Agricultural products still formed the backbone of the Taiwanese economy, as industrial and mining workers constituted a minority of the workforce, albeit a growing one, up from 92,424 in 1945 to 310,210 in 1954.[57] In rough order, dockworkers and farmers, industrial workers, and miners formed the backbone of the national economy in the early 1950s. Not so surprisingly, then, dockworkers at the two key ports received the first and most substantive American aid toward housing improvement in Taiwan.

Individuals played a critical role in facilitating this sort of aid as well. In Keelung and Kaohsiung, one young American supply officer and civil engineer named Albert Fraleigh made it his personal mission to raise awareness of local dockworkers' abysmal living conditions. Shocked and outraged by what he saw, Fraleigh took every opportunity to persuade Chinese and American officials to tour dockworkers' quarters. Indeed, Fraleigh had every reason to be appalled: some five hundred men shared a one-story dormitory of approximately 30 by 80 feet in 1952, and a subsequent typhoon erased even those primitive conditions. Thereafter, workers slept outside or under bridges. Fraleigh showed visitors "dockers' families living in empty crates and in sheds, packed so closely that no partitions separated them as they slept. Sick dockers stared dully out of the gloom as the parties probed through the area."[58]

On one such visit in the spring of 1953, touring officials finally vowed to take action. By July, the Chinese Council for United States Aid (CUSA), the MSA Mission to China, the Keelung Harbor Bureau, and Keelung Dockers' Labor Union had come to an agreement: they would pool money from the dockers' welfare fund (accumulated from automatic wage deductions), half of the rebate shippers gave to the American Foreign Operations Administration (FOA, 1953–55) for the unexpectedly fast work of Taiwanese dockworkers (roughly US $100,000), sixty days or 480 hours of unpaid labor from each worker (or his self-assigned substitute), and a government-donated long-time free lease on the land. Those families lucky enough to move into one of the first 102 houses would have monthly amortization payments set at 15% of family income. Payments would then go toward the construction of additional worker housing. Each family would own their brand-new home in less than a decade.[59]

From Improved Housing Quality to Homeownership in Taiwan

Initially, the emphasis on housing aid in Taiwan was on quality rather than tenure type. According to Roy Burroughs (HHFA), for instance, Communists achieved "rapid construction of capital goods" through the "heartless" denial of basic needs, but a democracy improved standards of living simultaneously with the growth of the national economy. For Taiwan, "strengthening of national defense necessarily [had] first claim on the time and resources of this island buttress against Communism. This defense, as well as the future improvement in the standard of living, required major emphasis on advancement of technology together with the amassing of the capital equipment to go therewith." Decent shelter was "a prerequisite to the good health of a family," and health was in turn "a necessity in the build-up for defense."[60] According to the FOA, American assistance for dockworker housing improvement made sense because it demonstrated the "Chinese government and Mission's concern for workers' living conditions" and therefore supported political stability.[61] Again, these arguments did not initially emphasize resident-owned units over rentals, but rather stressed housing quality.

Homeownership quickly became an equally important part of US efforts in Chinese housing improvement, however. There were a number of reasons why opening up homeownership to more individuals made good sense for a country at war with communism: first, it allowed the KMT to save money on expensive public housing projects in an era when the government needed the bulk of its spending to go to the military. Second, it made better use of what the government termed "leisure" hours, giving workers an incentive to repair and construct during their spare time when they would normally be "idle" (or more likely, resting). Third, it improved on-the-job performance to an astonishing degree. After the completion of the first round of housing units at Keelung, dockers halved vessel turnaround time and almost entirely stopped damaging and pilfering cargo. Fourth, this system of homeownership bound together government and labor unions into a system of mutual benefit, with the latter put in charge of many accounting duties, including the disbursement of all monies, the maintenance of progress records, and the issuance of periodic reports to the national government and the FOA/ICA. According to Taiwanese ILO representative, T. K. Djang, this kept "the labor union officials occupied and exert[ed] a centripetal force to the Union from hitherto apathetic members," since only the union could issue moratoria on mortgage payments in cases of illness or other personal emergencies.[62] The system worked so efficiently that the ICA rejoiced that the Dockworkers' Union had become "one of the best labor unions in Taiwan," and the US-aided housing projects, "excellent example[s] of Sino-American assistance to a Labor Union activity which directly benefits Asian Workers."[63] Fifth and lastly, homeownership allowed both governments to emphasize the "self-help spirit" of the venture, subsuming what would eventually become hefty US financial assistance (over NT$20 million in 1955 through surplus agricultural sales) under what the FOA/ICA asserted was the evacuees' much more important labor contribution. Evacuees contributed all un-skilled labor necessary to construct the homes, community buildings, and other facilities. The US downplayed the cash contribution necessary for these families to "be content with their choice of remaining in the free world."[64]

These early successes fueled more trans-Pacific exchanges. The Na-tional Housing Program Working Group subsequently requested specific information regarding American-style mass homeownership, including the legal mechanics of the Federal Home Loan Act of 1933, the National Housing Act of 1934, and the Housing Acts of 1949 and 1954. Although the Chinese Nationalists could not afford to offer government support for very lengthy amortization periods, they nonetheless strove to re-duce down-payments to 10% where possible, and interest rates to 1% per month over the period of the loan.[65]

From an American point of view, this type of assistance—"aided self-help" homeownership—could engender a "positive psychological impact on the people of Taiwan," according to the FOA. Joint hous-ing programs could "convinc[e] them of the aim and ability of Sino-American cooperation."[66] At the Kaohsiung opening ceremony on April 3, 1955, Fraleigh introduced a ceremonial gift of fifty-four mirrors in-scribed with the words "Abundance of Welfare by Selfhelp. Through this gift, "the US Government means to say that it firmly believe[s] that the welfare of people in any country is achieved by self help. . . . [This] new villa was entirely built up by the mighty two hands of each la-borer in Kaohsiung themselves, and what the US Government and the Chinese Government had done in its completion is merely some form of assistance."[67] Putting it in even simpler terms, Fraleigh exulted that Keelungers had learned "they can do something for themselves without waiting for the Chinese or US Government to come along and do it for them."[68]

This American emphasis on individual participation over government aid differentiated US rhetoric about aided self-help from other equally enthusiastic endorsements of the same. One year before Fraleigh deliv-ered his heartfelt speech, for instance, Danish and Swedish experts met with Latin American engineers, lawyers, architects, and economists in a special UN housing seminar, urging the latter to pursue economic de-velopment through national housing production and to nurture private investment through such techniques as the government assumption

6   Keelung dockworker families move to their new homes, May 1, 1954. The original caption to this image read, "We're glad we chose freedom." Source: Folder 1951–1954, box Chile-China, RAG 207, NARA.

of risk via a guarantee on low and medium-cost housing.[69] Unlike American counterparts in Keelung, Scandinavian housing advisors recommended that Latin American experts direct private interest toward nonprofit housing, since "the historical development of housing in Denmark has shown that private enterprise is too speculative to assure a regular supply of housing"; "housing is too important a commodity to be subjected to the same general market conditions as other goods"; "a housing shortage should never be exploited to the detriment of the tenants"; and "non-profit housing associations in the Scandinavian countries have proved to be the most effective means of helping to solve the housing problem."[70] In their view, local governments should work to actively reduce land speculation, and public revenue should continue to provide direct grants for social housing which "should not be made available solely on the basis of ownership."[71] In rural areas—the one sector where Danish authorities urged "small ownership"—individual investment was encouraged only because it would give tenant farmers and resident laborers "a refuge from which they will be able to bargain more freely for their labour."[72] If many experts urged aided self-help, then, Americans were unique in their emphasis on free-market ownership and a largely hidden government role. Scandinavian programs might have seemed similar to American aided self-help at first glance, but closer examination revealed fundamental differences in ideology and intention.

To be clear, American emphasis on a largely hidden government role did not equal a truly laissez-faire, free-market system. US housing programs required far more government action than self-help rhetoric might suggest. Fraleigh got it exactly wrong when he stated that Keelungers had learned they could "do something for themselves": the American housing project in Keelung demonstrated the utter *dependence* of improved shelter and accessible homeownership on government aid. Founding father and premier Sun Yat-sen valorized broader landownership as part of his principle of livelihood (Mínshēng Zhǔyì, or Three Principles of the People, 1905), but three decades after Sun's death, most Chinese families still lived in squatter settlements—many owner-occupied, but hardly the ownership society Sun had envisioned. Tenure type took second place when the shelter was of such low quality that it posed a health hazard. Unfortunately, the Yuan (legislature) had no money to back up the right of "every Free Chinese citizen to own and occupy adequate housing," and from 1950 to 1965, a tiny 0.1% to 2.3% of the annual national budget went to social welfare. Chinese Nationalists had little incentive to spend money on local housing when they intended to recapture the mainland as soon as possible. With no government-built housing, rentals out of reach, and an ever-growing refugee population competing for scarce shelter, squatter settlements were the only choice for most working people. The average laborer lacked not only capital and training, but also the basic tools and materials necessary to build efficient, long-lasting houses. The Keelung Labor Union drew up a ten-year housing project in 1952, but had to abandon it entirely on account of a "shortage of necessary funds."[73]

This inability was precisely the reason why US technical assistance funds flowed to Taiwanese ports in the first place. American aid went explicitly to "projects which were unlikely to have been financed by the recipients in the absence of technical assistance, thus avoiding to some extent the substitutability problem" where government aid might push out potential private investment.[74] At every level of Fraleigh's demonstration project, success depended on substantial state assistance. To give just a few examples, the project could operate on ten-year amortization cycles only because it received NT$651,890 of US counterpart grant money for Keelung.[75] The low cost of housing was made possible by the Keelung Harbor Bureau's donation of land, and only extensive US and KMT government action brought homeownership within reach: the US deposited NT$6.6 million of counterpart funds into the national Land Bank at 6% per annum, and the KMT government contributed NT$10 million at 18% per annum by the end of 1954.[76] By June 1955, builders, lenders, special trust funds, and more would join forces to deposit an additional NT$20 million on the KMT side, investments that were then matched dollar for dollar with US counterpart funds.[77] The Land Bank could thus invest the American contribution in the Bank of Taiwan at higher interest rates and average the domestic with foreign interest rates to a more affordable 10% per annum.[78] Again, the lower interest rate would not have been possible without government participation.

This critical government role did not elude free marketers. Although market liberals hoped aided self-help would eventually propel widespread private investment, they also understood current successes owed much to the flow of US aid dollars and they worried that Taiwan would develop an unhappy dependence on it. The American National Foreign Trade Council aired their concerns in 1951 as follows: "It cannot be expected that economic environments conducive to the investment of American private capital will be established in these foreign lands so long as the governments concerned have reason to believe—as they do have reason to believe—that *they will continue to be the beneficiaries of the hand-outs our own Government has given them for so long.*"[79] American officials continued to provide public assistance despite such concerns, and despite the alluring possibility that private enterprise might foster economic development on its own, for one simple reason: the struggle against global communism demanded close monitoring of economic health in vulnerable states. Nothing could be left to chance. As justification for public funding, Roy Burroughs (HHFA), George Reed (FOA), and other administrators very consciously emphasized their primary goal of national security in all manner of details, including the ranking of individual Taiwanese loan approvals from "workers and staff members in defense or related industries" at the top, and "common citizens" at the bottom, for access to mortgage assistance.[80] In addition, they strictly followed regulations on the use of counterpart funds. (Counterpart funds could only be used to provide rate-subsidized loans to builders or home financing for newly built houses, not for land purchase.) This attention to details helped justify US government assistance as a politically necessary, highly regulated form of pump priming, despite obvious contradictions with the larger ideology of self-help.

Unfortunately, the pump needed constant priming. In October 1955, the Taiwanese government's National Housing Commission led by minister Meng Chao-tsen planned to host a national housing exhibition showing off new model homes and selling a few of the samples at the end of the two-week long event for cash. The lucky buyers would be selected by lottery in order to prevent sellers from making profits over 10% of cost. Demand was high, and the demonstration seemed to have succeeded, but for one glitch: dismayed Americans Bert Fraleigh, Hugo Prucha (ICA/MSA Mission to China), and Roy Burroughs realized too late that the Housing Commission was having difficulties getting Chinese contractors to actually build more homes in line with the demonstration models. Contractors clamored to build the initial sample homes, since the Housing Commission provided land, roads, gutters, water, and electricity, and advanced them 70% of the construction cost. Only two contractors wanted to take on additional orders, however. In a desperate move to lure more private interest, the Chinese government offered construction loans drawn from the counterpart fund. Even there, the state was stymied again, as contractors could not secure land title and therefore had no need for construction money. The builders declared they would only be interested if the NHC made land available, secured cement from the government's Bureau of Supply, and agreed to finance half of the total cost over five years.[81] Not by any stretch of the imagination could the demonstration be labeled a successful revivification of private investment.

United States Operations Mission (USOM) officers saw no contradiction in government-backed private investment and profit. T. R. Bowden, deputy director of USOM-China, for instance, celebrated the exhibition as an unequivocal victory of free-market housing, a "great awakening among the people to the housing problem," a "local revolution" demanding "government plans and modern methods . . . formerly unknown in Taiwan or China."[82] To be sure, some 100,000 people traveled three miles from Taipei to visit the exhibition, and at least some of those 100,000 were excited about owning a new home. Bowden saw this excitement as an unambiguous call-to-arms for the government: the National Housing Commission would need to produce "large amounts of housing rapidly" lest it "suffer severe criticism"; contradictorily, "private builders have indicated increased interest in investing in housing,"

7   One of the lucky future homeowners in Taiwan's National Housing Exhibition, October 31,
    1955. Prospective homeowners had to post performance bonds in order to be included
    in the lottery. These houses were made affordable by government subsidies. Source: Folder
    1955, box Chile-China, RAG 207, NARA.

"builders and [the] house buying public [were] brought together," and
"hundreds of houses can be built by free enterprise without further NHC
assistance."[83]

Not only did USOM workers tolerate the cognitive dissonance of an
aided, managed market, they actually expected government funding
and management to increase through the late 1950s. The ICA declaimed
a determination "to [help] other countries solve their housing problems
with their own resources," preferably in ways that would stimulate private savings and international investment in local housing.[84] In the
same documents praising the Chinese for pulling themselves up by their
bootstraps, internal ICA proposal and budget sheets tellingly labeled
aided self-help homeownership in Taiwan a "Public Housing Program."[85]
The emphasis on temporary governmental support for private housing
investment resulted in a paradoxical "snowballing [of] housing affairs"

for the Yuan and a growing need for a larger, permanent, governmental national housing agency and staff.[86] The Taiwanese state grew with "free-market" housing.

Meanwhile, US aid continued with no clear end in sight. Since August 1954, the FOA had been funding a mobile demonstration truck showing coal-mine and salt-mine workers how to use a newly developed soil-cement block maker, and it provided technical assistance for the creation of the National Housing Authority (NHA), which had as its ultimate goal the "enabling [of] every Chinese citizen to occupy and own adequate housing." The Lowcost Housing Exhibition in December 1954 had introduced four different models of affordable, modern construction and officially launched the new national program that used counterpart funds to finance low-cost housing loans to urban dwellers in Taipei, Keelung, Kaohsiung, Taichung, and Tainan, and to a lesser extent, to workers, fishermen, construction firms, and farmers across the island.[87] American officials in the HHFA and FOA hoped this infant NHA would eventually secure "matching Chinese funds from non-[commercial] banking and non-governmental sources."[88] By late 1955, Prucha, Fraleigh, and Burroughs all urged amendments to Chinese national laws, changes necessary to successfully implement longer-term mortgage-financing schemes and to put into place the building society model used so effectively by "poor English families" a "century or more ago."[89] Americans had already learned from the British example, the three men argued. The US had established modern savings-and-loan institutions that pooled savings and "put them to work."[90] Taiwan could do the same to combat its intense capital shortage: individual savings should be funneled into down payments on homes and should generate ripple effects by attracting private capital and investment in housing. The NHA might also solicit foreign investment through the new American Housing Investment Guaranty Program.

Above all else, Americans underscored the importance of legal practices in the success or failure of state-aided homeownership. Foreclosure and eviction processes needed to be outlined if the new homeownership program was to be taken seriously. In order to give individuals "a valuable incentive for making savings," free title upon loan repayment would have to be guaranteed. FOA officials emphasized, "Citizens must be assured of their ability to own their own homes and do part of the labor work if they wish to lower costs."[91] Workers would resist using their off-hours to build new housing if they had no promise that the improved shelter would be theirs to keep. For these reasons, American administrators became caught up in all manner of legal minutiae, from the refinement of foreclosure and eviction laws (laid out in section 877 of the civil code) to the precise language of land titling.[92]

Throughout, the American justification for these costs continued in predictable fashion: "The citizens of Taiwan will be filled with hope and encouragement for a better future and their confidence in their government's concern for their welfare will grow as they rally behind a national housing program. 'Own Your Own Home' has as much appeal as 'Own Your Own Land'!" The FOA explicitly recommended the NHA remain "an advisory and policy supervising body for the Housing Program, patterned after the US Housing and Home Finance Agency. The NHA might insure bank loans if this step [was] considered necessary by [the] FOA." If the NHA adapted details of home financing and titling to suit local, capital-poor conditions, the National Housing Program could still showcase to "an impoverished Asia" the ways in which "the citizens of Free China [had] raise[d] themselves from hovels to clean, healthy homes built with their own hands from their own resources."[93] Whether new construction took the form of apartments in the cities or hillside family homes in the environs, the US would encourage the Taiwanese government to develop a "permanent program" under which citizens could "build, own, and occupy adequate housing."[94] Strangely, the difficulties experienced thus far did little to dampen American enthusiasm for mass homeownership and in fact seemed to make American advisors more determined than ever to achieve homeowning societies across Asia as part of the war against poverty and communism.

Why did men like Bert Fraleigh, who clearly understood the importance of US aid, speak publicly about the power of sweat equity and downplay the critical role of the Chinese and US governments in building a homeowning society?[95] Fraleigh provided the answer himself in a memo explaining a subsequent and possibly the "largest selfhelp housing plan undertaken under ICA assistance in Asia"—the resettlement of some 5,107 Tachen and Nanchi Island families into thirty-four new self-help villages. In this critical case, Americans needed to quickly and decisively showcase the power of private enterprise, whatever the facts of actual implementation. Evacuees had arrived en masse in Formosa in 1955 after the US pressured General Chiang to concede the Tachen Islands, a cluster of islands located two hundred miles north of Taiwan. Soon afterward, the Chinese Nationalists had also given up Nanchi Island to Mao's troops. The resulting refugee crisis tested the practical power of ideology. Could capitalism provide for those fleeing Chinese

8 Tachen residents celebrating the ICA-funded New Village Moving-In Day at Yu Ming, Ilan County, February 8, 1956, with village elders in foreground and new housing in background. ICA officials labeled this image, "The Tachen people resolve to defeat communism." Source: Folder 1956, box Chile-China, RAG 207, NARA.

forces and provide evacuees with decent homes and enough to eat? Would the government hand out necessities, or would it help people help themselves? Fraleigh understood the political ramifications of poor living standards and explicitly framed the resettlement program as an illustration "to those enslaved by communism that people who choose the free way of life can build a better life through their own efforts and the guidance of free governments concerned for their livelihood."[96] Much as dockworkers in Keelung and Kaohsiung benefited from a lower monthly installment system, so also could refugees benefit from affordable ownership programs in new villages surrounding Yilan in northeastern Formosa. Residents only paid one-third the actual cost of the new villages, and the ICA the balance, but US officials touted the plan as "most significant because the Tachen refugees are rehousing themselves." With seemingly unselfconscious sincerity, they added, "The project deserves adequate worldwide publicity as an evidence of Free World concern for refugees from communism."[97]

In the case of Taiwan, anticommunism was no mere window-dressing for economic development projects. Anticommunism was the underlying motivation for American foreign aid, and it profoundly shaped the type of assistance Americans gave as well as the spin they put on results. Housing aid could not have unfolded in the way that it did without a compelling Cold War agenda. Perhaps most tellingly, Americans chose to "phase out" their USAID Mission in China and to turn over housing policy and urban development planning work to the UN in the mid-1960s only once "the island economy [had] been characterized as being on the verge of 'take off'" and American foreign policy experts could rely on relatively stable governance by the KMT.[98] Homeownership was a Cold War weapon of sorts, and US housing advisors were able to wield it in Taiwan because it meshed well with local needs.

The Failure of Halfhearted Housing Aid in Burma

It is easy to observe the impact of American foreign policy on countries caught in the crosshairs of Cold War conflicts, but what happened to those nations eliciting weak American interest as second-tier sites for geopolitical strategy? Insubstantial, inconsistent American housing aid efforts in countries like Burma emerged as a byproduct of larger geopolitical concerns in East and Southeast Asia. The US consistently supported the Chinese Nationalist military from Mao's revolution in 1949 until 1954, and as a consequence paid some distracted attention to the overcrowded, degenerating living conditions found in Burmese urban centers like Rangoon. Following the broader pattern of postwar housing crises, Rangoon suffered a dearth of building capacity, scarce natural resources, a population explosion, nearly nonexistent planning staff, the remnants of a British colonial grid system within which Burmese families crowded together in increasingly untenable numbers, and a suburban push to accommodate the plethora of low-income laborers.[99] Burma was ripe for aid.

Alas, halfhearted American housing aid produced ephemeral results, proving that Point Four could not bring about housing improvement unless pressing national security concerns fueled a substantial, long-lasting US commitment. Within the first few years of Point Four, American advisors stationed in all corners of the globe came to the same conclusion: according to associate director George Reed of Burma's National Housing Board, "recipients of Point Four . . . are realizing more and more how little can be done in a year or two years and how the long-time projects are more necessary and more effective than some of the so-called impact projects."[100] Programs only worked when states made real long-term financial commitments to improve shelter. In a concurrent assessment of US aid programs' relative successes and failures in Western Europe, ECA workers agreed the West German housing program's astonishing success could be attributed to the fact that the average worker paid roughly 20% of his wage toward housing (as opposed to the French 3%, for instance) and because the state subsidized 80% of new housing starts in 1950, thus bridging the gap between an economic rent and what workers could afford.[101] Whether in Western Europe or East Asia, successful American technical assistance required heavy local government management and capital investment by the US, the host government, or both.

Despite these limitations, Jacob Crane hoped Burma might serve as a good place to experiment with new technical assistance ideas specifically targeting housing improvement with *reduced* state aid. According to Crane, the Southeast Asian nation was an ideal place to test out new ideas "since US-Burma relations are good and since it is a smaller and more manageable country."[102] (This despite the fact that Burma was the second-largest nation in Southeast Asia.) Initially, the ECA made standard commitments to help foster economic development, paying US$1.6 million to development projects "vital to the country's pacification," hiring a firm of American consulting engineers, and helping the Burmese government establish their national Rehabilitation Corps to "avert social unrest by training large numbers of people in trades" and to "get people accustomed to a normal life of peaceful pursuits," including the improvement of housing "and other enterprises of a public nature."[103] In an ECA meeting in Washington, DC, Crane broadened his assessment, noting that the US needed to adopt a "New Deal outlook" in South and Southeast Asia, one that weighed social welfare equally with development considerations. The Rehabilitation Corps was good, but not enough: "The tendency in Washington and in the field offices to assume that higher living standards, including better housing, will automatically result from economic development . . . [is] not necessarily true," and "in the case of housing, the situation may worsen under conditions of economic development," in Crane's words.[104]

Crane was right, but how to motivate American housing aid in addition to development? Congress had little interest in paying more to improve housing in a relatively unthreatened nation. A radical renewal program was out of the question. Still, Rangoon had been badly damaged during World War II and had the additional problem of approximately 200,000 new refugees out of a total population of 800,000 in 1950. This meant literally "hundreds of thousands of people . . . now squatting in *basha* (woven bamboo) huts,"[105] an obviously unsustainable state of affairs. It was in this context that Ellery Foster devised a housing tactic to test on the rough villages of the capital city. Why not adopt an even more incremental approach to aided self-help, one that "show[ed] people how to improve their condition in their present houses, even if those houses are terribly inadequate"?[106]

The Burmese National Housing Town and Country Development Board liked it. This was a low-cost, piecemeal program that did not daunt would-be participants with alarming bureaucracy or an overwhelming price tag. Under this new scheme, the board would sell towns or cities wholesale corrugated aluminum sheeting, a product obviously more fire-, vermin-, and rot-resistant than *basha* and proven in Panama to be comparatively cooler than iron. Each participating city would deposit one-sixth of the purchase price as down payment and pay even installments without interest over the course of the following five years. In addition to the interest, the board would subsidize the price when necessary to bring per user costs within reach of the average Burmese family. The board retained title until full payment was made, and if the borrower defaulted, the city would reclaim the sheets to be either resold or returned to the board. Ultimately, the individual family was beholden to the city, and the city, to the board.

The aluminum roof program seemed like a good idea, and the city of Prome bought the first major urban shipment of 19,001 sheets in April 1953.[107] Certainly, it was a creative technique: first, it made new building technology immediately available to any interested party. Second, it sought incremental improvement for wide swaths of the population, instead of dramatic changes for a few. Third, it effectively hid the government subsidy by reducing purchase prices and eliminating interest.

Why, then, did it produce such uninspiring outcomes? As it turned out, its greatest strength was also its most serious flaw: the program was by definition so incremental that it had no dramatic value, no ability to impress the general public or to earn the government political capital. The US provided a new building material that had no psychological connection to an improved housing type. American officials also complained that their loan program stumbled along in part because supplies had to be constantly redirected to emergency housing for fire victims. Emergency stopgap uses hardly glamorized corrugated aluminum in the public eye. Even worse, when it came to literal dollars, American effort was halfhearted at best, most likely because the US was more concerned with other pressing concerns in China and Korea and because, as Crane stated simply, US-Burma relations were good in 1951. USOM committed a paltry three men to the entire Burmese housing assistance program, and in a tour of various Burmese cities in the fall of 1954, Hugo Prucha (USOM-Burma) found that many municipal officers had never even heard of the aluminum roofing program.[108] In the middle of Prucha, George Reed (FOA), and B. Douglas Stone's (HHFA) efforts to roll the roofing program into a new national mortgage loan program, the Burmese government abruptly announced they would henceforth prefer to receive aid through UN channels in 1954. Such a weak housing program had little ability to counteract the much greater Burmese distaste for American military aid to Chinese Nationalists stationed in their country.

In the end, the roof scheme yielded few real benefits for either recipient or donor nation. Lackluster housing assistance programs could not disguise American geopolitical interests as humanitarian or development efforts. Aided self-help required a concerted public relations campaign and, more importantly, large-scale capital commitment in the form of increased staff and splashy, high-impact projects. Sadly, given Reed's very early awareness that little could be done in a one- or two-year program, what should have been long-term aluminum roofing and mortgage loan schemes both lasted less than two years.

According to a forlorn one-page assessment of the Burmese program in 1962, American advisors noted they had left behind "important new concepts" before withdrawing in 1954.[109] Ongoing embassy reports to the State Department belied this wistful retrospective: in contrast to the minuscule American roof and loan programs, the newly installed Ne Win government began a massive relocation campaign, building four immense satellite towns around Rangoon from October 1958 to February 1960, and spending nearly $28 million kyats (US$5.8 million) in the process. Colonel Yee Aye (retiring CEO of the board) commented in 1960 that even with such enormous government spending, "it would take ten years to clean up and modernize Rangoon."[110] UN aid programs proposed equally ambitious if unrealized guidelines: a 1961 plan recommended massive decentralization, dramatic reduction of density from as high as 636 persons per acre to two hundred persons per acre, small-house building plots with rooms for front gardens and kitchen gardens, greenbelts, and one playground for every neighborhood unit.[111]

American accomplishments seemed paltry indeed. Without substantial, sustained aid, US overseas housing programs had little hope of making an impact, and anticommunist considerations decided which countries would receive serious assistance. All other would need to cope with housing crises independently. American experiences in Burma proved that incremental aid would not yield incremental improvements.

From Aided Self-Help Architecture to Aided Self-Help Finance in South Korea

At the same time that Americans doled out housing aid to Burma, a very different pipeline was being set up for Korea. Unlike Burma, the Korean peninsula elicited a great deal of American concern. It would be reasonable to assume that given Cold War interests and the strategic and military importance of Korea, Americans might pursue housing aid programs in Korea similar to those in Taiwan, leaving Burma the under-funded exception. This did not happen, however, and the Korean case illustrates the power of local players in refashioning American housing aid to suit local needs. South Korea became an important benchmark in the evolution of American housing assistance because experiences in that country drove American experts, government officials, and private industry representatives to reevaluate their enthusiastic endorsement of aided self-help architecture in favor of new experiments with aided self-help finance—a shift that had critical repercussions for American interactions with other nations thereafter.

Like China after the Japanese surrender, the as yet undivided Korean peninsula suffered severe housing shortages aggravated by a mass migration of people. Roughly 1.6 million Koreans moved from 1945 to 1949, whether back to the motherland from overseas domiciles, away from the political domain of the North Korea Bureau of the Communist Party of Korea, or as part of the mass rural exodus to cities.[112] For most Korean migrants, the destination was Seoul, a city already destabilized

by variously challenged colonial land titles and uncertain housing markets. Even with a new construction rate of 5.9% during those five years,
Seoul could not come close to meeting overall housing need, and the
onslaught of war in 1950 again disrupted any attempts to address the
severe shortage.[113] At end of war in 1953, the southern Republic of Korea
(ROK) government estimated that 900,000 new or rebuilt homes were
needed for a total population of 21 million, with an average of five to
six persons per home. Cities like Seoul and Incheon were hit particularly
hard. Runaway inflation and food shortages wracked the nation, and
building supplies were in painfully short supply.[114]

Americans were well aware of these difficulties, and of the potential
unrest such conditions might breed. As early as September 1945, Government and Relief in Occupied Areas sent a shipment of US$502.5 million
of mostly consumer goods in order to make Korea "a strong, independent, and democratic nation that could serve as a balancing factor in
the East Asian region and as a showcase of free democracy to be emulated by other Asian nations."[115] The ECA took over the management of
aid to Korea by the end of 1948. Although its efforts were curtailed
by the onslaught of the Korean War, American aid dollars continued
through other agencies. In 1950, for instance, American dollars switched
streams to the multilateral United Nations Civil Assistance Command
(UNCACK) that was managing Civil Relief in Korea (CRIK, 1950–56)
funds, and the United Nations Korea Reconstruction Agency (UNKRA,
1951–60).

While American aid swapped institutional nameplates, in reality these
changes were not so dramatic. For instance, roughly 65% of UNKRA's
budget came from the US, and ECA staff remaining in Korea went directly to work for the new UNKRA.[116] The US government chose to operate under a UN umbrella at the time because it hoped to project an
image of international solidarity, to demonstrate that other nations—
even neutral ones—stood by Americans in giving aid to a "victim of
Communist aggression."[117] Political aims thus provided a sturdy core to
US-Korea aid programs that switched nameplates, but not necessarily
Cold War security interests.

When it came to housing assistance, American aid occupied a consistently critical position. Whether in the joint UN years up to 1956, or
in the subsequent bilateral aid years, US dollars played a singular role
in shaping housing policy for South Korea. Foreign aid contributed to
93.5% of all government-funded housing and 28% of all housing starts
in Korea from 1951 to 1960, and the US provided the lion's share of
those foreign aid funds. In fact, the US dominated many aspects of

the Korean economy, spending roughly $12 billion, or approximately $600 million per annum, in Korea from 1945 to 1965. According to scholar Woo Jung-en, the US gave roughly $600 "for every Korean man, woman, and child" from 1945 to 1976.[118]

In the immediate aftermath of World War II, Americans attempted to institute similar programs of aided self-help construction as had been done in Taiwan. Aid workers urged Korean leaders to consider a new architecture of earthen blocks that could transform the Korean countryside, moving destitute and desperate families into a more adequate form of shelter. This emphasis on compressed earth seemed particularly sensible given that wood shortages had stymied any effort at mass construction before, during, and after the Korean War. Domestic forests had been decimated by the Japanese and by the local population for heat and fuel, and while traditional Korean homes used readily available mud wattle, stones, and bamboo, they also relied on wood frames and heavy timber roofs with large beams and nails to adjoin the pieces. As a result, an unsustainable 90% of the national housing budget went to lumber imports in 1952. In response to this chronic wood shortage, UNCACK members counseled the Housing Division of the Social Affairs Bureau in the Ministry of Social Affairs to experiment with rammed-earth homes, realizing a 50% or more savings on cost and making new construction possible on a mass scale.

Despite the fact that compression machines were very much products of the industrial age, however, mud brick houses held little initial appeal for most Korean families and even less for a new government intent on proving itself. Unlike American advisors who thought of overseas housing quality as an academic problem answerable through scientific research, Korean officials understood the social and political meanings attached to the home, and they had little desire to urge citizens to build what appeared to be primitive mud structures, no matter how technically "improved" or innovative Americans claimed they were. The Korean Housing Division summarily rejected UNKRA's first housing proposal, noting that earthen construction was for poor people and not befitting a model demonstration project. Instead, the Housing Division argued, UNCACK should strive to put forward an aspirational standard of living for average Koreans and thus inspire greater housing improvement and modernization.[119] UNCACK advisors protested that "unfortunately the Korean people are poor" and "economies must be made," and they continued to urge earth construction in letters and reports. Only after UNKRA included the Institute of Korean Architects (IKA) in the design of the compressed-earth home did compromise become possible.

9 President Syngman Rhee and UNKRA head General John Coulter inspecting Landcrete earth-block makers for the 1953–1954 UN-funded housing program. Each home could be built with the unskilled labor of future homeowners, and cost $750, with roughly half ($380) going to imported materials. Source: UN UNKRA online exhibit S-0526-0350-5, United Nations Archives.

Together, UNKRA and the IKA taught families to make rammed-earth blocks with the South African Landcrete machine; the home was then plastered with a concrete-earth mixture and finished with a traditional-looking wood and tile roof. Ultimately, foreign advisors had to work within local design standards and expectations if they intended to build.

This compromise hardly ended the UN's troubles. There was the classic chicken-and-egg problem of domestically producing nails, glass, and cement, which required investment in industrial machinery, transportation lines, and oil or gas to fuel operations, all of which might produce jobs and better house workers so that they might more willingly produce more nails, glass, and cement. There were problems with housing standards and construction methods, both found to be "primitive" and "far below any . . . that would be permitted in the United States or Europe," according to UN surveyors. Overcrowding had "always been prevalent judged by western standards," and "houses [were] just too small and [had] too few rooms to accommodate the large households."[120]

10 A Korean home built with UNKRA funds. Note the smooth exterior, plastered with cement and earth, as well as the tiled roof laid on top of a wood base. Source: UN UNKRA online exhibit S-0526-0350-6, United Nations Archives.

American observers had little appreciation for the organization of the Korean home, including the *madang* (courtyard) and the multifunctional use of a single room. Wood problems persisted, too: even when UNCACK and ROK Office of Supply workers cooperated to bring desperately needed lumber imports to build new houses, supplies often got "mislaid," "borrowed," or sent to the wrong destination. Meanwhile, the overall picture became grimmer still: by 1953, 900,000 new or rebuilt homes were needed, and runaway inflation and food shortages wracked the nation.[121] Only a strong core of political interest could keep the Korean Civil Assistance Command (KCAC) workers motivated under these circumstances; they persisted because they were steadfast in their belief that "where there is lack of housing there is social unrest."[122]

From the start, then, South Korean urban housing efforts deviated from the Taiwanese dockworker program. Aided self-help programs with compressed earthen blocks would be used very differently in Seoul, Incheon, or Busan than in Keelung or Kaohsiung. Koreans also faced a greater housing crisis in terms of scale and scope because of the devastating impact of the Korean War from 1950 to 1953. President Dwight Eisenhower sent Henry J. Tasca to the South in the spring of 1953 to assess needs and to come up with concrete recommendations for postwar recovery. After surveying the leveled landscape, Tasca suggested a " 'three-year integrated economic program of military support, relief and reconstruction' totaling approximately $1 billion," increased Japanese trade with Korea in order to stave off any temptation to trade with "Communist areas," and the replacement of UN multilateral aid with direct US control.[123] Eisenhower subsequently redirected $200 million in remaining defense funds to the new, more centralized US aid agency, the Foreign Operations Administration (FOA).[124] American C. Tyler Wood became the head of the UN Office of the Economic Coordinator (OEC), an office that replaced KCAC and integrated US and UN aid to Korea.[125] Wood, although working for the UN, also served simultaneously in US agencies dedicated to managing overseas economic and technical assistance (the FOA and the International Cooperation Administration/ICA).[126]

11　UNKRA's earthen homes behind traditional Korean houses in Hweekeedong, East Seoul. Note the absence of the *madang* (interior courtyard) in the UNKRA homes. Source: UN UNKRA online exhibit S-0526-0351-19, United Nations Archives.

By the time Wood invited Keelung housing expert Bert Fraleigh to Korea in the winter of 1955–56, Americans unquestionably dominated Korean policymaking with regard to housing. Wood hoped Fraleigh would be able to find cost-cutting measures at a time of prospective dollar and counterpart stringencies, and he imagined that Fraleigh's successes with aided self-help in Taiwan made him the perfect man to recommend a future course of action in Korea. "ICA aid to a housing program in Korea might be justified on political grounds," since low-cost housing had the potential to deter "the spread of Communism," according to Wood, but ICA aid needed to be "limited to the importation of essential housing construction materials in short supply, plus such technical assistance as may be determined by OEC to be necessary."[127]

When he arrived, Fraleigh dismissed the multilateral UNKRA as "too much desk work, [and] not enough field work or supervision" and suggested the OEC take the helm, henceforth avoiding hiring former UNKRA workers.[128] US agencies like the ICA henceforth kept track of UNKRA's housing work in response. Still, the funding stream officially split after 1956.

More importantly, Fraleigh sought housing solutions that maximized private participation in the same way aided self-help had in Taiwan. At least a few American companies saw this as the opening they had been waiting for, a moment in which they might exhibit what the free market could do for development without massive government assistance. International housing investors joined together to create what became known as the American Korea Foundation (AKF), a private organization that incorporated government oversight through the FOA, any local governments involved in its programs, and South Korean president Rhee Syngman's administration (1948–60), but that also highlighted the ability of the private market to address mass housing needs.[129]

AKF members made no secret of the organization's explicitly political mission. The foundation joined with the US National Association of Home Builders (NAHB) and New York developer William Zeckendorf of Webb & Knapp to launch a "Homes for Korea" project touting the benefits of private philanthropy and investment while helping "this Asiatic bastion against communist aggression" help itself through the establishment of a home-building industry.[130] Through private donations, "all American businessmen [would be given] an unparalleled opportunity to . . . demonstrate the advantages of free enterprise . . . and [help] develop a basic private industry that [would] contribute to a strong, stable Korea."[131] The NAHB did not expect to make money directly through charity; instead, president Earl Smith noted that by

HOMES FOR KOREA

Homes For Korea
will help the Koreans
help themselves. It
offers all American
businessmen an unpar-
alleled opportunity to:

•
Support a private
industry program of
technical assistance for
a worthy and valiant
ally, The Republic
of Korea.

•
Demonstrate the
advantages of free
enterprise by showing
free enterprise
in action.

•
Help the Koreans
solve their severe
housing shortage and,
at the same time,
develop a basic private
industry that will
contribute to a strong,
stable Korea.

•
HOMES FOR KOREA
DESERVES YOUR
SUPPORT!

12 Depiction of undesirable Korean housing, according to a National Association of Home
Builders and National Housing Center's pamphlet. In the pamphlet are included the words
"This Asiatic bastion against communist aggression is desperately in need of homes for
its people and industries for its economy. A home building industry, introduced through
American private enterprise, is uniquely suited to fulfill both needs." Source: Folder 1946–56,
box 65, RAG 207, NARA.

paying to teach Koreans how to build better homes, the NAHB could essentially buy "insurance against war and [the] resulting disruption of the home building industry [in the US]."[132] The *Washington Post and Times-Herald* enthusiastically lauded the project as "Private Industry's Point Four."[133]

To the AKF's dismay, however, the 1955–56 Homes for Korea project struggled to become the privately driven housing program its sponsors had envisioned. The original plan met failure at every turn, most glaringly in the balance ledger: the AKF could not inspire enough American private donors, and the housing they did build cost much more than anticipated. Each unit required over $5,000 to construct, in contrast to the Korean Housing Administration's $1,500 per comparable unit. AKF rentals came to 40,000 hwan (US$80) per unit per month, "more than the entire monthly earnings of most Koreans in lower income brackets."[134] From the beginning, the AKF relied on both US and Korean state assistance to defray land and transportation costs. Even after the ICA's $600,000 subsidy of ocean transportation costs for foreign materials and the ROK's provision of 5.65 acres of land in a desirable part of northern Seoul near Dongnimmun (Independence Gate), the AKF managed to run up a debt of $300,000. Architectural details fell equally short: the AKF houses were small and lacked storage space for Korean essentials like grain, kimchi, and preserves. Seventy-five percent of all AKF units had showers instead of the preferred bathtub.

Homes for Korea ultimately proved an expensive liability for the ICA, which had to pick up the tab in order to preserve faith in American competence and good will. The lessons of the Homes for Korea project were threefold. First, ICA leaders learned the American government would be held accountable for actions by private American organizations, regardless of actual participation. For the South Korean public and the ROK government, American aid was American aid, regardless of whether it came through private or public funds. Second, private organizations lacked the wherewithal or the desire to competently manage substantive overseas aid, instead relying on critical government sponsorship and financial aid to achieve profitability. Third, private experiments came nowhere near having a real multiplier effect. The great majority of South Koreans still needed decent shelter after the devastations of war. (After this disastrous foray into investment in South Korea, the AKF went on to the much more manageable task of funding training for "older girls" providing "domestic service and child care in Korean and Western homes.")[135]

Americans needed to take a new approach to housing aid in South Korea. By spring of 1956, the fledgling nation had passed through the refugee stage, with UNCACK helping homeless families construct temporary dwellings. Typical were the 3,200 wood-and-cement self-made houses for 16,000 refugees in Chungcheongnam Province in the western part of South Korea. These would hardly suffice in the long run, however, as winters proved particularly bitter in uninsulated structures. The AKF had already proved unable to stimulate mass private investment, and it was clear the government would need to take the helm.[136] The ICA finally moved decisively in 1957, working cooperatively with the Korean government to create what USAID later called "one of its most comprehensive housing programs" on record.[137] With $2 million in American aid monies, 1.5 billion hwan of counterpart funds, and 4 billion hwan of Korean government funds, the two governments worked jointly to apply the aided self-help principle to housing finance instead of housing construction.

This was a dramatic change in the American approach to housing aid. The first stage of the new housing program showcased a new Housing and Home Development Fund (HHDF) within the Korea Reconstruction Bank that provided low-interest, long-term mortgages (3% during construction, 8% thereafter up to ten years) for "working people and [the] professional classes."[138] These terms were further liberalized to a uniform 4% for twenty years by 1963.[139] The new program would target home-building credit to "needy, non-indigent Koreans . . . who form a major portion of the country's population, to help themselves solve their own housing problems with their own modest resources."[140] In addition, the new program provided training for personnel in mortgage finance methods that "until this activity got underway, were completely unknown throughout the country." It placed emphasis on design and construction techniques as well as the stimulation of the building materials industry, prioritized information dissemination to the general populace including a "Why I Need a Better Home" essay contest for school children, funded the writing of new housing legislation and standards, and prioritized the curtailment of expensive commodity imports like cement within five years.[141]

To the great delight of the ICA, this multipronged, government-driven approach excited immediate interest from various cross-sections of the Korean population. New programs accurately assessed interest in improved housing finance and national legislation. In addition, the populace itself had begun shifting away from its earlier attitudes about homeownership and housing improvement: in the immediate post-war years of 1953–54, many refugees held onto a firm conviction that reunification would happen soon, and that they could then return to their former properties in the north. ICA workers observed a waning of this belief by 1956–57, as Korean families increasingly took on a more "realistic understanding that unification is very uncertain and that the best interest for them is the development of their projects to the point where they will become self-supporting in the shortest time."[142]

Loan application rates reflected these factors. From July 14, 1957 (the official start date for HHDF loan application submission) until August 30, 1957, 114,000 applications for over 16,000 new dwelling units came in. Successful applicants typically joined a large number of prospective owner-occupants under one cooperative, as in the case of the first HHDF-approved project for 200 new dwelling units in the neighborhood facing Seoul's main rail station. In this preliminary effort, area residents living in "shacks, tents, and other makeshift shelters" became owner-occupants of new houses built on the same land, with loan funds supporting both slum clearance and new construction. Geographically, HHDF received appeals first from Seoul City and the surrounding province of Gyeonggi, then increasingly from provinces and cities farther away from the capital.[143] For the first time, it appeared Americans had stumbled on a way to actually help large numbers of "non-indigent" Koreans better house themselves while also stimulating participation in depository savings institutions among a larger proportion of the population. Aided self-help could occur in housing finance, not just construction. So long as American aid continued unabated, aided self-help could fuel this particular form of burgeoning homeownership. From 1957 to 1961, ROK government funds constituted only 5.6% of the total amount of housing loans released, whereas US aid alone provided 55.7%. (General funds, vested property disposition funds, and UNKRA counterpart funds made up the rest.)[144]

Aided self-help finance had found one of its first success stories in South Korea, then, conditional on external US aid. Unfortunately such successes did not last, not because of any structural flaw with aided self-help finance itself, but rather because both the US and ROK governments wavered in their commitment at the exact moment that housing assistance gathered momentum and programmatic cohesion. The timing was bad: from 1957 to 1960, the ICA helped erect 32,239 new dwelling units and the national government conducted its first national housing survey in 1957–58. In April 1960 and May 1961, however, two successive political upheavals resulted in first, the ousting of the unpopular President Rhee by a student-led prodemocracy movement, and then a successful military coup d'état by General Park Chung Hee (1961–79). Regime change included massive administrative overhauls, as Park's government strove to eliminate corruption and inefficiency. Housing switched from the Ministry of Health and Social Affairs to the Office of National Construction (ONC), and then, to the ONC's successor, the Ministry of Construction (where it remains today). The Korean National Housing Corporation replaced what USOM-Korea advisor Guido Nadzo called a "retarded, inefficient, and discredited" Korean Housing Office (also called the Korean Housing Administration or Association) in 1962.[145]

Such changes might have had a positive impact on aided self-help programs, but General Park combined such streamlining efforts with a new focus on export-oriented industrialization and a personal preference for reformed rural living (as evidenced by his later Saemaul movement). These emphases put urban housing programs indefinitely on the back burner. While housing needs had not been resolved from 1953 to 1961, there had been some hopeful uncertainty about future policy; by 1962, development plans explicitly relegated urban housing to a second-tier issue of social provision. Park's administration did attempt some limited new construction, including notable early *ap'at'u tanji* (high-rise apartment complexes) in the early and mid-1960s, but even the larger-scale squatter clearance and resettlement programs of the late 1960s took their cues from economic development goals, clearing land only when needed for commercial and office spaces.[146] Up until 1971, the public sector built or financed a mere 16% of the total housing stock. Not until the 1972 National Housing Construction Promotion Law and the Plan for Construction of 2,500,000 Houses did the Park administration begin addressing issues of large-scale organization and supply of housing—and not coincidentally, at the same moment USAID became interested once again in Korean housing.[147] By that time, the already problematic urban density of the 1960s would reach crisis levels, demanding more concerted high-density urban planning and reconfigured American aid policies.[148]

Aided self-help finance programs did not die a premature death in South Korea, however. Nor was Korea the sole testing ground for such practices. As noted earlier with the Burma case, the Technical Cooperation Administration (TCA, 1950–53) had already begun urging similar aided self-help finance projects in South and Southeast Asia in the early 1950s, albeit without the same scale of development loan funds or direct aid and therefore without the same successes. Still, US interest in a region holding "one-fourth of the world's population and over one-third of the population of the Free World," covering 2.8 million square miles "strategically situated astride the Pacific and India Ocean lines of communication between the Near and Far East," and well "within the orbit of Communist Russia and of Communist China power expansion" had the potential to move quickly from low to high priority.[149] The region provided the Free World with the largest share of vital raw materials like manganese, rubber, tin, copra (coconut meat used to extract oil), fibers, and rice; it likewise served as a critical importer of US and European cotton, grain, and machinery. Any government failure to meet aspirations for improved living standards would undoubtedly result in increasing receptivity to "Communist or other extremist propaganda" and would jeopardize US access to raw materials and trade.[150] Although Korea received the lion's share of development loan funds in the 1950s, South and Southeast Asian housing programs began concurrently and would become critically important to US foreign relations in later years, carrying forward aided self-help finance programs begun in South Korea. Likewise, East Asian lessons would carry over into housing policies in other parts of the world like the Middle East.

It was in decolonizing countries first, and then Latin America soon after, that Americans would ultimately focus their greatest efforts in the late 1950s and early 1960s respectively. By 1962, Cold Warriors' concern with the Korean peninsula had tapered off almost completely; relatively stable stalemate and the decline of American involvement in Korean housing issues under General Park's administration freed the USAID office for more urgent programs elsewhere. Secretary of state Dean Rusk wrote a cryptic but revealing note to the Korean USAID office in 1963: "DLs [development loans] for housing in Korea should be of low priority in view of other current projects and potential projects forthcoming."[151] For Rusk, the next major development loans and extended risk guarantees would need to be planted in more politically volatile regions like Latin America. With aided self-help finance stalled in South Korea in the early 1960s, one phase of American housing aid ended and another began.

Worldwide Americanization?

Perhaps no other moment in Cold War housing rivalries is better known and studied than the famous "Kitchen Debate" between then vice president Richard Nixon and premier Nikita Khrushchev in 1959. The debate was memorable and eminently quotable, certainly; it captured the tone of US-Soviet relations from the start of the Cold War until détente in 1974, when President Nixon and premier Alexei Kosygin signed the US-USSR Agreement on Cooperation in the Field of Housing and Other Construction that launched a new era of exchange and shared technical expertise.[152] Throughout the first decades of the Cold War, American housing experts and government officials were intent on showcasing the accessibility of the suburban home to an international audience—in Nixon's words, "Any steel worker could buy this house!"—and to persuade others to emulate and reap the benefits of modern homeownership. Khrushchev debated Nixon with such vigor precisely because he understood the ideological importance of housing policies in a cold war.[153]

The Kitchen Debate was not the most important or even the first moment when housing became a site of political contestation, however. Clearly, American housing aid in "Free China" and South Korea set the tone long before Nixon set foot on Soviet soil. Early Cold War housing programs in Taiwan, Burma, and South Korea established that such programs would need to secure sustained, substantial state aid if they were to demonstrate the power of homeownership and private housing investment. American foreign policy analysts were troubled, "not [with] the rapid pace of worldwide Americanization but the lack thereof."[154] It remained to be seen what that "worldwide Americanization" might look like in decolonizing regions of the world.

THREE

Homeownership in an Era of Decolonization

To those peoples in the huts and villages of half the globe struggling to break the bonds of mass misery, we pledge our best efforts to help them help themselves.
JOHN F. KENNEDY, 1961[1]

American advisors may have exhibited an ideological commitment to homeownership, but they did not do so indiscriminately: politics mattered. Even as the Cold War unfolded in East Asia, Americans hesitated to intervene directly in regions still entangled in questions of imperial control. Cold War preoccupations dominated US and Soviet aid projects in the 1950s, '60s, and '70s, but for leaders in decolonizing regions, these years were also fundamentally about the eviction of former colonial powers, the fight for sovereignty and independence, and the articulation of a third world distinct from the first or second worlds. For many decolonizing regions, communist-capitalist rivalries occurred within the context of crumbling empires.

American housing experts had little choice but to learn this context. In engaging questions of building, finance, and design in conflict zones, housing experts came to see their role as a scientific one, one that might inspire new efficiencies and raise living standards across the decolonizing world. Experts wrapped what were in fact strongly ideological positions with what they believed was a neutral language of development. With this rhetoric, they sought to verbally distance themselves from any appearance of political interest or neocolonial intent. Instead, housing advisors couched their involvement as part of a larger humanitarian effort to help decolonizing regions help themselves. With aided self-help techniques, developing countries could not only improve the lives of their poorer residents, they could launch industrialization and install an orderly urban landscape legible to international investors.[2] American housing experts embraced aided self-help for its quintessentially capitalist, anticommunist ethos, but this language also provided a more palatable way for US planners, architects, and housing experts to insert themselves into debates about appropriate shelter policy in transitional and decolonizing countries—at least, from the viewpoint of the Americans themselves. The term "self help" denoted support for self-determination and national sovereignty, not a rising American empire.

Homeownership played a critical part in this story. There were simple, practical reasons for this: aided self-help—the notion that a future homeowner could contribute his labor to make better use of government assistance (whether in the form of land provision, basic utilities, and/or expert advice)—relied on participants having greater motivation to contribute that personal time and labor. US advisors hoped emotional investment could be acquired relatively quickly and painlessly with the promise of ownership. Even more importantly, the politics of decolonization required it. Years of colonial management and public health movements had established segregated cities with clearly demarcated, unequal spaces. Across the British, French, and Dutch colonies, poor living conditions in native quarters helped galvanize anticolonial and in some cases, communist movements at the end of World War II.[3] Americans hoped housing campaigns with literal buy-in would douse these political fires and give newly ascendant regimes an opportunity to build administrative institutions, trade networks, and industrial capacity, all of which would bolster global capitalism and American security. Traveling advisers feared the seductive power of public housing for new governments eager to prove themselves to their citizens and to the world. Direct provision might appear to be just as politically efficacious as a private housing system; if the US hoped to demonstrate the benefits of market over public housing, it would need to work quickly.

Not all private housing was worth owning, however. Some homes were built outside the regulatory and supervisory bounds of laws and tax codes. Others promoted values antithetical to a modern economy. In delineating what exactly constituted "good," "modern," "decent," "improved" shelter, Americans became active participants in international debates over such basic questions as, What was a good house? A decent home? What constituted a desirable community? Who had the right to build or destroy? These issues, while obviously concerned with the physical details of housing design and urban planning, also tapped into much more profound concerns with self-determination, national identity, and a rising development and modernization discourse that defined progress in culturally and architecturally specific terms. Housing policy could reshape how much power the state had vis-à-vis individual citizens, particularly with regard to land rights and forced relocation, and thus connect with politics as well. Houses became visual markers of the overall state of development in a nation, of the accomplishments of a particular political leader or party, of the worth of some residents over others. Architectural design and residential land use informed investors' ideas about value, profitability, and credit.

Debates over designs and plans thus offer insights into some of the fierce, competing visions of state and society unfolding in the 1950s, '60s, and '70s, connected as they were to processes of decolonization in many parts of the world. American experts participated in but did not control these debates; rather, they cooperated and competed with an international group of itinerant architects, planners, engineers, and scientists interested in shelter in decolonizing regions. In their various advisory capacities, US housing experts urged newly emerging states to increase access to homeownership through government incentives and reforms, and they demanded the right to participate in such discussions. Put more simply, Americans consistently injected questions of home-ownership and self-help into decolonizing regions through the "neutral" vehicle of tropical research.

This chapter begins by exploring US housing experts' attempts to make sense of decolonizing regions through the rubric of tropical housing studies. In establishing climatic relationships between decolonizing and postcolonial regions of the world, Americans tried to bring together otherwise widely varying locations and peoples into a category that could be better accommodated through scientific research and technical expertise. In this they were joined by architects, planners, and housing officials from around the world. With a seeming lack of self-consciousness about their own empire, prominent American advisors like Jacob Crane held up "successful" housing experiments in the semi-tropical US territory of Puerto Rico as an example for other tropical or semitropical regions across Southeast Asia, Africa, and Latin America.

From a broader description of tropical housing studies, this chapter moves on to detail the content and uses of the Puerto Rican model. Included in this discussion are the reasons why housing programs did not in practice yield predictable, rising rates of single-family, owner-occupied units, despite effusive mainland praise for aided self-help and homeownership campaigns. Irrespective of the fact that the Puerto Rican model included such surprising features as a large public housing program (envisioned as a stepping-stone to homeownership and at odds with the philosophy of aided self-help), American advisors regularly referred to Puerto Rican housing experiences in their work in other countries, promoting the tropical program as a model of self-help for such newly independent countries as the Philippines and Singapore. Contrary to expectations, however, the American "tropics" influenced Philippine and Singaporean housing policy less than mainland institutions like the FHA or Fannie Mae, or the homeownership and suburbanization campaigns led by iconic figures like William Levitt—developments and people that so utterly transformed the US urban landscape. Traveling American housing advisors did inform homeownership programs abroad, but more often than not, it was mainland institutions, construction, and finance techniques that newly independent countries wanted to learn about, not the transnational or tropical models US experts pushed so eagerly.

Each country had its own domestic politics to attend to, and these imperatives shaped responses to American ideas. In the Philippines, for instance, government officials built new national housing institutions designed to support upper-income homeownership. Modernization efforts worked hand in hand with controversial relocation programs that moved squatters from central Manila to semiurban or rural aided self-help or core housing sites, usually in nonelection years. In other words, Philippine policymakers set up a split homeownership system, with the affluent making use of increasingly sophisticated housing finance to buy their homes, and with poor families shifted out of the way of modernization campaigns and offered conciliatory homeownership in sub-urban or rural locales. In Singapore, by contrast, the ruling party worked hard to build one policy through housing policies. It made a point of differentiating its homeownership programs from the racially segregated, unequal housing systems promoted by the US government, pointedly embedding its own mass homeownership program within an explicitly *public* housing system and touting the egalitarian nature of government provision with no hidden subsidies. In Singapore, public housing had political power that could not be matched by homeownership alone. What emerged from various American engagements in decolonizing regions, then, was not a single practice of homeownership or even a steady advancement of American interests through emerging development discourses, but rather a plethora of homeownership programs that engaged similar questions and that used parallel language but that also put forward distinct versions of "homeownership for all."

The Tropics as Entry Point for American Experts

From the outset, the "tropics" were no simple fact of environmental science, but rather an invented unification of vastly different regions by mostly European and American actors, and of relatively recent genesis.[4] In the mid-nineteenth century, Europeans and Americans used the tropics as a way to classify and comprehend other worlds; in historian David Arnold's words, "Calling a part of the globe 'the tropics' or some equivalent like 'equatorial region' or 'torrid zone' became a Western way of delineating something culturally alien as well as environmentally distinctive from Europe (especially northern Europe) and other parts of the temperate zone."[5] The idea of the tropics traveled between colonial regimes, creating a new conceptual space of racial, geographic, and cultural identity that alternated between "moral miasma," lush paradise, and raw state of nature.[6]

This conceptualization of a tropical landscape continued well into the postwar decades. For G. Anthony Atkinson, a British architect and highly influential colonial liaison officer of the Building Research Station, economic and social "backwardness" played the greatest role in defining the tropics, although he concluded somewhat facetiously that "the greatest single characteristic of a tropical climate is that it is hot."[7] The ongoing struggle to define the tropics reveals just how troublesome the "science" of the tropics was in practice: UN advisors wrestled with various problematic measures before mapping the "tropical zone" as a nebulous region spreading erratically from the equator, transgressing the Tropics of Cancer and Capricorn to inexplicably include northern India, Iraq, and South Africa.[8] Anatole Solow, the chief of the Division of Housing and Planning in the Organisation of American States, limited his definition of the tropics in 1949 to regions "characterized in the main by relatively high temperatures combined with excessive humidity."[9] Alas, Solow then muddied this relatively straightforward definition with an inclusion of the whole of Africa in his list of tropical regions. Meanwhile, British staff officer for the Tropical Medicine Survey Dr. Curt R. Schneider forthrightly confessed his own troubles with the term *tropical*, admitting that sites were arbitrarily chosen for his research

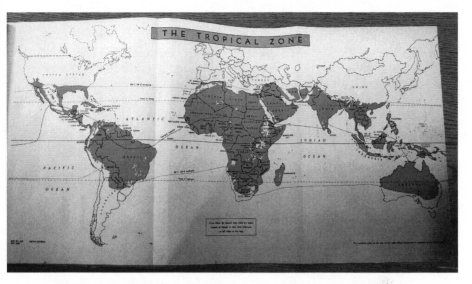

13 The UN's 1952 map "The Tropical Zone" delineated a climatic region that spread out erratically over countries roughly situated between the Tropics of Cancer and Capricorn. Source:
UN Housing and Town and Country Planning Bulletin 6 (May 1952): back page.

in a sweeping study that encompassed 170 countries, all economically
underdeveloped. By Schneider's logic, nonindustrial areas offered a
more "convenient research 'field.'"[10] German climatologists Wladimir
Köppen and Rudolf Geiger's five climate types set up an international
reference point in the late nineteenth and early twentieth centuries;
still, experts employed an ad hoc, highly variable system when conducting individual studies, and Catherine Bauer Wurster concluded that the
world required an internationally uniform census and a "universal yard-
stick" to measure tropical housing.[11] Despite all of the acknowledged
inconsistencies, Bauer asserted in 1963, "no one questions the fact that
most of the people in Asia, Africa, and Latin America live in very low-
standard homes, and little documentation is needed here."[12] Such comments captured the imperfect construction of the tropics as a distinct
region. Tropical housing needed to be studied because of the unique
effects of climate on shelter, yet those regions not neatly fitting clima-
tological definitions still needed to be part of a tropical study because of
obvious, if undocumented poverty.

Tropical architecture evolved alongside tropical hygiene and health
movements. T. Roger Smith's 1868 paper on tropical architecture for the
Royal Institute of British Architects (RIBA) first launched climate-centered

design experiments for expatriates in British colonies, and the study of cross-ventilating breezes and climate fatigue quickly gained momentum with the advent of germ theory and mosquito breeding studies, again primarily aimed at improving the health of colonial officials working in foreign climes. Early theories often produced a strange amalgamation of construction practices: in a segregated suburb of Freetown, Sierra Leone, for example, British colonial officials chose to elevate housing on columns and pour cement below, ostensibly to stop mosquito breeding while also "prevent[ing] malarial poisons that might rise from the soil."[13] Deeply racialized ideas about environment and culture also played critical roles in shaping architectural practices. The secretary general of the French Society of Town Planners argued in 1952 that tropical architecture should consider the needs of the tropical "native": "The African body react[ed] better to the tropical climate than that of the European, and thus required somewhat different ventilation devices [in homes.]"[14] Likewise, British architect Atkinson unabashedly connected climate with cultural-racial characteristics and building types, arguing that the "Arab" dweller responded to his hot, dry climate by devising light clothing to protect from radiation and to provide insulation against the desert air, building homes with thick walls and small openings to keep heat out, while the "Negro" found comfort in nakedness and inactivity, constructing his home with thin, permeable walls and large open spaces to allow airflow.[15]

Intense anticolonial struggles in the late 1940s, '50s, and '60s gave new urgency to tropical housing research. The French Congrès International de l'Urbanisme aux Colonies et dans les Pays de Latitude Intertropicale (1932) had already begun expanding the geographic reach of tropical research beyond colonial interests, as had the International Federation for Housing and Town Planning's subgroup on Housing in Tropical and Sub-Tropical Countries and the British Department of Scientific and Industrial Research's (DSIR) Tropical Products Institute.[16] Organizations birthed in an age of empire hastened to rename themselves, as in the case of the Vereeniging Koloniaal Instituut (Dutch Colonial Institute, 1910) which became the Koninklijk Instituut voor de Tropen (Royal Tropical Institute, 1950) while also broadening its mission "from studying the 'Dutch Overseas Territories,' to [examining] the tropics in general, including 'cultural, economic and hygienic issue(s).' "[17] Atkinson unsubtly advised British architects to "remember that our clients are [now] more the people of the Tropics not Europeans: that we have to work there as equals, only privileged because of our special knowledge."[18]

For the British, assertions of technical expertise coincided with deepening concerns that "a critical situation" would arise if Malayan communists stopped the export of regional rubber, tin, and coffee. The British depended on proceeds from rubber sales to repay wartime debts to the US, and complete withdrawal from the region could spell financial catastrophe for the British economy. The US for its part depended upon Southeast Asian raw materials to fuel "the booming civilian automotive tire industry, the core of the American Dream," with the US singlehandedly purchasing nearly half of Malayan rubber exports in 1946 and 90% of its tin exports in 1949.[19] Ports like Singapore experienced some of the greatest congestion and poverty to date, as displaced workers, impoverished rural dwellers, and regional migrants flooded into the city, taking low-paid dock work and a wide array of service and transportation jobs that made the Lion City the bustling entrepôt of the region. Singapore Improvement Trust manager J. M. Fraser observed, "With rubber and tin fetching the highest prices ever, money is flowing fast and yet the mass of the population is living in filthy slums. It is a crazy situation and reflects the craziness of the world around us."[20]

Americans assumed a more active role in tropical research during these years of uncertainty. Twenty-three American corporations donated $78,100 toward tropical housing research in 1943, and private grants supported work at the Army Medical Museum, the *Journal of Parasitology*, and universities such as Cornell, Duke, Nebraska, New York, Pennsylvania, Stanford, Texas, Tufts, and Yale.[21] Working alongside international organizations like the International Co-operative Alliance, the World Health Organisation, FAO, UNESCO, the International Labour Organisation, the Organisation of American States, and more, American leaders in mining, oil, banking, airlines, agriculture, manufacture, and other "major industries operating in the tropics" organized conferences and research groups.[22] The Industrial Council for Tropical Health held conferences from 1950 to 1974, for instance, convening interested scientists, experts, and industry members to coach "corporate decision makers and . . . their agents based in the tropics."[23] Besides advisors from the US Public Health Service and the Rockefeller Foundation, and scientists from Harvard's School of Public Health, the list of participants read like a who's who of America's most important industries: among them were representatives from US Steel, American Cyanamid Company, Firestone Plantations Company, Socony Mobil Oil Company, Standard Oil Company, Sylvania Electric Products, First National City Bank of New York, and the United Fruit Company.[24]

American housing experts competed and cooperated with American industries, European business interests, intergovernmental agency representatives, humanitarians, ambitious local and regional political leaders, and more to shape postwar tropical cities. Jacob Crane was very clear about his reasons for doing so: Americans should "give a little push to enormous housing problems" and thereby "strengthen the role of the USA and the HHFA in a lot of countries."[25] Crane simply and unambiguously aspired to make the HHFA "one of the chief domestic *and* international agencies of the US Government," protecting the "interests of the USA" at home and abroad. From Crane's vantage point, American expertise in modern housing construction and urban planning gave officials the ability and right to share technical know-how and best practices.

Alas, effective aid required knowledge of local conditions and resources—an expertise that was in short supply among international housing experts. Like European counterparts, American advisors faced the daunting challenge of designing affordable homes with a modern, industrial sensibility in communities they knew little about and feared were starkly different from any in the US or Western Europe. Men and women like Jacob Crane, Anthony Atkinson, Otto Koenigsberger, Jacqueline Tyrwhitt, Jacobus P. Thijsse, Antonio Kayanan, Charles Abrams, and William Wurster understood that questions of form were critical in achieving resident satisfaction and staying within budget—but which building materials were readily available? How would they react to humidity or heat? And how skilled were local workers?

In part, American attention to tropical housing design fit with a domestic movement to design houses that took heed of the basic principle that "different places need different houses."[26] Architects like Bernard Wagner—an ECA representative in Germany in the 1950s and HHFA and USAID housing advisor in India (1964), Jordan (1965), Brazil (1966), Guatemala (1967), Nigeria (1967), and the Philippines (1968)—also encouraged American builders to consider environmental design at home, and the magazine *House Beautiful* brought together an FHA economist, Yale professors, the research director for the American Institute of Architects, and Army climate and environmental health specialists to publish a series of articles on climate-specific construction techniques and energy-conserving methods for domestic housing markets.[27] Tellingly, however, profitable American housing practices of cheap mass production and tract suburban development precluded the expansion of generally more expensive environmental design ideas that the American public perceived as architecturally restrictive and more often than not, aesthetically displeasing. By the early 1960s, HHFA and USAID workers exerted greater energy pursuing environmental design abroad than at home.

Tropical Housing in Transition

At the international level, the perceived need for basic knowledge about local climate, economies, materials, and labor in the tropics fueled a series of research initiatives and conferences, the first of which was the UN Social Commission's meeting of experts on tropical housing in Caracas, Venezuela, in December 1947, a meeting that then funded the UN's first Mission of Experts on Tropical Housing (November 21, 1950, to January 22, 1951). Predictably, the "tropics" remained a fluid geographic space in this mission, determined more by member interest and background than by any consensus over terms. Led by American Jacob Crane and including fellow experts Jacobus P. Thijsse (a Dutch civil engineer, planner, and professor at the University of Indonesia), Robert Gardner-Medwin (a Scottish architect trained at Harvard and Taliesin and advisor to the British West Indies 1944–47), and Antonio Kayanan (an architect trained in the Philippines and at MIT who worked in the Cleveland Regional Planning Association and in Puerto Rico in addition to serving as chief planner for the Philippines), the UN Mission chose to visit India, Indonesia, the Federation of Malaya, Pakistan, the Philippines, Singapore, and Thailand—an itinerary that neglected entire continents and included dry, arid regions within South and Southeast Asia. By the team's own admission, a wholly tropical itinerary remained elusive, since "parts of India and of Pakistan [were] neither tropical nor humid; and, of course, this [was] true of other countries in Asia."[28]

The UN team had its reasons for pursuing this particular configuration of tropical research. Most likely, the four men felt obliged to consider countries as a whole, despite regional variations. More compellingly, the group wanted to focus on the Asian continent because their personal experiences and a jumble of anecdotal evidence from different Asian countries convinced them that the continent faced the worst housing crises of the world.[29] Despite admitting their paucity of knowledge about housing conditions in the Middle East, Africa, Latin America, or even the majority of Asia, the team argued that "the magnitude of the Asian housing problem [was] far greater than that of any other part of the world," and there were around "100,000,000 Asian families (perhaps as many as 150,000,000) . . . in crowded, unsanitary, sub-standard quarters, urban or rural."[30] Estimates that varied by as much as 50 million families revealed just how little the men actually knew about housing problems in the region. Worse, Crane had made earlier assertions that 200 million families in tropical and semitropical regions inhabited mostly inadequate huts.[31] Despite the ignorance of any hard facts, the team persevered, boldly putting forward more generalizations, including comments that "proper, even very simple, arrangements for the storage of food and the washing of dishes, clothes and persons [were] almost unknown" in Asia, that Asian housing problems had little difference "from other regions of the world" in issues of "organization, manpower (both professional and labour), materials, and finance," save for magnitude, and that improvements in Asian housing might prove especially useful to Latin Americans and Africans, the latter of which lived almost entirely in "huts of grass and mud and wattles."[32] The Tropical Housing Mission repeatedly underscored the importance of "the Asian people and the Asian Governments . . . decid[ing] which western methods can be adapted to the evolving way of life in their countries," but in the end, "modern," "well-rounded," "appropriate," "good," and "effective" programs demanded the immediate installation of a "well-rounded technical team" with financial administrator, town planner, architect, specialist engineers, and housing manager as "commonly engaged in European and American countries," and requiring the counsel of visiting foreigners who could "stimulate new developments and new ideas" much as Patrick Geddes did for Bombay University in the 1910s.[33]

Homeownership played a pivotal role in the UN team's assertions of expertise. The mission understood that most governments could not afford to provide all families with dwellings that had "hard, clean floors; better types of roofing; and larger, better divided inside space" with emphases on privacy and gender segregation.[34] Given that warm weather required little insulation, housing experts reasoned, governments could make use of lighter construction methods and building materials while providing basic services in a "core unit." Without homeownership, governments would be responsible for maintaining rudimentary facilities that residents had little incentive to use carefully.[35] With homeownership, cash-poor but labor-rich families would have incentives to invest savings, time, and labor. Homeownership, therefore, was essential. Aided self-help—government assistance (whether in the form of land provision, basic utilities, and/or expert advice) in conjunction with self-construction and maintenance—only worked in the tropics if joined with homeownership, according to relentless aided self-help advocates like Crane.[36] In no small part because of Crane's dogged determination, international and domestic bodies like the UN's ECAFE, the Housing and Home Finance Agency, and the Ford Foundation came to endorse aided self-help housing. As geographers Richard Harris and Ceinwen Giles put it, "US agencies promoted self-help to anyone who would listen."[37]

Aided self-help was a response to the tumultuous politics of the day as much as it was a response to financial exigencies. In an era of violent decolonization struggles, transitional and postcolonial leaders across Asia and Africa strongly opposed any hint of colonial arrogance. The term "self-help" put national sovereignty and self-determination at the center, leaving aid as a temporary measure to promote independent development. European and American tropical housing researchers felt compelled to give repeated verbal nods to the importance of local knowledge, and some officials went so far as to chide governments for copying instead of adapting Western "dwelling types and methods of construction used in the temperate zone where housing techniques are generally more advanced, but not necessarily appropriate to tropical needs." The "slavish" imitation of modern forms in the tropical zones was not only "unwise" but also "unscientific."[38]

Instead of imitation, United Nations Technical Assistance Administration official Howard T. Fisher proposed a "tropical housing in transition"—a government-assisted, owner-built and owner-maintained home that used available resources and that laid the groundwork for more expensive, regionally tailored modern housing programs.[39] It was patently obvious to men like Crane and Fisher that the tropical hut could not continue in its current state. Still, unmodified Western technology fit equally poorly in a tropical landscape. The solution was simple: western science could help develop housing that was tailored to tropical conditions. Fisher explained that "scientific knowledge and advanced study" were necessary not only in developing an "improved metallic curtain wall" in "highly industrialized areas of the temperate zones," but also in formulating "a superior solution for the problem of a low-cost, rain-tight, vermin-proof roof for tropical housing."[40] Western architectural forms suited temperate or continental zones' weather patterns, material resources, and living requirements, while indigenous tropical practices, if unaltered, were limited in method, "inextricably mixed with religious requirements and taboos," and linked to traditional economies that were rapidly becoming extinct.[41] Modern tropical housing programs should henceforth combine the strengths of each while rejecting backward practices or climatically inappropriate elements.

This formula may have sounded like a practical compromise between a carefully constructed "tradition" and "modernity," but in practice it failed to resonate with the needs and desires of host governments. Politicians often rejected proposed intermediate "tropical" designs and lowered building standards, exhibiting little interest in the "native" materials and forms European and American experts fetishized as quintessentially "tropical." Nor were leaders eager to adopt advice wholesale. In newly emerging countries, governments fashioned housing programs first and foremost around their own perceptions of modernization and development, whether in the financial infrastructure beneath built forms, or in the literal architecture itself. Tropical housing devices were employed only when useful to these primary aims, and homeownership took on many different, highly localized forms.

Homeownership in the "American Tropics"

While the UN team traveled around South and Southeast Asia surveying tropical housing conditions, substantive experiments with aided self-help programs had already begun on the other side of the world in the so-called "American tropics" of Puerto Rico. Puerto Rican housing programs began at roughly the same moment that the Home Owners' Loan Corporation (HOLC), Federal Housing Administration (FHA), and Public Works Administration (PWA) inaugurated mass mortgage-driven homeownership for the mostly white middle class in the continental US; unlike HOLC, FHA, and PWA programs, however, the US territory's experiments directly targeted low-income families and broke new ground in implementing one of the most widely inclusive, systematic, and long-lasting programs of government assistance for self-help housing in the world.[42] Puerto Rican housing officials established the first land-and-utilities program and then aided self-help program whereby families could use their own labor to build government-provided facilities in the former, or core housing units in the latter.

With little regard for political and historical context, American housing advisors latched onto Puerto Rican housing successes as particularly compelling evidence that the US had know-how of value to other tropical nations. Puerto Rico's aided self-help housing programs could only have taken place in a hot environment, they argued, since small indoor spaces were made tolerable by the extensive use of the outdoors, and since self-help construction depended upon less rigorous wintering. Compared to a concurrent "low cash-cost housing" program by the Tuskegee Institute in the "semi-tropical climate" of Alabama, Puerto Rico more precisely replicated the urban housing problems seen in the developing world.[43] Like leaders in developing nations, Puerto Rican officials also had to address a wider range of needs, including those of low-, middle-, and upper-class residents in urban, suburban, and rural areas. Unlike developing nations, however, Puerto Rico had the advantage of being able to call upon US resources directly. As a territory, the island received regular advisory services, and the island's housing officials observed continental programs first-hand and could apply for and claim the benefits of US federal housing laws. Puerto Rico could be an excellent laboratory for American housing experts to observe experimental housing efforts without the encumbrances of diplomatic relations or hostile local governments. Ultimately, it would serve as the perfect showcase of what might be done to improve housing in the entire tropics.

Puerto Rican housing programs began predictably enough with land reform. Like their counterparts in Taiwan, South Korea, and many other countries, Puerto Rican officials had to grapple first and foremost with questions of unequal landownership when addressing the housing crisis in the early 1920s. Along with the creation of the Homestead Commission in 1921, the Puerto Rican government issued 4,219 loans to rural peasants and urban laborers for rural lots and new urban housing projects until the Puerto Rico Reconstruction Administration (PRRA) took over the commission's operations in 1935. In the two decades following, the PRRA distributed over 10,000 lots in addition to building a more modest 1,460 urban units.[44] Amid massive reorganization, the local authority in Ponce devised what would become a globally significant technique known as land-and-utilities. The 1939 program worked as follows: while emphasizing the role of the owner-builder and the temporary, declining role of outside subsidy, Ponce's planners paradoxically began by converting private slum dwellings into semipublic housing. The city built lots equipped with water and sewage lines; shanty owners were then encouraged to relocate their houses by truck-trailer to the site, sell their homes to the authority for $1 each, and pay a monthly rate with accompanying lease terminable by either party with thirty days' notice.[45] Should residents choose to terminate, they would reclaim their homes but not any increase in land value. This system, while temporarily suspending ownership rights, bestowed badly needed services and gave families the financial stability to invest in improvements.[46] Split ownership also fostered new inflexibilities: since local authorities qualified for loans and annual contributions from the Public Housing Administration under the 1937 Housing Act, residents had to be relocated when they rose above public housing income limitations. Residents could take their homes with them—being owners of the unit, not the land—but the physical movement of improved units inevitably deflated house values, and owners lost permanent improvements like concrete porches.[47]

Local authorities experimented with a form of partial public provision because high land prices made lower-income private development nearly impossible. The issue of land tenure had to be addressed first if the government wanted to produce real, substantive housing improvement. Senate president Luis Muñoz Marín and governor Guy J. Swope understood this, and together they tackled the problem in a 1941 Ley de Tierras (Land Law).[48] Set up to protect the "fundamental human right" of agricultural workers to own their land and homes, the law granted perpetual usufruct to relocated families in new villages complete with schools, health centers, parks, churches, and basic services like streets and water. These measures were explicitly intended to achieve "higher production and consumption levels" throughout the island.[49] The new legislation also established the Social Programs Administration within the Department of Agriculture and Commerce that subsequently assumed the massive technical and administrative duties associated with organizing new rural communities under an island-wide master plan. While not a total solution, the Ley de Tierras took a decisive step toward individual, smaller-plot landownership.[50]

The Ley de Tierras did not immediately solve all rural and urban housing affordability problems, of course. Two issues in particular plagued lower-income housing development. First, the ongoing cultivation of sugar restricted the availability and affordability of undeveloped land that did not require expensive grading, filling, and drainage. Second, the Puerto Rico Planning Board set strict site improvement standards and zoning regulations that raised prices for development projects.[51] Private contractors' experiments with mass production techniques could not overcome these two issues, and most new houses remained above the affordable $6,000 per-unit price tag. Meanwhile, banks disliked small loans due to high servicing costs, and an uncertain secondary mortgage market cut off further routes to home financing.[52]

It was because of these limitations that land-and-utilities programs became an island-wide practice expanding far beyond Ponce's borders, albeit with important adjustments in tenure options. The Puerto Rico Land Authority's Social Services division and Community Programs of the Ministry of Agriculture mimicked some of Ponce's best features while moving away from split ownership in island-wide land-and-utilities schemes: they acquired sub-urban land, installed facilities such as sanitation and roads, and leased serviced plots to relocated families. Importantly, local housing authorities wanted to "maintain the desire for ownership of the shack" while operating within cost limitations. As a result, the Land Authority provided loans to land-and-utility owners for home improvement (from $500 to $1,200 in 1955), and shack owners were permitted to either continue paying ground rents (roughly $.50–$4.00 per month), or to transition to a lease purchase plan with higher monthly payments (roughly $7.00) for twenty years.[53] Approximately 65% of slum residents owned their physical housing units in the 1950s, and loans could help the majority of shack dwellers build on their moveable investment while expanding into landownership.[54]

As a modified version of the aided self-help programs launched in Asia, the Puerto Rican program achieved success on a scale not seen before. US housing experts spread the news with alacrity, carrying the concept through a multinational Caribbean Commission (including the US, UK, France, and the Netherlands) to the insular or local governments of Antigua, Barbados, British Guiana, British Honduras, Surinam, and Trinidad and Tobago in the early 1950s. Chairman of the Puerto Rico Planning Board Rafael Pico and officials like Puerto Rican agriculture secretary Luis Rivera Santos traveled the world, providing key addresses in forums like Jacqueline Tyrwhitt's 1954 UN Seminar on Housing in New Delhi.[55] By the end of the decade, US housing advisors had helped develop a national aided self-help housing program in Guatemala and organized the Nicaraguan Colonia Managua (funded and organized by the Nicaraguan Institute of Housing and the US Operations Mission to Nicaragua), with key elements directly patterned after Puerto Rico.[56] It was no surprise to see Americans like Crane along with chief of the UN Housing and Town and Country Planning Section Ernest Weissmann, British architect Atkinson, Greek architect Constantinos Doxiadis, and others concurring that the Puerto Rican and Caribbean experiences with aided self-help would prove "most useful for Asia" in the 1950s and '60s—this time in the increasingly politically sensitive regions of Southeast Asia rather than in China/Taiwan or South Korea.[57]

The use of Puerto Rico as a model fit with broader trends among social science researchers. In the 1940s, the University of Puerto Rico's Social Science Research Center (SSRC) helped bring reputable American researchers and opened up funding for experiments in Puerto Rico, boasting that the island was "virtually a social science laboratory where in the compactness of 3,435 square miles and two and a quarter million people the scholar may study all of the facets of rapid social change as well as the fusion and conflict of cultures," according to an SSRC director.[58] The US government program Operation Bootstrap (1948) rapidly industrialized the island, transforming it into "A Study in Democratic Development," and by the early 1950s, State Department officials regularly referred to the island as a model site and a counterweight to the Cuban revolution unfolding some six hundred miles away.[59]

Perceived successes encouraged more experimentation in Puerto Rico, this time with *urban* aided self-help and mutual aid housing programs. The latter also incorporated loans, this time from the Puerto Rico Housing Authority (PRHA), in order to foster the same "sounder social attitude" encouraged by the Land Authority in land-and-utilities offerings.[60] Since private building and financing proved difficult in most cases, the PRHA subsidized up to 50% of the cost of new construction materials and offered the remaining 50% in no-interest, ten-year loans amounting to roughly $2,300 each in 1955 ($1,200 in materials and $1,100 in cost of lot). Typical improved urban houses consisted of rudimentary 600-square-feet concrete units on 2,712-square-feet lots (252 square meters). In another innovation, the Social Programs Administration encouraged groups of fifteen families to cooperatively build new cement-block homes, thus realizing a savings of 50% in labor costs. American observers exulted in the results, praising the conversion of some 25,000 families "from the literal state of peons to that of subsistence homesteaders."[61] For those who could not participate in these schemes, the Social Programs Administration added a minimum urbanization program wherein squatters could relocate to cleared land organized in small lots with minimum amenities on the outskirts of large cities. Relocatees were again given the choice between land rentals and long-term loans. In most cases, the very nature of aided self-help construction encouraged families to opt for ownership, since families invested countless hours dismantling old shacks and erecting new units through cooperative labor.

Aided self-help programs directed families into a much more streamlined, state-managed form of homeownership than ever before. They also gave the Social Programs Administration and the PRHA new control over where Puerto Rican families would live, and how. Astoundingly, officials segregated 600 square feet into two or three bedrooms, a kitchen, a bath, and a living-dining room. Many of these officials emphasized the almost farcical segregation of such small spaces space by gender and use as a necessary improvement over previous, communal living arrangements with multipurpose rooms. In one of a number of outrageous comments, PRHA director of planning Pieter Pauw emphasized the pressing need for division of space "in tropic and semi-tropic climates, in which the female species mature much earlier than those in colder climates."[62]

14 "Typical low-cost housing built by private enterprise and an example of the improvement process." César Cordero Dávila, executive director of the Puerto Rico Housing Authority, remarked on the "unusual pride" residents displayed in remodeling their homes. Source: César Cordero Dávila, Executive Director of the Puerto Rico Housing Authority, memorandum to the Staff Director of the House Banking and Currency Committee, regarding Housing Problems and policies of the Commonwealth of Puerto Rico, fig. 9, December 16, 1955, folder PRHA/Housing Problems, box 2, Jacob Leslie Crane Papers 2646, Division of Rare and Manuscript Collections, Cornell University Library.

Residents had their own reasons for accepting new living arrangements. The expansion of living space and accoutrements—including extra rooms, porches, and ornamental features built around and above the core unit—offered the obvious labor-saving, bodily comforts of amenities like running water. Such improvements could also signal a desirable rise in class status exceeding any satisfaction found in previous ownership. Naturally, the families featured in official publications demonstrated pride in their new homes. Government officials steered families toward a specific form of "decent shelter" and deliberately tried to imbed a modern aesthetics for a new middle class.

From the north, HHFA officials applauded these developments, marketing the "Puerto Rican model" to other governments around the world. In marketing land-and-utilities schemes more broadly, Crane argued that the island had successfully adapted US models to a tropical context, thus serving as a perfect example for other aspiring nations in the tropical zone:

The development of housing policies in the Caribbean island has been related to that in the rest of the United States, particularly since 1933; but the adaptation of these policies to Puerto Rican conditions has produced principles and methods which may be of more interest to other countries than to the continental States of the United States. The problems of housing and sanitation in all the tropical and semitropical areas . . . have much in common with those in Puerto Rico.[63]

Indeed, another report crowed, the land-and-utilities scheme had successfully set up a method by which countries in the developing tropics might integrate themselves with global capitalism: "This program creates extensive economic activity in its requirements for cement, reinforcing steel, and machinery, both domestic and imported. While the investment and the materials going into each house are small, in total the programs will stimulate a great demand for materials and machinery and hence promote economic development on a broad scale."[64]

As perhaps the best evidence that ostensibly climate-oriented innovations really had more to do with integration into global markets and economic development than with weather, the model spread quickly beyond hot, humid locales to subtropical and temperate countries like Iran and Greece. Governments around the world watched Puerto Rican experiments intently, soliciting information and requesting training visits. Even American USOM-Iran representative William Warne's insulting comments about Iran's "cave dwellers" and inferior local housing codes did not deter prime minister Fazlollah Zahedi from repeatedly

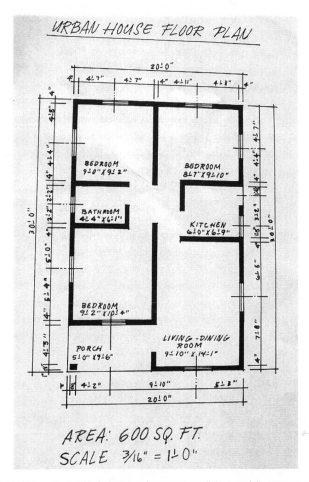

15 The Puerto Rican aided self-help housing design was small, but carefully segregated by use. This particular floor plan included three bedrooms, one for the parents, and two for the male and female children. Source: Puerto Rico Housing Research Board, *Aided Self-help and Mutual Aid: A New Approach to Low Cost Housing in Puerto Rico* (Rio Piedras, Puerto Rico: 1959), 34.

requesting intensive, on-site training in Puerto Rico for Iranian technicians so that they might replicate the "better planned, better built homes [that were] chiefly owner-occupied."[65] Public Housing Authority and former Ponce worker George Reed likewise referred to Puerto Rican ideas in his advisory work in Greece. According to one HHFA document, the Greek example of "international cooperation" with Puerto Rico would further encourage self-help construction and the use of governmental assistance to insure low-interest loans rather than grants "as a means of both stimulating private investment in housing and also bringing the cost of credit within the reach of more families."[66] This would make Greeks "stronger adherents of the ways of freedom and democracy."[67] Crane and others may have first thought of Puerto Rican innovations as tropical housing solutions, but these programs ultimately exceeded expectations, offering a homeownership model for all manner of regions and climates.

Looking back, it is tempting to accept the Puerto Rican story at face value. Certainly land-and-utilities and aided self-help programs reduced maintenance issues and increased individual investment in housing via homeownership. There is more to the Puerto Rican housing story, though. Less publicized but equally important, public housing grew in tandem with the emphasis on government-supported homeownership. Although counterintuitive, the explosive growth of public housing from 1940 to 1970 in fact strengthened—not weakened—the government's emphasis on a homeownership society. An astounding 75% of all slum clearance relocatees qualified for federally supported public housing, and rates of public housing residency rose significantly during these three decades—in retrospect, what sociologist Zaire Dinzey-Flores notes was "the highest production of public housing in Puerto Rican history."[68] (The remaining 25% of slum relocatees who did not qualify for public housing could avail themselves of land-and-utilities or urban aided self-help programs.) Homeownership rates also steadily rose during this period, from 61.8% owner occupation of all occupied dwelling units in 1940, to 65.4% in 1950, to 67.8% in 1960—significantly higher than mainland rates and seemingly indicative of a highly successful homeownership experiment.[69] Puerto Ricans demanded and got a Federal Home Loan Bank Board (FHLBB) charter for the First Federal Savings of Puerto Rico in 1950; by 1963, the bank had nearly 100,000 accounts and provided home financing on nearly the same terms as the fifty states.[70]

In the simultaneous expansion of public housing and homeownership can be seen the aspirations of Puerto Rican policymakers like Luis Muñoz Marín (first governor under the Constitution of the Commonwealth, 1949–65), and more importantly, of the Puerto Rican people themselves. Public housing programs proliferated for those who could not afford modern dwellings, but these units in no way infringed on the expansion of homeownership at the upper-income levels. Muñoz Marín believed public housing to be compatible with owner aspirations, serving as a transitional stage from slum dwellings to private, single-family homeownership. Muñoz Marín, the PRHA, and the PRHA's successor agency, the Corporación de Renovación Urbana y Vivienda

(CRUV, 1957–91), all tried to "integrate public housing into the popular psyche and make it more palatable both to slum dwellers and to government officials" by arguing for its impermanent nature.[71] If many public housing residents were ultimately resistant or unable to view their new accommodations as a temporary way station between slum dwelling and modern single-family homes, massive public housing construction nonetheless failed to weaken a broader idealization of homeownership.[72]

Urban renewal programs often worked in conjunction with public housing to nurture upper-income homeownership. Like realtors and private builders in the continental US, private Puerto Rican investors quickly realized that the powers of eminent domain could be used to facilitate slum removal and to open up land to higher-income site development.[73] Urban renewal would accomplish two goals at once: it would relocate slum dwellers from unsavory homes into transitional public housing or loan-driven self-help projects, while it simultaneously freed up property for more upper-income homeownership. Unclear or nonexistent titles to substandard properties helped smooth the process. In the San Juan neighborhood of Río Piedras, for instance, the PRHA launched a 1956 "El Monte" Redevelopment Project that became one of its largest Title I projects, with 38 acres and 1,500 families cleared and replaced with private, higher-income units for purchase. According to the executive director of the PRHA, "this slum [was] arresting the sound growth of [an] adjacent, stable high-class residential district."[74] The Slum Vigilance Act (1950) provided further legal ballast for these sorts of programs by supplying the housing authority with annual appropriations to prevent squatters from building new shacks in urban areas.

In 1960, the HHFA helped launch a series of housing initiatives that shared one common trait: they were all dedicated to modernizing shelter and increasing homeownership. It had become obvious to the local government that critical problems remained in Puerto Rican housing as a whole, despite all the aided self-help units, transitional public housing, urban rehabilitation programs, and homeownership assistance. Chairman of the Housing Research Board Luis Rivera Santos identified the "hottest aspect" of the Puerto Rican housing problem as early as 1957, when he wrote to Crane about the need for "financing arrangements for new aided self-help, owner-occupied housing," and in particular, the need for a local market of small, low-interest, long-term mortgages insured by the FHA and purchased by FNMA.[75] By 1960, the CRUV actively sought a more coherent system to organize its many housing programs while also considering a Commonwealth loan guarantee or loan acceptance program to expand low-income homeownership. Even with the aided self-help programs and various public and publicly aided housing initiatives, the prospective small homeowner still had little access to housing finance, and public housing could not single-handedly resolve the Puerto Rican slum problem even if units continued to be built at the current pace. Worse, CRUV consultant George Reed doubted that even the inadequate numbers of public housing units would continue to be funded at the federal level, as "the general attitude toward public housing has deteriorated in the Congress as well as in the administration and under the most favorable conditions it would take several years to recover the kind of enthusiasm for low income group subsidized rental housing, which activated the 1937 legislation."[76]

As a first step in seeking creative solutions, Reed convinced Crane to conduct a study of state legislation facilitating financial aid for low-income families to own homes. In his conclusion, Crane found all five states involved in any supplemental measures (Pennsylvania, California, Connecticut, Massachusetts, New York) shared one key characteristic: each state designed its low-income homeownership programs to "supplement and to assist, but *not to compete with* or to damage the role of private enterprise in the provision of housing."[77] Federal institutions like the FHA, FHLBB, and FNMA had a much more powerful role in opening up accessibility, while states merely facilitated ground-level enactments. Consequently, Crane recommended Puerto Rico simply develop more "intensive use of the federal facilities" already existing for the sale of Puerto Rican mortgages.[78] (These included the mainland sale of CRUV notes and bonds, FHA insured mortgages, mortgages purchased by local S&Ls, and mortgages sold to FNMA. The FHA's 213, 220, 221, and 231 programs were all still at the trial stage.)[79]

The status quo was not enough. Neither public housing nor federal government mortgage assistance had yet stemmed slum growth in Puerto Rico, despite all the international praise and attention. Finally in 1961, the Housing Bank and Finance Agency was created to provide financing for low-income homeownership. The bank would generate a positive cycle of support for owner-builders, leading to sounder investments in housing, with resultant security of investment on the part of the Housing Bank. Reed projected long-term benefits, enthusing, "The crystal ball shows me: better small homes; better compliance with regulations; less slum building; better use of Island as well as metropolitan industry and commerce; advance toward our social as well as economic goals."[80] With the new bank, Reed urged Puerto Ricans to continue formulating "a new kind of land reform," this time to open up real estate procedures and practices to make homeownership reasonable, practicable, and economical.

"Home buying," he concluded, "can be made as simple as buying a car or a TV set."[81]

Tropical housing programs were meant to help underdeveloped regions transition from informal ownership of "shacks" and shelter of varying quality, to formal, government-managed, debt-driven ownership of modern housing.[82] For those looking closely, however, the Puerto Rican model demonstrated the inequalities embedded in a mass homeownership society, and the intractable problems with fair housing that would plague both American and Puerto Rican housing systems in the coming decades.

Applying the Puerto Rican Model in the Philippines

American interest in the Philippines, like its interest in Puerto Rico, had a long trajectory, formally beginning with the Treaty of Paris in 1898 and including nearly fifty years of colonial rule. American architects like Daniel Burnham and William Parsons influenced city-planning practices, most notably with modernist plans for Manila and Baguio in the early twentieth century.[83] Just a few short months before independence on July 4, 1946, the US continued to exhibit considerable interest in Filipino urban planning and housing issues, dispatching a housing advisory team to the archipelago to survey and advise the new administration on future policies.

The US advisory team of 1946 consisted of three men: Earl Gauger served as the head of the mission and a technical advisor, John Tierney as the legal advisor, and Roy J. Burroughs as the economic advisor. Upon arrival in Manila in March of 1946, the team found a city reeling from wartime destruction, with "squalor and congestion" in urban areas that would "shock the national conscience."[84] Refugees and displaced urban residents erected informal shelter across the capital in places like Intramuros, Ermita, Malate, Harrison Plaza, Barrio Fugoso, Magat Salamat Elementary School, North Harbor, and Casbah within Binondo.[85] Amidst such chaos, the team surveyed Philippine housing conditions and issued two reports, one a formal advisory to the housing manager of the National Housing Commission (recently created by the National Housing Act of 1941), and the second, a confidential memo to the US government.

Both in its preparation and in its recommendations, the team relied heavily on Puerto Rico as a point of comparison. This was no accident: Crane made sure Gauger and other potential mission members spent time in Puerto Rico before going to the Philippines, and he even considered director of the Puerto Rico Housing Authority César Cordero Dávila as a potential member of the mission.[86] Tropical Puerto Rico offered the most compelling and pertinent example of land-and-utilities projects in this specific climate, according to Crane. In its final recommendations, the team encouraged government support for homeownership but urged the concurrent construction of subsidized rental units for very low-income families.[87] The report also underscored the importance of rentals over sales in initial slum clearance schemes such as the one in Diliman, Quezon City, for low-salaried employees and laborers. If land were sold, the men reasoned, similar experiences in Puerto Rico showed resale speculation could run wild and it would be impossible to control subsequent use.[88] Alternate methods should be sought for satisfying what HHFA-trained housing economist Cesar Lorenzo called a "peculiar psychological demand" for homeownership.[89] Philippine government subsidy was absolutely necessary to acquire and clear slums like Tondo in Manila; more funds were required for low-rental housing throughout the archipelago. Above all, research in tropical housing was urgently required, and the Philippines ought to participate, but probably not lead, such research.[90] (The leadership role would presumably go to Puerto Ricans, being further along in their experiments with tropical solutions.) Immediately after the publication of the report, Crane urged more Philippine officials to inspect "housing projects designed for climatic conditions similar to those of the Philippines," persuading men like congressman Atilano Cinco and ambassador Eduardo Quintero to visit Puerto Rico. Crane further smoothed the way with well-prepared itineraries and introductory letters to the Puerto Rican governor, Jesús Piñero.[91] Eventually, funds from the Smith-Mundt Act (1948) helped pay for an ongoing flow of experts between the Philippines and the US, almost invariably including Puerto Rico.

If American advisors thought of Puerto Rico as a parallel tropical site of experimentation, it was clear Filipino government officials did not feel the same. Climate mattered very little in the face of pressing development needs, and while Americans did influence Filipino housing policies, it was rarely if ever under the rubric of climatic studies. When US advisors were able to make a mark, it was because they gave suggestions that complemented domestic ideas about homeownership, or because American advice furthered domestic plans for rapid economic development and modernization. The Philippine government did follow some of the 1946 US mission's advice—for instance, merging the People's Homesite Commission (an agency devoted to stimulating home building and thrift as well as to aiding "persons of moderate means" in the purchase of lots and homes [1938–47]) and the National Housing Commission (NHC; an agency devoted to providing for "destitute individuals," "paupers," and those who were unable otherwise to live in decent shelter [1941–47]) into a new People's Homesite and Housing Corporation (PHHC, 1947–75).[92] The 1947 Joint Philippine-American Commission built on this momentum, successfully arguing that restrictive laws be amended to permit banks and financial institutions to issue more long-term, low-interest loans. (Commercial banks had been kept to five-year and savings banks to ten-year maturities.) The 1947 commission also persuaded Philippine officials that the Rehabilitation Finance Corporation—a body that had provided loans to residential and business owners to repair their property after World War II—should move into the secondary mortgage market, operating as a rediscounting facility for mortgage loans, providing greater liquidity to banks and building-and-loan associations, and incentivizing small-scale loans at low interest rates (below 6% in 1947) with building standards set by the RFC in cooperation with the NHC. These moves were explicitly designed to help "salaried people in the moderate income groups" become homeowners.[93]

The Philippine government followed suggestions from the 1946 team for various institutional changes, including that the Housing Commission's exercise of eminent domain (Public Act 648, section 11) be expanded to include condemnation of lands for all slum clearance purposes, regardless of subsequent use.[94] These suggestions fit with government efforts to decentralize Manila, such as the roughly concurrent National Land Settlement Administration's (NLSA, 1939–50) attempt to relocate families from self-made structures on public or unused private properties to new developments in the relatively underpopulated southeastern island of Mindanao in the mid-1950s.[95]

Conversely, the 1946 team's suggestion that the national government build subsidized rental units fell on deaf ears, and the few socialized housing units built in Quezon City and Caloocan City only provided shelter for government workers. Likewise, total number of units provided through multistory tenement housing projects like the Bagong Barangay Housing Project in Pandacan, Vitas and Del Pan in Tondo, Punta in Santa Ana, Fort Bonifacio in Taguig, and Philippine North Avenue Apartments in Quezon City was small, even if the projects themselves were well publicized.

Filipino perceptions of American housing programs mattered as much as direct advice. Rhetorically, the Philippine government echoed

American calls for universal access to decent shelter. President Ramon Magsaysay verbally underscored the importance of "enabling the greater mass of our people to *own decent homes* in [a] suitable living environment" in an echo of the 1949 US Housing Act's call for "a decent home and suitable living environment."[96] The newly created Home Financing Commission (HFC, 1950–), however, offered mortgage financing that targeted middle- and upper-, not low-income consumers, and that explicitly modeled itself after the American Federal Housing Administration (FHA), all too closely reproducing the exclusion of poor families—in the case of the Philippines, the "greater mass"—from homeownership. Acting chairman and general manager of the HFC commodore Jose V. Andrada celebrated the Philippine-American connection and labeled HHFA international housing finance advisor Roy J. Burroughs the "brains" of the Home Financing Act.[97] Much like the American FHA, the Filipino HFC could stimulate the home construction industry—"the mother of all other industries," according to Andrada—and bring an estimated 300 million in private savings into formal bank accounts, developing a national pool of revolving home loans by "provid[ing] liberal financing through an insured mortgage system, and develop[ing] thrift through the accumulation of savings in [an] insured institution."[98] For the first time, a government agency (the HFC) insured mortgages at 90% to 95% of the appraised value with a 1% premium.[99] Such insurance extended average repayment periods from fifteen to twenty-five years and drove down average interest rates. Even more than the FHA, the HFC took a direct role in stimulating homeownership, directly issuing loans up to 80% of the appraised value, with generous mortgage terms.[100] A Government Service Insurance System issued loans to government employees beginning in 1955, and a Social Security System did the same for private employees beginning in 1957.[101] All of these programs required participation in a formal labor market, of course.

The mechanics of state-supported homeownership were as follows: government insurance funds would finance HFC projects with $10 million every year for five years, with the hope that private finance would pick up after the initial trial. In these initial HFC projects, private developers would receive loans in order to build twenty or more housing units at a time, with minimum standards set by the HFC (including site, location, utilities, and community facilities). The developer would then sell individual houses and lots on terms and appraisal mechanisms set by the HFC. The HFC would ensure that home values did not spiral out of control by setting sale price at cost plus 10% profit. Buyers had to put from 5% to 10% down, with the remaining balance on loan from the

Government Service Insurance System at 5% to 6% interest for twenty-five years, and an HFC insurance of mortgage at 1%. The RFC, meanwhile, sold bonds with insured HFC mortgages as security. All of these mechanisms were meant to "promote homeownership . . . [through] the development of new communities by subdivision builders."[102]

Various intergovernmental and international reports noted the absence of a viable housing program for low-income urbanites and urged comprehensive national housing needs surveys, land and utility programs for low-income families, and public encouragement of private investments whether in affordable rental units or in mortgage financing.[103] Reports like a 1958 UN study by Charles Abrams and Otto Koenigsberger suggested adaptation of the "patterns and traditions of the barrios" into an urban core house suiting the habits and climates of the Philippines, and other UN technical assistance teams recommended soil construction, soft volcanic stone walls, and pressed coconut fiber roofs.[104]

None of these hit the mark. Philippine planners and Manila City Council members exhibited far greater interest in the potential advice of private developers like William Levitt, and the flood of UN and US advisory reports in the 1960s yielded few real dividends for the urban poor.[105] World Bank reports summed up 1960s and early 1970s government housing efforts for slum dwellers and squatters as "a series of *ad hoc* projects generally involving major relocations to distant sites, which have not been very successful."[106] In 1968, HHFA and USAID officer Bernard Wagner declared aided self-help housing in central Manila an untenable idea for the future because of ever-rising real estate prices. American homeownership programs had influenced Philippine housing policies, but not quite as expected. Perhaps out of desperation, Wagner suggested Philippine officials consider Hong Kong and Singaporean housing as potentially more realistic models.[107]

Singapore's Rejection of American-Style Homeownership

Wagner's recommendation was odd, to say the least. Of all countries located between the Tropics of Cancer and Capricorn, Singapore was in the process of building one of the most unique and explicitly *public* housing programs in the world. This feat was all the more remarkable given that Singaporeans were decisively capitalist in their outlook, and that they grappled with problems as intractable and immense as those faced by any other emerging nation in the postwar period. The city-state contended with massive urban in-migration, dense self-built squalor, and limited government funds in the midst of a turbulent transition from colony to independent nation. Unlike most, however, Singaporeans used international advice and drew from overseas models to create a visually stunning, socially transformative, structurally hybrid, and above all else peculiarly Singaporean system that utterly changed how all citizens lived. The ruling People's Action Party (PAP) set up a massive public housing system—a system seen elsewhere at this scale in this time period only in Hong Kong—and developed the first massive homeownership program within a public housing system.[108]

What role did Americans play in this remarkable evolution? As in many other decolonizing regions, tropical housing studies provided a language by which Americans could join other interested players in articulating a vision for the city. British colonial workers underscored the importance of site- and climate-specific research in the face of shrinking funding from the Colonial Office in London; Singaporean architects, planners, and intellects used tropical housing debates to critique and challenge the PAP's one-size-fits-all vision of modernization and development; Americans asserted politically neutral scientific expertise in tropical housing in order to protect regional trading interests and Cold War geopolitical concerns. While the Puerto Rico and Philippine cases offer insights into American housing interventions in areas under direct territorial or indirect, postcolonial influence, Singaporean housing debates afford a view of negotiations in areas less directly tied to American interests.

In Singapore, it took some time for a vocabulary of tropical housing to develop and take hold. In the immediate postwar moment, architectural design placed a distant second to other, more pressing questions of governance and reconstruction. No "imagined community" held together countryside and urban center, and the island's future leadership remained undetermined. Originally a smattering of rural settlements along the coastline, the arrival of the British in 1819 transformed the island into the empire's star port and the administrative hub of Southeast Asian trade. From the beginning, the Crown separated Singapore from the larger British Federated Malay States (FMS), which had ruled from a central government in Kuala Lumpur. Singapore, Malacca, and Penang were put together and named the Straits Settlements; this structure remained in place from 1826 until the Japanese invasion in 1942.[109] Singapore was further alienated culturally, ethnically, and economically from its Muslim neighbors by a steady influx of Chinese merchants who soon composed a majority of the population and who kept the port in motion. World War II wreaked havoc on an economy so heavily dependent on trade: with unemployment high and labor abundant, self-made workers' villages crammed together in unprecedented numbers on Crown land in the city center, aggravating already dire shortages in basic utilities and welfare services.[110] In 1947, town population figures surpassed 800,000, up from 490,155 in 1936, and the slums of Covent Garden, Havelock Road, Calcutta Road, Victoria Street, North Bridge Road, Kampong Silat, and Henderson Road reached unprecedented densities with an accompanying rise in public health nuisances.[111]

For over a century, British imperial control precluded any American involvement in Singaporean housing issues. After the successful independence movement in India, the British renewed efforts to retain Singapore. Esler Dening, head of the Far Eastern Department in the Foreign Office, wrote in 1947 that Singapore would henceforth serve as "a strategic link between the United Kingdom, Africa, and Australia" because of the loss of the subcontinent. A Special Commission of the Foreign Office added in another memo that a regional system would "not only strengthen the political ties between the territories concerned and facilitate a defensive strategy, but also prove of considerable economic and financial benefit to the United Kingdom."[112] Returning British colonists had much to prove, however; many Chinese Singaporeans had spent three years agitating against Japanese colonists and building anticolonial political organizations, and the Pan Malayan Federation of Trade Unions and Singapore Federation of Trade Unions had persuaded 70% to 80% of organized workers to become communist by 1945. The old dominant Malayan Communist Party and the Malayan People's Anti-Japanese Army had grown stronger, also, as had the Malayan Democratic Union.

The colonial housing agency, the SIT (1927–60), faced the difficult tasks of increasing provision and more generally demonstrating the sincerity of the British to a skeptical native population while also convincing Labour leaders at home that the British government should continue to fund their work in Singapore. In trying to persuade all parties, returning imperialists argued, first, that the British had to address housing conditions that were in a state of crisis; second, that in order to begin solving these problems, "tropical housing" needed to be studied separately from shelter in colder climes; and third, that these actions proved the SIT was there to aid "development," not to colonize per se. SIT workers walked a careful line between arguing that British models did not work in the tropical context and defending British control over Singaporean housing policy.

The SIT had already led the International Federation for Housing and Town Planning's (IFHTP, 1938–) subgroup on Housing in Tropical and

Sub-tropical Countries and displayed its tropical housing innovations in a 1938 Empire Exhibit in London. After 1945, returning colonial workers argued for more vigorous tropical research using this same justification. Municipal health officer N. A. Canton put the matter simply: "To base housing standards here on somewhat the same lines as in the UK seems to me to be completely unscientific, as the problem there is to allow of sufficient sunlight and air changes in rooms without causing droughts or undue lowering of the temperature in the building, whereas, here, the problem is more or less the converse."[113] Canton added, "Practically no information with any scientific basis to go on is available for the tropics," and even the Rockefeller Foundation and Harvard University's Graduate School of Engineering had done very little research in this direction. At present, then, "The UK [was] miles ahead of . . . the USA."[114]

Miles ahead or no, colonial officers had a basic problem: they needed money. Architect Bruce Martin succinctly outlined the biggest stumbling block for tropical housing improvement in a 1950 Royal Institute of British Architects (RIBA) meeting: "On the one hand, people are saying that we need high standards, better standards, scientific standards, standards suited to the actual conditions in any given place, to satisfy problems of temperature, wind, heat, and warmth, and so on. On the other hand, we are told that these standards must not be followed, that we must not build to them because it will be uneconomic to do so."[115] In Singapore, the SIT had already considerably expanded its role from simple improvements and town expansion to the preparation of a diagnostic survey and master plan; in 1950, manager J. M. Fraser set out to find more creative ways to save money while building climate-specific architecture and leading tropical housing research globally.[116] After American Jacob Crane encouraged Singaporeans to participate in the UN's worldwide housing and town and country planning affiliations, Fraser ambitiously contacted UN secretary for economic affairs Andrew Gilmour to promote a future Regional Building Research Station, preferably sited in Singapore.[117] By the winter of that same year, the UN Secretariat had issued a report encouraging Asia to develop its own policies and to participate in a "worldwide exchange of experience."[118] Determined to keep Singapore "abreast of the times and the modern trends," Fraser persuaded SIT chief architect Stanley C. Woolmer to use his 1951 Commonwealth Fund Fellowship to study American mass production, prefabrication, mechanical equipment, and new materials, and he praised Woolmer's efforts at innovations in the colony, for such work would undoubtedly result in designs of use "to many other countries in the Far East and most of the tropical areas of the world."[119] Soon after,

SIT architect Lincoln Page followed up in 1955 with attendance at the first International Conference on Regional Planning and Development, a British-led attempt to forge "closer contacts between the various professions concerned with regional planning and development" and to begin discussing a single center "attempting comprehensive work in this field."[120]

Despite these ambitious forays, it was difficult for the SIT to establish dominance in the field of tropical housing, especially when others contributed in equal or greater numbers. Throughout the 1950s, for instance, the American Society of Heating and Ventilating Engineers continued to dominate cooling and ventilation studies, providing data that Singaporean colonial officers relied on to improve tropical housing design.[121] In another telling example, Crane spoke at the Singapore Rotary Club in 1951, praising the "wonderful experience [you have] to draw upon within the British Commonwealth," but underscoring the importance of studying other tropical housing experiences in the Philippines, Indonesia, and "some good new experience in Puerto Rico and Hawaii and Panama, all tropical dependencies of the United States."[122] Woolmer verbally downplayed the usefulness of American housing techniques in the tropics but nonetheless quietly studied in detail potential uses of American floating slab foundations, rammed earth, ready-mix concrete, and contractor organization techniques, to name a few.[123] By 1958, the US would send over 1,449 experts and help set up training facilities for 4,833 students in South and Southeast Asia; the Ford, Rockefeller, and Asia Foundations played large roles in funding these exchanges. Americans also actively participated in international forums like the joint Technical Assistance Administration and United Nations Economic Commission for Asia and the Far East Programme of the Regional Seminar on Housing and Community Improvement in New Delhi in 1954. At the latter, modernist architect and prominent member of the British Modern Architectural Research Group (MARS) Jacqueline Tyrwhitt brought together international experts like Crane, Atkinson, MIT professor Frederick J. Adams, Puerto Rico Planning Board chairman Rafael Pico, and planner Charles Abrams in an international exchange of ideas and techniques of particular relevance to the tropics.[124]

Americans were beginning to make some progress in joining discussions about Singaporean housing when all plans came to an abrupt halt with the beginning of self-governance and the replacement of the SIT with a new Housing and Development Board (HDB) in 1960. HDB officials indicated very little interest in tropical housing research with the exception of limited studies on low-cost reinforced concrete and

16 Clearance was a critical part of the PAP's rehousing campaign. Here, earthmovers arrive in Toa Payoh, 1963. Source: Media Image 19980005152-0080, courtesy of National Archives of Singapore.

multistory structures in the tropics, or in priming and curing paint in hot, humid environments.[125] A new era of modern home construction had begun, and first prime minister Lee Kuan Yew, finance minister Goh Keng Swee, and minister of national development and HDB chairman Lim Kim San made clear their priorities in the Homeownership for the People Scheme in 1964: all future housing development would help Singaporeans live in modern accommodations, mobilize domestic savings for industrial development, ensure political buy-in, and—after full independence in 1965—help transform a fractured migrant community into a functioning, multicultural modern nation. Planner Jacqueline Tyrwhitt may have argued, "Where there is home ownership there can be no objection to temporary housing being built by the owners because they are going to keep it in repairs,"[126] but in the case of Singapore, self-built housing was completely out of the question, and the tropical aspect nearly irrelevant.

The PAP's housing program makes for a particularly compelling case study of failed American housing diplomacy because its leaders so deliberately, openly embraced homeownership and the architecture of modern housing even as it rejected any imitation of American housing. The PAP embraced transparency and honesty in housing allocation, explicitly eliminating any hint of corruption or favoritism via a British- or American-style "hidden subsidy." The principle began as a public relations campaign to differentiate HDB transactions from the opaque dealings of the SIT, especially at such notorious estates like Tiong Bahru, but it quickly expanded to include the American housing system as well. When the American Consulate sent publications on US housing programs to the HDB secretary, CEO, and chairman in the fall of 1961, for instance, chief architect Teh Cheang Wan carefully reported on the details of the American public housing system but added that US citizens tended to be far better equipped to buy or rent, and that Singapore could not undertake the type of massive central government subsidy seen in the US public sector. Teh observed, "The extent and scope of aid given by the American Government to public housing authorities in America is interesting. However, so long as the principle of 'no hidden subsidy' is to be followed in Singapore, existing financial arrangements here will have to continue."[127]

17 The Housing and Development Board taught Singaporeans how to live in new, modern flats through such devices as furniture exhibits, as seen here. This particular exhibit at MacPherson Road Housing Estate on August 12, 1961, encouraged participants to walk through rooms with models and to learn how they might conduct family life in high-rise apartments. Source: Media Image 19980001628-028, Ministry of Information and the Arts Collection, courtesy of National Archives of Singapore.

18 Commemorative stamp design winner, 1962. The government clearly wanted to project an image of order and modernity in its vision for Singaporean *perumahan* (housing). Source: Media Image 19980005642-0087, Ministry of Information and the Arts Collection, courtesy of National Archives of Singapore.

By 1965, Singaporeans had become extraordinarily savvy about the details of American homeownership. Rejection of American systems was undergirded by careful study, often through fact-gathering missions sponsored by American private and public institutions. HDB members successfully appealed to the Asia Foundation, the Ford Foundation, the HHFA, and USAID to sponsor housing, transportation, and urban renewal tours in the US. Of course, American institutions had their own motives for funding Singaporeans: the Asia Foundation, for example, thought such tours would showcase appealing capitalist housing systems while giving the Asia Foundation "a good position to watch future developments" in "this highly political field" of urban renewal and housing policy.[128]

In one Asia Foundation-funded summer study trip, Malaysian representatives Alan Choe Fook Choong, Chua Peng Chye (both from the Singaporean Ministry of National Development), and Chung Weng Foo (state planning officer for Penang, Kedah, and Perlis) toured planning departments around the US, including those in San Francisco, Los Angeles, New York, and Washington, DC. The Singaporean contingent was well versed in the basics of American federal housing laws and institutions, and they came with specific questions about government techniques for recruiting private participation in FHA programs, the role of government-insured loans in urban renewal programs, sources of financing for insured mortgages, the Below Market Interest Rate Program, 221(d)(3), the interest rates, debenture issues, yields and related financial matters of the Federal National Mortgage Association (Fannie Mae), Community Facilities Programs, the Area Redevelopment Administration Program (1961), the Accelerated Public Works Program (1962), and public relations operations of the Urban Renewal Agency, among others.[129]

It is absolutely certain that these men took back lessons learned from the US context, primarily as a series of inapplicable or unattractive policies to avoid. Architect Alan Choe and HDB chairman Lim Kim San believed this understanding of American experiences was critical to the evolution of Singaporean housing:

America at that time was the leading country in the field of urban renewal because they were the ones that saw to it that you had to renew your cities otherwise the decay would just stifle the growth of the city and like a cancer degenerate the whole city if you don't do anything quickly. So they were the first in the world to embark on urban renewal in a systematic matter. So those who wanted to study urban renewal, that was the place we would go to because you can see examples of what they did.[130]

Singaporean planners used this knowledge to reject what they viewed as a disastrous policy of ghettoization and segregation. In Choe's opinion, Americans employed a bulldozer approach that used eminent domain against the poor. The lesson for Singapore was to not "go in" before preparing adequate public housing facilities for relocation, and to design public housing that did not bear the stigma found abroad. Furthermore, Choe added: "We devise[d] something that nobody else had done—not in America, not in England, nowhere. . . . After clearing the land, we'd make the land available on a very transparent system for people to come in and bid for the land so that there [would] not be the same kind of stigma or accusations leveled on urban renewal. . . . It was an extremely transparent system."[131]

This new, transparent system would "entice the private sector" with equally transparent incentives. If Americans had begun the discussion and had even provided some of the critical vocabulary, Singaporeans ultimately used these to reach distinct conclusions. Legal techniques of slum designation and compulsory acquisition of land as well as relocation processes, redevelopment payment schemes, and the like mimicked key American legislative and institutional precedent, but unlike

Americans, Singaporeans set up an unparalleled Homeownership for the People Scheme (1964–) that encouraged private ownership of public housing and that circulated forced savings through the housing industry. Throughout, the PAP deliberately claimed credit for government subsidies, labeling public housing "public" and inveighing against the hidden subsidies of the American "private" system.

By the 1980s, the PAP had so successfully transitioned residents to modern mass homeownership that the city-state had itself become a model for newly independent countries and rapidly modernizing economies around the world. In an interesting twist, the US's international division of the Department of Housing and Urban Development expressed great interest in the creative and "highly successful" tenant ownership program within public housing—so much so that president Ronald Reagan and secretary Samuel Pierce (1981–89) discussed "learning as much as possible about Singapore's experience." Pierce eventually visited major housing sites in Singapore to discuss the island's homeownership program in detail with the city-state's minister of national development. Nor was the US the only major world economy to take notice of Singaporean housing successes. A decade later, Beijing would mimic Singapore's forced savings plan, or Central Provident Fund (1955–), which required employer-matched employee contributions that could then be used toward housing or education. The Zhufang Gongjijin (Housing Provident Fund) was first tested in Shanghai (1991) before being expanded in 1994 to fuel homeownership across all of China.[132]

In the process of becoming a different kind of homeownership model for the world, the PAP largely neglected tropical housing in favor of rapid industrialization and modernization. Tropical housing studies took on new life with a different group instead: architects and intellectuals resisting the seemingly inexorable modernization campaigns of the ruling party and the high-rise, slab-block monotony of HDB architecture adopted the language of tropical housing in order to demand diversity in the housing design process. Housing could not be churned out like a product in a factory. Architecture needed to be tailored to climate, to the tropical context of Singapore, they argued. These architects and planners organized lively debates outside the walls of the HDB in a collective known as the Singapore Planning and Urban Research Group (SPUR, 1964–73)—a group "seek[ing] involvement in the physical planning process of the newly independent nation state."[133] Architects like Tay Kheng Soon, William Lim Siew Wai, Liu Thai Ker, and others hoped to create a distinct "design language for tropical Asia,"[134] one that emphasized "the discovery of a design language of line, edge, mesh and shade rather than an architecture of plane, volume, solid and void."[135] "Tropical housing" no longer hid colonial aspirations or signaled aided self-help programs for the very low-income. Instead, it provided a language for Asian intellectuals to debate the character of their transforming nations.

Because Singaporean architects had trained in European methods, an "unlearning process" constituted the first necessary step toward genuinely tropical architecture. Tropical architecture no longer prioritized the wall—that key component of Western architecture separating people from extreme outdoor weather. Instead, it focused attention on the roof—the source of shade and shelter from rain—as well as on cross-ventilation and deliberately unplanned spaces like void decks. In the late 1960s and early 1970s, Jacqueline Tyrwhitt's Asian Planning and Architecture Collaboration group facilitated exchange between architects like Charles Correa (India), Tao Ho (Hong Kong), Sumet Jumsai (Thailand), William Lim (Singapore), and Koichi Nagashima and Fumihiko Maki (Japan), all of whom were intent on understanding and shaping a new Asian urbanism.

Tyrwhitt believed that "'the wisdom of the East' encouraged a focus on process and frameworks that allow[ed] for citizen participation."[136] Despite this orientalist framework, Lim and others did in fact use Asian Planning and Architecture Collaboration meetings to better theorize challenges to Asian planning and to demand access to the process. In the case of Singapore, tropical housing studies opened up critical approaches to HDB design: Tay's Development Guide Plan for Kampong Bugis and his Revised Concept Plan for Singapore both applied principles from Tay's 1989 critical tract, *Mega-Cities in the Tropics*, for instance, and the HDB's Urban Renewal Department eventually hired Lim, Tay, and Koh Seow Chuan to design People's Park, a vertical building of internal "streets" that challenged single-use zoning while "recaptur[ing] the atmosphere of the informal bustling activity of Chinatown" by creating a "space for people."[137]

Still, truly community-driven planning remained at best an occasional part of the HDB's design process. For the PAP, the distinctly Singaporean system of homeownership provided the most important organizing principle for all discussions about design. Homeownership did not have to be silently subsidized. The state could take credit for homeownership by embedding it within a large public housing program. The state could openly manage the population through homeownership policies. As an obvious counterpoint to the American "homeownership for all," Singapore provided a compelling model for those not interested in following in American footsteps.

No Tropical Homeownership

Americans promoted homeownership in the decolonizing world, but the language of "tropical" difference did not ultimately yield housing programs that cohered within climatic regions. When American housing officials like Jacob Crane repackaged "Puerto Rican housing" into a code word for successful aided self-help in the tropics, Philippine policymakers summarily rejected it. Instead of the more rudimentary structures promoted by tropical housing experts, Philippine housing officials put into place modern home financing institutions that mimicked American mainland counterparts and that remained largely out of reach for the urban poor. The Puerto Rican example was itself a complex one given the concurrent, substantial public housing effort and the resulting tensions and inequalities within housing provision. In Singapore, the transitional and independent government straddled the public-private divide by building an enormous, majority homeownership system within public housing. In so doing, the PAP deliberately rejected both the US homeownership system and tropical housing models. In retrospect, perhaps what is most remarkable about the story of American efforts in the tropics is the persistent, almost blind determination American officials exhibited when promoting mass homeownership abroad.

FOUR

Homeownership as Investment

Foreign aid is not charity; it is sound business management.   PAUL G. HOFFMAN,
FORMER MARSHALL PLAN ADMINISTRATOR, 1962[1]

In 1956, Sadashiv Kanoji Patil traveled from the tropics to Wichita, Kansas. He came as part of an Indian mission, but Patil was no ordinary participant. A spritely fifty-five-year-old peasant's son cum political boss and mayor of Bombay, Patil had just brokered one of the largest grain transactions in history. Using president Dwight D. Eisenhower's Agricultural and Trade Development Act (Public Law 480, 1954), Patil negotiated a shipment of 600 million bushels (roughly 16 million tons) of American surplus grain to be sent to India in exchange for local currency. By the time Eisenhower actually signed the deal in 1960, that number would rise to 16 million tons of wheat plus another million tons of rice over four years to the tune of $1.3 billion—the largest US aid package since the Marshall Plan.[2]

At least one avid listener understood the magnitude of this deal and its potential consequences for international housing aid. Willard Garvey was the son and heir of Ray Hugh Garvey's enormous Kansan grain, oil, and real estate empire. The senior Garvey had already made the family one of the world's largest producers of wheat at 1 million bushels annually in 1947, and he had built the world's largest grain storage units with a capacity of 150 million bushels by 1959. The federal government encouraged this sort of entrepreneurship, offering five years' worth of tax write-offs for the storage bins and paying $14.7 million per year in 1958 to warehouse government-owned surplus grains.[3]

In the federal exchange of surplus grain for counterpart funds, Willard Garvey saw an exciting new real estate prospect to supplement his portfolio. Garvey's Wichita property holdings had not proved profitable of late, yielding "substantial deficits."[4] In fact, the entire state's housing development activity appeared to be at least momentarily on the decline. The turn to overseas opportunities could add practical business interests to ideology: Garvey had already served as the head of the National Association of Home Builders in the late 1940s and had made a name for himself urging politicians and businessmen to embrace the political benefits of American homeownership, that most "measurable freedom." Now, Garvey passionately argued for mass homeownership programs worldwide. Much as Albert Fraleigh had done in Taiwan and South Korea, Garvey pushed the US government to use capitalism's superior standard of living as a weapon against global communism: "Food and housing are Russia's vacuum. Let's hit them where they live, housing, and food."[5] Unlike Fraleigh, Hugo Prucha, Roy Burroughs, and other government officials, however, Garvey approached the matter from the viewpoint of big business. By encouraging American companies to promote homeownership in other friendly nations, the US government could spark entrepreneurial activity abroad and yield reasonable profits for US industries. When Patil spoke of US government-sponsored, surplus grain shipments to India, Garvey immediately pondered how housing might be included, and how a profit might be made.

According to the junior Garvey's calculations, $3 billion was at stake. The Department of Agriculture's Commodity Credit Corporation purchased US surplus grains and "sold" them at below-market interest rates to countries with little foreign exchange (gold or convertible currency); buyers would slowly repay the Commodity Credit Corportation through installments in their local central bank, and the US government would acquire soft (nonconvertible) currency. Title I of PL 480 (1954) stipulated acceptable US government uses of that soft currency, including the purchase of military equipment, acquisition of sites and buildings, and the funding of US-sponsored schools.[6] The Cooley Amendment of 1957 widened legal uses by setting aside 25% of counterpart funds for US businesses "promoting balanced economic development and trade among nations." (Foreign firms could access some of that 25% if their use would increase the consumption of American agricultural goods.) By

1959, members of Congress—including senator Harold D. Cooley (Dem-NC)—came to see housing finance as a legitimate use of these counterpart funds. "Cooley loans," as they came to be known, served as one of the first major government programs to entice American investors into international housing, and by the end of 1967, yielded roughly $90 million in housing aid.[7]

Willard Garvey liked the American government's proactive stance on both business overseas and agriculture at home, but he wanted to do more than distribute bread and use up local cash. Why give a one-time handout, when you could make the counterpart fund regenerative? Why not allow American homebuilders to build new homes in these countries, with local currencies going toward a "revolving fund for mortgage insurance to underwrite housing . . . just like the FHA had done here in the 1930s"?[8] This "Wheat for Homes" program could fulfill the existing goals of PL 480 by reducing American grain stockpiles, saving tax money currently spent on storage fees, and addressing overseas food and dollar shortages, all while using local cash in a way that would build on itself, that would create new investment opportunities for American homebuilders *and* accomplish political anticommunist objectives.

This was not the same self-help, project-based approach to overseas housing aid taken in Taiwan and Korea in the late 1940s and 1950s. Garvey did not believe American investors should concentrate first and foremost on mass, low-income housing or on do-it-yourself construction techniques. Nor was it a broad attempt to touch the hearts and minds of residents in decolonizing, "tropical" regions. Rather, Garvey emphasized "middle-class" customers' long unmet needs for decent shelter and pursued low-*cost*, not low-*income* housing. American businessmen like Garvey wanted to create customers and partners in world trade, not address the human rights of a poorly housed multitude. These potential partners would consume modern houses, generating all sorts of sales for American investors. Although Garvey claimed all architectural designs were "100% adaptable" to local traditions and desires, in reality the contractor-designed units relied on standardized floor plans with only minor individualization in extensions, landscaping, and interior décor.

"Wheat for Homes" never became the official name of US overseas housing assistance programs under PL 480, but the idea—the notion that the US government should woo private investment into home construction and financing abroad—did become a concrete reality. Garvey's infectious enthusiasm for "productive" housing aid, for investments that could regenerate and be self-sustaining, had support from the highest echelons of policymakers, including Walt Rostow (development economist and presidential advisor), Don Paarlberg (agricultural economist and coordinator of PL 480 from 1958 to 1961), Osborne Boyd (director of the Housing Division, International Cooperation Administration), Dan R. Hamady (Housing and Home Finance Agency), Richard Nixon (vice president from 1953 to 1961), and Joseph Rand (secretary of the Council on Foreign Economic Policy from 1956 to 1961).

In 1961, the National Association of Home Builders (NAHB), the US Savings and Loan League, and the National Association of Real Estate Boards (NAREB) added another critical piece to the arsenal of home-owning democracies: it lobbied for and got congressional support for a Housing Investment Guaranty insuring private US ventures into overseas homeownership programs. Together, PL 480's Cooley Amendment and the Housing Investment Guaranty provided low-risk ways for American entrepreneurs to invest in homeownership programs around the world.

This was no simple policy. Just as Point Four unexpectedly strengthened the role of governments in improved housing for Taiwan and South Korea, so also did Wheat for Homes and the Housing Investment Guaranty tighten the bond between corporate and government interests, with consequent contradictions in American foreign aid policies. One of the most important contradictions occurred in the distribution of improved shelter: Congress had political reasons for seeking better mass housing, but private investors usually found slum dwellers too risky and less profitable than the professional classes. As a result, the "low-cost" housing that politicians funded to defuse the communist threat rarely went to the impoverished majority; many poor people around the world heard promises of impending housing aid but witnessed—indeed, often helped build—shiny new dwellings designed for the top 25% of the population. Objectives became muddied, as congressmen and businessmen talked about stimulating overseas consumption, bolstering middle-class capitalism, and nurturing mass homeownership. No single homeownership campaign could have accomplished all these objectives while spending almost no public money. Ultimately, this supposedly private market solution ended up costing over a half billion dollars of US government money to cover overseas defaults, and yielded some of the highest mortgage failure rates in history among the vaunted "middle class" abroad. The late 1950s, '60s, and '70s saw an explosion of global exchange in housing finance, institutions, and consumer rights, then, exchanges that produced a new set of political and social costs.

Corporate Interest in the 1950s

At its inception, Willard Garvey's idea inspired because it directly addressed one of the central concerns of postwar international housing aid: it did not require much cash. Both the Democratic Truman and Republican Eisenhower administrations wanted to jumpstart overseas housing construction and investment with the larger aim of launching national economic development, but endless handouts were out of the question, and neither administration wanted to issue excessive loans. Both believed a heavy debt burden could sink an emerging economy. Aided self-help demonstration projects provided a seemingly grassroots solution. Unfortunately, progress was maddeningly slow and new construction rates showed no signs of catching up to spiking rural-to-urban migration and population growth. Even in Taiwan, one of the oft-referenced success stories of self-help construction, "private housing wasn't meeting the need" and "obviously a massive increase in housing production is required."[9] More importantly to Garvey, aided self-help and community development programs targeted slum dwellers, leaving the professional class to fend for itself.

Garvey loudly proclaimed a "vendetta" against Rooseveltian, "socialist" government and made unequivocal statements that "the government is the enemy—always has been, always will be," but he also encouraged and profited from US government involvement in middle-class housing, an interest that eventually focused on Latin America. Even the most devout market liberals succumbed to government incentives, apparently unselfconsciously. The Committee for Economic Development (CED, 1942–), a nonprofit public policy organization led by some of the country's wealthiest corporate executives, openly supported soft loans and an increased public investment fund by 1956–57. These executives increasingly occupied top civilian positions in foreign policy-making agencies and included such business elites as Paul Hoffman (Studebaker Corporation and Economic Coordination Administration director), Eugene Black (Chase National Bank and World Bank executive director), and Clarence Randall (Inland Steel Company and Council on Foreign Economic Policy).[10]

Garvey, for his part, made no secret about his partisan agenda, and he urged Republicans to take advantage of homeownership programs' "natural affinity" to conservative economics and politics. Practical business interests also motivated Garvey; in the late 1950s, he briefly contemplated direct sales of his Midwestern wheat surpluses to developing countries before quickly giving this up when he realized how thoroughly Big Six grain exporters commanded global sales.[11] PL 480 offered a more appealing opportunity in overseas home construction and financing—a potentially bigger and certainly less competitive field than grain export.

It is hard to see the line between government and business in Garvey's dealings. Garvey moved seamlessly between corporate and government organizations to push his ideas, and he often met key private investors in public venues. For instance, Garvey joined the Commerce Department's Committee on Foreign Economic Practices in 1959 in order to market his ideas to other committee members such as the heads of the Mortgage Bankers Association, Owens-Corning Fiberglas (producer of air conditioning parts, screens, insulation, and plastic reinforcement), and most importantly, President Eisenhower's friend, Stephen Bechtel, the head of the behemoth global engineering firm. According to Garvey it was precisely his work on this committee that triggered Bechtel's interest in Garvey's "Every Man a Homeowner" ideology and that led to Bechtel taking Garvey under his wing. Garvey also actively nurtured relationships with "ivory tower boys" like Charles Abrams, kept tabs on innovations in other industries like sheet roofing in India by Alcan Aluminum, Ltd. (the international division of Alcoa), brought his "gun to bear" on government officials like Don Paarlberg, all the while fiercely pursuing allies in the Council for Foreign Economic Policy and the National Advisory Council.[12] Regional connections occasionally worked to Garvey's advantage: after the newly inducted president John F. Kennedy appointed former Kansas governor George Docking in 1961 to direct the Export-Import Bank—the bank that managed all PL 480 loans—Garvey successfully acquired his first loan for a pilot homeownership program.

Without question, the biggest names in corporate America and Congress consulted each other, borrowed each other's ideas, and promoted mutual interests. Together, they urged others to draw from their collective wisdom. Much as the federal government and a powerful real estate lobby ended up crafting a two-tiered domestic housing system with a residualist public housing program for the most needy and hefty government-supported home financing for the middle and upper classes, these same actors worked together to bolster homeownership for white-collar professionals in the developing world on a scale not seen in aided self-help projects for low-income families.[13] To Garvey's own surprise, government interests would initially redirect his time and money to homeownership programs in a region much closer than India.

Starting in Latin America

Corporate America actively participated in policymaking, but politicians played an equally potent role in determining where and how much private investment would occur. The process was simple: government incentives and protections determined the level of profit and risk in specific overseas ventures, which in turn determined where investors put their money. PL 480 began as a government response to costly domestic agricultural subsidies and perceived waste in storage fees, but it also essentially funneled private investment money to some homeownership programs and not others.

Up through the mid-1950s, the US government intervened militarily and politically in Latin American affairs, but showed less consistent care with development aid.[14] When the US helped topple popularly elected Guatemalan president Jacobo Árbenz Guzmán in favor of Carlos Castillo Armas in 1954, for instance, development aid did rise to $90 million total from 1954 to 1957, but that money came in spurts, was poorly managed, and stopped abruptly in 1958 because—as ambassador Lester DeWitt Mallory explained—Guatemalans needed to understand that "some self help, some local pulling of the boot straps, some honesty and responsibility are important."[15] The Mutual Security Administration generally shied away from aid commitments in Latin America, stating that the "more realistic approach" to the region's housing problems was to "realize that the responsibility for improving housing conditions rests with the individual countries themselves," and that the US did not see "the necessity for financing from external sources."[16] Mid-decade, Latin America received significantly less than other regions: in 1956, for example, the US gave net $155 million in aid to Latin American countries as compared with $1.36 billion for East Asia, Southeast Asia and Africa or $542 million for Western Europe.[17] West Germany alone received $160 million in counterpart and special funds for housing, provoking at least one international housing advisor to comment, "One is inclined to wonder whether an equal amount of money spent in Latin America . . . in connection with housing might not have had a greater impact . . . One could also ask the same question concerning the Arabian countries in the Middle East."[18]

Private investors likewise showed little interest in flooding Latin America with housing improvement money. With the exception of extraordinary places like Puerto Rico, the sale of small-denomination government bonds had not proven particularly effective at channeling individual savings into housing in the region. As a US territory, Puerto Rico had the advantage of a mainland demand for tax-exempt bonds and an FHA mortgage insurance program. In fact, Nelson Rockefeller's International Basic Economy Corporation (IBEC, 1947–77) used these advantages to launch a unique housing program there in 1956. In most of Latin America, however, no sane investor would leap at the chance to buy bonds *and* "a paper every morning to keep up with the composition of the government so you know whose signatures ought to be on the bond," in the words of prominent Miami-based S&L president Jack Gordon.[19] Inflation also discouraged long-term investment in mortgage or other bonds, insurance policies, savings deposits, and the like. Other private investments proved far more enticing than housing, with billions of US dollars flowing annually toward industries like oil, minerals, and coffee.[20] By 1958, these sorts of exchanges made Latin American trade the second-most important for the US economy (behind Western Europe) with over one-third of all US direct overseas private investment going to Latin America.[21] Latin American investors likewise put their money into more lucrative venues to the neglect of housing finance, preferring to "put their money into idle land where they believe it is more secure, or into speculative luxury buildings for a quick resale, or— too often the case—into Zürich or New York bank accounts" rather than in affordable housing or local savings institutions.[22]

The International Cooperation Administration (ICA, 1955–61)—a State Department agency set up to administer foreign aid after the dismantling of the Mutual Security Agency (1951–53) and Foreign Operations Administration (1953–54)—did launch one of the first US technical assistance programs to raise homeownership rates in Latin America in 1956, but the effort was small and ended quickly. In this important but small project, executive director of the US Savings and Loan League Morton Bodfish led an ICA Savings and Loan advisory group to Peru and, together with the Peruvian Commission for Agrarian Reform and Housing, wrote and enacted S&L legislation by March 1957. Laws were necessary but not sufficient to build up credit institutions, however, and newly birthed S&Ls stumbled along for the next few years in Peru.[23] Bodfish's attempt to amend the Home Owners' Loan Act (1933) was met with little enthusiasm from the international division of the HHFA, even though Bodfish argued such a measure would allow federal S&Ls to invest in equivalent institutions abroad and possibly jumpstart local savings "in the way that the Treasury-HOLC pattern started so many now successful institutions in the financially blitzed areas in the early 30s."[24] When IBEC Housing Corporation tried to replicate its successful construction of 1,500 San Juan houses in other parts of Latin America, it quickly found itself stymied by a lack of adequate long-term financing in non-US territories. The US Mutual Security Act of 1957 created a Development Loan Fund within the ICA that firmly committed the US to soft lending in development aid but allocated few of its resources to shelter and categorized housing again as a nonproductive investment.[25] HHFA acting administrator Walker Mason anticipated troubles with weak American interest in 1958, arguing that an undesirable explosion of "multiunit, state-run housing" might become the norm in Latin America "unless US aid policies helped to make private homeownership more feasible for the average worker."[26] Nonetheless, PL 480 funds issued up to 1959 favored other, nonhousing investments in Turkey ($7.8 million), Greece ($2.9 million), Israel ($10.2 million), Pakistan ($16.4 million), and India ($14.2 million). Peru and Ecuador received a mere $1.5 and $0.5 million respectively, and again, in nonhousing investments.[27] In fact, Latin America received only 3% of all development aid under the Truman administration, and 9% under Eisenhower.[28]

Only those American corporations selling specific building components actively participated in the mid-1950s Latin American housing scene, and they did so in a very limited way. The New York–based international division of Owens-Corning Fiberglas, for example, sold housing products in Venezuela, Colombia, Ecuador, Peru, Bolivia, and parts of Central America by 1960, but they did not dictate where or for whom these goods would be used. Most likely given the nature of the products themselves—Fiberglas provided insulation for modern electrical systems and appliances or reinforcement for plastic furniture—these investments affected only the most elite housing.[29]

Ultimately, it took large political events like street-level hostility to vice president Richard Nixon in Latin America (1958) and Fidel Castro's revolution in Cuba (1959) to tip the scales. Much like Mao Zedong's victory opened the door to American housing investments in East Asia a decade prior, the fearsome "cult of Castro" now galvanized congressional members once leery of what they perceived to be social development spending.[30] President Eisenhower responded to security concerns by supporting the formation of an Inter-American Development Bank (IADB) in 1959; he went further a year later with the Act of Bogotá (1960), allocating $394 million for clean water, sanitation, and low-income housing projects in a Social Progress Trust Fund managed by the newly created IADB.[31] By 1962, IADB had provided over $117 million in loans to Brazil, Chile, Colombia, Costa Rica, Ecuador, El Salvador, Guatemala, Nicaragua, Panama, Peru, Uruguay, and Venezuela for the construction and sale of new homes.[32] Meanwhile, Congress amended the Mutual Security Act of 1954 so that the Development Loan Fund could use more of its $1.95 billion (1960) assets to develop "free economic institutions and [encourage] the stimulation of private investment, local as well as foreign, in the field of housing."[33] The Development Loan Fund acted on this new legislative mandate by encouraging savings-and-loan associations in Ecuador and Chile, alongside the first test program in Peru. Both the IADB and Development Loan Fund initiatives supplemented and bolstered smaller Cooley Amendment housing loans starting in 1959.

At the same time that Latin American programs were beginning to push forward, American development experts for a very brief moment considered African sites for parallel self-help experiments. Beginning in the fall of 1961, the Agency for International Development launched three aided self-help projects in Rhodesia, Zambia, and Mali—all three promoting homeownership, the first in urban Dzivaresekwa, the second and third, in rural Mukobeko and Djoliba.[34] In these early programs, AID introduced a language of homeownership that resonated with ad-

19 Part of US technical advice missions centered on helping others "visualize development works at the planning stage." In this US-supported Ghanaian Technical Advice Centre, local staff helped participants build model houses. Source: Folder Ghana, box 2 of 8, RG 286, NARA, n.d.

20 In Dzivaresekwa Township near Salisbury, Rhodesia, HUD and USAID worked together to "train urban workers to assume more responsibility for managing their own affairs through home and land ownership." Only married, employed men "of good character" qualified to participate in this homeownership program. Here, Self-Help Home Builders' Brotherhood members receive cloth badges and paper certificates indicating their successful completion of 100 hours of "spare time work." Source: Department of Housing and Urban Development, Division of International Affairs, Aided Self Help Housing in Africa—Prepared for the Agency for International Development, Ideas and Methods Exchange 65 (Washington, DC: DIA, 197?).

ministrators' needs in a wide array of African nations, and that would persist well after American aid had faded. By 1965, for instance, United Nations Economic Commission for Africa (EC-Afr) worker A. A. Carney emphasized to the Kenyan government, "One important field in which African ownership must be encouraged is housing. . . . In the future . . . projects promoting [low-income] African ownership of houses will be given highest priority."[35] These first projects in Rhodesia, Zambia, and Mali had long-lasting impacts in terms of the rhetoric of aided self-help on the continent, and the emphasis on homeownership within aided self-help programs received reinforcement over successive years through various paths, undoubtedly because it appeared to require minimal internal or external government funding. In 1968, for example, the Netherlands' Bouwcentrum launched a housing mission in cooperation with EC-Afr that urged governments to "execute [their] housing policy in such a way as to make it the personal interest of the individual people concerned to proceed in the direction as considered necessary from the government's overall point of view."[36] This could include such indirect mechanisms as a mortgage insurance system, such as "in the United

States of America, where such a system is administered by the Federal Housing Administration."[37]

African programs ultimately fell by the wayside as Latin American programs took off, however. The reason was simple: unlike Latin American counterparts or even the Greek, Taiwanese, and South Korean housing programs that preceded them, the Rhodesian, Zambian, and Malian projects lacked a compelling political component for American aid givers. The contrast between African and Latin American programs illustrates just how critical American political interests were to international housing assistance, despite rhetoric about basic human rights and decency in "teeming slum quarters" around the world. If assessment had been based purely on need, the tumultuous independence movements in Africa that stimulated capital flight and disinvestment from former European colonial powers would certainly have made the world's second-largest continent a top contender for housing assistance. EC-Afr regional advisor R. E. Fitchett griped in 1965, "Africa is still far behind in the matter of assistance when compared with that received by Latin American countries through the Social Progress Trust Fund of the Inter American Development Bank."[38] Latin America dominated US aid in the 1960s: "Thanks to US support, the FSO [Fund for Special Operations, IADB] was exceptionally well endowed with resources in comparison with the Asian Development Bank and the African Development Bank," one IADB history recounted.[39] If African leaders experimented with the general principles of aided self-help, "no really bold and imaginative attempt [was] made to use the enormous possibilities inherent in this system to the best advantage of the African people," even in the programs begun in Kenya, Nigeria, Togo, Chad, Somalia, Libya, and Algeria.[40] EC-Afr workers had little choice but to focus on the "self-help" aspect of "aided self-help" and to not expect much from the "aided" component. Africans would need to find African solutions to unprecedented problems of urbanization and centralization (or "urban drift," as they were called by AID workers).[41]

Meanwhile momentum in the Latin American aid programs continued to build. The first dramatic augmentation came in March 1961, when president John F. Kennedy opened both doors wide with his Alliance for Progress, headed by Teodoro Moscoso, previously head of Operation Bootstrap in Puerto Rico. The Alliance for Progress promised $20 billion in public and private loans and investments in the coming decade for the US's southern neighbors, and $100 million of that fund was earmarked for homeownership programs in self-help construction and aid for savings and loans. Both self-help and savings-and-loan assistance explicitly required all US-supported units be 100% owner-occupied.[42] Within seven months of the Alliance for Progress's launch, an American investor named William Luce had begun a 5,200-unit project in Guatemala, and former US housing administrator Norman P. Mason had founded the American International Housing Corporation with special interest in Latin American possibilities. The Rockefellers' IBEC encouraged a Puerto Rican building affiliate to sell its mass production techniques to Jamaica, directly launched its own 700-unit project in Peru, and began construction on a 750-house, "middle-class" (US$7,000–8,000 per unit) community in Santiago, Chile, with the hope of "demonstrat[ing] that United States industrial [building] methods and techniques are applicable abroad," all while ensuring that the "Latin middle class is loyal to the Western concept of government" through the fulfillment of "normal material rewards that the middle class expects in the United States."[43] The Brazilian government used Alliance funds to build Vila Kennedy, Vila Aliança, Vila Esperança, and Cidade de Deus for low-income residents cleared from favelas, "the supposed hotbeds of communism." Argentinians built housing in Villa Lugano I–II and Ciudad General Belgrano, with the "transformation of the squatter dweller into a homeowner" serving as a critical justification and operational principle of the new complexes.[44] As Ernesto (Che) Guevara predicted in a speech at Punta del Este in August 1961, "It is said: 'Cuba is the goose that lays the golden egg. Cuba exists, and while there is a Cuba, the United States will continue to give.'"[45] This statement was especially true for housing aid.

Garvey, like other investors, found his attention directed to Latin America by foreign relations interests. Initially, the businessman conducted a wide survey of potential prospects in the mid- and late 1950s, reading mortgage finance reports from First National City Bank of New York offices in South Africa, Jamaica, Japan, and Germany, to name a few; he also visited potential pilot sites in South Asia, Central America, and South America before narrowing his choices to India and Pakistan. When Export-Import Bank (Exim) loan administrators urged Garvey to consider Peru instead, however, Garvey put his Asian plans on hold and redirected his attention southward. It was in this way that World Homes, Inc., finally selected a small settlement on the outskirts of Lima to use its historic 1960 Exim loan of S/.4,000,000 (Peruvian soles, equivalent to US$143,000) at 8% interest—the first US government loan to a private building firm for the purpose of home construction outside the US.[46] Garvey created a subsidiary of World Homes called Hogares Peruanos S.A. (Peruvian Homes), and with it, dreamed of building a new middle class, a "bulwark of Democracy in Peru."[47] The first step would be a set of long-term mortgages using counterpart funds for roughly 2,400 Limeños (400 families).

Building a Middle Class in Peru

That Garvey thought his plans fit readily into vastly different locales, and that he knew so little about Peruvian society before aspiring to create a new middle class there, reveals the formulaic approach adopted by at least some international investors. What fit in one country would fit in another; Levitt and Sons of Puerto Rico, for instance, built Levittown de Puerto Rico in complete communities and with similar housing models as those found in other Levittowns across the US.[48] Garvey, for his part, did not distinguish much between a Peruvian and Indian middle class, nor did he give more than a passing glance at local perceptions of status vis-à-vis shelter type. For Garvey, World Homes' modern units were intrinsically desirable and superior to any indigenous building types, and they would satisfy the class aspirations of a rising middle class. The only cultural differences that counted were those that impacted sticker prices or consumer strength. Garvey shared developmental theorists' belief that the "middle classes [were] the bounty of economic modernization and growth," and he believed these middle classes would share a taste for modern housing that matched their ambitions and aspirations.[49]

Although Garvey did not know it at first, he was fortunate in that Hogares Peruanos's efforts dovetailed with an already well-established interest in American urban planning as well as a burgeoning savings movement in Peru. World Homes was thus able to ride the wave of interest in US-style homeownership already cresting in that country. The Corporación Nacional de la Vivienda (a government agency) had previously built a low-cost housing project of 1,112 units in suburban Lima utilizing mostly private capital. The project's street layout and placement of housing vis-à-vis schools, stores, playgrounds, and other services closely modeled Radburn, New Jersey, in a deliberate imitation of US-style garden city development.[50]

In the realm of savings, Peru had an unlikely early banking maverick in the mid-1950s: thirty-four-year-old American missionary Father Dan McLellan argued that a "free man" needed to not only own his home, but also participate in the "thrift institutions for capital accumulation."[51] Following this conviction, the self-proclaimed "capitalist priest" launched Peru's first credit union in 1955 in Puno, an indigent community on the shores of Lake Titicaca at the southeastern border

with Bolivia. After witnessing the severe poverty of this Andean com-
munity, McLellan came to the conclusion that "you can't do a very good
job of saving a man's soul if you're going to leave his body in hell."[52]
Instead, McLellan aspired to secure "decent homes" for the indigent and
turn "poor people . . . into capitalists with a credit rating."[53] By 1967,
McLellan had persuaded nearly 350,000 Peruvians to deposit almost
$40 million in approximately 600 regional unions organized under a
Peruvian Federation of Credit Unions, supplemented by a $1 million
Inter-American Development Bank loan, and with its own total accumulated loans at $150 million.[54] By 1966, this money had funded 742
housing loans, in addition to public water and sewerage projects and
agricultural loans.

After two of prime minister Pedro Beltrán's US-sponsored national
savings-and-loan efforts (Mutual Lima and Mutual Peru) both flopped
miserably, Beltrán and US S&L experts persuaded McLellan to expand
his credit union work to savings and loans, promising a government
match in credit to all personal savings and $7.5 million in Development
Loan Fund funds (later replaced with Inter-American Development Bank
loans).[55] In 1961, McLellan helped open Mutual El Pueblo and within
sixteen months had 3,605 members and S/.17,458,000 in savings, supplemented by a $1 million Inter-American Development Bank loan
in 1963.[56] By 1966, the total number of savers had jumped to 21,000
with $13,954,979 in savings and 4,732 new homeowners provided with
mortgages.[57]

McLellan's work promoted the idea of a better life through homeownership, and Garvey benefited from the broader idealization of economic
advancement through mortgage-driven ownership, as well as by the rising discontent of a professional class untouched by McLellan's programs
and still living in small, poorly equipped urban quarters. Garvey believed
he was building a brand-new professional class, but in actuality he inadvertently tapped into the aspirations of *empleados* (white-collar workers)
already claiming middle-class status in urban Peru. World Homes' motto,
"Todo hombre puede tener su casa" (Every man can own his home),
struck a chord with these professionals who had protested their relative
economic misfortune compared to the *obreros* (manual laborers) since
the 1920s. They believed themselves sorely used in a class system that
required them to pay more to keep up appearances, "to live in decent
houses, to dress with relative elegance and to eat with some comfort"—in
short, to "maintain themselves within a social situation that, for their
very modesty, they cannot possibly abandon."[58] These protests were,
to some extent, disingenuous, however, since most middle-class young

professionals had yet to achieve visibly superior housing standards. The class divide was not as large as they may have wished: many middle-class families lived in cramped city apartments or subsections of relatives' homes, not unlike their American or British counterparts in the late 1940s.[59] These accommodations were a step up from the *barriadas* (shanties), but not by enough. Hogares Peruanos's affordable modern units meant that professional Limeños could at long last articulate their class standing through their homes and no longer suffer the indignity of renting hovels while McLellan's poor began owning in Puno.

From a US perspective, the major problem with linking homeownership to middle-class respectability was that the Peruvian middle class did not resemble the US version. In Peru, the middle class constituted a

21 It was never exactly clear who the "middle class" was in Peruvian homeownership campaigns. Image of a worker going into a house. Source: Drawn by Ernesto Aramburú Menchaca, Arquitectos for Viviendas de Interes Social, February 1959. Lima, Peru. World Homes Collection 94-9, box 58, folder 3, Special Collections and University Archives, Wichita State University Libraries.

22 Proud new homeowner Francisco Tarazona with his family in 1960. Tarazona lived in a two-room apartment with his wife, sister, and young child before Hogares Peruanos S.A. offered ten-year financing for this home in a northern suburb of Lima. Hogares Peruanos was able to offer this sort of financing because of an Export-Import Bank loan under the provisions of the Cooley Amendment to PL 480. Source: World Homes Collection 94-9, box 94, folder 7, Special Collections and University Archives, Wichita State University Libraries.

small fraction of the total population and was relatively wealthy. Hogares Peruanos's manager, Howard Wenzel, struggled to define it: "Hogares' market might be defined as ranging from the lowest paid steadily employed worker . . . to the white-collar employee holding junior executive positions in Peruvian Industry and Commerce," he reported in one loan application to the Exim Bank. "Hogares' market is what will eventually become the middle class of Peru. In other words, those interested in Hogares' houses have some education and generally wish to improve their present status."[60]

Business-wise, it made more sense for World Homes to delineate class status based solely on income, without regard for education or social aspiration. In order to purchase a home using no more than 25% of the monthly salary of the homebuyer, families had to earn between S/.2,400 and 6,000. According to the FHA–Latin American division, the average Limeño white-collar worker brought home S/.2,371 a month; since white-collar and high-wage blue-collar workers often operated in multiple-earner households, both could afford the units built by World Homes or any other American builder.[61] According to the Peruvian Ministry of Labor, however, only 50,000 of the total workforce had base salaries in the S/.2,400–6,000 range in metropolitan Lima, a city with a total population of about 1.5 million.[62] This definition meant that a mere 3% of all metropolitan residents qualified for Garvey's homes. The FHA's claim that these white- and blue-collar workers together constituted a growing "middle class" in Lima was further qualified by the fact that the average per capita monthly income in 1967 was roughly S/.223.[63] Even if one homeowner provided for an average family of six, and even if Hogares Peruanos actually supplied the necessary 50,000 units (which it did not), it could hardly claim the benefits of mass home-ownership. A vast cohort of deeply impoverished citizens shared the city with a "middle class" whose income was over ten times theirs. Nonetheless, Wenzel argued, "this potential middle class group" could later serve as the "bulwark of Democracy in Peru," help Prime Minister Beltrán with the pressing political problem of indecent shelter, and have an appealing trickle-down effect, opening up urban slums to former shantytown dwellers while the middle class moved out to new suburban communities.[64]

In fact, what the American company Hogares Peruanos (and indirectly, the FHA and USAID through their proposal analyses and recommendations) was effectively doing was building a new geography of class. This spatial reordering played out very differently from the US's experiences with mass suburbanization: by 1959, Peru's primate city, Lima (1.3 million), and its much smaller second city, Arequipa (140,000), faced intense rural in-migration, burgeoning informal settlements in the outer ring of the city, increased subdivision of existing homes centrally with concomitant increase in core population density, and flight of the wealthy to new planned communities on the outskirts of the city. Hogares Peruanos encouraged the minuscule professional class to join the wealthy and the very poor in developing socially segregated communities on the edges of the urban core, thus pushing at the boundaries of the city and feeding metropolitan sprawl. While Wenzel and Garvey believed they were growing a US-style homeowning suburban middle class, in reality they were developing relatively small, affluent, and isolated residential communities with markedly better access to urban services than the *barriadas* nearby. (Indeed, sometimes the *barriadas* were so close that homeowners could stand on their paved roads and see them spreading across the horizon.) Like Santiago, Recife, São Paulo,

Rio de Janeiro, or Buenos Aires, Lima's businesses and substantive services still proliferated within an ever-denser urban core, but the reach of these megalopolises also grew ever larger as communities pushed at the boundaries while relying on the city for urban services, jobs, and consumer goods.[65]

Class prejudice or past experience does not solely explain the American propensity to encourage this sort of sub-urban, decentralized development for the middle class. Economics mattered at least as much. Large sub-urban projects worked better because they standardized production and reduced overhead costs for international investors. When unexpected political events or financial disasters struck, multinational corporations could much more easily shut down operations without long delays and expensive drag time. The very structure of overseas financing gave strong disincentives to renovate or infill buildings in the existing urban topography.

The perfect example of this was Hogares Peruanos's central-city "Package Homes" project. In this early 1960s venture, director Howard Wenzel attempted to replicate Jim Walter Corporation's US Shell Homes in Peruvian urban communities by providing contractor-built housing with complete exteriors, all basic services, raw interiors, and 100% financing. In theory, the prefabricated, individualized character of each unit should have facilitated urban uses, singly replacing decrepit houses without disturbing larger urban communities. Unlike Shell Homes in the US however, Package Homes had to cope with a sudden, dramatic change in political fortune when it lost mortgage financing in 1962 after Ricard Pérez Godoy's successful military coup. While Jim Walter reaped over $9 million in profits in his first five years of operation in the US, Package Homes quickly slid into the red within the first two. Project director Wenzel concluded that when long-term financing was uncertain, single or small clusters of construction made a company vulnerable because of the cost of fixed overhead in multiple locations:

You cannot shut down your operations very readily. However, if you are building a large group of houses in one place, you either have the financing or you don't go ahead, and if you have the financing, since all your houses are concentrated in one place and are of the same type, you can keep your staff on a relatively low level and keep your overhead low. . . . I think that contractor-built homes, in other words, homes built by the contractors for the people, is really the only answer. . . . A regular self-help project takes way too much administration and one of the problems of the under-developed countries is that they are short of capable administrators.[66]

After this first failure, WHI only ventured into sub-urban, mass con-struction sites in Peru and in its expanded operations in Mexico, Bolivia, and Chile. These peripheral urban developments might have looked very similar to post-1945 American suburbs, but they reflected a calcula-tion of political risk specific to international investment in the devel-oping world. American workers had to deal with a distinctly local and national mix of class identity and political instability as they carved out new communities with the tools of US home finance. Again, this inter-est was explicitly in low-cost rather than low-income housing. It made perfect sense that Garvey would never reference or consider British ar-chitect John F. C. Turner's enormously influential work on the self-help efforts of squatters, despite the fact that both men were active in Peru at roughly the same time.[67] Indeed, Turner's emphasis on local know-how and the potential for self-construction amongst the lowest classes had little resonance with Garvey's view of housing as investment.

Rather, considerations like land availability played a large role. In La Paz, Bolivia, for instance, most of the flat center of the city was com-pletely occupied, with vacant lots broken up into small, dispersed plots. The Jockey Club had one of the few large tracts of metropolitan land that could hold 700 or more new homes, albeit six miles outside the central district. In addition, the club's land abutted the higher-class resi-dential district of Calacoto, a fact that developers rejoiced would stabi-lize land value and motivate buyers looking to "move up."[68] Time and time again, cheaper, larger tracts of land could be had three to ten miles outside the central city.

Fringe land was not an uncontested site for new development, how-ever. American companies worked hard to make sure no squatters could establish their own communities in this emerging "middle-class" do-main, whether in Bolivia, Peru, or any other investment site. In sub-urban Lima, World Homes converted the hill between two of its largest middle-class housing developments into a park lest informal dwellings "mar the scenery" from Sol de Oro and Villa Los Angeles.[69] A global settle-ment pattern was emerging, then, one that visually reflected the struggle for land and home as it played out between the classes. The familiar grid of single-family "middle class" homes may have looked like tract hous-ing in the US, but in Latin America, this sort of peripheral development constituted an expansion of the metropolis rather than a dispersion. In fact, the process was not called "suburbanization," despite the sub-urban locations of new settlements; instead, they were labeled "urbanization" schemes because companies provided city services like sewage, water, streets, and electricity, and usually became subject to local taxes.

23 In the Sol de Oro project, World Homes worked with Peruvian firms to build with the assistance of USAID loans. This 500-unit project was located north of Lima along the Pan American Highway. Source: World Homes Collection 94-9, box 94, folder 1, and box 58, folder 5, Special Collections and University Archives, Wichita State University Libraries.

24 In the Sol de Oro project, World Homes worked with Peruvian firms to build with the assistance of USAID loans. This 500-unit project was located north of Lima along the Pan American Highway. Source: World Homes Collection 94-9, box 94, folder 1, and box 58, folder 5, Special Collections and University Archives, Wichita State University Libraries.

American corporations and host governments deliberately promoted this sort of decentralized urbanization as a solution to the massive urban in-migration to developing-world cities in the postwar period. Hogares Peruanos stationed its headquarters in downtown Lima, hoping to woo prospective purchasers currently living in one- or two-room apartments in the central city. After completing its first profitable 72-house pilot project, aptly titled "Operation Guinea Pig," Hogares Peruanos used earnings to fund a new subsidiary named Hogares Chavarria. This subsidiary built a much larger 1,120-house community in the aforementioned Sol de Oro, four miles northwest of downtown Lima and outside the ring of slums surrounding the city. Another project, Hacienda Chavarria, also skipped over undesirable fringe settlements in favor of a site along the Pan American Highway five miles from the center of Lima. The Peruvian government encouraged such developments, publishing maps of uncultivated agricultural lands available to "resolve the housing crisis."[70] The resulting settlements added a new ring of residential communities to the city where farmlands and undeveloped lands had once existed.

With the exception of dense, circumscribed cities like Hong Kong or Singapore, this pattern of metropolitan sprawl spread like wildfire across the developing world.[71] By 1964, UN housing advisor Gerald Desmond believed housing standards had become implicated in global flows of investment capital, and that rising concerns with inflation, concomitant shortage of long-term funds, and escalating demands for long-term credit from "unprecedented rates of urban growth . . . [were] among the foremost problems of public officials" in Latin America, according to Desmond.[72] Private innovations like indexing to inflation and wage-based mortgages (mortgages that were not set as an actual dollar amount but rather as a percentage of the homeowner's income) directly addressed international investors' concerns, and the UN for the first time contemplated a role in Latin American home financing even as AID, the Organization of American States, and the Inter-American Development Bank all failed to adequately address the credit crunch. (Interestingly, one of the first UN housing finance experts to serve in Central America, Panama, and Mexico argued that more needed to be done along the lines of USAID's studies in Pakistan with regard to formal study of climatic zones and the influence of climate on "type of house, . . . shape of roof, orientation, ventilation, isolation, and other qualities.")[73]

Meanwhile, World Homes projects continued apace: the company completed a 400-house community near the Bogotá airport in Ciudad Techo with funds provided by a Cooley loan and local S&Ls. (The name of the city was changed to Ciudad Kennedy after the president's assassination, much to Republican Garvey's dismay.) World Homes also launched a 600-house project in the outer ring of Mexico City, a 400-house project in La Paz, Bolivia, and new projects in suburban Taipei and Bangkok.[74] Developers routinely transformed raw peripheral land into small, single-family homes: just twenty minutes' walking distance outside Santa Cruz, Bolivia, Equipetrol Ltd. provided Hogares Bolivianos 385,000 square meters (95 acres) of heavily forested raw land for development into 450-square-meter lots of two-, three-, and four-bedroom houses.

Time and time again, American builders chose sub-urban properties over already developed urban areas. One of World Homes' more colorful competitors, an ad man turned real estate investor named Alan Carnoy, first made his mark constructing a controversial, racially integrated homeowning community in White Plains, New York. Soon after, Carnoy decided to set up seven single-family homes "based on United States standards" in Lomas de Sotelo, roughly six miles east of central Mexico City, with the hope of demonstrating what "private enterprise could provide if builders and the public could obtain mortgage loans."[75] In 1964, Carnoy attempted valiantly, if unsuccessfully, to persuade USAID to help him launch similar homeowner communities on the outskirts of Saigon. USAID finally did support Carnoy's efforts in Tunisia, where his International Building Corporation used a $5 million loan from three American insurance companies and a USAID guaranty to build in El Menzah, a "suburb" (now district) three miles north of central Tunis. All 500 homes sold quickly, with "excellent publicity for the US," but alas, only with what Carnoy believed to be a "middle class," since the 10% deposit of $1,300 excluded most Tunisians, the average per capita annual income being $128.23 in 1960.[76]

None of this overseas investment would have been nearly as attractive without government initiatives. From 1959 to 1972, the IADB's Social Progress Trust and Development Loan Fund, PL 480 currencies, and Cooley loans gave investors added incentives to reshape the urban landscape in Latin America and, eventually, parts of North Africa and Southeast Asia. Eventually, loans extended beyond the usual construction of new homes to fund "slum improvement" projects such as the massive 1962 favela clearance and urbanization effort in Rio de Janeiro—a project with high visual impact, razing entire informal settlements and erecting evenly spaced tract housing in enormous "vilas"—all of which was funded by PL 480 monies at a price of 1 billion cruzeiros (roughly $2.8 million). A similar project in Venezuela garnered $30 million of USAID support.[77] Only with the Food for Peace Act of 1966 did the Cooley Amendment portion of overseas housing assistance end; the new Act required dollars for all grain sales starting in 1972, drastically reducing demand for American agriculture.[78] The end of PL 480 did not mean that housing programs abated, however. Besides other loan programs, another federal government incentive created shortly after the Cooley Amendment offered a different kind of support for improved housing in overseas democracies. This tool was used in combination with Cooley funds beginning in 1961, and then independently after 1972.

The Housing Investment Guaranty of 1961

Ambitious American businessmen welcomed loans to experiment with various housing pilot programs. The federal government wanted to devise more and varied incentives, though, and in 1961 it came up with what became known as the investment guaranty. There had been some limited private insurance against commercial risks as early as the nineteenth century (e.g., insurance against borrower defaults due to poor business practices). The largest obstacle to overseas investment in the late 1940s and 1950s still remained nonbusiness risk, however. The Foreign Assistance Act of 1948 launched the first government investment guaranty against losses due to inconvertibility in Europe only, a guaranty that by 1950 included losses due to expropriation. The geographic limitation officially ended in 1951, when the Mutual Security Act opened the program to all aid-receiving nations. (Still, the first year after the act's passage saw an exclusive approval of European applications.) Congress further extended what became known as specific risk guaranties to include war, revolution, or insurrection in 1956.[79]

Exim, meanwhile, began covering limited political risks (e.g., defaults due to regime change) for a few export items like cotton and tobacco held abroad on consignment beginning in 1953. In 1960, President Eisenhower demanded Exim cover 90% of short-term credit losses due to risks caused by "political or catastrophic causes not privately insurable."[80] President Kennedy further stretched coverage in February 1961 to add commercial credit risks neglected by Eisenhower in the year prior. Under Kennedy's amendments, Exim split coverage of 85% of all commercial risk with a newly created, voluntary organization of qualifying US insurance companies called the Foreign Credit Insurance Association

(FCIA). (Exim would continue to be solely responsible for no more than 95% coverage of political risks.) Neither political nor commercial risk was covered fully, since "this insurance [was] intended to reinforce rather than replace sound credit evaluations by the exporter."[81]

By 1960, Exim, the Development Loan Fund, and ICA each tested the government insurance idea in some fashion, offering loans to private enterprises and foreign governments for development projects abroad with full or partial US government guaranties of loans by private lenders at interest rates of 3.5%–6% and for amortization periods of seven to forty years.[82] Certainly, the US was interested in stabilizing Latin American economies; it was also interested in larger questions of development and Rostovian "take off." (American economist Walt Rostow posited five stages of economic growth from a traditional to a mass consumer society, with "take off" occurring when economies experience rapid, self-sustaining growth.) Exim, Development Loan Fund, and ICA's investment guaranties did not directly target housing or mortgage finance development, but they did highlight broader policy questions that would prove critical to future overseas housing policy: could a government guaranty against various risks stimulate large-scale American private investment abroad? Could that investment in turn stimulate economic development and take-off?

The National Association of Home Builders (NAHB), the US Savings and Loan League, and the National Association of Real Estate Boards (NAREB) thought yes, and yes again. Capitalizing on the momentum behind government-aided private investment, they actively lobbied ICA's successor—the US Agency for International Development (USAID, 1961–)—to open up investment guaranties to include residential financing in the Foreign Assistance Act of 1961. The 1961 act itself represented a reorganization and consolidation of government insurance for private investors: it supplanted previous Mutual Security Acts, setting up a new two-part system with all foreign aid henceforth falling under either the Development Loan Fund's emphasis on productive and self-generative economic growth, or under the Development Grant Fund's focus on technical cooperation.[83] Eventually, USAID took charge of economic aid (FAA 1961, part I) while the State Department managed military aid in consultation with the Department of Defense (FAA 1961, part II).

In Title III, section 221(b)(2) and section 224, of the 1961 Foreign Assistance Act, the federal government finally responded to housing advocates' exhortations by creating a Housing Investment Guaranty, offering protections for investment in international housing projects much as the FHA did at home. Legislators and private industry wrangled over the extent of the guaranty, with NAHB arguing for 100% and the Senate, 75%; both concurred, however, that US guaranties ought to grease the wheels of private investment. With private dollars coming in, savings-and-loan industries could get off the ground, mobilize local savings, and issue mortgages to new homeowners across Latin America. New emphasis was made on programs as opposed to specific projects; best of all, the guaranty would be almost subsidy-free.

Specifically, section 221(b)(2) permitted "low-cost housing" activity as part of the broader emphasis on "economic development projects which further social progress" delineated in section 221 of the 1961 act. These projects explicitly had to have a "favorable impact on a *broad segment* of the public."[84] While section 221(b)(2) provided general guaranties for organizations involved in financing overseas S&Ls, housing cooperatives, and the like, section 224 provided specific guaranties for pilot or demonstration private housing projects "of types similar to those insured by the Federal Housing Administration and suitable for conditions in Latin America."[85] These demonstration projects should nurture homeownership, whether in condos, cooperatives, or single-family homes, and thereby "assist in the development of stable economies" in Latin America.[86]

The guaranty program's administrators intended to use FHA techniques, but to take more risks. At first glance, the new legislation might appear to simply expand extant FHA programs into other countries; however, HHFA clarified that the program was in actuality "an economic development tool rather than a mortgage insurance program" designed to entice "private enterprise to join the US government in its attempt to resolve the housing problems of developing countries."[87] This served to loosen risk assessment, as "the usual conservative mortgage insurance criteria of 'economic soundness' must be replaced with a more liberal attitude toward assuming increased risks if new housing techniques in developing countries are to be developed."[88]

The mechanics of the guaranty were fairly straightforward: USAID would give US investors an incentive to put their highly mobile capital into targeted overseas housing markets by guaranteeing 75% to 100% of that investment at a rate of return of between 0.5 and 1 percentage point higher than the current FHA-insured mortgages, plus a 0.5% to 2% fee to USAID, depending on the amount of coinsurance issued by the host government.[89] (Coinsurance was encouraged but not required as a way to lower insurance premiums.)[90] This guarantee protected against all risks such as default and devaluation, with the only two exceptions being fraud or misrepresentation on the part of the investor.[91] A local version of the US's Federal Home Loan Bank Board would collect all monies and relend to local associations. Meanwhile, newborn S&Ls would cultivate local savings and make use of these USAID "seed" loans to issue mortgages to "competent" borrowers, as determined by the American FHA's standards. The mortgages would have amortization periods of fifteen to twenty years and would require a down payment of 10% to 25%. When individual homeowners made monthly payments on their mortgages to the local S&L, that money would be channeled back to American investors (plus the fee to USAID). As in the US, the local Federal Home Loan Bank Boards would facilitate a standardized national savings and mortgage issuance system in addition to providing a critical layer of oversight. If homeowners became delinquent on payments, the local institution would borrow from their reserve funds (with temporary shortfall) and continue payment to the US lender until the mortgagor caught up with his payments. If the local project administrator had to put the homeowner into foreclosure for serious delinquencies, the house would be seized and resold, hopefully with significant recovery of owed funds. If, in the worst-case scenario, local S&Ls completely depleted their reserve funds for delinquencies, USAID would pick up the tab and attempt recovery through the host government, depending on the extent of the coguaranty. (Congress allocated reserve funds to USAID, held pro tempore by the US Treasury.)[92] The NAHB and US lawmakers believed the Housing Investment Guaranty would provide newborn S&Ls with enough fast cash to issue mass mortgages immediately before public enthusiasm for saving faltered. Eventually, they predicted local savings deposits would provide the bulk of funds needed to sustain this system.

Theoretically, there was something for everyone in the guaranty program. Whether overseas homeowners paid or defaulted, the federal government promised American investors a low-risk opportunity in international housing at better rates than the domestic FHA program. This investment was not only guaranteed, it was potentially limitless, as more and more of the world's citizens made their way to the urban slums and provoked security concerns. The US government, for its part, paid less than an out-and-out capital aid program, gained political stability, and reinforced middle-class growth in the developing world. Last but not least, developing world governments gained access to US capital (albeit with attached guaranty fees) and could use the same to build higher-quality housing and a modern S&L and Home Loan Bank Board system. At the very least, foreign governments had a new option; as HHFA worker Richard Metcalf put it, they could "either take it or leave it."[93]

The NAHB tapped the right nerve in the Senate and House by arguing for security through capitalism—an irresistible promise for the US government and for other capitalist nations around the world. By the NAHB's logic, single governments could not guarantee they would stay in power, but individual homeowners in a developing nation would carry on with their mortgage payments "just as purchasers of comparable status and income in the United States have made their obligations on FHA-insured loans. . . . The likelihood of default would be no greater than in the United States," promised Paul Burkhard, chairman of the NAHB's Committee on International Housing and former mayor of Glendale, California. It went "without saying" that only the full weight of the US government could foster this sort of stability.[94] Equally important, the cooperating government would need to play a carefully circumscribed role along the lines of the FHA's insurance (not direct loan) system, since the whole point was to activate a capitalist economy rather than to secure one particular government. States should save their money for other critical resources like highways and schools—resources which private enterprise could not be expected to provide.[95] In a rare moment of agreement, the AFL-CIO and American Auto Workers concurred with builders' prescriptions, albeit for broad principles of worker rights rather than the possibility of direct profit, as was the case for NAHB members.[96]

It is not surprising that nations eagerly jumped on board, given the incentives. Peru's 1956 savings deposit insurance was the only Latin American program of its kind to predate the Housing Investment Guaranty, but it lay relatively dormant until the guaranty mobilized savings and mortgage issuance in 1961 with a US$9.5 million allocation. By 1962, Peru had 9,500 savings accounts and 850 mortgage loans totaling $2.4 million. In Chile, USAID advisor Harold Robinson and the Instituto Chileno del Acero had argued in 1959 that the country had an annual savings potential of $100 million and debt service capacity of $200 million. With Investment Guaranty providing $5 million in loans, $5 million in grants, and $1.5 million in Public Law 480 funds, local S&Ls at least partly lived up to this prediction, holding $100 million in total savings ($41 million net) and issuing 23,000 loans by 1966.[97]

A wide array of US private investors also found the prospects alluring, including, for instance, a large Wall Street securities firm named Carl M. Loeb, Rhoades, & Co., which created a subsidiary International Housing Capital Corporation that invested roughly $7 million in its initial housing venture in Cali, Colombia, in 1962 with the first ever extended risk investment guaranty for homebuilding in Latin America.[98] International

Housing produced 2,000 two- and three-bedroom stand-alone homes selling at $5,000–$6,000 each with "major public improvements and utilities such as are found in project developments in the US," and in truly international fashion hired a Puerto Rican corporation, Viviendas Pan Americanas, to supervise and manage construction.[99] Loeb followed up this investment with another in metropolitan Lima, this time using a Peruvian subsidiary of the Delaware construction corporation, Development Corporation International (partly owned by Long Island developer Fred Epstein's Development Corporation of Puerto Rico). Loeb also used as his local fiduciary a home loan bank (Banco de la Vivienda del Peru) that had been established a few years prior with USAID assistance.[100] For the 915-unit single-family middle-class housing development in Lima, USAID issued a 100% guaranty of $4 billion, allowing Loeb to ultimately reap an 11% profit on all direct costs of construction and urbanization.[101]

Like convertibility, expropriation, and war risk investment guaranties in general, the Housing Investment Guaranty focused on Latin American needs above others, aligning with the regional focus of other Alliance for Progress projects in the early 1960s. All guaranty loan money went to local Federal Home Loan Bank Boards (also known as National Housing Banks) before going to S&Ls, and most host countries matched US funds. Mexico, for instance, matched USAID and IADB's collective $30 million loan to its Housing Trust Fund at a two-to-one ratio (two Mexican for each US dollar) in 1963. The fund used these monies to "support mortgage lending operations by the savings departments of commercial banks, mortgage banks, and savings and loans banks," repaying the US in dollars over a term of thirty years with annual interest at 2%.[102] In countries where Federal Home Loan Bank Boards did not exist, new ones were created. Legislation created the first National Housing Bank in Ecuador and Venezuela in 1961, and in the Dominican Republic in 1962.[103] The HHFA also encouraged less industrialized countries to establish savings-and-loan associations "with an understanding of United States practices," in the words of James Moore, assistant administrator to the Office of International Housing. Although each lending institution needed to decide its own threshold for acceptable mortgage risk "depending largely on the varying influence of different cultures," the HHFA also offered the FHA's *Underwriting Manual* as a positive example of risk assessment in American mortgage insurance.[104]

With these encouragements, homeownership programs built momentum. At the suggestion of senator John Sparkman, USAID administrator David Bell called upon experts like Charles Abrams (UN housing consultant), Alexander Bookstaver (AFL-CIO economic advisor), W. Evans Buchanan (NAHB president), Neal Hardy (former FHA commissioner), Lloyd Rodwin (MIT planning professor), Robert Weaver (HHFA administrator), and Joseph McMurray (Federal Home Loan Bank Board chairman) to guide the agency through housing assistance provisions of the foreign aid legislation, including housing investment guaranties, S&L development, and mortgage structuring.[105] To HHFA officer James Moore's delight, the advisory committee and USAID's Osborne Boyd agreed with the HHFA that future policies needed to include greater consideration of urban development (not just housing), that US agencies should help train foreign nationals in planning, and that the US should pay more attention to countries outside Latin America.[106]

Only Charles Abrams and HHFA staffer Morton J. Schussheim seemed to notice the pitfalls in building an explicitly middle-class, exclusively homeownership-oriented program. Rhetorically these programs were designed for the masses and meant to open up better housing access for more deserving families; in reality such housing remained out of reach for the vast majority of impoverished residents. Echoing similar statements by Abrams, Schussheim warned in a memo to James Moore, "If we dictate our rigid private-ownership, no subsidy housing program as a price for our assistance in developing countries, we may be identified with the provision of housing only for the well-to-do."[107]

The protests went largely unheard, however, and in the meantime, so many countries leapt at the chance to participate in USAID's pilot demonstration programs that the agency had to temporarily block new applications in May 1964. During the first three years, an astonishing $700 million worth of applications had come in. This was far more than anticipated, and secretary of state Dean Rusk outlined new procedures to streamline the application process beginning in 1964, including more detailed USAID recommendations on desirable price ranges and geographic areas as well as "specific guidance, to the degree possible . . . [on] reserve fund requirements, readjustable mortgages, prevailing interest rates, and other items which vary from country to country."[108] Homeownership also excited interest from NGOs, too. The Peace Corps "branch[ed] into finance" when the National League of Insured Savings Associations began recruiting volunteers with business degrees to help set up marketing cooperatives and credit unions in Peru, Colombia, Sierra Leone, and the Dominican Republic, and to assist in the creation and operation of new S&Ls.[109]

The total number of US dollars flowing southward was, of course, a mere drop in the bucket compared to the need. American aid programs never intended to provide all necessary shelter. Instead, they sought demonstration or leveraging effects. The problem lay in determining precisely how much would be enough to yield those effects; USAID had $780 million in housing guaranty authority by 1972 and had spent $187 million on nonguaranty housing aid worldwide from 1949 to 1970. Senator William Proxmire (Dem-WI) computed the per capita expenditure to 87 cents in a somewhat specious exercise of simple division.[110] (Obviously this was misleading, as the US executive director of the International Bank for Reconstruction and Development pointed out to the senator, since housing guaranties were not equally distributed across all of the needy.) Nonetheless, Proxmire used his "statistic" to effect: World Bank and USAID officials admitted American housing aid was quite limited and favored the top quartile despite claims to help the masses. In the larger scope of overseas capital assistance, housing also constituted a small portion of the total spent in foreign aid, and predictably lagged far behind the $6 billion allocated for military aid to Latin America during the same time frame.[111] The main thrust of American housing assistance was not a massive capital transfer, but rather a creation of institutions and a modernization program that put homeownership center-stage—emphases that would persist in World Bank programs in the 1980s. The idea was that modern homeownership should not remain a relatively inaccessible fee-simple system. Instead, it should be opened up to more consumers through bank-managed, government-regulated, long-term debt, and incorporated into an international market of housing credit.

This was simultaneously global capitalism and international relations. The role of US housing officials should also be noted here. Because domestic agencies best understood American housing "precedent," they quickly became the gatekeepers and regulators of foreign aid. USAID depended upon the FHA for all technical processing of guaranty applications by 1963, with the latter agency's workers conducting all technical evaluations and making recommendations for approval or denial to USAID.[112] USAID's David Bell and HHFA's Robert Weaver concurred that this system exploited "FHA's long experience and knowledge gained through 30 years of mortgage underwriting" in the US.[113] HHFA, meanwhile, coordinated and used the "skills or resources" of the Public Housing Administration, the Federal National Mortgage Association, and any other housing agency that might assist the FHA in assessing proposals.[114] USAID, for its part, supplied both the FHA and HHFA with necessary foreign policy guidelines. After 1965, HHFA's replacement— the Cabinet-level Department of Housing and Urban Development (HUD)—directly received all applications for the Housing Investment Guaranty, with an explicit mandate from Congress to focus more on institutions than pilot demonstrations. The FHA's International Housing Division conducted field inspections and issued feasibility reports that HUD used to make final selections in consultation with USAID. Private investors worked closely with public agencies, and some private entities like Washington Federal Savings and Loan in Miami Beach, Florida became disproportionately powerful as the right arm of USAID's Latin American housing guaranty programs. Washington Federal gave guidance to overseas financial institutions on how to conduct credit analysis, mortgage closings, collection of monthly payments, handling of reserve funds, and foreclosures.[115] When Congress amended the 1933 Home Owners Loan Act in 1965, allowing American S&Ls to invest 1% of their assets in programs under the purview of the Housing Investment Guaranty, these S&Ls grew in importance and power. Another amendment in 1967 allowed regional Federal Home Loan Banks to facilitate private investment in guarantied projects, while the Foreign Assistance Act of 1967 flatly stated the importance of homeownership in foreign aid, noting that the "first objects of assistance" would be "to support the efforts of less developed countries to meet the fundamental needs of their peoples for sufficient food, good health, homeownership and decent housing."[116] The first two actions in particular were stimulated by intense lobbying from the S&L industry, and resulted in a near total dominance of the housing investment guaranty program by American S&Ls by 1968.

Did the guaranty work? Did savings increase alongside American private investment in homeownership programs? Early results trended positive. By 1970, Latin American countries collectively boasted 170 S&Ls, one million savers, and a total savings of roughly a half billion dollars. In addition, S&Ls had become "the most important and largest suppliers of housing finance in the hemisphere . . . [for] the new and vitally significant middle class," according to Stanley Baruch, director of the Office of Housing at USAID.[117] As Baruch noted in Senate hearings in 1972, "All of Latin America is blanketed with a network of savings and loan systems that finance all of the private housing in Latin America, except that tiny part which is built for cash and the smaller amount of private housing that is built by public housing agencies and sold with subsidies to low-income families. There are a few exceptions to the rule but the incontrovertible fact is that none of this financing existed before the foreign aid program."[118] Raymond P. Harold of the International Union of Building Societies and Savings Association boasted that never before had the world seen such global acceptance of US-style homeownership:

Never in the history of the savings and loan business has there been such a world-wide acceptance of the idea of our type of institutions by people in authority. Every country is hungry to learn how we did it. . . .

We have to think big today. We have the responsibility for selling our system for financing housing, for financing homes, to parts of the world where it does not exist. If we do not give the people . . . the chance to have their own homes, we shall be responsible, in part, for upheavals and people who are deprived are therefore desperate. We have the solution for a bright future for the ordinary man and we cannot, in justice, hide this key.[119]

In making such grand claims, Harold conflated greater access for the upper quartile with a system of equal opportunity across all classes, closing his eyes to the fact that, by his own logic, the US was still "responsible, in part, for upheavals" among the deprived.

In any case, the US economy felt the impact of over $880 million in authorizations by 1974. Foreign aid programs generally required export of domestic commodities such as steel and iron, bringing over $148 million to New York City alone in fiscal 1971, or $10 million to smaller cities like Pittsburgh. American companies like Lockheed Aircraft Service Company and Continental Homes, Inc. (a division of Continental Airlines) benefited from some of that $880 million, obtaining Cooley loans and Housing Investment Guaranties to set up local manufacturing and production facilities for Lockheed Panel-Lock housing components, first in California and Puerto Rico, then across Latin America, and by the mid-1960s, in Ceylon, earning in 1967 approximately $172 profit per house after all land, materials, and labor costs.[120] Continental Homes director and vice president of IBEC Richard S. Aldrich facilitated profitable low-cost housing projects in Argentina, Brazil, Chile, Colombia, the Dominican Republic, Paraguay, and Tanzania under the extended risk guaranty.[121] For these reasons, Richard Knight of the National Savings and Loan League argued that foreign aid should be viewed "not only as an assist to the developing countries of the world, but also [as a part of] the development of our markets overseas, which in turn benefits the domestic economy."[122] Indeed, US housing aid helped create a new spatial order to globalizing metropolises, and it also pumped cash back into American cities via overseas markets.[123]

The Problem with Middle-Class Homeownership

Guaranties were not pure benefit for all, of course. The Housing Investment Guaranty program faced all manner of pitfalls, many anticipated by HHFA workers in the early 1960s. One worker described the program as "fraught with dangers," and he was not wrong in this assessment: dishonest builders with inflated cost figures could obtain higher guaranties, creating incentives for them to foreclose and collect on the higher guaranty payment.[124] Graft could be both necessary to function in a local economy and deeply problematic if brought to light as a part of US aid. Low-cost housing could be shoddily constructed if costs were reduced overmuch in an attempt to reach the truly impoverished classes. Language and cultural barriers could lead to unanticipated troubles.

Ultimately, it was one particular fatal flaw that plagued American homeownership projects abroad and that brought about the demise of the guaranty program. The slippery nature of the "middle class" proved its undoing: policymakers, politicians, and the general public never explicitly agreed upon who constituted this class, and the confusion between low-income and low-cost housing programs raised all sorts of contradictory expectations about who would benefit from American housing aid. In fact, in an utter defeat of the foreign aid goals of the State Department, it often appeared to the poorer classes that US housing aid programs provided for affluent families with apparently little concern for the truly needy. This assessment was not entirely off the mark, either; projects backed by the Housing Investment Guaranty often did not even attempt to address the needs of the lowest-income segment. Section 221 of the Foreign Assistance Act of 1961 explicitly and repeatedly asserted the supposedly low-income focus of the guaranty, stating that Congress wanted "carefully designed programs involving United States capital and expertise [that] can increase the availability of domestic financing for improved housing and related services for *low-income people* by demonstrating to local entrepreneurs and institutions that providing *low-cost housing* can be financially viable."[125] Yet Dean Rusk unhesitatingly described the Housing Investment Guaranty program in 1962 as one "intended to stimulated private home ownership for middle- and lower-middle income families by means of guaranties of housing projects . . . similar to those provided in the United States by the Federal Housing Administration."[126] Robert Weaver, HHFA administrator and future first secretary of HUD, agreed that low-income housing needs were not being addressed, but defended the largely upper-income assistance as necessary since it served the "urgent needs of a group with incomes which are somewhat higher, but which are nevertheless very low by American standards."[127] Still, Congress expected the Investment Guaranty to address the housing problems of the masses, and it did not. Nor did it appear that the guaranty's benefits would ever trickle down to the "pathetically, miserably, grindingly, cruelly poor."[128] This was true during the period of pilot demonstration homes from 1961 to 1965, and still true after USAID shifted to institution building after 1965. Legislative edicts like the lower-income housing clause in the 1965 amendment (Foreign Assistance Act, 1961) could not change prohibitive prices or finance terms with high minimum annual income requirements. One Government Accounting Office report on Central American conditions criticized the Investment Guaranty program in simple terms:

Our report does not imply that the HIG program is building luxury houses. We merely point out that it is only people in the top 25 percent of the economic stratum that can afford even the lowest priced HIG houses. . . . The Office of Housing [in USAID] may prefer to describe families that can afford HIG houses, as well as those receiving the benefits, i.e., mortgage financing, as being in the middle- or lower-middle income bracket. However, this does not change the fact that they are in the upper 25 percent of the economic stratum in the Central American countries.[129]

In a country-by-country breakdown of affordability in Central America, Nicaragua and El Salvador posted the highest percentage (87%) of urban families unable to purchase the lowest priced Housing Investment Guaranty house. Central American project administrators openly admitted not even attempting to finance packages for the bottom 75% in the region. Instead, they sold guaranty homes at a minimum cost of $3,500 to families with annual incomes up to $34,000 and some owning multiple guaranty homes—this, in countries where low-cost housing units typically cost less than $1,000 each.[130] No private builder or governmental agency had submitted a proposal for a home costing less than $3,500, even with explicit USAID promises to give "special consideration" in the ratings process to the lowest selling prices.

According to Stanley Baruch, the price remained stubbornly high because future consumers in developing countries—"the little people, middle-income people, even the poor people"—wanted amenities including sewer, water, and sex- and age-segregated spaces.[131] In reality, Americans investors often refused to engage in what they perceived to be far riskier low-income housing projects, instead reshaping programs to fit middle- and upper-middle-income consumers and relabeling units "low-cost" housing. These decisions were fueled by class prejudice rather than solid research proving a greater or more reliable market in middle-class housing. The Panamanian Kheel-Gilbane project of 1963 was a classic example of this. Named after the primary contractor, Gilbane Construction Company of Rhode Island, and the attorney Theodore Woodrow Kheel representing the National Maritime Union that committed up to $10 million in construction loans, the Kheel-Gilbane project aimed to build 1,200 single-family homes in the northern community of Pan de Azucar in Panama City. Problems began when USAID and the State Department put pressure on the Panamanian National Assembly to issue bonds to secure the $10 million loan, effectually rendering that government a "full guarantor on a loan by the US labor unions to Panama," according to one Congressional Staff Survey Team.[132] The National Assembly initially complied, passing a law that was approved by president Roberto Chiari Remón in April 1963. Alas, the directors of the Kheel-Gilbane project almost simultaneously veered the project away from its initial low-income focus and instead decided to construct upper-middle-income homes, apparently out of sheer faith that upper-middle-income families had a greater propensity than lower-income counterparts to buy and not default. No survey had been made of the possible demand for 1,200 homes at $8,333 apiece, and at least one housing advisor later found the price high in comparison to other, similar housing.[133] When the public learned of this change, Panamanian politicians and the press widely condemned their government's role, forcing it to stop bond issuance and to cut off any guaranties for future Kheel-Gilbane construction. Needless to say, USAID/Panama's image suffered greatly as a result of this incident, and neither low-cost nor low-income housing was effectively provided.

Confusion reigned, as commentators and legislators in both hemispheres used the terms "low-cost" and "low-income" interchangeably. Again, much of this confusion stemmed from a lack of clarity about who constituted the "middle class" in various Latin American countries. Equally important, US guarantors and investors tacitly pursued different objectives, leading to discrepancies between promised low-income housing and produced low-cost housing. It should also be said in HUD and USAID's defense that the two agencies faced a difficult set of conditions under which they were expected to provide better low-income housing. Developing-world cities had relatively high central land costs, limited debt-carrying capacity, and insufficient foreign exchange, yet Congress demanded that housing assistance be self-paying and demonstrate a multiplier effect while addressing the needs of the poor and raising living standards. Investors, too, demanded guarantied profits and low risk. Even allowing for all of these challenges, however, USAID "action" was hardly impressive. Instead of tackling the absence of low-income housing aid head-on, USAID suggested host country governments solve their own problems by taking out market-rate loans and financing housing for lower-income families. Poor people's shelter might constitute too great a risk for a housing guaranty, but USAID officials still lauded their own agency's "demonstrated ability to influence overall national housing policies and programs to provide for greater emphasis on lower-income housing" on these risky terms.[134]

The housing guaranty's delineation of risk proved faulty on multiple levels. All too often, foreign policy objectives and good business did *not* go hand in hand. Under the Housing Investment Guaranty system, American investors no longer had to bear the brunt of risk assessment for their own investments, nor did host governments always follow through on their matching guaranties when borrowers defaulted. Ultimately, the US government had to pay investors if others did not, thus forcing taxpayers to assume the greatest risk and to pay for others' missteps. As a result, the US government took responsibility for all manner of minutiae in assessing and managing overseas risk, including instituting building standards set by international FHA representatives and measuring the default risk of intermediate guarantors and individual borrowers. The US government sought to standardize international housing loans, construction, legal frameworks, and the like, but in the process became involved in managing details for which its workers had no prior experience or knowledge. Not surprisingly, overextended FHA and foreign aid staff sometimes produced inaccurate data that was then used to incorrectly assess risk. After shocking default rates (38.2% for Latin America in 1972) jolted guaranty administrators, USAID tried to recoup losses by using rollover mortgages, where the administrator would replace a delinquent mortgage with an eligible one, thus avoiding default but skewing data on delinquency.[135] USAID so inaccurately assessed potential defaults that it carried only a fraction of its loan values in reserves. By the end of the program in 1995, USAID held at least $400 million in bad loans but only $50 million in reserve.

Given these appalling financial troubles, as revealed in a particularly damning 1995 GAO report followed by an oversight hearing, Congress decided to formally shut down funding for the Housing Investment Guaranty program—a program that had clearly been reeling from its troubles for some time. In its place, Congress set up the

Housing Investment Guaranty with an Urban and Environmental Credit Program in 1998; the new program would provide "long-term financing to developing countries for innovative urban investment programs in areas such as shelter, potable water, wastewater treatment, solid waste disposal, environmental improvement of poor urban neighborhoods, and energy distribution."[136] Housing administrators focused on reducing massive liabilities and balancing their ledgers. Eventually, the Urban and Environmental Credit Program trimmed over $2 billion in guaranteed loans outstanding in the liquidating account at the beginning of 1996, to $847 million by the end of 2008.[137]

The Housing Guaranty limped along for two decades, but mercifully it was not the whole of USAID housing efforts in the developing world. After a congressional mandate in 1973 directed the agency to focus on the basic needs of low-income families, USAID issued a new Shelter Sector Policy (revised October 1974) that emphasized minimum housing standards and gradual improvement, permitted incomplete units, emphasized technical assistance for savings mobilization, facilitated transfers of technology, encouraged sites and services, and explored alternative interest rate policies and cost recovery. In these emphases, USAID joined forces with the World Bank, a body that had up until the early 1970s remained largely disengaged with questions of shelter. As the World Bank slowly took a lead in setting global housing aid policies over the course of the 1970s, USAID began following policy trends set by the Bank, launching slum upgrading programs in 1976, joining shelter development with community development programs in 1978, and expanding from its Latin American sites to open regional offices in Nairobi (1975), Tegucigalpa (1975), Seoul (1976), Santiago (1976), Tunis (1977), Panama City (1977), Bangkok (1979), and Kingston (1980).[138] Like the Bank, USAID believed governments ought to "provide the environment for private resources to resolve their own problems," including an "investment policy that recognizes the significance of shelter production to the national economy; [a] high degree of reliance on private market systems and private development of housing . . . ; cost recovery in the provision, maintenance, and financing of housing and urban services, . . . [and] adoption of rational administrative procedures that encourage private investment in housing and land development."[139] By the 1990s and 2000s, USAID's programs had shifted to a greater emphasis on Poland, Eastern Europe, Russia, and the Newly Independent States, with new efforts like the Housing Sector Reform Project echoing Bank insistence on privatization, regularized property titles, mortgage finance, cost recovery, and limited subsidies, and also maintaining

USAID's historical insistence on maximum homeownership as a symbol of American capitalism and as a way to "give Russians a stake in market reform."[140] Approaching housing problems as they did, USAID programs soon ran into the same difficulties as those experienced by the Bank. Most critically, transplanted ideas and institutions failed to connect with domestic perceptions of tenure security, since Russians did not generally view mortgaged property as true homeownership. The US model traveled, but the long-term results were unpredictable.

The Bottom Line

In 1993, interviewers asked Willard Garvey what he considered to be World Homes' greatest successes and failures. Garvey paused, hesitated, then said, "The bottom line is what counts, and sometimes the bottom line and the best project don't coincide. So I don't even know right now . . . bottom line which one was the best."[141] This was a strange answer from a highly successful businessman. Surely profits or losses should clearly indicate the bottom line for World Homes? Yet time and time again, investors and foreign policymakers became implicated in each other's business when attempting to craft better housing programs—so much so that goals became mudded, and assessments of success and failure, obscured.

This messy interaction between business and politics, the melding of economic with ideological goals, had significant consequences for sprawl and urban development in communities around the globe. Housing financiers also played a critical role in defining appropriate, desirable housing forms in their determination of mortgage eligibility. Although World Homes went out of business and USAID's efforts in Latin America petered out by the late twentieth century, clearly US-promoted, mortgage-based, mass middle-class homeownership lived on, albeit in ever-evolving forms. As such, the history of American overseas housing finance reflected a much larger debate about appropriate modern housing in the developing world. This debate did not stay unidirectional, but instead brought new ideas back home to stricken districts of American inner cities and to impoverished Native American reservations.

FIVE

Fair Homeownership

Clearly, for our industry, the minority and low-income sectors are the "emerging markets" that we can and must develop. ANGELO R. MOZILO, CEO OF COUNTRYWIDE FINANCIAL CORPORATION, 2003[1]

The National Savings and Loan League may have claimed "spectacular" successes in Latin America, with "savings and loan type institutions . . . successfully operating in almost every Latin American country" by the early 1970s. Yet one fatal flaw continued to undermine American authority as international advisors and aid givers. That flaw was racism. To many dismayed planners and politicians around the world, the increasingly visible plight of American minorities in the late 1950s and 1960s undermined the image of an egalitarian society and undercut any claims that the US housing system should be emulated. Scenes of race riots in deeply segregated communities and images of shocking urban decline exposed the weakest points of domestic housing policy to international scrutiny. In the immediate postwar years, US government officials attempted prominent displays of racial equality in an attempt to project a particular image of American democracy. By the tumultuous 1960s, the John F. Kennedy and Lyndon B. Johnson administrations for the first time brought the federal government directly into questions of fair housing enforcement, and eventually, fair homeownership. Domestic upheaval and civil rights struggles made the federal government willing to seriously contemplate overseas housing lessons for local application, and homeownership rates came under scrutiny as a potential metric for assessing minority and low-income housing access. Lost in the discussion were the broader conditions by which low-income and minority families purchased their homes, including critical questions about where, what type, and through what financing mechanisms individuals became homeowners.

The demand for fair housing in the US pushed the federal government, experts, real estate industry leaders, and bankers (among others) to reconsider circuits of exchange. By the late 1960s, officials experimented in earnest with local applications of internationally tested techniques, participating more fully in a global circulation of home-ownership-building practices like mutual and aided self-help, government-backed savings and loans (S&Ls), and mortgage guaranties.

Mutual aid had played an undocumented and undoubtedly crucial part of American homebuilding history since the colonial era, much as aided self-help had its origins in European experiments of earlier decades. There was nothing new or particularly American about either technique, but what was remarkable and different about civil rights–era applications in the US was the emphasis on racial equality as well as the direct reference to recent American foreign aid efforts. Ideas about self-help moved in transatlantic circuits first, then extended to the developing world, and finally circled back to the housing needs of people of color in the US, although with different labels.[2] Like self-help, government-backed S&Ls and mortgage guaranties began in the US as white middle-class housing assistance undergirded by institutions like the Federal Home Loan Bank system, the Federal Deposit Insurance Corporation, the Federal Savings and Loan Insurance Corporation, the Federal Housing Administration (FHA), the Veterans Administration, and the Federal National Mortgage Association (FNMA/Fannie Mae). American housing experts and aid organizations promoted similar institutions abroad and especially in the developing world immediately after World War II, and then cycled back to the domestic sphere with adaptations for low-income, disproportionately minority housing markets in the US. Critically, new policies targeting urban, minority, and Native households focused on the potential profitability and financial viability of increased ownership rather than on spatial integration. In the words of Countrywide CEO Angelo Mozilo, "emerging markets" had appeared at home.

Fighting Discrimination, Not Segregation

The fair housing movement had always been international to some degree. Well before "the whole world is watching" became the standard cry of civil rights and antiwar demonstrators, the whole world did indeed watch American policymakers struggle with the intractable problem of race, even as fair housing advocates understood and used this attention to push specific legislation. Politicians and world leaders articulated connections between once colonized peoples not only in well-known events like the Bandung Afro-Asian Conference in April 1955, but also in the fight for better housing in Africa, Asia, and Latin America, and in the inner-city neighborhoods of Chicago, New York, or Los Angeles.

This transnational exchange flowed in all directions. Many experts and even some investors actually began their careers in domestic low-income fair housing struggles before extending their activities to housing in the developing world, while others tested investment ideas first in the developing world before bringing such projects home. At least some Americans came to see domestic problems with segregation as part of a larger global pattern of class and race inequality. Charles Abrams, for instance, began his career as a lawyer and fair housing advocate. In a pivotal 1936 court case *New York City Housing Authority v. Muller*, Abrams defended the New York City Housing Authority's right to take private land through eminent domain when erecting public housing. He believed in public housing in great part because he thought it had "done more to point the way to real nonsegregation than any other measure in our time."[3] Years before flying on his UN missions to the Philippines, Singapore, and Ghana, Abrams worked with Algernon D. Black and others on the City-Wide Committee on Harlem to fight restrictive covenants on private property.[4] Abrams articulated some of his concerns with the rapidly evolving meaning of land and landownership and urged specific government actions to move toward a more just land policy in his *Revolution in Land*—a publication that eventually caught the eye of UN director of the Housing, Building, and Planning Branch Ernest Weissmann and inspired Weissmann to ask Abrams in 1952 for a formal study of international land problems ("Urban Land Problems and Policies".[5] After this first UN project, Abrams's interests permanently widened to include global concerns, and he quickly became one of the key players in a postwar community of housing experts. Not surprisingly, Abrams carried fair housing principles with him as he traveled and advised the world. In a UN Regional Seminar on Housing and Community Improvement held in New Delhi in 1954, for instance, Abrams and fellow committee members urged close integration of "all sections of the community" and "opportunities for day to day social intercourse." According to Abrams, "balanced, healthy development" was only possible if "the population in an area or colony represent[ed] the cross-section of the society or the community."[6]

Abrams may have been extraordinarily agile in navigating various aspects of housing policy, including finance, design, and law, but he was hardly exceptional in the international character of his work. In addition to other internationally minded intellectuals and public officials like Catherine Bauer and Elizabeth Wood, businessmen like Alan Carnoy also made the connection between foreign and domestic work. Carnoy began as a domestic builder, erecting a controversial, integrated community in Westchester County in the 1950s.[7] By the 1960s, Carnoy had become an avid proponent of mass homeownership around the world, with projects across Latin America and increasingly voluminous writings expounding the democratic virtues of "homeownership for all."[8] Carnoy argued that affordable mortgages and low-cost housing could accelerate the development and growth of a middle class in developing nations, much as it might in the domestic sphere for African American families. He noted the larger class implications of his successful sale of a thousand homes worth $5 million total in 1967 in El Menzah, a suburb of Tunis, and observed the tragic missed opportunity in Saigon in 1964, when USAID refused to support a demonstration program there. "Even a few sample homes might have had a tremendous psychological impact and promoted democratic goals," Carnoy mourned.[9] All components of Carnoy's homeownership formula "have been or are now practiced in the US"; if applied evenly, they could transform the slums at home and in "black Africa."[10]

It took more than a handful of internationally and transnationally oriented housing experts to yield real changes in domestic housing inequalities, however, and the federal government showed at best, great passivity and at worst, active support for such segregative tools as racial designations in FHA applications during the 1950s. Federal positions were often articulated as interventions in an otherwise free-market process despite the fact that the government facilitated decades of racial zoning, racial deed restrictions, and restrictive covenants. As late as the Eisenhower administration, Housing and Home Finance Agency (HHFA) administrators Albert M. Cole (1953–59) and Norman P. Mason (1959–60) asserted that "federal intervention is incompatible with our idea of political and economic freedom" and that the federal government should only enforce fair housing "by persuasion."[11] The FHA refused to deny loan guarantees to prejudiced builders "even when it possessed massive evidence of wrongdoing," so long as the builder was not actually convicted of discrimination under state law.[12] The federal government likewise refused to ensure equal market access to loans in discriminatory private mortgage lending cases, and the Federal Home Loan Bank Board did not declare a nondiscrimination policy until 1961. After 1961, the board did little to enforce such a statement.[13]

The little legislative progress that was made was motivated primarily by Cold War concerns. The Justice Department became involved for the first time in a Fifth and Fourteenth Amendment case involving restrictive covenants (*Shelley v. Kraemer*, 1948), underscoring the critical impact of housing discrimination on foreign relations.[14] Subsequent propaganda wars demonstrated just how clearly the US Information Agency and Soviet propagandists understood the damaging impact of segregation on the image of American capitalism.[15] Soviet and Chinese strategists repeatedly combatted potentially appealing images of the "American way of life" with facts about American segregation and sexism, while US experts and politicians urged a "domestic containment and . . . therapeutic corollary [that] undermined the potential for political activism and reinforced the chilling effects of anticommunism and the cold war consensus."[16] Clearly, Cold War imperatives fueled federal government interest in minority access to decent shelter—a topic that had thus far elicited little real state action and which the government had in fact actively undermined in earlier policies.

This newfound sensitivity was global in scope. American and Soviet strategists were not alone in realizing the potential international implications of unequal housing conditions. European powers became equally if not more responsive to issues of racial inclusion and integration, and some even sought solutions by studying US housing practices. British officer Stanley Woolmer, for instance, traveled from Singapore to Cambridge, Massachusetts, through a Commonwealth Fund and Research Fellowship at Harvard University, only to conclude with some schadenfreude that "the attitude of the average white American, in areas where there are any considerable numbers of nonwhites, is certainly no more liberal than is the case in the British Far Eastern colonies today, in fact often less so," and that problems with racial segregation permeated American communities as much as British colonial cities.[17] According to Woolmer, the nonwhite standard of wealth and education in the US was irredeemably low compared to the white one, and the "mixing of races having different habits, customs, and outlook, built up over hundreds of years, even if desirable, [could not] be rapidly achieved." Integration would result in "increased mixed marriages producing half-caste children, who have difficulty in assimilation into either of their parent's racial groups."[18] Despite such gratifying discovery of a common

Euro-American "race problem," the British Colonial Information Policy Committee also emphasized the deleterious effects of segregation on colonial policies across a vulnerable empire, and it sought immediate address, with or without American models. By the late 1940s, segregation in the UK proper had become deeply problematic as well, with separate accommodations in London making colonial "guests" more susceptible to communist doctrines and giving rise to "unfavourable publicity in the Colonies themselves," according to the committee.[19] Prominent leftist journals like the *New Statesman* similarly worried about the potentially devastating impact of "distinctively Negro quarters, on the American model"—often called "Little Harlems" in local parlance.[20]

This heightened awareness of racial inequality flowed freely across the Atlantic, leading to the common refrain that "something" ought to be done, even if it was unclear what that something was. In the US, awareness of a global audience did not always lead to consistent propaganda, and some public relations attempts went sadly awry: a US Steel–backed traveling "People's Capitalism" exhibit of 1956, for example, set out to showcase the benefits of American housing but then displayed an all-white family living in the all-white community of Fairless Hills, Pennsylvania. This inadvertently honest display earned the loud criticism of the American Friends Service Committee and other prominent national organizations and individuals as an unwittingly truthful demonstration of race relations in the US, but the exhibit went abroad without modification despite these protests, as US Steel had donated the exhibit and "one doesn't look a gift horse too hard in the mouth."[21]

Other public relations campaigns went more smoothly. The federal government helped organize Edith Sampson's 1952 Scandinavian tour, for instance, in which Sampson argued that African Americans "owned homes that were the envy of the world, including the Soviet Union."[22] Government agencies like the Technical Cooperation Administration also made a concerted effort to send African American representatives to postwar housing conferences and study tours. According to advisor Bernard Loshbough, "top-flight Negro personnel" should be found for all community-building posts in India, not only because this gave the appearance of equal rights, but also because African Americans ostensibly intuited developing-world experiences better than their white counterparts. More than "name guys," African Americans were "young people with vision, imagination, and the capacity to understand what promotion of human welfare means."[23] Jacob Crane concurred, stating, "We know a good number of Negroes whom I think would do well [in India]."[24] Meanwhile, NAACP executive director Walter White paid close attention to the international dimensions of segregation throughout the 1950s, as did Nigerian newspaper editor Nnamdi Azikiwe and other intellectuals, politicians, and common citizens around the world.[25]

It was not until the 1960s, however, that development came into vogue at home and abroad: President Kennedy established the US Agency for International Development (USAID) in 1961, and acting secretary-general U Thant called for a UN Development Decade, even as Walt Rostow put forward a seductive theoretical-historical narrative of development in 1958 with his lectures "The Stages of Economic Growth."[26] Meanwhile, social scientists at organizations like the Southeast Asia Development Advisory Group joined foreign and domestic problems under the rubric of "consequences of underdevelopment"; the Peace Corps created a domestic Volunteers in Service to America program replicating overseas work at home; and the Office of Economic Opportunity (1964–70) applied international community development principles to community action plans in the US.[27]

Alongside such globalizing development work, new laws changed the landscape of discriminatory housing practices within national boundaries. One of the first steps came in the form of sections 220(h), 203(k), and 221(d)(3) of the 1961 Housing Act, which indirectly targeted discriminatory mortgage lending by legislating FHA mortgage insurance for urban renewal sites. A year later, President Kennedy's Executive Order 10063 (1962) prohibited discrimination in federally owned or operated housing; the Civil Rights Act of 1964's Title VI to a lesser extent, and the Civil Rights Act of 1968's Title VIII (the Fair Housing Act) to a greater extent further transformed the day-to-day practice of segregation by barring discrimination in the sale, rental, and financing of all dwellings, public or private. The FHA, for its part, responded to unrest and an increasingly volatile civil rights movement by loosening underwriting practices in inner-city lending with commissioner Philip Brownstein announcing the end of discriminatory insurance in 1965. The Demonstration Cities and Metropolitan Development Act of 1966, meanwhile, authorized FHA insurance for loans failing the test of economic soundness if "the dwelling covered by the mortgage is situated in an area in which rioting or other civil disorders have occurred or are threatened."[28] Two other programs fueled the trend, although they remained small in scale: HUD launched a tiny homeownership program for public housing tenants in 1965, and one year later an equally minuscule section 221(h) program (Public Law 89-754) allowing low-income families to buy rehabilitated homes from nonprofit sponsors.[29] Further rioting gave a bigger push to these initially timid acts, with President

Johnson commissioning three separate studies of housing problems (the National Commission on Urban Problems with chair Paul Douglas, the President's Committee on Urban Housing with chair Edgar Kaiser, and the National Advisory Commission on Civil Disorder with chair Otto Kerner, Jr.). All three observed that nonwhite families paid on average one-third more than white families for rural and metropolitan housing, and that the federal government had built a mere 800,000 public housing units from 1937 to 1968 as opposed to the 10 million units built with FHA insurance and VA guarantees from 1934 to 1968. The Kerner Commission went so far as to argue that "the rent supplement concept should be extended to provide homeownership opportunities for low-income families."[30] At long last, Congress put into place the first major homeownership program for the nonrural poor with the section 235 Mortgage Insurance and Assistance Payments for Homeownership Program of 1968. Section 235 provided federal subsidies for interest rates on privately originated home mortgages, resulting in the sale of 465,972 new and used homes—sales that proved disastrous for many of the buyers, who faced hidden bank charges, poor-quality housing stock, and racially circumscribed neighborhoods.[31]

This history of early reverse redlining remained wholly absent from government retrospectives, however, and according to one history by Fannie Mae, such fair housing laws reflected the "twinge of conscience" felt by increasingly "comfortable" white Americans, as their affluence grew in contrast to the housing plight of families of color.[32] Perhaps some middle- and upper-class Americans did feel this "twinge," and senator Hubert Humphrey was surely not alone when he noted the hypocrisy of American foreign aid in his 1964 observation that "before we teach everyone else in the world how to live . . . we could well do a little better at home."[33] The actual mechanics of passing and enforcing laws, however, revealed a federal government reluctant to vigorously pursue equal access to decent shelter. Instead, Washington repeatedly deferred to local interests. Homeowners became outspoken representatives of these local interests, employing a language of property rights to justify racial exclusion, transforming overtly racist positions into a "new language about difference about metropolitan economics, and about the politics of property that justified exclusion by a means that seemed genuinely nonracist."[34] This property rights movement had a distinctly segregationist agenda despite free-market rhetoric, offering new tactics for conservatives to fight racial integration, especially in rising Sunbelt cities. In California, various realty boards and neighborhood and homeowner associations banded together to end fair housing laws

like the Rumford Act (1963), a California law rendering illegal any discrimination based on "race, color, religion, national origin, or ancestry"
and granting the Fair Employment Practices Commission the power to
adjudicate grievances.[35] In the anti-Rumford campaign, the California
Real Estate Association successfully campaigned against "forced housing" and for freedom, opportunity, and choice to dispense of property
as property owners saw fit through a ballot measure known as Proposi-
tion 14, overwhelmingly approved by California voters in 1964.[36]

Conservatives did not oppose government aid for private homeownership in the same way they did other social welfare programs.[37]
Government-backed private housing expanded at an exponential rate
and elicited little criticism—unlike public housing, which was plagued
with accusations of socialist design from its legislative inception and
which took massive body blows from white middle-class resistance and
activism, poor architectural and policy decisions (such as large, racially
homogenous high-rises in inner cities and a concentration of youth),
and federal neglect (including pared-down construction, poor crime
management, and disregard for maintenance needs).[38] As a result, many
Americans ignored the contradictions of federal aid for "private" homeownership, instead positing unequal homeownership rates between
white and nonwhite, wealthy and poor Americans as a market function rather than a result of deliberate policies—this despite overwhelming evidence that "the average housing subsidy in an elite suburb . . .
exceed[ed] by several times the average subsidy to a welfare family in
the inner city" and that the overall federal subsidy to that middle-class
homeownership was "staggering and exceed[ed] by four or five times
all the direct expenditures Congress grant[ed] to housing" by the early
1980s.[39] The stigma faced by "public" housing residents in contrast to
the praise heaped upon "private" homeowners was indeed, a "cruel but
telling irony," in the words of scholar Lawrence Vale.[40]

Within such a divided housing system, the fight against unequal housing often emphasized access to homeownership. There were some small
but important legal protections put into place during the 1970s and
1980s: the Society of Real Estate Appraisers and the American Institute
of Real Estate Appraisers signed a consent decree with the Department
of Justice in the 1970s ending explicitly racist policies, and the Federal
Home Loan Bank Board adopted regulations prohibiting racial discrimination in lending in 1973 and 1978.[41] Congress, meanwhile, passed
the Equal Credit Opportunity Act in 1974 (with amendments in 1976),
prohibiting home lending discrimination and requiring banks to keep
track of the racial background of all applicants. The Home Mortgage

Disclosure Act (1975, amendments in 1989) required banks to report which neighborhoods were issued mortgage or home-improvement loans, while the Community Reinvestment Act (1977) stipulated that banks must prove they were providing adequate credit services to low-income areas.[42]

While important, these legislative acts lacked the social, political, or economic power to end segregation. During the 1960s and 1970s, sociologists Douglas Massey and Nancy Denton observed "a sharp improvement in racial attitudes among whites" and the development of a "large and increasingly affluent black middle class," but these improvements eroded little of the white-black physical divide: "The forces of racial change that transformed American society during the 1970s have had a marginal impact on the spatial behavior of blacks and whites in American cities. . . . The segregation of blacks in large cities hardly changed. . . . Most blacks continue to reside in predominantly black neighborhoods."[43] Indeed, Denton and Massey declared some cities "hypersegregated," despite modest declines in indices of dissimilarity from the 1970s to the 1980s.[44]

Segregation proved an intractable problem for a government unwilling to force integration. Federal laws gave the appearance of equal access to homeownership, but these same laws outlined only negative rights—the right to be protected from discrimination—not the positive right to live in integrated communities nor the right to equally vibrant housing markets. Because housing laws did not acknowledge segregated markets (much less address them), patterns of neighborhood racial composition ultimately told a much more truthful story about access to housing than new legislation. Regardless of ongoing residential segregation, improved access to homeownership had political appeal for both Republicans and Democrats, and minority homeownership became an accepted goal in federal policies—a "market" approach to fair housing that was more palatable to business interests and many middle-class homeowners than any forced integration.

Even when fair housing legislation was present, enforcement proved difficult. Flaws in the original Fair Housing Act, for instance, constrained HUD's power to conduct investigations and the Justice Department's ability to ensure compliance.[45] When the FHA loosened regulations and accepted an unprecedented number of nonwhite applicants, this change actually worsened the situation as rising rates of FHA lending became "a surrogate indicator of racial change" in a neighborhood (ostensibly from white to black or Latino), and as appraisers began equating rising numbers of FHA loans in an area with higher risk.[46] Other laws of the 1980s and 1990s continued the trend of reinforcing antidiscriminatory but not integrative housing policies: the Civil Rights Restoration Act of 1987 amended Title VI and related statutes with a more expansive definition of "program or activity"; the Fair Housing Amendments of 1988 broadened protected classes to include disabled persons and families with children and added more enforcement mechanisms, including stiffer penalties for violations of the 1968 Fair Housing Act; and president William Clinton's Executive Order 12892 (1994) required federal government departments and agencies to affirmatively further fair housing under the HUD secretary and to set up a President's Fair Housing Council to "review the design and delivery of Federal programs."[47] Even the weighty Fair Housing Amendments of 1988 did not improve segregation, and the expansion of the mortgage market and concomitant downscaling of public housing continued pulling or driving more low-income families into the private sector, even as the color line persisted and the real rewards of homeownership fell disproportionately to the upper and middle classes. Better enforcement of the Community Reinvestment Act in the late 1980s and early 1990s led again to better minority access to homeownership but not to integrated neighborhoods, and the increase in subprime and predatory lending in the 1990s created new vulnerabilities for low-income homeowners.[48]

This shift into unequal homeownership systems (instead of the previous renter-owner divide) moved the struggle for "fair access to credit," to a struggle for "access to fair credit."[49] If minority and low-income families were mostly excluded from the prime mortgage market earlier, now more families of all backgrounds could buy homes, but with vastly different terms of credit and in neighborhoods with highly unequal rates of appreciation on housing investment. Worse, these initiatives increased homeownership possibilities for low-income families and families of color by opening them up to poorly understood credit risks and challenges. Even before the meltdown in subprime lending, the encouragement of low-income homeownership rested on questionable assumptions that home purchases were good investments for families of all income levels, that owner-occupancy would improve maintenance costs, and that homeownership would buffer the owners from steep changes in monthly housing expenditures.[50]

In response to the urban crisis of the 1960s and growing alarm over urban rioting, Congress passed the Housing Act of 1968 that launched a powerful new tool: the mortgage-backed security. The 1968 act, and in particular, a short-term program called Section 235, directly responded to the low-income housing question by offering more low-income loans and converting record numbers of renters to homeowners. Mortgage-backed securities allowed investors to buy risk-rated securities that required no knowledge of actual properties or mortgage but that nonetheless produced higher returns than government securities and that had the appearance of full government backing. By 1973, Fannie Mae was "next to the Treasury, the largest debt-issuing institution in US capital markets."[51]

Perhaps no single case better illustrated the problems with this sort of increased access to homeownership than the reverse redlining program of the Boston Banks Urban Renewal Group, when a group of twenty-two area banks agreed in 1968 to provide $50 million in loans for what would ultimately be 2,000 mortgages exclusively to black families within the set boundaries of a renewal area. Within a few short years, roughly 70% of the new homeowners could no longer afford their mortgage payments because of dishonest appraisals, excessively high purchase prices, and/or poor matches of income to debt.[52] Needless to say, temporarily increasing black homeownership rates in this manner did little to equalize housing access or improve segregation in Boston.

As fair housing programs evolved over the course of the 1970s and 1980s, then, both government and private housing industry officials made abundantly clear their preference for increasing homeownership opportunities without directly tackling the thorny issue of spatial integration. African Americans, Native Americans, Latinos, and other racial minorities could be "integrated" into a homeowner society without necessarily living side by side with white, middle-class families. Naturally, this new orthodoxy failed to address the real inequalities of owning a home on stagnant reservation land or an inner-city block versus a booming suburb, nor did it account for highly unequal mortgage packages.

The application of international experiences played an important role in strengthening the physical and policy divide between middle- and upper-class American homeowners on the one hand, and working-class and poor American homeowners and renters on the other, with a disproportionately negative effect on racial minorities. By the 1970s, HUD housing officials viewed American inner cities, migrant labor communities, and Native American reservations as anomalous "problem areas" that "parallel[ed] overseas problem areas for which successful organized aided self-help housing programs have been devised."[53] As such, places disproportionately inhabited by indigent, racial, and ethnic minorities came to be seen and categorized as exceptional places that could benefit from shared international knowledge. "Just as the Puerto Rican experience was able to be transferred to other countries," former chief of HUD and the Latin American Bureau for USAID Harold Robinson noted in 1976, "so their varied experience can be transferred back to Puerto Rico and this country . . . in the Indian and migrant worker projects."[54] Even if housing programs for Native Americans were small and restricted in scope, they still had greater significance because they could not only draw from lessons abroad but could eventually assist in "formulating and testing approaches, methods, and techniques which could relieve the social tensions within inner city areas."[55] This approach to housing problems in the inner city, on Native American reservations, in migrant laborer communities, and in US territories like Puerto Rico and the Virgin Islands further divided an already split housing system. One side quietly enjoyed ongoing federal tax deductions and mortgage insurance, while the other was expected to achieve rapid housing improvement through temporary public subsidies, an aided self-help approach, or problematic, risky loans. On the surface, low-income households were gaining ground, but in reality they were participating in vastly different forms of homeownership with correspondingly dissimilar risks.

The confusion of heavily subsidized "private" homeownership, underfunded "public" dependence, and seemingly equal access to mortgage loans was made only more bewildering by the divergent forms of self-help rhetoric that pervaded each. For instance, while the federal government urged Native American reservation dwellers and migrant farm workers to participate in self-help construction projects, the private industry used the same do-it-yourself language to market home improvement to middle-class suburbanites.[56] As a result, some international housing experts erroneously assumed that self-help was "generally a middle class undertaking" in the US, Sweden, and Australia—"more like a hobby, often competing with television, hunting, boating, etc., than a real necessity."[57] One Australian housing expert added, "Do-it-yourself is primarily a sales gimmick." Meanwhile, this same group of experts noted that low-income families in the developing world required aided self-help and mutual aid programs that would instill in them "a genuine desire for self-improvement rather than a feeling of dependency." It was a double irony that the American middle class required no self-help because of extensive government support for homeownership, and thus could participate in private market do-it-yourself hobbies, while lower-income Americans received little comparable government assistance and thus needed to participate in paternalistic aided self-help programs that would teach them to become "the competitive, self-sufficient, independent citizens depicted by the Protestant ethic."[58]

Even as the chasm between profitable upper-income and risky lower-income homeownership yawned wider, Wall Street innovations like the adjustable-rate mortgage and collateralized mortgage obligations opened up more opportunities for homeownership. Federal government programs exhibited little caution in the 1990s and early 2000s: Fannie Mae launched the Opening Doors to Affordable Housing Initiative (1991), the Trillion Dollar Commitment (1994), and the Partnership Office Initiative (1994), while HUD laid out "explicit goals for Fannie Mae and Freddie Mac to promote affordable housing for moderate-, low-, and very low-income families and to provide financing for homebuyers and renters in underserved areas" through a Federal Housing Enterprises Financial Safety and Soundness Act (1992). After 1999, newly appointed Fannie Mae chairman Franklin Raines (1999–2004) sought creative ways to "penetrate" the minority segment, including but not limited to the American Dream Commitment (2000) and a new strategy of directed promotion, in which marketing experts like Vada Hill (of Taco Bell's Chihuahua campaign fame) helped match minority consumers with "appropriate" mortgage products.[59] In part inspired by Hernando de Soto's theories about homeownership in the developing world, Raines believed his "risk-based pricing" system was not only good business, but would in fact permit low down-payment lending to "democratize homeownership in America"—to equalize access to that critical marker of middle-class achievement.[60] Despite clear warnings against fetishization, homeownership had become shorthand for better housing both in the US and abroad.

Residential integration, meanwhile, remained equally elusive in both. It was all the more alarming, then, that HUD officials believed themselves qualified to advise the postapartheid South African government on fair housing and fair lending practices. Through the US–South Africa Binational Commission, housing secretary Andrew Cuomo, technical experts, US Treasury Department officials, and housing industry representatives traveled to South Africa to share American best practices in 1999. Together, the American delegation persuaded minister of housing Sankie Mthembi-Mahanyele and eventually, the South African Parliament, to adopt a Home Loan and Mortgage Disclosure Act modeled explicitly on the US's Home Mortgage Disclosure Act in 2000. The South African government requested additional advice about "public-private partnerships in lower income neighborhoods, particularly the relationship between banking institutions and community-based organizations and residents," potentially stimulating more legislation along the lines of the US's Community Reinvestment Act.[61] The flow of ideas and techniques continued in the twenty-first century, circulating from nation to nation and group to group despite the mixed record of such efforts.

Native American Homeownership

In the US, the first large-scale experiments with self-help (aid for family-based efforts) and mutual help (aid for community-based projects) were initiated on Native American reservations. These experiments came relatively late in the international history of aided self-help and mutual help. Although the federal government contemplated Native American housing improvement well before the 1960s, it did so without a clear connection to foreign policy or international housing assistance before World War II. (The latter was an obvious absence given the near non-existence of housing aid pre-1945.) Native American land and housing policies became a domestic issue for the federal government only after the formal conquest of the American continental empire, and late nineteenth and early twentieth-century experiments with landownership failed to yield positive results for Native populations. The devastating policy of land allotment (Dawes Severalty Act, 1887–1934) converted large tracts of Indian land to individual family homesteads of 160 acres apiece, theoretically yielding greater agricultural efficiencies, economic self-sufficiency, and cultural integration, but in reality stimulating massive land loss and a precipitous decline in living standards for many Native American families. (Homesteads were subject to local and state laws rather than remaining under tribal jurisdiction; high taxation, unscrupulous officials, and a policy of selling some lands to non-Indian homesteaders reduced Indian landholdings from roughly 138 million acres in 1887 to 48 million in 1934.)[62] The dwelling type that the federal government urged alongside these improvement programs likewise failed to revolutionize Native American housing conditions. If new architecture broke dramatically with previous shelter in its standardized, machine-cut horizontal siding and large glass windows, such houses were few in number and largely out of reach for most Native American families.

Any improvement in Native housing conditions would need to come from substantive, sustained federal government subsidy, and that action did not come readily in the late nineteenth or early twentieth centuries. Centralized state action was predicated in part on the federal government's recognition of special obligations to American Indians and Alaska Natives. There were also legal and institutional reasons for Native housing to fall squarely in the lap of the federal government: the Snyder Act of 1921, for instance, mandated that all services to reservation communities—including housing—needed to be provided through the Bureau of Indian Affairs.[63] Since the federal government interacted directly with recognized tribes in a sovereign-to-sovereign relationship rather than in the typical hierarchy of federal-state-local relations, Native American tribes found themselves at once dependent on the federal government and yet unable to participate in the national programs created by the Housing Acts of 1934, 1937, and 1949. Furthermore, the BIA held in trust a large portion of tribal land, disqualifying Native families from applying for FHA-insured housing loans for repairs, improvements, or building of homes, since the "Regulation No. 1 governing such loans" stipulated that "promissory notes must be signed by an owner of the real property to be improved."[64] In this way, government ownership blocked access to federal assistance for Native families while also frustrating the development of a vibrant private housing market.[65] Unlike states or even territories like Puerto Rico, national housing acts were not applied to Native American tribal areas for many years, and the federal government felt little need to address the widespread and increasingly dire housing problem on Indian lands beyond the minimal improvement programs of the BIA.

Not until the mid-1950s did the Department of Health, Education, and Welfare start a water and sanitation program through the Indian Health Service (IHS). It took another five years for the Bureau of Indian Affairs commissioner to write to the Public Housing Administration (PHA; a predecessor agency to HUD, 1947–65) requesting an Indian housing program.[66] These small positive steps facilitated a devastating termination policy in which the federal government ended federal trust responsibilities and delegated criminal and civil jurisdiction to states after establishing sanitation and water facilities and supplying land titles. Henceforth, it was assumed Indians "were integrated into the social and economic life of the local community, and that termination of the special relationship between them and the Federal Government would impose no particular hardship on them," according to commissioner of Indian Affairs John Crow. "To assume otherwise, the Government would be placed in a most embarrassing position of fostering termination and leaving the rancheria [rural land parcels in California held in trust by the federal government] residents to face possible eviction from their homes by application of local health and safety laws."[67] Under these new policies, Indian urban populations jumped from 27,000 in 1940 (8% of the total Indian population) to 56,000 (16%) in 1950, to 146,000 (28%) in 1960, to 356,000 (45%) in 1970, and finally to a majority 807,000 (53%) in 1980.[68]

The rhetoric of homeownership became part of the justification for termination. According to a BIA report in the same year as the California Termination Act of 1958, "persons holding assignments on Rancherias in California have been anxious to have clear title to the lands they are occupying so they can feel secure in the ownership of their homes."[69] Termination would finally give them that full homeownership. The details were unsavory, though: after a check of federal records of Indian names with land rights in the designated reservation, individuals were offered land titles and termination agreements; for those who refused, the state would sell their rancheria or reservation land and use the funds for the benefit of all Indians in the state. In addition, termination meant forfeiting educational subsidies and enduring county health inspections and residential taxes. "Mixed-blood" Indians "terminated" as part of one tribe surrendered claims to all other tribal rights. Half-Indian teenager Jon L. Adams explained the consequences in personal terms: "When they checked my records they found that my tribe was terminated and so was I. Asking what it ment [sic] they told me that I was ineliledgible [sic] for the grants to continue my education. In short my name on a piece of paper made me a white man."[70]

For those left without their own property, the Office of General Council in the PHA recognized tribal governments as legal "municipalities" in 1961, thus granting them the right to create public housing authorities under the Housing Act of 1937. Public housing access was more complicated than homeownership, however, and the Low Rent Program (as public housing was known on Indian lands) posed two issues in particular: first, Indian families tended to be suspicious about any government-funded housing program that removed them from their land. Second, public housing rent was still too high for most families, given that they were paying nothing on their current properties. If most Indian families could not afford a private home and mortgage, they also could not pay rent for a new public housing unit while buying other basic necessities, no matter how simple the amenities in that unit. Many families were accustomed to paying little or no rent on their rudimentary shelters, according to PHA economist Richard Metcalf. The Oglala Sioux created the first Indian Housing Authority (IHA) in 1961, and Metcalf characterized the PHA program at Pine Ridge Reservation, South Dakota, as a cautious "experiment in improving social conditions of a people whom society has treated cruelly," but still not one that would reach the poorest families on the reservation.[71] For the few that did receive accommodation through the PHA, Metcalf anticipated culture shock. At Pine Ridge Reservation, most lived in rudimentary squatter "shacks," and bathroom and kitchen utilities were virtually unknown to many members of "this relatively primitive tribe."[72]

Conditions were so poor in fact, that Metcalf believed the reservation presented an "ideal social laboratory" to ask social science questions intended for application in the developing world. Leo Grebler, a professor of urban land economics at UCLA, had proposed a study of the relationship between housing and productivity in underdeveloped countries. Such studies had been conducted before by other social scientists, but they had failed to yield conclusive results because of the difficulties acquiring pertinent, accurate data. Metcalf believed Pine Ridge provided the perfect venue to ask these same questions, being simultaneously a "quasi-ward of the federal government" with detailed records covering such topics as job attendance and medical data, and also a distinct group with socioeconomic and housing conditions mirroring those found in Asia, Africa, and South America.[73] "It is doubtful," Metcalf opined, "whether similar data could be found anywhere else for any large number of persons living under primitive conditions."[74] Metcalf's ideas eventually took physical form in a 1961 pilot study funded by USAID and assisted by UCLA researchers, BIA officials, and US Public Health Service officers. In this first study of its kind on Pine Ridge, Metcalf worked with Wright & McGill Company (a producer of fish tackle) to "acquaint research workers with the technical problems of identifying, assembling, reconciling, and interpreting the information required for a detailed examination of the housing-productivity relationship"—techniques that were rapidly applied to concurrent and subsequent USAID/UCLA studies of the housing-labor relationship in Hambaek, South Korea (Dae Han Coal Corporation); Monterrey, Mexico (Instituto de Investigaciones Industriales de Monterrey and the Fundidora de Fierro y Acero de Monterrey); Zacapu, Mexico (Celanese Mexicana, Construccion Popular, and Instituto Mexicano del Seguro Social); Guayana, Venezuela (SIDOR steel mill); and Limuru, Kenya (Bata Shoe Company).[75]

In the same way that developing world policies could emerge from Pine Ridge, Metcalf believed Pine Ridge could learn from lessons abroad. Public housing would be too expensive to address the entire housing problem on Indian reservations, so Metcalf urged the federal government to explore programs "of the kind the government sponsors overseas, such as aided self-help housing."[76] At long last, the Housing Assistance Administration (later located within HUD), the BIA, and the US Public Health Service jointly launched a Mutual Help Homeownership Program (1962–96) that lowered costs with "a lease and a repayment schedule eventually leading to home ownership." The program constituted the "first serious effort to carry out a large-scale, federally-sponsored and as-sisted, organized aided self-help housing program within the continen-tal United States . . . [that] drew very heavily upon overseas approaches and methods."[77]

Mutual Help Homeownership modified the installment contract sys-tem commonly used with minority families by adding mutual help com-ponents tested in the developing world.[78] The Housing Assistance Administration and the BIA agreed that very low-income Indian families needed a "strong incentive for self-help in building and maintaining their homes." Under this program, even the poorest families priced out of conventional public housing could benefit from government hous-ing assistance.[79] In the Mutual Help Homeownership Program, families contributed a set dollar amount of land, personal labor, or materials in return for HAA-funded building materials and/or skilled labor. (Usually, the tribe provided land on behalf of families.) Then, occupants depos-ited roughly 15% of their adjusted income into an operation and main-tenance account held by the Indian Housing Authority. Once they built up enough savings to purchase, they would become homeowners. Until then, the tribe held the title, and residents could not sell units, claim federal tax deductions, or enjoy any equity increase.

Even the Treasury Department and HUD had to admit this form of ownership bore "little resemblance to homeownership as it is gener-ally understood off Indian Reservations."[80] PHA general counsel Joseph Burstein turned a blind eye to the costs of this sort of homeowner-ship, arguing that the mutual help program used a "completely unique [system] . . . of public housing financing to weld together the pride and self-help of the individual, the incentives of home-ownership and the enthusiasm and abilities of Indian Tribal organizations, the Bureau of Indian Affairs and the Public Health Service."[81] Like informative furniture shows and home economics programs abroad, Mutual Help programs also included educational aspects to "train occupants of new homes in housekeeping skills."[82] Wyoming home economist Helen John Wright, for instance, used "magazines, home demonstrations, and slides" to help Indian families with "color schemes, draping, furni-ture, and general home arrangement." She also "toured furniture stores grouply" and commended "the Indian people" on their "natural ability." Ultimately, BIA officials agreed, the purpose of the program was to cultivate self-respect and to guide participants toward "a real desire for a home."[83]

There were some basic problems with this narrative, however. Mutual Help housing served only a fraction of needy Native populations, failed to meet the expectations of some of those within that small group, and suffered mortgage default rates of "crisis proportions," according to HUD Regional Office IX, the southwestern states responsible for 51% of the nation's Native population. "The homeownership concept of the Mutual Help program has serious implementation problems," the HUD Region IX Office noted in 1981. The All-Indian Pueblos IHA experienced 70% delinquency in 1981, with over 20% of delinquents being federal employees. The primary obstacle to timely payment was the "failure of the IHAs to enforce strong collection and eviction policies."[84] Enforcement was difficult, given that self-determination mandates required Indian Housing Authority officials to pursue collections and evictions through independent judicial systems with opaque, cumbersome procedures.[85] Nonetheless, HUD concluded that the projects "support[ed] the assumption that home ownership is a primary 'felt need' of the Indian people."[86]

Interestingly, the PHA general counsel observed greater federal government enthusiasm and concrete action for the Indian Program than for comparable innovations in inner-city, urban areas.[87] Perhaps congressional support for Indian housing initiatives stemmed from a stronger consensus that the US government "owed" something to Native Americans as opposed to, say, indigent inner-city dwellers. Given the weak response to the housing needs of Native city-dwellers, however, it is more likely IHA problems were seen as manageable, conscribed as they were by reservation boundaries. Whatever the reason, both the low-rent and homeownership schemes were ultimately devised and managed by the PHA in conjunction with the BIA, and President Johnson earmarked 3,200 housing units within the PHA in 1964 for Indian reservations in the continental forty-eight states—roughly half low-rent and the other half, mutual self-help.[88] The BIA also stepped up efforts to help Indians obtain private home loans, doubling total loans from $2.9 million in 1962 to $6.2 million in 1963, and the Office of Economic Opportunity began a basic housing program with centrally heated, weather-tight units on the Rosebud Reservation in hopes of creating jobs in the prefabrication plant and providing minimum basic structures.[89] In Alaska, the BIA and PHA worked with the Alaska State Housing Authority to

launch a low-income mutual self-help and prefabricated housing demonstration for Indians, Aleuts, and Eskimos from 1963 to 1966. Like
those at Rosebud, most native Alaskans could not afford the rent of low-
income housing, and "were it not part of the United States, [the state]
could qualify for assistance from the World Bank or our own Agency for
International Development," according to Charles Abrams.[90]

The connection between domestic and foreign aid programs could
not have been clearer. In the language of the self-help project assessment by the Alaska State Housing Authority, the demonstration project was an attempt to modernize "extremely primitive shelter" and help
native peoples "make the transition to a western culture."[91] Rodman
Rockefeller (vice president of the International Basic Economy Corporation) brought floor plans, construction techniques, and repayment
schedules to discuss possible collaborations in Cherokee mutual-help
housing with Ervan Bueneman (BIA) and Marie McGuire (Housing
Assistance Administration, HUD) in the mid-1960s, eventually producing formal domestic IBEC programs.[92] Bueneman himself would publish a
special report in which he exhorted American cities to make use of US experiences in Puerto Rico, the Virgin Islands, and on Native reservations.[93]

Homeownership played a critical part in other Indian housing programs as well. The Bureau of Indian Affairs' Housing Improvement Program (1965–) targeted those with "exceptionally low" or "no income at
all" by encouraging impoverished Indian families to use the proceeds of
supervised land sales, claim monies, or judgment funds to pay for materials to improve their own homes if possible, or to build new homes
if their current abode was beyond repair.[94] If families rented, they were
shown modern single-family dwellings and persuaded to use their funds
to become homeowners. While the BIA received some complaints that
this program penalized "the more industrious" in favor of welfare recipients, government officials responded that the houses were built primarily "for the children, to provide them [gender-segregated] privacy
in a sleeping area and to provide a quiet study area . . . [as well as]
to teach them the benefits to be derived from clean, warm, adequate,
sanitary housing, and possibly deter these children from becoming welfare cases themselves."[95] The financing of the Housing Improvement
Program was certainly striking: Pawnee claims monies, funds on deposit
at the Treasury to pay a judgment by the Indian Claims Commission
to the Northern Cheyenne Tribe, and money from unspecified "land
sales" now went to "modernize" or purchase single-family residences
for Native families. Some homes were modest but equipped with new

25 According to BIA reports, every effort was made to encourage individual Indians to "modernize" their homes through self-help. Material costs were usually paid with land sales and claim
monies. Here, Lamont Warrior inspects his renovated interior walls and ceiling in Anadarko,
Oklahoma. 1964. Source: Folder Anadarko 2 of 2, box 3: Albuquerque Area, Albuquerque Mutual
Help to Anadarko, NARA-DC.

porches, paint jobs, uncracked foundations, or modern plumbing. Others
were almost extravagant, with two-car garages, seven bedrooms, and
upper-story balconies. Whether humble or grand, each house was meant
to accommodate one nuclear family, one owner-occupier.

The Homeownership Improvement and the Mutual Help Homeownership Programs looked good in photographs. Couples smiled in front
of gabled homes; children played on porches while mothers sat beside
them. Photographs hid the inadequacy of such programs, however.[96]
Despite the visual and ideological appeal of the two programs, Congress
allotted insufficient funds, and BIA area offices were "fully aware of the
deplorable housing conditions" experienced by most. Any progress thus
far—in the BIA's words—"falls far short of what is needed."[97] Indian
housing reached a new state of crisis by the late 1960s, resulting in a
flurry of legislative and regulatory action: in 1968, Congress put into
law the 1961 and 1962 court decisions, and HUD, BIA, and IHS signed

an Interdepartmental Memorandum of Understanding (1969) stating a determination to produce 40,000 units a year for the next five years—the largest public provision to date.[98] Section 701(b) amended the 1954 Housing Act, mandating federal government assistance for low-income families in Indian areas. Meanwhile, a home purchase program for qualified urban relocatees provided a grant of up to $1,000 to help with home purchase, since "an Indian does not cease being an Indian simply by moving from the reservation" and since he required assistance to become self-supporting and self-dependent.[99] Their state of extreme deprivation made "Indian reservations in the United States . . . the equivalent of underdeveloped, isolated nations," one HUD report concluded.[100] HUD subsequently launched a Model Reservation Program that prioritized development aid and comprehensive site planning, and it began a preliminary study of the development potential at the second-largest reservation in the US—the Pine Ridge Indian Reservation in South Dakota.

26 Mr. and Mrs. Theodore Walking Eagle participated in an experimental low-cost housing demonstration at the Rosebud Indian Reservation in South Dakota. In this program, HUD worked with the BIA, the Public Health Service, the Department of Labor, the Office of Economic Opportunity, and the Sioux Tribal Council to test, among other issues, whether or not homeownership, "coupled with a choice of site selection, [could] . . . revive individual responsibility, create a sense of achievement, and promote dramatic community improvement." Source: US Department of HUD, Low Income Housing Demonstration Program, Report on the Transitional Housing Experiment—Rosebud Indian Reservation (Washington, DC: Government Printing Office, c. 1968), 17, 21.

Conditions at Pine Ridge were dire by the end of the decade. Despite a small population (roughly 10,000) and immense landholdings (1.7 million acres), median family income only reached $1,910 per year (1968). Forty-two percent of the work force was unemployed, less than 12% of all families could afford electricity, only about 3% of Indian homes had telephones, and roughly 25% of the population received water and sewage facilities through the Public Health Service.[101] The sheer size of the reservation could be a liability, given the vast distances—sometimes as much as a hundred miles—from home to shopping, with no public transportation and only 150 out of 530 miles of roads graded, drained, and hard-surfaced by the BIA. Reservation poverty exceeded conditions found in the worst inner-city slum, with 58% of the housing stock deemed dilapidated beyond repair, and half of the population hauling water over one-quarter mile or from a polluted source. In fact, living conditions at Pine Ridge did more closely echo problems with rural poverty in the developing world.

The National Savings and Loan League (NSLL) drew explicit connections between conditions on Indian reservations, urban centers in the US, and developing world cities in the early 1970s. The league had begun in 1943 as a coalition of private home financing institutions and state and regional associations of housing professionals with the objective of promoting greater thrift and homeownership. The national organization quickly expanded to include countries outside the US, with the subsidiary National League, International (NLI) providing underwriting and inspection services to twenty-six countries by 1956, working under formal contract with the US Department of Commerce and eventually by 1963, under contract with USAID. The NLI wanted to "implement US foreign policy directives in the areas of housing and housing finance" by selecting, briefing, and supporting American S&L executives to then go overseas and help set up comparable housing finance institutions.[102] The league explored ways to increase minority development projects, including low-income housing, by linking businesses with financial institutions. It set up an Inner City Committee with HUD to produce legislative proposals addressing the problem of financing for low- and moderate-income households, and it had already begun providing technical assistance to seventy minority-owned S&Ls by 1974.[103] The NLI saw all three—homeownership for middle-class Americans, inner-city residents, and those living on Indian reservations—as intertwined projects. In one of many statements, the National League argued, "Because of [our] experience with the fostering of private savings institutions in developing countries, [we have] little doubt that given adequate support on a scale commensurate with available resources a viable mortgage credit mechanism within selected reservations is workable."[104] The *Washington Post* rejoiced, "Savings and Loan Group Aids Housing Abroad and Now in US Too."[105]

The NLI would not have pursued reservation housing with such enthusiasm had the federal government not provided the same incentives as for overseas investments or for suburban middle-class white homes in the US. Director of Knickerbocker Federal Savings and Loan Association Paul G. Reilly noted, "The response of the private sector is dependent upon adequate promotional activity directed at it, coupled with a sufficiently interesting profit margin, security of repayment, and reduction in the efforts requested to initiate and close the transaction."[106]

In 1972, those incentives were not yet in place, although the NSLL noted nascent possibilities for investment and profit. In November of the same year—just days before the American Indian Movement's BIA occupation in Washington, DC—a National League of Insured Savings Associations planning team traveled to Rosebud Reservation, South Dakota, to discuss the possibility of an S&L to promote thrift and homeownership. Interestingly, Harold Tepper served as one of the two directors for the project; Tepper was the vice president and deputy director of international operations, and clearly meant to bring his international experiences to bear on Indian housing. The team observed that existing federal programs encouraging minority economic development might also be used in Indian housing programs.[107] At the time, planning team members hoped Indian-owned and managed S&Ls, greater individual savings rates, and more widespread homeownership would help the transition from a "barter society" to a "money society" while "lessen[ing] some of the frustrations which were evident during the Indian occupation of BIA Headquarters."[108] While the Wounded Knee incident in February did eventually dampen enthusiasm for the Sioux reservation, the NSLL did bring to fruition their plans for a first Indian-owned and operated S&L association on the Navajo Reservation at Window Rock, Arizona.

The NSLL believed homeownership could better utilize trust lands and open up private investment on Indian reservations if three conditions were met: first, land alienation (the process by which trust lands became individually owned and transferable from current occupant to new owner by mortgage or deed) needed to be regularized; second, the process of foreclosure on reservation land needed to be instituted in the law; third, investors' "distorted view of the Indian adherence to the values of a money society" needed to be rectified. Instead of forcing the issue of land alienation through the writing of new legislation, the NSLL took the interesting step of recommending a federal insurance or guarantee system instead. If the government could guarantee against losses from an investor assuming alienation, the latter would be much more motivated to participate in reservation housing. This suggestion drew explicitly on the NSSL's work in Latin America as well as referencing standard FHA/VA practices in the US.

Congress passed an Indian Finance Act the next year (1974) that followed the same pattern as overseas investment guarantees in Latin America. President Richard Nixon explained the logic behind the 1974 act: "The loan guarantee program is the Administration's way of backing up our conviction [that Indians are good loan risks] with Federal money. I hope that enactment of this bill will greatly enhance the financial attractiveness of Indian borrowers in the private sector."[109] As in the international scene, the federal government chose to emphasize economic development first, with housing subsumed within that broader framework. Section 215 of Title II specifically encouraged investment in land within a broader discussion of terms by which loan guaranties and insurances would operate. The NSSL believed the Finance Act could help assimilate Indian mortgages with standard practices in the US:

In any system designed to invite the participation of the private sector, there has to be a concept of adequate rate, appropriate credit standards, and liquidation readily available to the lender. We also think the guarantee ought to be as broad as any present FHA guarantee. In terms of the subsidy provisions of the Indian Finance Act the system could provide for a variable or subsidized rate to the borrower but at the same time give a minimum guaranteed rate to the lender. Assuming that the instruments evidencing the debt were comparable to those of the private sector then the means could be found for those securities to obtain the benefits of the present secondary markets through the medium of GNMA, FNMA, and FHLMA and their cooperation should be invited.[110]

The BIA, meanwhile, encouraged NSSL executives to use the Finance Act to help meet initial S&L capital requirements and to investigate potential "application of the Financing Act to housing programs in general."[111]

Still, there was much that made housing problems in tribal areas distinct from those found in major metropolitan areas or even rural regions. The federal government held much reservation land in trust, and if that land was held in trust for a tribe, it could not be mortgaged. If it was held for an individual, it could have a lien put on it only with federal approval.[112] Foreclosure remained a sticky affair; household incomes were often untenably low; and above all, many Native Americans simply did not embrace mortgage-driven, single-family homeownership. In response, HUD began opening Indian Program offices in the late 1970s, and finally set up the Office of Indian Programs in Washington, DC, in 1980—the same year that president Ronald Reagan attempted to effectively eliminate the Indian housing program by a budget "reduction" eliminating 96% of federal funding.[113] (The remaining 4% would be used to finish as yet incomplete projects.)[114] The Reagan administration justified the drastic cuts as a promotion of Indian self-sufficiency and free enterprise on reservations, continuing the process of separating Indian housing from national programs while decimating federal funding.[115] Interior secretary James Watt put the blame for abysmal living standards squarely on the shoulders of Indians themselves: "If you want an example of the failure of socialism, don't go to Russia. Come to America and go to the Indian reservations."[116] New programs under housing secretary Samuel Pierce's Joint Venture for Affordable Housing initiative permitted HUD to make single-family mortgage insurance available to Commonwealth of the Northern Mariana Islands residents and to native Hawaiians residing on Hawaiian Home Lands in 1987.[117]

Throughout the 1970s, '80s, and '90s, HUD consistently emphasized less federal provision and more private initiative. The Community Development Block Grant (CDBG) model established by the Housing and Community Development Act of 1974 required grant recipients to make "all reasonable efforts . . . to maximize participation by the private sector," including loan guarantees for notes issued by tribes to finance affordable housing.[118] Indian Housing Authorities used the section 8 Certificate and Voucher Program (Housing Act of 1937) funds to help qualified families rent privately owned units. Organizationally, the 1988 Indian Housing Act began consolidating all laws and formally separating Indian from public housing, a process made complete by the Native American Housing Assistance and Self-Determination Act of 1996.

By 2000, Native American homeownership rates in Indian tribal areas stood at 68.5% as opposed to the rate for Native Americans nationwide (55.7%) or the national average (66.2%).[119] The high rate of ownership in tribal areas was affected to a small degree by the Mutual Help housing program, but more likely owed its numerical strength to the ongoing predominance of poor-quality housing units, especially mobile-home ownership, which stood at twice the national rate.[120] Private mortgage financing, meanwhile, continued to be difficult throughout the 1980s, 1990s, and early 2000s. The FHA's section-248 Mortgage Insurance Program (1985) tried to address the risk of foreclosure on trust land, but it attracted few borrowers or lenders. The Housing and Community Development Act of 1992's section-184 Indian Loan Guarantee Program subsequently complemented the section-248 insurance approach, guaranteeing private loans to Indian families and Indian Housing Authorities (IHAs) for the "purchase, construction, or rehabilitation of one- to four-family dwellings on restricted lands and in Indian areas," thus overcoming private lenders' wariness of homeownership on restricted lands.[121] The program offered "true homeownership"—an improvement on the Mutual Help homes that remained on lease from the Indian Housing Authority until completion of the full amortization period—and it targeted middle-class Native American and Alaska Native families with the goal of galvanizing savings, building equity, and stabilizing housing costs.[122] HUD's Office of Native American Programs emphasized that the program merely built on preexisting, even primal desires for homeownership; it did not create them. As one document averred, "Your ancestors have always made the home the center of their existence."[123] Office of Native American Programs writers indulged more than once in sweeping generalizations about Native American culture, noting that Native American families could use time-honored "trading" skills to seek out the best private loans to be subsequently guaranteed by the federal government. "Don't hesitate to 'horse-trade' a little with them to get the most for your money," one brochure advised. "No one is a better trader than a Native American."[124]

In addition to employing offensive stereotypes about Native American behavior, documents pertaining to section 184 also blindly elevated homeownership without any indication or understanding of the realities of this tenure type for Native Americans. By the 1990s, it was clear from HUD's own documentation that the majority of Native American families living in Indian areas[125] owned poorly equipped homes. The problem was not with tenure type but with the housing itself. Some HUD studies even explicitly addressed the burgeoning problem of mobile-home ownership, including discussion of the declining living conditions within such units as well as the obvious problems with weatherproofing and overcrowding. At the same time, a HUD guidebook emphasized, "many families in Indian country have worked hard to achieve success, and now want to own a home of their own."[126] Part of this confusing combination of high rates of homeownership and perceived need for homeownership promotion could be attributed to HUD's reluctance to engage explicitly with class issues. Had HUD been willing to critically examine the costs and benefits of tenure types in relation to housing quality, homeownership statistics would not have masked poor living conditions. As in the tropics, though, American housing experts were inconsistent in thinking about homeownership of dilapidated, self-built structures with no utilities.

Location mattered just as much and received equally inconstant attention. It was questionable how much HUD housing rehabilitation grants mattered if the land had little appreciable value or was contaminated, as in the case of the California Elem Pomo Indian Colony's homes. This particular California reservation received housing rehabilitation loans in 1986 and 1987. Therepaired units were part of a reservation built next to the Sulphur Bank Mine, however, and homes actually utilized the mine's "tailings" (old rubble) for piles before the dangers were fully understood. Residents were subsequently advised by the Department of Health Services not to visit the old mine site or neighboring ponds, and to only rake or clean up the yard when the grounds were wet for fear of stirring up mercury-laden dust—hardly homes worth owning, by any stretch of the imagination.[127]

Section-248 and section-184 housing programs stumbled along through the 1990s, tripped up by administrative failures and the fact that most Indian Housing Authorities were unaware of their existence. Both programs ultimately failed to produce the sort of homeowning communities sought by lawmakers. Meanwhile, a Farmers Home Administration (now Rural Housing and Community Development Service) program (section 502, 1949/1990) provided direct loans to very low-income families for the construction or purchase of single-family homes, with an emphasis on self-help and other low-cost methods—but again, with 80% of all IHAs claiming little or no knowledge about these Farmers Home Administration (FmHA) programs, and the programs themselves serving very few families.[128] Home purchase loan denial rates from 1993 to 1999 reflected the difficult path prospective owners faced: 38.6% of American Indian applicants were denied, exceeding even the high rejection rate of African American households (36.4%) during that same time period.[129]

The Office of Native American Programs and HUD continued to attribute problems with private lending to the unique character of American Indian land, especially to the problem of recouping losses when a borrower defaulted. Together with ICF Kaiser International (an international consulting firm), the Office of Native American Programs and HUD addressed the difficult problem of eviction and foreclosure, developing a comprehensive Tribal Housing Code that might be adopted by individual tribes.[130] In this way, Native American homeownership campaigns replicated the problems of predecessor programs in the developing world:

instead of acknowledging the already present, widespread, and complex configurations of ownership, government officials pushed hard for higher rates of "modern" middle-class homeownership. By 2000, such thinking had translated into homeownership programs like the Oglala Sioux Tribe Partnership for Housing, which helped middle-income Pine Ridge families finance down payments, cover closing costs, and obtain a mortgage—once again, to the neglect of the most destitute.

Aided Self-Help for Impoverished Migrant Workers and Inner-City Dwellers

Inner-city programs replicated the same emphasis on modern middle-class homeownership found in BIA antecedents. Minority housing programs in the US should be understood in the context of a broader trend of aided self-help promotion and acceptance; by the early 1960s, for better or worse, the idea of aided self-help had become largely uncontroversial in policymaking circles.[131] As a sign of just how commonplace the technique had become, the World Bank finally joined HUD, USAID, and various intergovernmental and nongovernmental organizations in pushing for its own variation of aided self-help in 1973, altering the principle only slightly into what it called sites and services programs.[132] To some extent, aided self-help transitioned from outlier to orthodoxy in American urban housing programs of the early 1970s, with housing experts and community leaders learning from each other in diffuse ways, sharing assumptions about the perceived benefits of mass homeownership and relying on the practical appeal of aided self-help. As such ideas and practices became commonplace, it became more difficult to identify single, direct points of exchange. Networks became increasingly transnational and global, and idealized notions of citizen investment through homeownership, aided self-help techniques, and technical assistance programs became part of the basic vocabulary of most housing experts and city planners.

While the exact transmission points of international exchange may have become more difficult to pinpoint, it is unquestionable that "urban" (in the US, a code word for mostly working-class, nonwhite) aided self-help programs drew from and contributed to international forums. As HUD documents freely acknowledged, "many of the organization and orientation techniques, management methods, and project implementation practices used overseas in new aided self-help construction are applicable to urban aided self-help rehabilitation projects [in the US]."[133]

Like projects abroad, American aided self-help projects struggled to reconcile race and class tensions, and as a result, had much to learn from overseas techniques and methods. Homeownership played a vital role in the application of aided self-help to domestic American problems: as journalist and aided self-help housing advocate Richard Margolis put it concisely, "It is not just the house, it is *owning* it that does the trick."[134]

From their conception, American aided self-help programs served communities ill-served by the market. If "self-help is usually associated with crises in capitalism, when the state is hard-pressed to provide housing for urban workers," then certainly the Depression was enough of a crisis to stimulate this response.[135] Private nonprofits and local governments, and later the federal government, all stepped in to assist low-income households after the private market failed to do so, beginning most notably with two Depression-era housing projects for unemployed coal miners (Pennsylvania Relief Board housing project in Westmoreland County, Pennsylvania [1933] and the American Friends Service Committee (AFSC) community of Penn-Craft [1937]).[136] After 1945, other projects like the Flanner House Homes' mutual aided self-help program (1950) focused on the needs of poorer communities of color. In the case of the Flanner Homes, director Cleo W. Blackburn enlisted the help of the AFSC and converted an old settlement house into a "do-it-yourself" home-building and owning operation for an impoverished community near Indianapolis's Northwest Side. Blackburn's nonprofit bid on condemned tracts of "blighted" land and then collectively built new homes, with male heads of households contributing "muscular investment." Each man was required to contribute twenty hours a week of labor for a year to earn "sweat equity" of roughly $3,500, to be applied to the purchase of a three-bedroom ranch house estimated at $13,800 total value.[137] In addition, the FHA and VA offered financing by the early 1960s. Affirmation of African American masculinity played a key role in this scheme, as Blackburn believed "lasting improvement [could] result only from a strengthening of man's self-esteem and pride and from his personal investment in his own welfare."[138] The program required no public subsidy—a source of great pride for Blackburn—and it demonstrated African Americans' desire to "upgrade themselves" through homeownership.[139] Local businessmen provided construction material loans, while private banks issued mortgage loans.

Even though Flanner House eventually suspended construction in 1965 because of problems with rising mortgage interest rates and increasingly scarce affordable land, the program nonetheless inspired others. The

27 American Friends Service Committee advertising announcing a self-help homeownership
program for the North Eighth Street/Fairmount Avenue/Franklin Street/Brown Street block.
Philadelphia, 1952–1953. Source: Box 82, folder 4, American Friends Service Committee, Archives,
Philadelphia, PA.

Flanner Homes demonstrated that, given the right incentives, working-
class families and private investors could "join hands" to effectively address the housing problem in inner cities. If the government stepped
in and helped maintain conditions favorable to private investment,
more mutual aided self-help projects could flourish across the country;
Blackburn urged the federal government to open Model Cities Program
(1966–74) coffers to these sorts of initiatives, arguing that federal loans
to aided self-help programs could serve as a revolving fund of interim
financing for homeowner-builders.[140] The Flanner Homes had already

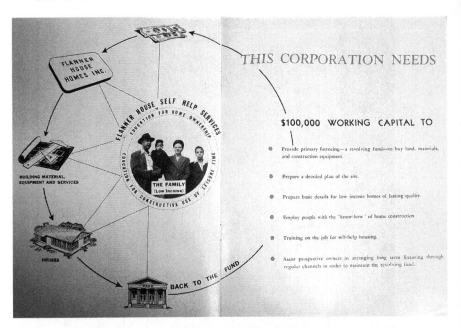

THIS CORPORATION NEEDS

$100,000 WORKING CAPITAL TO

● Provide primary financing—a revolving fund—to buy land, materials, and construction equipment.

● Prepare a detailed plan of the site.

● Prepare basic details for low income homes of lasting quality.

● Employ people with the "know-how" of home construction.

● Training on the job for self-help housing.

● Assist prospective owners in arranging long term financing through regular channels in order to maintain the revolving fund.

28 Diagram explaining the general principles behind Flanner Homes' mutual aided self-help program. Source: Box SIS1946-RRD, American Friends Service Committee Archives, Philadelphia, PA.

demonstrated the safety of such an investment, since 400 houses had been built with precisely this sort of revolving fund. It was critical that the federal government pursue "good relations between our segmented populations" by helping all Americans "see themselves as legitimate shareholders in the Great American Dream."[141] Republican Michigan governor (1963–69) and future HUD secretary (1969–73) George Romney was so impressed with the potential of this "Indianapolis technique" that he argued in 1967 that it ought to be extended nationwide.[142]

The active involvement of the AFSC ensured that the Flanner Homes and concurrent experiments would connect with parallel national and international projects, eventually becoming sustained, institutionalized efforts backed by the federal government. Two years after the start of Flanner Homes, the AFSC and the Friends Neighborhood Guild launched a self-help rehabilitation project (1952) in Philadelphia that applied similar concepts of "muscular investment" but with an emphasis on rehabilitation rather than new construction.[143] Bard McAllister (secretary for the Farm Labor Project, AFSC) worked with the secretary of the Commission on Agricultural Life and Labor to draft and pass legislation expanding Farmers Home Administration (FmHA, 1946–94; Rural Housing Service, 1994–) loans from farmers to farmworkers and non-farm rural residents (section 502, 1961). Once passed, the AFSC again took the helm in applying for and using section 502 loans. Choosing an impoverished migrant worker community in Goshen, California in the San Joaquin Valley, AFSC leaders set up an aided self-help housing program that gave predominantly migrant laborer communities the ability to build and own their own homes in the Golden State. The AFSC and other likeminded Californians built on this successful experiment to found Self-Help Enterprises (1965–), an organization dedicated to supporting self-help housing for low-income families everywhere. By that same year, sixteen states had launched FmHA-backed projects; Self-Help Enterprises boasted at least 5,000 new self-help units; and the AFSC and Ford Foundation organized an international conference of self-help organizations out of which was formed the International Self-Help Housing Association (1966). Attendees at the international conference referred to aided self-help projects in Puerto Rico, the Pine Ridge Reservation public housing program, HHFA Office of International Housing's Ideas and Methods papers, and UN publications dealing with soil cement and compressed earth, among others, to draw inspiration.[144] Meanwhile, Margolis helped publicize these burgeoning domestic aided self-help housing efforts with expositions on the living conditions of migrant laborers, the rural poor, and Native Americans.[145]

In this way, foreign aid became entwined with Indian, migrant labor, and rural poor housing issues, each informing and influencing the other. HUD secretary Robert Weaver's Turnkey III program (1967) was a perfect example of this, establishing a non-Indian public housing program that moved residents toward homeownership much like the Indian Mutual Help Homeownership Program, a program which itself borrowed from Mutual Help programs overseas. In Turnkey III, residents of subsidized, publicly owned rental housing could contribute maintenance labor ($350 worth of sweat equity) in exchange for HUD's providing credit toward a down payment in a lease-purchase contract with the Local Housing Authority.[146] The tenant then contributed 20% of income until earned equity equaled the balance, at which point the tenant acquired title.[147] "Turnkey" methods brought FHA-FNMA financing mechanisms to public housing; according to HUD, the turnkey method

sets up a method of development and construction financing by private lending institutions with a "take-out" upon completion analogous to the FNMA purchase of an FHA mortgage when a development is completed. Under this arrangement, the permanent financing "take-out" is accomplished with the proceeds from the housing authority's sale of its bonds secured by the pledge of PHA annual contributions, or, where necessary, with the proceeds from a PHA loan to the housing authority. Should the LHA default on its contract with the developer-seller, the "take-out" will be made through direct payment by the PHA. Thus, the developer-seller and his financing institution during construction are assured of an ultimate "take-out."[148]

Put more simply, Turnkey III allowed eligible low-income families to buy public housing units through a lease-purchase system that would guarantee developer-sellers long-term financing. By the end of the program in 1996, Turnkey III programs also enabled Indian Housing Authorities to help low-income families achieve "self-sufficiency through home-ownership."[149] Cycles of knowledge were important: overseas mutual aid programs drew on FHA-FNMA experiences to support homeownership abroad, then used these ideas to inform Indian homeownership programs, which in turn, shaped low-income homeownership programs for inner-city residents in a truly global circulation of ideas about low-income homeownership.

Large-scale changes in the global economy also profoundly shaped American housing programs, and in particular, low-income homeownership efforts. Waves of suburbanization, shrinking industrial cities, and collapsing urban industrial economies across the northeast heightened the housing crisis for low-income households. Decades of fair housing agitation added to the fire, and in 1968 Congress passed one of the first government programs designed to bring home financing within reach for low-income families (section 235, Home Mortgage Interest in the Housing and Urban Development Act of 1968). Unfortunately, the law missed the mark in at least two respects: first, it provided greater subsidies to those families purchasing more expensive homes, since the subsidy paid for the difference between cost of debt service at market rate and 1%.[150] This meant that those receiving the largest subsidy through section 235 were not truly low-income. Second, and even more damning for inner-city customers choosing to invest in existing urban communities, artificially high demand for inner-city property led to escalating home prices on older units. Owners were often startled to discover these older houses needed extensive, expensive repairs—repairs they were ill equipped to make, given that they had built little to no equity in their homes and had no way to immediately resell at inflated prices in order to recoup realtors' and related purchase fees. Given these untenable options, many families chose to abandon their homes, and the defunct properties became part of HUD's inventory, making HUD the largest real estate owner and manager in the entire country by the early 1970s. Section 235 was suspended in 1973, reactivated in 1976, and finally terminated in 1989.

In an attempt to shed its unwanted role as real estate mogul, HUD tried to tap into American affection for homesteading by transferring select foreclosed properties in its inventory (generally those with value less than $5,000) to local governments for $1 each under a 1974 Property Release Options Program (PROP), with properties to be reused for either homesteading or other public purposes. Under HUD rules, however, all qualifying units had to have no remaining market value, leaving essentially only the most severely damaged properties available for this sort of reclamation. With such limitations, cities often refused to take on such properties for homesteading, arguing the program did not prove cost-effective for cities, given that the cost of rehabilitating severely dilapidated units often exceeded the value of the house itself. In the rare instances where individuals actually showed an interest in buying these properties, the renovation and rehabilitation of that housing unit did not result in more low-income stock, since only wealthy individuals could actually afford the high costs. And realistically, such scenarios were too rare to have any real impact on policy. Given these disincentives, many cities chose instead to demolish properties and to create parks or open spaces. In much the same way many developing nations found it more practical to raze rather than rehabilitate slums, so also did HUD's actions trigger further governmental disinvestment in low-income housing provision.

Even with these results, HUD continued to prioritize homeownership and aided self-help techniques over any large-scale reconsideration of this tenure type as a universal ideal. HUD officials removed the requirement that properties have no remaining market value under PROP, and instead put forward a Housing and Community Development Act (1974) that allowed HUD to transfer one- to four-unit properties once owned with mortgages insured by the FHA, FmHA, or VA and since foreclosed by lenders and repossessed by the government, without cost, to local governments for reuse in homesteading programs. (Section 810 of the act removed the zero-value condition.) This new policy opened up nearly all single-family HUD inventory for potential homesteading, and cities could henceforth give title to abandoned public property in exchange for the new homeowners' promise to repair, maintain, and live in the home.[151]

As a first step in this program, HUD developed the Urban Home-steading Demonstration in cooperation with interested local govern-ments. Between 1975–77, thirty-eight cities signed demonstration agree-ments with the federal government. Local governments made most program design and operation decisions, thus allowing municipal gov-ernments to be more creative in their approach to homesteading.[152] The demonstration included $5 million initial authorization for cities to acquire HUD-owned, vacant property. In addition, the federal gov-ernment provided funds for technical assistance as cities chose a "tar-get neighborhood" for an upgrade of public services and facilities. The new owner, meanwhile, applied for one of three types of rehabilitation and home improvement loans: they could choose from private, city agency, or section-312 federal government loans. (The federal govern-ment strongly preferred the first option, of course, since the purpose of the program was to encourage more private investment in housing rehabilitation.)

By the 1980s and '90s, low-income homeownership had become the favored policy of all politicians, whether Democrat or Republican. Homeownership constituted a laudable, uncontroversial goal that showcased concern with poverty and racial inequalities while still en-dorsing government-backed "private" housing over any openly public provision. Low-income homeownership made unlikely bedfellows of the National Association of Home Builders, the Enterprise Foundation, mortgage bankers, government officials, community organizations, and low-income housing advocates, most of whom agreed that "despite its problems, [the] FHA is still needed, particularly the credit enhancement qualities it brings to underserved populations needing housing."[153] If the FHA worked together with private sector institutions, they could "bet-ter manage known risk" and "spread the risk associated with lending in underserved communities." This would lead to the beneficial "deliv-ery of private capital to underserved areas and offer the opportunity for both the FHA and private institutions to learn more about lending in un-familiar markets."[154]

New mortgage instruments facilitated "underserved" clients' access to what was now regularly referred to as the American dream of homeown-ership. Some early efforts in the 1980s included the Graduated Payment Mortgage program (1980), which reduced down-payment requirements and made initial payments affordably low; the Nehemiah Program (1987) which promoted low- and moderate-income homeownership by allowing grants to nonprofits for loan programs and by providing up to 6% of total sales cost for those qualifying for an FHA loan; and last but not least, the adjustable-rate, price-level-adjusted, shared appreciation, and reverse annuity mortgages, which all offered more accessible loans. By the 1990s, government-sponsored enterprises were also responding to the congressional affordability goal as established by the Federal Housing Enterprise Financial Safety and Soundness Act of 1992. The act "set targets for the share of loans purchased by the GSEs that should be made to low-income individuals and in low-income neighborhoods . . . [and] made it easier to justify investments in securities backed by subprime loans that had been targeted to low-income borrowers and neighborhoods."[155] President George H. W. Bush's Homeownership and Opportunity for People Everywhere program (HOPE, 1989) helped the private sector to build more affordable housing, with $3.9 billion in budget authority and over $750 million in local, state, or nonprofit matching funds. Meanwhile Title II of the Cranston-Gonzalez National Affordable Housing Act offered formula grants to states and local governments for more low-income housing (both owner-occupied and rental), while HOPE I (1992) provided $161 million for grants to fund activities to develop and implement successful homeownership programs for public and Indian housing residents. (British "right-to-buy" policies provided an important model for HOPE's conversion of some public housing into owner-occupied units.)[156]

Rental assistance and public housing programs, while important, nowhere approached the scale of homeownership programs. By 1995, FHA insured over 23 million mortgages at a total value of $751.7 billion, and by 2007, mortgage interest deduction cost the federal government $73.7 billion in forgone taxes, making it arguably the single largest government housing program. Homeownership in multifamily housing also increased steadily from the 1960s to the 2000s.[157] By comparison, HUD provided rental assistance to only 4.7 million families, of which 1.4 million were in public housing units.[158]

National homeownership programs reflected a complex process of policymaking that included economists, private actors, politicians, and community leaders. While each program deserves closer scrutiny in separate studies, here it is perhaps most on point to highlight homeownership's connection to broader perceptions of risk, the health of the national economy, and more subtly, to American perceptions and promotion of their country as a land of equal opportunity. Even in the 1920s, homeownership had been excellent politics, but now it became so popular that cautionary signs went unheeded. When homeownership rates went into a downturn in 1994, president Bill Clinton directed HUD secretary Henry Cisneros to convene public and private housing industry representatives to devise "creative" financing strategies to overcome financial barriers for low-income potential buyers.[159] A Homeownership Zone Initiative (1996) provided federal seed money for local municipalities to build new neighborhoods of mixed-income, single-family homes around employment centers. A Self-Help Homeownership Opportunity Program in the same year made funds available for land acquisition and infrastructure improvement for housing projects using self-help or volunteer construction labor. Homeownership had developed a seemingly unstoppable momentum.

Some federally insured lenders responded to the more ambitious nationwide homeownership campaign by lowering mortgage underwriting and risk-assessment standards, provoking Federal Reserve chairman Alan Greenspan to advise lenders to look beyond computer-generated models of risk: "Human judgments, based on analytically looser, but far more realistic evaluations of what the future may hold, are of critical importance in risk management," he noted.[160] Still, corporate leaders like executive vice president of the Federal Home Loan Mortgage Corporation Michael Stamper believed homeownership was good business, and he argued that targeted, affordable-housing lending was "no more risky than traditional products for higher-income borrowers" when done well.[161] The Clinton administration and HUD secretary Andrew Cuomo forged ahead with a new goal of 67.5% homeownership rate by 2000, up from the already record-setting 66.4% in 1998. The same year, HUD enthusiastically launched a national Homeownership Week (1998), with 1,200 events in over 600 locations, bringing together America's Community Bankers, Neighborhood Reinvestment Corporation, National Community Development Association, the National Association of Realtors, and HUD, among others, in a cooperative effort to increase homeownership through the "successful efforts of a partnership of public, private, and nonprofit organizations."[162] Warnings were issued, to little immediate effect. In March 2000, for instance, a HUD-Treasury Task Force investigated predatory lending practices, yielding a series of reports "documenting the explosive growth in subprime mortgage markets and the accompanying rise in foreclosures, demonstrating that low-income and minority communities are more likely to be victims of predatory lending."[163]

The shift to a Republican administration was smooth from the point of view of homeownership advocates. A national homeownership program within section 8 (2001) opened up more avenues for low-income access by providing vouchers for any mortgage costs above the usual

30% of income, and George W. Bush reaffirmed the federal government's commitment to an "ownership society," including most importantly, homeownership. The FHA began issuing zero-down-payment mortgages through the American Dream Downpayment Initiative in 2003, and it offered more flexible requirements under the American Homeownership Act in 2006.[164] There were few limits on the potential expansion of homeownership to thus far underserved populations; even the residents of so-called *colonias* along the US-Mexico border lambasted for being "pathological aberrations visited upon urban areas" and sources of "vice, crime, indigence, and illegal-immigrant residence that above all presented a major public-health problem"[165] became part of a HUD and Federal Deposit Insurance Corporation program (Money Smart Financial Education Curriculum, 2001–) to educate potential borrowers about credit and banking services.[166] The more they knew, "the more likely they [would be] to build real assets in the form of savings, a down payment on a home, and other benefits of good financial health," HUD literature argued.[167]

HUD publicized the benefits of increased minority homeownership, noting in 2002 that 5.5 million more homeowning families would generate $256 billion, primarily through taxes and new manufacturing and construction jobs, and that minority homeownership could fuel billions in new wages, state and federal tax revenues, and interior appliance and décor purchases.[168] The following year, Angelo Mozilo observed the critical role "minority and low-income sectors" would play as "emerging markets" for companies such as his Countrywide Financial. An ever-widening search for mortgage customers resulted in a rapid expansion of subprime mortgage originations from 2003 to 2005, with Countrywide Financial Corporation becoming the single largest mortgage origina-tor from 2004 to 2007. According to a New York Stock Exchange ar-ticle in May 2005, Mozilo was an "American Dream Builder" valiantly pursuing low-income and minority customers, with nearly half a mil-lion loans made to African American, Hispanic, Asian-Pacific Islander, American Indian, Alaskan, and Native homeowners in 2003 alone.[169] Even after the subprime mortgage meltdown and the financial crisis, Mozilo staunchly defended his company and his lending practices to a government Financial Crisis Inquiry Commission, stating his toxic loans helped 25 million people buy homes and "prevented social unrest by extending loans to minorities, historically the victims of discrimi-nation."[170] No homeownership crisis could change the fact that mass homeownership yielded so many political benefits. For Mozilo, the mass homeownership ideal was alive and well, all evidence to the contrary.

Resilient Ideology, Vulnerable Homeowners

American ideas about homeownership evolved tremendously from the 1960s to the early 2000s. Because of world events and a watchful global public, homeownership became a way to demonstrate the equal opportunities available to people of all colors and classes in the United States. Native reservations and homeownership programs became important sites of experimentation and implementation of globally shared practices, while homesteading and low-income homeownership programs likewise built on the momentum of developing world programs.

Low-income homeownership did not yield touted benefits to low-income families, but it was immensely profitable. In fact, low-income homeownership was advantageous for almost everyone except the new homeowners themselves: politicians could claim to be helping the poor without building public housing. The middle class benefited from second-tier investments while enjoying the moral satisfaction of their own, "earned" position in the social hierarchy. Bankers and investors thrived. It was left to low-income homeowners to learn in the most direct and profound ways what the costs of mass homeownership might be.

SIX

A Homeownership Consensus?

Owning a home is a universal dream. US OVERSEAS PRIVATE INVESTMENT
CORPORATION, 2010

Ten years after creating the term "Washington Consensus,"
economist John Williamson ruefully observed its unexpected popularity: "While it is jolly to become famous
by inventing a term that reverberates around the world,"
he wrote, "I have long been doubtful as to whether the
phrase that I coined served to advance the cause of rational
economic policymaking."[1] Rather, Williamson suggested,
phrases like "universal convergence" or "one-world consensus" might have better conveyed the sense of intellectual
agreement that lay beneath many economic policy discussions at the end of the Cold War.

Indeed, "universal convergence" and "one-world consensus" are equally tempting descriptions of the homeownership ideal at the end of the twentieth century: by the late
1980s and early 1990s, single-family, owner-occupied housing with some form of government support seemed an unquestionable good for international housing aid programs,
eliciting little debate or controversy in UN housing discussions, USAID policies, World Bank debates, or any number
of other international forums. Homeownership seemed a
natural goal with obvious benefits rather than a tool of American soft power or a US system forcibly replicated around
the world. Hidden in this language of self-evident value
was the long history of American interest. Under secretary

of the Treasury for international affairs Timothy Geithner observed the state of the Washington Consensus in 1999—"I don't think anyone believes there is a universal model that can or should be imposed on the world—Washington consensus, post Washington consensus, or not"—but the preponderance of a very specific homownership ideal belied Geithner's claim to diversity.[2] Mass homownership had and continues to have considerable allure as one potential path to modernization and middle-class growth across the global South—a fact that reflects the aggressive marketing of American-style capitalism and democracy rather than any sudden "natural" recognition of mass homeownership's intrinsic values.

This last chapter turns to the question of consensus in World Bank housing and asks how Bank programs affected the way policymakers in the developing world saw mass homeownership. Did a "universal convergence" exist in the late twentieth century? By looking closely at the World Bank's sites and services and slum upgrading programs of the 1970s and 1980s and the transition to market-enabling strategies in the 1980s, and then to sector-wide initiatives in the 1990s and 2000s, it becomes clear the consensus existed more at the level of ideology than practice, and more with policymakers than with new homeowners. Low-income homeowners often had little choice but to accept their new status and the heavy costs exacted from them for this privilege. Details from specific cases reveal the ways policy-level consensus resulted in widely varying experiences of homeownership on the ground. The Bank was not the only international financial institution or intergovernmental organization interested in such questions, of course, and so the chapter also includes a brief discussion of the ongoing activities of USAID, the Overseas Private Investment Corporation (formerly within the foreign investment operations division of USAID), and HUD's Office of International Affairs in the 1990s and 2000s.

Why a Washington Consensus?

The World Bank often used the language of consensus—language that implied acceptance of the inherent virtues of homeownership—from the 1970s on. While the Bank was not the direct mouthpiece of the American government, American officials and experts both within and outside the Bank certainly informed evolving ideas about appropriate housing aid programs. Even as a relative latecomer to international housing efforts, the Bank was a disproportionately powerful player by the

1980s and '90s as one of the fastest growing and largest funders of housing aid globally. Bank policies could determine the options available to developing countries as they struggled to address domestic housing shortages. Even in countries that did not receive direct housing assistance, Bank policies could exert considerable influence: "If Washington played no direct role in establishing the new housing policy," geographer Alan Gilbert observed of Colombia in the 1990s, "one point must be remembered. The basic tenets of the new housing policy were quintessentially neo-liberal. . . . Local housing experts considered outside experience but looked only at appropriate experience."[3] The Bank also carried disproportionate weight as the "'flagship' of all development banks in the world": the actions of regional development banks and other international financial institutions often followed the models set by the World Bank, and together they compelled national governments to accept "the confines of an ideological corset," to borrow Gilbert's phrase.[4] Bank economist Joseph Stiglitz may have exhorted governments to "scan globally and reinvent locally," but in practice there were many layers of political pressure and economic persuasion shaping housing policies.

From the start, the US made sure to protect national self-interest in the structure of the Bank, exhibiting little interest in diluting or dispersing decision-making power for loans primarily fueled by American dollars. When developing nations urged the creation of an internationally governed Special United Nations Fund for Economic Development from 1953 to the 1960s, for instance, the US blocked their efforts and instead pushed for the formation of an International Development Association (IDA, 1960–) within the World Bank as a largely autonomous agency more directly under the control of the US.[5] (As a concession, the US supported the creation of a more international Special Fund in the UN under Paul Hoffman.) The IDA almost immediately began recommending the Bank expand into "welfare" provisions and start "loosening IBRD discipline" in line with American foreign policy interests, particularly in Latin America in the 1960s.[6] By one account, "after striving for fifteen years to achieve Wall Street respectability, the Bank watched as IDA suddenly materialized and conjured up the 1940s' augury that the Bank would grow up to be a soup kitchen."[7] This somewhat uneasy coexistence of "looser" IDA and "tighter" IBRD lending persisted throughout the 1960s, as the IDA and Bank entered "new activities and countries" driven "less by sentimentality than by political fear, intellectual innovation, and the Bank's own organizational urge to expand."[8] The IDA encouraged more "social" and "soft" lending programs, while the Bank sought to "assure investors in Bank bonds that their interest in the Bank would not be diluted by the diversion of funds into the softer IDA channels."[9]

In addition to the IDA, Bank officials maintained other practical and ideological bonds with the US government—in particular, the State Department—as the Bank depended on the latter for "reports and advice on developments in borrowing countries that are of interest."[10] Bank officials like vice president Burke Knapp insisted the Bank "strongly maintain[ed] our autonomy and independence," but Knapp could hardly deny that the US Treasury secretary served as the governor for the Bank, the US was the principal shareholder, and "de facto the United States government could always mobilize a majority of the board against any operation on which they wanted to impose a political veto."[11] Knapp added, "If there is any doubt as to whether the United States government will support an operation by the Bank, it's just as well for us to know that at an early stage of the game, and the way we usually find that out is through contacts with the State Department."

Even with various American inputs and explicit IDA interest in soft lending, it took time for urban and housing issues to become part of the Bank's overall agenda. Not until the early 1970s did the Bank finally begin addressing low-income shelter needs, and then, mostly as a way to rationalize urban growth and to in some way address the problem of swelling informal settlements. Again, compared to other intergovernmental organizations and international financial institutions actively engaged in questions of housing, including the US Agency for International Development (USAID), the Inter-American Development Bank (IADB), the Asian Development Bank (ADB), the United Nations Centre for Human Settlements (HABITAT), and the United Nations Development Programme (UNDP), the Bank was a relatively late contributor. Key individuals like Robert McNamara were responsible for this institutional change of heart. By the logic of those pushing for urban programs, homeownership required clear land titles and better government records; the system drew a line between legitimate and illegitimate occupation, between profitable and marginal property. Homeownership could bring largely unregulated land uses into alignment with official bureaucratic and legal practices, benefiting its proponents, in particular politicians, investors, and elite urban residents. Even more importantly, homeownership at various income levels and with a wider range of affordable, low-cost, low-income housing options could fulfill the primary goal of "mobiliz[ing] private savings and . . . reliev[ing] the public sector of most of the financial burden for urban services."[12] By this logic, homeownership would increase family savings and motivate greater labor force participation through debt, primarily in the form of mortgages. It would open up access to credit, security, and social mobility for poorer families, helping them plug into the benefits of a capitalist system while enjoying ever-increasing living standards based at least in part on their own efforts. At least in theory, homeownership could organize all manner of unruly properties and people into a coherent, capitalist system that benefited those who managed it.

A closer examination of key moments in housing aid at the end of the twentieth century reveals a much more complex story than that of a triumphant homeownership ideal, however. While many planners, housing experts, and government officials in Southeast and South Asia, Latin America, and sub-Saharan Africa tested techniques that relied fundamentally on mass homeownership and on owner occupation, they did so not because they bought wholeheartedly into the rhetoric of equal opportunity and larger societal investment through owner occupation per se, but rather because they were "persuaded" by outside pressures and because more often than not they needed politically viable ways to dodge what they perceived to be the crushing costs of public provision. When governments could afford public housing and when they felt such largesse was politically necessary, they easily switched from one tenure type to another. Tellingly, few policymakers relied exclusively on homeownership experiments; instead, they tested them in conjunction with other programs in social housing, cooperative living, and a wide array of mixed tenure types. While the actions of international organizations like the World Bank, the UN, USAID, or regional development banks might fit within a narrative of global consensus, then, a fuller account of actors, motives, and methods reveals all too quickly how complicated and multilayered this seeming meeting of minds was in reality.

The opinions and experiences of slum dwellers and squatters only further muddied the waters. From a grassroots perspective, homeownership could be a weapon as much as a reward or dream. Government officials and business leaders often enacted homeownership programs whose purpose was to better regulate, control, and more often than not reduce the costs of rehousing poor people and evacuating unsightly informal settlements from prime urban real estate. It was not readily apparent what value semirural or sub-urban homeownership had when taken as compensation for the written promise to never return to informal urban settlements, for instance. Few families would deny the desirability of owning their own home, but affordability, location, access to informal urban jobs, and a sense of the familiar also worked as

countervailing forces in their shelter decisions. Furthermore, the benefits of homeownership were not as clear given the varieties of that ownership, the experimental nature of early programs, and the volatility of
many political regimes.

Given this context, it makes more sense to think about the evolving
uses of consensus language in the late twentieth century than to try
to write an objective timeline of when individuals and countries sub-
scribed to this ideal, whether or not there were enough adherents to
make it a truly global consensus, and whether or not motives aligned
perfectly with each other. Consensus was never an immoveable fact.
When governments and housing officials found the language of univer-
sality and inevitability useful in attaining certain political, social, and
economic goals, they employed it. The appearance of consensus could
help governments court international aid and navigate domestic political pressures while wooing foreign investors and seeking competitive
advantage in a global marketplace. Conversely, when individuals and
families found homeownership policies coercive or detrimental to their
interests, they spoke of their new tenure security as a form of forced
exclusion from the center city. In those moments, homeownership represented an upper-class "consensus" to lock away helpless relocatees on
remote land they did not want, in houses they could not pay for.

Given the contentious nature of homeownership campaigns, it is
difficult to assess whether or not title actually improved the lives of
poor urban residents. Here again, World Bank housing programs reveal
just how complex homeownership was, not only ideologically but in
implementation. Bank housing programs repeatedly ran into troubles,
whether because of deliberately obstructionist acts by opponents, the
sludge of bureaucracy, larger political and societal upheavals, or any
manner of other roadblocks. These multifaceted experiences give a much
fuller understanding of homeownership in the late twentieth century:
while ideas of personal investment, increased savings, "bootstraps" capitalism, and the like made homeownership a seductive ideology, in reality
this tenure type did not always give people more stability or security; it
did not always result in more class mobility for low-income families; it
did not consistently inspire squatters with a stronger sense of community or citizenship, or it did so in ways that the ruling government did
not find desirable; it did not always produce a sustainable, low-cost, private solution for governments overwhelmed by mushrooming informal
settlements. The World Bank pressured many government officials and
policymakers to attempt its housing techniques, but it could not guarantee results, nor could it bypass processes of local negotiation. Often,

those policymakers and officials still embracing the homeownership ideal did so not because it had proved successful, but rather because other options—for instance, substantive government redistribution or pricey public provision—proved far more distasteful. Lastly and perhaps most importantly, the Bank did not always act as the direct mouthpiece for American foreign policy (although it often did), nor did it successfully impose American homeownership ideals to all its loan recipients (although it often did).

Tackling Urban Poverty

The World Bank's urban housing–related lending programs are typically grouped into distinct phases. The first period, from 1945 to 1972, was marked mostly by neglect, as the Bank focused on European recovery (1945 to 1948), investment in infrastructure (especially energy and transportation) in the developing world over any "social" or "unproductive" investments in urban housing (1948 to the late 1950s), and poverty in the agricultural sector (1960s) stemming mostly from the popularity of the competitive-advantage thesis (again, to the neglect of both urban problems and housing issues). In the second phase, starting in 1972, the Bank began actively considering urban poverty and basic housing needs. In that year, the Bank published the influential *Urbanization Sector Working Paper* and created the Urban Development Department. In the process of looking for "urban analogues" to the small farmer of previous rural development projects, the "frustration of that search left housing for the poor, by default, as the principle vehicle for an urban poverty effort."[13] Bank officials began with aided self-help and then slum upgrading schemes, but failed to meet their own goals, most notably in the arena of cost recovery. In the third phase of activity from the mid-1980s to the early 2000s, the Bank inaugurated a sector-wide integrative strategy that focused on private-sector development and greater access to market-based housing finance.[14] Most recently, the Bank has added a renewed call for attention to low-income housing access.

Without diminishing the importance of these shifts in housing policies, Bank officials have remained remarkably consistent on one point since 1972: homeownership is a preferred tenure type, and increased access to that homeownership, an intrinsically desirable goal. Debates have centered on what role homeownership plays in the development process (is it the end result or a tool?) and what specific steps the Bank should take to address housing inefficiencies and inadequacies, but rarely have

Bank officials reflected on the demerits of homeownership or contemplated large-scale public or cooperative housing as an alternative. Rental housing is necessary to a vibrant private housing system but has less political and emotional appeal than homeownership.

Bank interest in such issues, and more generally, in the explosive growth of cities in the developing world, began under the leadership of a few individuals. Most Bank reports highlight the importance of president Robert McNamara's concern with issues of urban poverty as first formally articulated in his 1975 address in Nairobi. Equally critical, David Henderson and Douglas Keare (Development Economics Department), Robert Sadove (Special Projects Division), Edward Jaycox (Transportation and Urban Projects Department), and Michael Cohen (Urban Poverty Task Force and later director of the Bank's Urban Division), among others, urged the Bank to become more directly engaged with urban housing issues. Together these men built on the experiences of Jacob Crane, Ernest Weissmann, Charles Abrams, John Turner, William Mangin, Janice Perlman, Otto Koenigsberger, and other predecessors in the field of international housing aid to formulate a new urban program for the Bank. Urban advocates faced skepticism both internally and externally, and they worked hard to convince developing world governments and fellow Bank workers that antipoverty measures could, in fact, generate greater economic productivity and not merely drain precious resources into endless welfare provision. Well-crafted housing programs could further macroeconomic aims while improving the lives of the urban poor, they argued, whereas inaction would exacerbate already dangerous problems of rapid urbanization, explosive slum proliferation, and an ever-widening income gap.[15] Bank officials advocating urban lending carefully set apart their proposed programs from earlier bilateral aid programs, critiquing previous experiments even as they borrowed terms and techniques like aided self-help. For example, USAID-backed single-family homes in Latin America "were actually responsive to prospective middle-class homeowners but were prohibitively expensive to the urban poor," according to Cohen, whereas "the Bank began to ask much more basic questions about how to actually 'reach the poor.'"[16]

In an important first step, executive directors decided to fund an experimental fifty-year urban development loan of US$8 million for a sites-and-services project in the Cap Vert region of Senegal. This demonstration project made clear from the outset how important homeownership was to the test case of Senegal and how central it would be to subsequent Bank housing loans. The project itself was a massive endeavor, relocating roughly a quarter of Dakar's 1970 population into a new town built on large sand dunes six miles from central Dakar south of Cambérène and west of the city of Pikine.[17] Despite the fact that homeownership "ran counter to both the legal context and the country's political philosophy," Bank officials maintained that for the new town of Parcelles Assainies (translated, Sanitary Plots), "ownership was a necessary incentive to private investment in shelter," and all relocatees needed to be granted freehold on sites-and-services plots.[18] Homeownership was no mere detail: Bank officials were specifically interested in seeing if low-income homeowners would invest in their housing given tenure security. For the Bank, that security could only come in the form of freeholds, not government occupancy permits.

Bank insistence on free title came as something of a surprise to the Senegalese government. Prior to Bank involvement, the French colonial—and after 1960, independent Senegalese—government had begun large-scale resettlement projects in Pikine, Guédjawaye, and Grand Yoff, removing squatters from downtown Dakar and granting permanent occupancy permits on *domaine national* (state-owned land) fitted with basic infrastructure. The colonial administration engaged in a "process of dialogue and negotiation with traditional landlords [that] stemmed from the tacit acknowledgement by the colonial authorities of the rights of the Lebou people over the land in the Cape Verde peninsula"—a tradition of negotiated land rights that continued after independence.[19] In postcolonial urban decentralization efforts, the national government converted cleared central urban land to various uses, in particular, to the development of middle-income public housing provided by the Office des Habitations à Loyer Modéré (OHLM) and upper-income public housing provided by the Société Immobilière du Cap Vert (SICAP). The longevity and established character of these programs were in fact the main reasons Bank officials selected Senegal as a first location for its sites-and-services funding. The Senegalese government for its part welcomed a Bank loan as a potential expansion of existing programs, with external funds feeding but not fundamentally changing existing relocation and public housing programs.

Despite this history, Bank officials immediately insisted on freehold over occupancy permits for all sites-and-services homes, slum upgrading over slum eradication, and the gradual elimination of all public subsidies to SICAP and OHLM upon entry into the housing scene. Even when Senegalese government officials aired concerns over the potential deterioration of Parcelles Assainies into an enormous *bidonville* (slum) of 140,000, the Bank insisted on immediate occupancy through temporary wooden shelters and asserted the project would "reduce the risk of social unrest precisely because it offered an opportunity to the urban poor to find employment, own their own homes and live better."[20] Senegalese officials resented the stubborn insistence on titling, suspected that the Bank harbored "a political, even ideological motivation that concern for the proper implementation of the project alone did not warrant," and deplored the "expert mentality" that "impose[d] analyses, concepts, and philosophy options that not take sufficient account of the country's own choices."[21] Ultimately, though, Senegalese officials succumbed to Bank conditions after "much discussion and intense Bank pressure."[22]

Bank officials did in fact bring a "political, even ideological motivation": they saw sites-and-services programs as a way to promote private over public systems of housing production and improvement while also demonstrating to skeptical Bank colleagues the productive possibilities of low-income housing loans. A Bank economic mission visiting Senegal in 1972 openly remarked that "one of the main reasons the Bank participated in the Site and Services project" of Cambérène was to rein back public investment in low-income housing through a "new orientation to lower cost dwellings."[23] To the Bank's dismay, however, the sluggish pace of intergovernmental negotiations, institutional reorganization, and household savings all slowed project implementation and resulted in confusing declarations of success and failure from both the Bank and the Senegalese government. Assessments were complicated by the fact that "the Bank as a whole had invested so much of its institutional prestige that it could not afford a failure."[24]

Despite this somewhat unsteady beginning, World Bank urban housing programs gained momentum after the Dakar project, with small sites-and-services loans to low-income countries across Africa, Asia, and Latin America. Programs from 1972 to 1981 included but were not limited to India, Nicaragua, and Botswana (1973), Tanzania, Zambia, Jamaica, and El Salvador (1974), Kenya (1975, 1978), Peru (1976), Thailand (1978, 1980), and Brazil (1979), and together they amounted to US$1.5 billion in sixty-two projects affecting, by some estimates, 10 million individuals.[25] If housing projects constituted a proportionally tiny fraction of total Bank budgets, "in absolute terms . . . the amounts were huge," and "it was clear that by the mid-1970s the World Bank's lending activities overshadowed those of predecessor agencies."[26] As noted earlier, president Robert McNamara further paved the way for the Bank's involvement in 1975 when he formally announced the expansion of Bank antipoverty programs to include urban problems.[27]

Even as experiments continued, however, Bank officials feared that rising housing standards and ongoing dependence on subsidies would preclude the successful expansion of homeownership for truly impoverished urban communities. As a next attempt at targeting neglected populations, the Bank helped launch slum upgrading programs that focused more on improved access to services in informal settlements (for instance, roads, water, and street lighting) as opposed to building new units, increasing housing stock, and relocating populations, as was generally done with sites-and-services projects. Upgrading programs were meant to directly target the very poorest residents of urban centers where they lived. By eliminating the disruption of resettlement and by tackling poverty where it occurred, the Bank hoped to have greater impact than relocation-oriented aided self-help projects had thus far. The further reduction in housing standards in upgrading schemes also fit with the Bank mantra that governments needed to move away from higher quality, unaffordable public provision and toward smaller-scale personal investment in housing improvement schemes through more secure tenure (i.e., homeownership).

As part of the effort to target low-income urbanites, the Bank distinguished distinct income levels within the category of "urban poor." In one of its first slum upgrading efforts in Francistown, Botswana (1974), Bank workers tied different housing assistance programs to each level. The lowest tier would utilize minimally equipped settlement plots; the middle, slum upgrading; and the top, aided sites-and-services. According to the Bank, this system would "accommodate even the poorest sections of the population and ensure affordability" even as it transformed informal settlers into homeowners.[28] Unfortunately, even such fine-grained measurements of poverty could not mitigate the cost recovery issues that plagued the Botswana program from beginning to end. The Bank praised it as a success with "widely perceived benefits (and resultant credibility) of [an] approach to urban development" that emphasized, among other points, "the preparation of an urban investment program that would be simple, practical and low cost and would not require subsidies."[29] It was hard to imagine how subsidies could be avoided, however, and the same problems of loan defaults and poor repayment rates appeared repeatedly not only in Francistown but also in subsequent projects in the country, including two USAID programs in Gaborone and Lobatse. This repetition should not have surprised USAID officials, given that both the Gaborone and Lobatse projects were initiated in response to the Bank's experiences in Francistown, and that the Bank and USAID collaborated throughout, sharing data, maps, technical knowledge, and best practices.[30] With default rates high and cost recovery elusive, the neoliberal emphasis on government aid for private housing and investment looked uncomfortably similar to straightforward subsidies.

Intimately tied to low cost recovery was the enormous challenge of land titling. Bank officials believed families would not pay back loans or invest in their homes if they did not feel some degree of tenure security. In the case of Botswana, however, tenure security depended heavily on a well-funded, technically and administratively competent land board. The State Land Act of 1966 conveyed all British colonial titles to the newly independent state, and the national Department of Surveys and Land still needed to rationalize and demarcate plots and then issue certificates of rights before any building loans could be issued by the World Bank.[31] For those lands under tribal ownership, separate boards needed to be consulted and use rights, secured. These sorts of titling issues were hardly unique to Botswana. In another Bank project begun the same year as the one in Francistown, the Tanzania Housing Bank required title for any house loan in sites-and-services and upgrading efforts, with resulting bureaucratic delays of three years on average (Tanzanian First National Sites and Services Project, 1974).[32] In the Zambian informal settlement of Chawama (Lusaka), Bank-funded sites-and-services and upgrading programs required the Department of Lands to verify all claims to occupancy licenses (Housing [Statutory and Improvement Areas] Act of 1975). By the time government workers actually did so, the supposed beneficiaries had little interest in claiming these legal rights, as residents already felt considerable security from their extended length of stay; collection required full payment of service charges; financial institutions did not consistently recognize licenses in mortgage lending in any case; and even the government did not accept licenses as proof of eligibility for homeowner allowances.[33] Clearly, every country had its own peculiar combination of challenges when it came to tenure security, including but not limited to a shortage of trained surveyors, government resistance to aerial surveys for security reasons, a maze of preexisting bureaucracy, and nonconforming "traditional" renting and homeowning practices. Much as homeownership did not mean exactly the same thing from country to country, so also did titling benefits and rights change depending on the legal and cultural context.

Even more perplexing for Bank officials, housing programs were vulnerable to people acting precisely the way economists might expect. Families lived in their homes when they thought they could save more money doing so, and they rented or sold their homes when they found that path more lucrative. In Dandora, Kayole, and Mathare North (eastern

Nairobi, Kenya), a twenty-year (1971–91), US $424 million "incremental housing model" aimed at promoting owner-occupant housing ended up "help[ing] improve the efficiency of rental markets by keeping rent-to-income ratios at an affordable level in low-income areas."[34] It did so through a process of "gentrification," in the World Bank's words: poor households were first allotted land parcels with core units at cost rather than at market price. They were then encouraged to slowly upgrade with loans and technical assistance, thus minimizing public housing subsidies. Enormous demand for housing sharply raised the value of these units, giving parcel holders strong incentives to sell their properties at profit to land speculators and return to renting status. Speculators rented Bank-supported upgrading units to a higher tier of low-income families, increasing the overall rental market and displacing the very low-income families with a "gentrified" new class of residents. For the small minority of original plot owners in Dandora who did not sell, most decided to become absentee landlords themselves, renting out their units and renting cheaper housing for themselves elsewhere. At best, then, the Bank's homeownership efforts failed to stop a broader trend of declining owner occupancy from 29% in 1983 to 7% in 1993, and at worst, actively created the conditions by which truly low-income Nairobians would become renters.[35] While homeownership and secure title seemed like good ways to meet the needs of the poorest urban dwellers, each local housing system operated differently and no general formula had been proven effective by the late 1970s.

Community, People's Power, and Homeownership

The closest the Bank came to a model technique was in its slum upgrading programs in Southeast Asia. In its Kampung Improvement Programs in Jakarta and Surabaya (1974–79), and an upgrading program in Tondo, Manila, the Bank encouraged community participation in urban planning as a way to encourage personal investment. Both became early showcases for successful urban upgrading techniques, demonstrating effective avenues for nurturing community and individual investment via tenure security. In the case of Indonesia, the Bank argued that the complex, four-part *hak milik* (right of ownership), *hak guna bangunan* (right to build), *hak sewa* (tenant rights), and *hak pakai* (right of use) confused residents and took away potential benefits of ownership. In its place, the Bank urged a single legal system of government-managed paper certificates that replicated the US system of titling. The Bank also provided loans to continue government Kampung Improvement Programs already in the process of adding roads, water and sewage, schools, and other amenities to poor urban *kampungs* (villages). Additionally, the Bank helped establish two new urban institutions, the National Urban Development Corporation and the National Mortgage Bank.[36] By the end of the fourth and last urban development loan (1992), the Bank had invested US$438.3 million in the Kampung Improvement Programs, and both Bank and Indonesian government reports proudly touted gains in health, services, and urban infrastructure. By streamlining titling procedures and improving amenities (as well as funding for those amenities), the Bank hoped residents would naturally recognize the benefits of homeownership.

As an attempt to smooth the transition from prior housing systems to Bank-sanctioned ones, Bank and government officials claimed to be making use of local traditions of mutual cooperation and aid; they were simply building upon the timeless Javanese principle of *gotong royong* and Filipino *bayanihan*, or mutual help. Modernization campaigns were anchored in native practices of community cooperation and local civil action, they argued, and global housing systems shared core ideals with ongoing domestic practices. In putting forward this sort of "history" and context, Bank workers and politicians constructed a path to participation in a global capitalist marketplace, one that progressed naturally from "traditional" values to capitalist, modern housing systems. Mutual aid served as a sort of bridge from tradition to modernity. The Bank workers observed *gotong royong* only among the lowest classes in Indonesian cities. As families raised incomes and standards of living, mutual cooperation and consensus-making practices broke down in favor of highly atomized household decisions.[37] One of the key findings of the Kampung Improvement Programs was that "community consultation and participation in the early stages of project preparation and design was important for instilling a sense of project ownership by the community," and that this community ownership would eventually become unnecessary as single-family households achieved greater degrees of tenure security and economic upward mobility through homeownership.[38] Successful projects required ideological and practical consensus among "senior policymakers and key officials" in the host country and the Bank—a homeownership consensus of sorts, but certainly nothing approaching the actual spirit of community cooperation in *gotong royong*. Ultimately, the Kampung Improvement Program's version of mass homeownership dissolved older bonds of community obligation and mutual aid.

Homeownership and community played out in equally complex ways in the Tondo case. Located in the northwestern corner of Manila, Tondo claimed upward of 180,000 residents, making it one of the largest informal settlements in the world. Given the site's size and political significance, it was natural that the Bank contemplated a project there. Startlingly, however, instead of endorsing the wholesale relocation and rapid redevelopment preferred by the Marcos administration, Bank officials worked closely with resident community organizations to reduce the number of families forcibly removed from the community and supported slum upgrading on-site when possible. Since density issues could only be resolved by some relocation, the Bank did believe some families needed to be shifted. In its choice of resettlement site, however, the Bank again showed consideration of resident needs, selecting a site five kilometers north of Tondo at Dagat-Dagatan so that individuals could still commute to work and stay in contact with friends and family. For those remaining in Tondo, Bank workers emphasized improved living conditions with better access to loans. These funds could be used to make self-help improvements and to install minimal services with community participation in both planning and implementation stages. The Bank intended to take a "people-centered approach" to the project, according to internal memos. As one official observed, "The essential element of this project is reaching an agreement on a scheme for renewal with the large, strongly organized inhabitants of this squatter area. . . . Without the cooperation of these people there can be no project."[39]

The Bank's "people-centered approach" was a practical one, and one that worked only because Bank interests in homeownership meshed well with informal dwellers' demands for tenure security. Long before the Bank took an interest in Tondo or Philippine housing, informal dwellers had sorted themselves into tenant organizations and had fought, sometimes separately, other times in a unified fashion, for landownership rights. As early as the 1950s, individual ownership had become a critical demand of increasingly marginalized squatters (I use *squatter* because the term captures the precarious legal position of Tondo residents): according to one resident collective known as Zone One Tondo Organization (ZOTO, 1970–), they were "haunted by the threat [of forcible ejection] and spurred by the strong desire to get themselves a small place in the sun, be it hell or otherwise."[40] From 1940 to 1969, land values in the National Capital Region of Metropolitan Manila increased an astonishing twenty-seven times as opposed to twelve to fifteen times across the rest of the nation.[41] Impoverished rural newcomers had little choice but to occupy the margins of formally owned land, building illegally or extra-legally on unused, unoccupied public and private property. After living sometimes for decades in such precarious and unhealthful circumstances, tenants began demanding title to the lands they occupied, in the process rejecting limited, often multifamily state housing schemes that left most residents vulnerable to relocation and that clashed with their own beliefs about decent shelter. In Tondo in particular, residents grew in numerical strength and organization, and by the 1970s various squatter groups had collided repeatedly with a national government interested more in modernizing the city and redeveloping the port and bay than in improving the lives of its poorest citizens. Squatters would no longer fall "easy prey to the soothing message and deadening effect of 'community development' programs," ZOTO proclaimed. Instead, they would collaborate with allies of all kinds—the Japanese International Cooperation Agency, the German government, Catholic Church leaders, and Jesuit priests, to name a few—and they would fight clearance schemes and demand more land rights.[42] The Bank's ideas about gradual improvement and tenure security made sense to squatters battling their illegal status.

In the midst of fierce battles between Tondo dwellers and the national government, Typhoon Gloring struck. Flooding was a routine occurrence in a country located in a tropical storm region and in a capital city with entire neighborhoods below the flood line (12.5 meters above sea level). The July 1972 storm exceeded all others that year in its ferocity, however, bringing much of the city to its knees. Communicable diseases and visible health crises spread rapidly, and the newly homeless and affluent alike struggled with impassable roads and widespread power outages. The floods could be attributed to a longer process of urbanization, including the installation of impermeable surfaces and the excessive use of ground water, but Marcos blamed informal dwellers for much of the trouble. According to the president, illegal shanties and refuse had clogged the Pasig River's *esteros*, making the city vulnerable to such catastrophes. All public lands and waterways needed to be cleared of illegal construction. One week after Marcos declared martial law on September 21, the military raided ZOTO headquarters and arrested leaders. Two weeks later, the government began demolition in Tondo. To add to the squatters' legal plight, Marcos issued Presidential Decree No. 722 in 1975 rendering all squatters criminals.

The World Bank became important in this context. The Bank did not introduce mass homeownership as an utterly foreign ideal to Tondo

29 In order to create a more orderly streetscape in Tondo, the World Bank launched a reblocking program in the mid-1970s. Reblocking entailed the movement of homes into organized
"blocks" and "neighborhoods." Such movement inevitably included the remote resettlement of some families. Manila, 1977. Source: Manila Urban Development Project—Philippines—
P004445—Loan 1272, Loan 1282—Correspondence—vol. 11, File Unit 30192945, ISAD(G)
Reference Code WB IBRD/IDA EAP, World Bank Group Archives, Washington, DC, United States.

residents; settlers had been demanding land rights for decades. Indeed,
according to the Bank's 1973 survey, "the reason why Tondo is overcrowded with houses is because the people prefer to live in a very small
barung-barong [shanty] that is their own rather than rent a place."[43] Nor
did the Bank launch community development programs for the first
time. Residents had already set up elaborate networks and knew how to
get media attention for their efforts. What the Bank *did* do was provide
financing and help build new institutions. With the newfound stability
brought by martial law, Robert McNamara expressed interest in deepening Bank investments in housing projects in Manila and in Tondo in
particular. Earlier Bank programs had faced roadblocks in the Philippine
legislative approval process. With Marcos firmly in charge, "the Bank
was fully prepared to more than double its current rate of lending if an
adequate number of projects could be prepared in time."[44] According to
one Brookings Institute retrospective, "Martial law triggered the takeoff
of Bank lending."[45]

Martial law also permitted large-scale institutional overhauls in the realms of urban planning and housing policy. Up until the early 1970s, seven housing agencies conducted ad hoc resettlement and rehousing projects.[46] In 1975, president Ferdinand Marcos replaced these agencies with a single National Housing Authority (NHA) charged with building medium-rise housing in central urban locations for low-income families, enacting slum upgrading schemes, and setting up new sites-and-services and resettlement programs. Other newly formed agencies focused on improving housing finance, including the development and management of a secondary mortgage market (National Home Mortgage Financing Corporation, 1977–), the management of forced savings (Home Development Mutual Fund/Pagtutulungan sa Kinabukasan: Ikaw, Bangko Industriya at Gobyerno or PAG-IBIG Fund, 1978–), and the regulation of land use and real estate (Housing and Land Use Regulatory Board, 1981–).[47]

While squatter groups won small victories and concessions from 1972 to 1977, by and large the regime had little interest in supporting informal settlements that had potentially volatile political groups embedded in them—groups that resisted development and modernization plans in an organized fashion, and that resisted the wholesale redevelopment of what Marcos saw as a large eyesore in a city with rapidly rising real estate values. When one of the larger groups, Zone One Tondo Organization, protested an April 1977 resettlement scheme that aimed to replace squatters with tourist hotels, ZOTO leader Trinidad Herrera was captured, interrogated, and tortured with electric shocks until she could no longer speak. News of the incident spread rapidly, and the international community—journalists, priests, Amnesty International, and humanitarians—condemned what appeared to be a joint World Bank–Marcos program of repression. In American congressional hearings, the World Bank became further implicated, with Representative Burke testifying, "Ms. Herrera had been detained by authorities after having expressed some concerns about aspects of the World Bank project in Manila's Tondo slum district."[48]

Internal World Bank records offer little insight into what officials must have thought at the time. The Bank repeatedly denied any involvement in Marcos's resettlement programs, but it stayed silent on the regime's approach. Later reports erased this moment completely, instead holding up Tondo as an example of how slum dwellers might improve their own homes if given security of tenure and various small incentives like improved services. A year later, the Bank funded a Second Urban Development Project that included a Slum Improvement and

Resettlement component (known as the Zonal Improvement Program in Metro Manila) directing 24% of all funding to upgrading in Philippine cities—"a major shift in Government emphasis from costly and subsidized programs of resettlement to improvement in situ with recovery of servicing costs."[49] Upgrading would cost a mere $505 per family versus $1,500 under resettlement programs; lease-purchase contracts would allow the government to fully recover costs.[50] The Bank applauded the national government and the NHA in particular for their "new approach" to shelter, and the president's Letter of Instruction 557 (similar to an American executive order) adopted slum improvement as national policy and promised to use relocation sparingly and only when public infrastructure necessitated it. The second LOI 555 (amended LOI 686) went further, empowering the NHA to organize upgrading nationally with local government units.[51] Bank officials believed the Tondo project was a success, not only because it kept costs down, increased homeownership, and brought "substantial parcels of urban land with clouded title back into the urban economy," but also because it "brought the area to the 'take-off' point . . . stimulat[ing] private investment by residents to an even greater extent than previously predicted."[52]

The Cost of Success

According to the World Bank, Indonesia and the Philippines were exceptional success stories. In most of its aided self-help and upgrading projects, by contrast, repeated difficulties achieving cost recovery and maintaining housing standards, as well as logistical mishaps in the implementation of bricks-and-mortar programs all led to a general reevaluation of Bank strategy by the mid-1980s. Of all these failures, Bank officials focused on cost recovery as the most critical, since no housing project would be able "to expand the access of low-income groups to home ownership by recirculating funds recovered from original beneficiaries to new ones" if there were no funds to recirculate.[53] With these lessons in mind, Bank officials began moving away from sites-and-services and urban upgrading, or what it called "largely physical objectives" oriented around questions of design or cost reduction, to a "sector-wide initiative strategy" that emphasized housing finance and broader institutional reform. The new accepted wisdom among Bank analysts became that sites-and-services and to a lesser extent, slum upgrading programs, had failed to achieve cost recovery, could not easily be replicated by the private sector without subsidy, and did not consistently benefit the most needy.[54]

Despite the critique of sites-and-services programs, however, redesigned aid programs did an even poorer job of addressing the most impoverished classes. Through its sector-wide initiative, the World Bank emphasized the creation of "self-supporting financial intermediaries capable of making long-term mortgage loans to low- and moderate-income households" while "reduc[ing] and restructur[ing] housing subsidies."[55] World Bank senior housing finance advisor Bertrand Renaud's words in 1987—"Cities are built the way they are financed"—became the new accepted wisdom, and the UN General Assembly endorsed this emphasis on enabled private markets by the end of the decade.[56] According to the Bank, slums only proliferated in "savage" markets where states failed to regulate and protect property rights. "In countries with underdeveloped housing finance systems," another report noted, "most households either build their house individually over long periods or settle for a low-quality structure that does not comply with planning and building regulations."[57] Instead of small projects or test sites piloting low-cost construction or aided self-help, the Bank turned to housing finance liberalization, privatization of production, and consideration of housing in macroeconomic planning as more effective, wide-ranging solutions to the problem of slum proliferation. Henceforth, low-income housing project reports emphasized the primary goal of "provid[ing] access to sustainable housing finance for low-income households, to purchase, build, or upgrade their dwellings."[58]

In the mid-1980s and 1990s, this meant individual loan sizes would increase and some regions would benefit more than others. Individual Bank loans quintupled in size from 1972–75 to 1985–90, with each recipient receiving much more substantial aid, even as total Bank lending climbed first to a record $12.3 billion in 1981, and then even higher to $16 billion worth of loans for over ninety countries by 2006.[59] There were regional consequences, also: African nations received far fewer loans. For Bank officials, the fall of the Berlin Wall in 1989 and the dissolution of the Soviet Union in 1991 only confirmed "how poorly nonmarket approaches to the provision of shelter performed."[60] When the American housing bubble burst, the resulting financial crisis rocked so-called market fundamentalism, introducing new critiques of the regulatory failures of the American subprime system and a second look at rental housing. Bank Director Loïc Chiquier observed the need for more policies directed at that "segment of the population that cannot afford to buy a home, should not qualify for a mortgage, or simply does not want to own a home at a certain stage in their lives."[61] Chiquier added, "Rental residential markets have remained the orphan child of any comprehensive and affordable housing policy, whereas home ownership has been the object of all the attention, sometimes at the price of stretching the frontiers of accessibility beyond sound financial or fiscal rules. Now the rental sector deserves greater attention and deployed expertise."[62]

USAID and HUD in the 1990s and 2000s

USAID had a longer history of engagement than the World Bank in such questions of homeownership and low-income housing aid. In the 1960s and '70s, it initiated a housing guaranty program that was meant to foster precisely the sort of private housing investment the World Bank sought. Although that specific program died a slow death until the mid-1990s, the Foreign Assistance Act of 1969 had already created a federally chartered agency under the secretary of state with a public-private board of directors, an agency that would become critically important for overseas homeownership aid in the 2000s. Called the Overseas Private Investment Corporation (OPIC, 1971–), the agency would "reorganize and operate selectively on a business basis US Government incentives to the investment of American private capital and know-how in projects which contribute to development."[63] Specifically, OPIC took over the USAID's Office of Private Resources functions, providing four key services: preinvestment assistance; investment insurance against risks of inconvertibility, expropriation, war, revolution, or insurrection; investment finance through guaranties of private loans or direct loans; and technical assistance. Although OPIC initially focused on nonhousing investments, by 2000, OPIC seemed to have come full circle, displaying a classic case of historical amnesia. While acknowledging prior USAID efforts, OPIC's housing report indicated little understanding of that program's struggles. Instead, George Muñoz, president and CEO, declared private investors' "new" interest in overseas housing:

Because the United States is widely viewed as the most successful housing market in the world, many developing countries have looked to the US as a model for their own housing markets. . . . And the US housing industry is increasingly interested in finding the best mechanisms for using [their] knowledge and skill base to tap into the opportunities that are beginning to take shape internationally.

Given the crucial role of private home ownership, and the concerns of the markets to address the housing gap, OPIC has been working with US housing industry experts on how to best bring their know-how to the developing countries and how OPIC can mitigate and cover some of the political risks.[64]

Muñoz believed OPIC was particularly well suited to deal with the demand for private homeownership in the developing world because it knew best how to "mitigate these risks," and as a branch of the US government, had "great influence in advising governments on how to best adapt their laws and policies to facilitate foreign direct investment in their countries."[65] Owning a home was "not just an American dream," declared another OPIC housing pamphlet. It is "a universal dream."[66]

Granted, the terms had become more complicated by the 2000s: the International Finance Corporation in the World Bank now actively participated in the creation and maintenance of secondary mortgage markets, where second-tier lenders sold bonds and bought long-term local loans. Local governments also built more institutions to guarantee, fund, and securitize mortgages. International housing had become big business, with finance markets demanding the specialized services of global insurance companies, private label servicing, due diligence workers, ratings companies, investment bankers, and more.[67] Even the process of determining value had become standardized at the global level: the US-based Appraisal Institute played a decisive role in international discussions of real estate valuation, for instance, setting up appraisal courses and certifying Members of the Appraisal Institute (MAIs) in the early 2000s in Korea, Turkey, Germany, Japan, Mexico, China, Egypt, Cyprus, and Vietnam. An ever-widening circle of countries and agencies joined soon after, and the widespread interest in Market Value and Mortgage Lending Value as well as the resulting International Valuation Standards reflected just how global these questions had become.[68] Appraisals, like land titles, played an important role in standardizing housing value and transforming a necessity into a commodity.

Despite these exponentially greater numbers of participants and their accompanying complications, today's OPIC products look awfully familiar: in the greater Accra region, for instance, OPIC issued a $30 million loan to a local credit subsidiary of Ghana Home Loans, Ltd., a company subsumed within the larger Massachusetts-based Broad Cove Partners, Inc., investment firm. Much like World Homes in Latin America decades ago, Broad Cove currently focuses on "increas[ing] the supply of housing affordable to Africa's booming and underserved middle class."[69] With OPIC assistance, Ghana Homes intends to create up to 600 mortgages for single-family residences and to increase the number of Ghanaians participating in a modern housing industry.[70] In Tanzania, OPIC's

$12.4 million in insurance aid to another company named Enterprise Homes, LLC, in 2007 helped jumpstart a residential housing program where 5,000 new homes should be completed by 2014 in clusters of single-family houses roughly twenty miles outside major cities' central business districts.

Much like OPIC's most recent housing aid echoed and continues to echo the themes of the preceding sixty years, so also does HUD's Office of International Affairs continue to promote American techniques and ideas abroad. Created by HUD secretary Andrew Cuomo, the Office of International Affairs launched such efforts as the 1995 secondary mortgage market program in Mexico with the US's Office of Federal Housing Enterprise Oversight, Fondo de Operación y Financiamiento Bancario a la Vivienda (a government-run trust fund), the Mexican Government, USAID, and a bevy of private financial institutions, bankers, and mortgage industry service providers. The program was meant to help Mexico develop better low- and middle-income access to mortgages as well as to learn how the American FHA, Ginnie Mae, Fannie Mae, Freddie Mac, and private mortgage insurers measured credit risk for low-income mortgage recipients. In a related housing aid effort, HUD helped organize a Nuevo Milenio housing program in Chiapas using aided self-help techniques to transform *ejidos* into "carefully planned, individually held plots of land" after the devastating El Niño rains in 1998.[71]

Other programs like the Mortgage Securitization Pilot Project in China in July 2000 provided "advice on developing a market-based system of mortgage finance, including the creation of secondary mortgage markets, to facilitate China's transition to privately owned housing" primarily by "tapping the expertise of the US private sector," including representatives from Bear Stearns, Countrywide Credit Industries, Ernst & Young, Latham & Watkins, Freddie Mac, and the Mortgage Bankers Association of America. Together, various American industry experts spoke with Chinese counterparts from the Ministry of Construction and Finance, the People's Bank of China, and the China Construction Bank (the largest state-owned mortgage lender) regarding the development and operations of primary and secondary mortgage markets. HUD also encouraged US cities to set up housing demonstration projects with international "sister cities" that made use of each city's architects and planners. The Department of Commerce was "a key partner in the initiative," bringing American building materials manufacturers into this potentially lucrative project.[72]

Andrew Cuomo had no difficulty articulating the international significance of these programs:

Many countries and millions of their citizens face the same social and economic challenges, and even the basic human need for safe, affordable housing remains elusive.
Because of increasing industrialization, a quarter century from now 60 percent of the
world's population will live in cities—deepening the difficult challenges. . . . These
problems know no national border and are found from China to Mexico . . .

One of the highlights of my tenure as HUD Secretary has been to meet with my
counterparts from around the world and, at President Clinton's request, travel to many
of their countries to share ideas with them on how to best address these global challenges. I became convinced that President Kennedy's original vision for the Department
of Housing and Urban Development as a promoter of justice requires that we play a
vital role in thinking through and solving these international problems.[73]

In other words, housing challenges were "global," "international," and
above national borders.

Given the basic facts of foreign financing for American mortgages,
it would be difficult for the HUD secretary to describe them otherwise.
Mortgage-related securities are now a significant and growing part of
Asian—especially Chinese—investments in the early twenty-first century, with overseas demand for high-grade debt and GSE securities sky-
rocketing in the first decade of the twenty-first century. Economist Paul
Krugman told the Financial Crisis Inquiry Commission in 2010, "It's
hard to envisage us having had this [housing] crisis without considering
international monetary capital movements. The U.S. housing bubble
was financed by large capital inflows. . . . It's a combination of, in the
narrow sense, a less regulated financial system and a world that was increasingly wide open for big international capital movements."[74]

Added to these bilateral exchanges, intergovernmental and nongovernmental organizations continue to bring policymakers together. The
World Bank, for instance, periodically organizes conferences and produces reports commenting and advising on the details of Chinese urban
and suburban growth. If "the Bank has the ear of even the most powerful governments," it remains to be seen what China will do with what
it hears.[75]

Contested Consensus

Looking back, the late twentieth century was undoubtedly a culmination
of American efforts to promote homeownership around the world. From
the perspective of agencies like USAID, OPIC, or HUD, countless individuals from all corners of the world now knew of American techniques

30 Philippines homeownership programs relocated families to sites hours away from the center city, bringing new challenges to former urban dwellers. In this image, a model home stands abandoned next to completed blocks. NHA Southville, 2013. Source: Author.

and borrowed American language to formulate policies that valorized homeownership, at least on paper. Once the World Bank finally entered into urban planning and housing policy debates in the 1970s, it did so firmly on the side of market solutions to low-income housing crises, with a preference for owner-occupied homeownership.

Was this a consensus? Certainly, governments around the world adopted policies and erected institutions that referenced American ideals. Many NGOs embraced the logic of mass homeownership, with organizations like Habitat for Humanity promoting aided self-help homeownership around the world. These were not small efforts: as of 2014, Habitat alone built or repaired over 800,000 homes, affecting 4 million individuals. Other NGOs and religious charities like Catholic Charities took up similar programs to facilitate low-income, self-owned, self-improved homes. Even philanthropic divisions of banks like Citi Foundation helped sponsor such efforts. By the early twenty-first century, the homeownership ideal had without question gone beyond bilateral aid agreements and small demonstration programs.

Looking at specific cases in the late twentieth and early twenty-first centuries, however, terms like *consensus* and *convergence* still seem inadequate. The words obscure class difference; not all low-income homeowners shared the "dream" or believed homeownership could be anything other than a crushing burden. In the case of one widowed homeowner in Northville 5 in Batia, Bocaue, Bulacan (roughly nineteen miles north of central Manila), homeownership was merely punishment for being poor—a status put upon her by a government agency intent on reforming squatters and removing them from central city sites. The NHA claimed to have improved her condition by offering her secure tenure on this remote resettlement site, but for the widow, the personal cost of homeownership was great indeed: "I used to wash clothes and make 150 pesos a day [in Manila]—just enough for one meal. Now I have no income. If I can't eat every day because I have no money, if Meralco [power company] is going to cut off my electricity, how am I going to pay my mortgage?"[76] In this context, it makes more sense to conclude mass homeownership was a deeply contested ideal—one that many knew of, urged upon others, and implemented in various housing policies—and that also benefited people very differently depending upon their circumstances.

Conclusion

If I were to underscore the main weaknesses in our aid program, I would say it is the lack of expertness. CHARLES ABRAMS, 1963[1]

A few short years before the start of the subprime mortgage meltdown, I stopped by a small shop in Singapore's Changi International Airport on my way home from a research trip. Making small talk, I asked the clerk where he lived and whether or not he liked his home. He told me he lived in one of the large New Towns built by the ruling People's Action Party, and that he shared a comfortable flat with his wife and young boy. They had room enough and he owned the unit, but his face took on a wistful look as he added, "Of course, I would like a garden and a house all of my own. But we cannot all be like you Americans." His comment surprised me. I myself was heading back to a small rented apartment in New York City and I knew all too well that not all Americans wanted or could afford to live in a detached, single-family suburban tract home. What was more significant in this moment, however, was the image: for this Singaporean clerk, the vast majority of Americans lived in idyllic suburban homes with individual gardens and various enviable comforts. This was the American Dream.

To some extent, this book has been about this tension between American homeownership as image and ideology versus the realities of homeownership as policy and practice. Many individuals and countries embraced the ideal of a universal "homeownership for all," but actual homeownership programs remained deeply contentious and incompletely realized even in the US context. This paradox—a contentious consensus of sorts—helps explain how a country so passionately endorsing home-ownership might have lower domestic homeownership rates than, say, Romania (96.6% in 2011), Norway (84% in 2011), or Finland (74% in 2012), and how homeownership rates themselves serve as poor compar-ative indicators of housing quality, standards of living, or even housing finance mechanisms from one country to another. What, ultimately, do homeownership rates tell us about comparative quality of life, savings, stability, class mobility, or any other critical measure of successful hous-ing policy?

In the end, homeownership rates hide as much as they reveal.[2] High rates might mean a satisfied, largely middle-class citizenry with consider-able savings, but it might also mean heavily subsidized land titles, large rural populations with inherited titles, sudden privatization after the end of socialism, mass ownership of substandard shelter, majority own-ership within a very small formal housing sector (with the rest of the masses living in unregulated, informal shelter), or even majority own-ership within public housing, as in the case of Singapore. Much as the divide between "public" and "private" housing is generally murky, so also do homeownership statistics require more depth and detail in order to yield meaningful comparison across nations. Simple homeownership rates can say more about what image governments would like to project than the actual proportion of state-to-market involvement, as in the Singapore case where the People's Action Party deliberately labeled state-aided housing "public." We can accept such seemingly contradictory categories as "ownership of public housing" or "government-supported homeownership" because we understand the political and conditional nature of such terms.

When looking back over sixty years of American homeownership pol-icies and overseas aid programs, one fact becomes startlingly clear: ideas traveled. For most of the postwar period, the United States sought to pro-mote a particular vision of homeownership worldwide. Initially it did so through its own advisors and agencies. Increasingly, its vision was articu-lated and endorsed by international agencies, notably the World Bank. Sometimes it met with active resistance; just as often (if not more), the United States found itself pushing at an open door. But despite the inevi-table variety of outcomes, the American version of housing was general-ized and, for better or worse, came to have an enormous influence on governments and peoples around the world.

American motives for urging this sort of homeownership are an im-portant corollary. Americans pursued homeownership for all first as a

Cold War strategy to control radical elements in geopolitically critical regions of the world, and then as a way to install capitalist institutions like savings and loans and as a stimulant for American overseas investments. At home, American homeownership proponents believed increased access to mortgages would quell urban unrest and racial tensions. Both in the international and domestic spheres, US advisors wielded mass homeownership as a tool to achieve political calm and to advance capitalist networks, regardless of the long-term consequences for new homeowners themselves. It should be added that many—perhaps even most—genuinely believed homeownership could yield the physical and spiritual benefits they promised. Willard Garvey did not speak only as a businessman when he worried about communist, socialist housing programs in Latin America. Nor did Jacob Crane, Charles Abrams, or any number of other technocrats and specialists feign concern with the well-being of others. On the one hand, then, simultaneous self-interest *and* humanitarian concern drove Americans to carry this homeownership ideology around the world.

On the other hand, homeownership never worked exactly as planned or promised. The ideal was never transplanted in its entirety; it was always adapted to suit local politics, geopolitical concerns, and Cold War imperatives. Local officials, informal dwellers, corporations, small shopkeepers, women, and men all contested aspects of homeownership, sometimes in its ideological, other times in its practical dimensions, but always in every country and in every decade. Long before "housing pessimists" like Dean Baker, Karl Case and Robert Shiller, and Paul Krugman warned of a housing bubble in the early 2000s, even before securitization transformed housing finance and introduced American homeowners to new vulnerabilities and risks in the late twentieth century, homeownership was a contested ideal—one that housing experts and advisors had to grapple with in a multidimensional, global way after World War II.[3]

Not surprisingly, then, each case of exchange resulted in vastly different housing policies: in "Free China," both the US and Taiwanese governments had to spend an enormous amount of money to sustain what they thought would be low-cost, low-income housing demonstrating the virtues of private initiative; the US government had to bail out a private housing project in South Korea originally designed to showcase the benefits of private market provision. In Puerto Rico, a supposedly successful self-help system operated alongside massive public housing provision—the second-largest public housing authority in the nation. The Philippines, meanwhile, rejected the American tropical example of Puerto Rico, instead copying the FHA, Fannie Mae, and other mainland institutions, with the long-term result of heightened disparities between rich and poor and a largely inaccessible homeownership system. Singapore refused to follow American examples, instead building an alternate national system of "homeownership for all" that existed within a public housing program. Peruvian middle-class homeownership programs did not promote class mobility and in fact heightened spatial disparities in Lima, while the American developer launching the housing project as part of his fight against communism lost sight of his own bottom line. Housing investment guaranties abroad shared key characteristics with loan guaranties in the domestic sphere, as American taxpayers incentivized high-risk, high-yield investments abroad and at home, in all cases picking up the tab when investments fell through. Last but not least, Native homeownership programs often left families in worse shape than if they had been given public housing provision, while predatory and subprime lending opened up low-income families to new levels of risk and financial uncertainty.

American aid givers and advisors could not ultimately control how their "influence" would actually shape other nations' housing programs. They affected and influenced, but not always to their own benefit and almost never in the ways they predicted or wanted. The experts were often surprised themselves; paraphrasing Abrams, the real problem was that the experts lacked expertise. This history of housing aid has attempted to foreground some of the longstanding questions facing governments and citizens, with discussion of the sometimes problematic, other times innovative answers devised in response.

The story of homeownership is not over, of course. Developing nations continue to struggle with inadequate housing for a rapidly urbanizing populace. Gated communities proliferate globally, offering unique, fortress-like experiences of ownership that further divide the wealthy from the poor. Vastly unequal housing investments confound the ill-informed buyer. A single history of the homeownership ideal cannot address all policy questions of such magnitude, but perhaps it can begin a more rigorous conversation about who should own which homes, and with what assistance.

Acknowledgments

There are many reasons why I am delighted to be done writing this book, not the least of which is that I can finally thank everyone who helped me along the way.

First and foremost, I thank Ken Jackson, my graduate advisor and mentor in the truest sense of the word. It was Ken who encouraged me to pursue the transnational dimensions of my story before I even realized they were there. Ken always reminded me to convey my ideas in simple, clear sentences and to write history that had meaning for ordinary people. I still aspire to reach this standard.

Alan Brinkley, Betsy Blackmar, and Owen Gutfreund provided important feedback on earlier iterations of this manuscript. I owe a particular debt of gratitude to Gwen Wright, who spent countless hours reading drafts and discussing ideas with me, and to Vicky de Grazia, who provided intellectual and literal nourishment for so many of us. At the University Seminar on the City, I had the good fortune of meeting and working with Lisa Keller—an irreplaceable source of wisdom and guidance, and humor, too.

As any historian knows, a knowledgeable archivist can make all the difference in a difficult research project. This study would never have made it off the ground without the assistance of Shiri Alon and Sherrine Thompson (World Bank), Mary Nelson (Wichita State University Special Collections and University Archives), Joelle Miller (Rockefeller Archives), Romain Ledauphin and Amanda Leinberger (UN Archives), Scott Taylor (Georgetown University Special Collections), Kenneth Cobb (New York Municipal Archives), Donald Davis (American Friends Service Committee Archives),

Carol Leadenham (Hoover Institute), and the staff of the Herbert H. Lehman Archives and Oral History Office at Columbia University, the National Archives in DC and College Park, the JFK Library, the London Municipal Archives, the Singapore National Archives, the National University of Singapore Library, the World Health Organisation, the George Marshall Archives, Cornell University Library's Rare Books & Manuscripts Division, the Bancroft Library, the British Public Records Office, the Philippine National Library, and the National Housing Authority of the Philippines.

Chua Beng Huat at NUS met with me very early in this project and opened my eyes to the vibrant world of Southeast Asian housing research. In the Philippines, Michael Pante helped me get my foot in the door and provided entry to new research sites. Florian de Leon and Elsie Trinidad (NHA), Len Barrientos, Cromwell Teves, and Ana Mirador (HUDCC) spent many hours explaining the ins and outs of Philippine housing policy. I owe a special thanks to Eleiza Recaro (NHA) who introduced me to relocated families and who made possible my conversations with them. I am still surprised and grateful for Frank Quilas (ABS-CBN), who spent nearly a full day showing me the various ABS-CBN housing efforts in Bayanijuan, and for Bebot Corpuz (Kapit Bisig para sa Ilog Pasig) who walked me through the Estero de Paco cleanup site and introduced me to homeowners. To the residents of Northville 5 and Southville 7, many thanks again for welcoming me into your communities and for sharing your personal relocation experiences.

Institutional funders paid for research trips, most of which I could not have afforded otherwise. In particular, I would like to thank the Fulbright Institute of International Education, the Lehman Center for American History at Columbia University, the Social Science Research Council's Inter-Asian Connections Program, the Graham Foundation, the UC Humanities Research Institute, the Hellman Fellows Fund, the Center for Humanities at UCSD, UCSD's History Department, NYU Polytechnic School of Engineering, and Columbia University.

At the University of Chicago Press, I had the extraordinary good fortune of working with Richard Harris and a second, anonymous reviewer. Both provided a close reading and an astonishingly detailed set of suggestions and feedback—not once but twice! It is an understatement to say the book benefited immensely from their expertise. My editor Tim Mennel likewise provided invaluable, substantive editorial comments in addition to shepherding me through the process. I am indebted to Becky Nicolaides for her editorial feedback and even more for her support of this book from beginning to end. Thanks also to my copyeditor Carol

Saller for her meticulous, painstaking corrections, and to Nora Devlin and Jenni Fry for managing all details with such efficiency and good cheer.

Many others have read chapters or given critical advice on the over-arching framework. Bob Beauregard, Sven Beckert, Nick Bloom, Tim Borstelmann, David Engerman, Richard Greenwald, Joseph Heathcott, Carola Hein, Amy Howard, Chris Klemek, Jennifer Luff, Carl Nightingale, Kavita Philip, Wendy Plotkin, Sean Purdy, Neil Rosendorf, Andrew Sandoval-Strausz, Pierre-Yves Saunier, Andre Schmid, Oliver Schmidt, Jonathan Soffer, Larry Vale, and Alex von Hoffman all helped me think more carefully about the relationship between politics and built form, between housing and the people who live in it.

I could not ask for better colleagues at UC San Diego. In the history department, Dave Gutierrez prepared me for every aspect of my life as a junior faculty member. Truly, he is one of the hardest-working people I know. I am very grateful also to Seth Lerer, Stefan Tanaka, Pamela Radcliff, Natalia Molina, Steve Erie, Rebecca Plant, Nayan Shah, Todd Henry, Bob Edelman, and Matthew Vitz for their support and warm collegiality. I am proud to say the title is straight from the brilliant mind of Patrick Patterson.

Friends kept me sane as I revised, scrapped, and started over again. Nobody knows the agony of my writing better than Jan Traflet, since she has read nearly every draft. I have enjoyed every minute of every debate with Lisa Ramos, Karine Walther, Betsy Herbin, Claudine Leysinger, Tim White, Dominique Reill, and Jim Downs, and their encouragement continues to keep me afloat.

My family is and always has been my center. My sister Sally Kwak and brother Lawrence Kwak have cheered this project on for many, many years—probably too many years. I am relieved to tell them it is finally done, yes really! My mother Soonup Kwak and father Dochan Kwak are unusual first-generation parents: they never pushed me toward the typical "immigrant" occupations. Instead, they encouraged me to find a career I enjoyed and even now enthusiastically applaud my obscure victories. I am more than lucky to have parents like these. Thank you, Mom and Dad. My babies, Subin and Joon, continue to give me a reason to work harder and better. They are the chocolate in my pudding, the apple in my pie. Now that the book is done, I will do something extra-special with my little monkeys! And last but not least, my husband Brian Byun has heard more overenthusiastic monologues and tirades about housing policy and academia than any human being should have to endure. You truly are the better half, and I count my blessings every day. None of it would be any fun without you.

Abbreviations

AFSC	American Friends Service Committee Archives
AKF	American Korea Foundation
AIAN	American Indians and Alaska Natives
BIA	Bureau of Indian Affairs
BNL	British National Library
CCC	Carl Coan Collection, Georgetown University Library Special Collections
CDBG	Community Development Block Grant
CRIK	Civil Relief in Korea
CRUV	Corporación de Renovación Urbana y Vivienda
CUOH	Columbia University Oral History Archives
CUSA	Chinese Council for United States Aid
DSIR	Department of Scientific and Industrial Research
ECA	Economic Cooperative Administration
ECAFE	United Nations Economic Commission for Asia and the Far East
FHA	Federal Housing Administration
FHLBB	Federal Home Loan Bank Board
FmHA	Farmers Home Administration
FMS	Federated Malay States
FNMA	Federal National Mortgage Association or Fannie Mae
FOA	Foreign Operations Administration
HDB	Housing and Development Board
HFC	Home Financing Commission
HHDF	Housing and Home Development Fund
HHFA	Housing and Home Finance Agency
HIA	Hoover Institute Archives, Stanford University
HLURB	Housing and Land Use Regulatory Board
HOLC	Home Owners' Loan Corporation
HUD	US Department of Housing and Urban Development
IADB	Inter-American Development Bank

IBEC	International Basic Economy Corporation
ICA	International Cooperation Administration
IFHTP	International Federation for Housing and Town Planning
IHA	Indian Housing Authority
IKA	Institute of Korean Architects
JCRR	Joint Commission on Rural Reconstruction
KCAC	Korean Civil Assistance Command
LCC	London County Council
LMA	London Metropolitan Archives
MARS	Modern Architectural Research Group
MCLGU	Makati City Local Government Unit Records
MFA	George C. Marshall Foundation Archives
ML	George C. Marshall Library
MSA	Mutual Security Administration
NAHB	National Association of Home Builders
NAHO	National Association of Housing Officials
NAHRO	National Association of Housing and Redevelopment Officials
NARA	National Archives and Records Administration II (College Park, MD)
NARA-DC	National Archives and Records Administration I (Washington, DC)
NARA-San Bruno	National Archives at San Francisco (San Bruno, CA)
NAREB	National Association of Real Estate Boards
NAS	National Archives of Singapore
NHA	National Housing Authority
NHC	National Housing Commission
NLP	National Library of the Philippines
NLS	National Library of Singapore
NLSA	National Land Settlement Administration
NSLL	National Savings and Loan League
NUS	National University of Singapore
NYMA	New York Municipal Archives
OEC	Office of the Economic Coordinator
OHLM	Office des Habitations à Loyer Modéré
ONC	Office of National Construction
OPIC	Overseas Private Investment Corporation
PA/HLA	British Parliamentary Archives, House of Lords Archives
PAP	People's Action Party
PHA	Public Housing Administration
PHHC	People's Homesite and Housing Corporation
PRO	British National Archives
PROP	Property Release Options Program
PRHA	Puerto Rico Housing Authority
PRRA	Puerto Rico Reconstruction Administration
PWA	Public Works Administration
RFC	Rehabilitation Finance Corporation

RIBA   Royal Institute of British Architects
RPAA   Regional Plan Association of America
SICAP   Société Immobilière du Cap Vert
SIT   Singapore Improvement Trust
SPUR   Singapore Planning and Urban Research Group
SSRC   Social Science Research Center, University of Puerto Rico
TCA   Technical Cooperation Administration
UNA   United Nations Archives
UNCACK   United Nations Civil Assistance Command, Korea
UNKRA   United Nations Korea Reconstruction Agency
UNRRA   United Nations Relief and Rehabilitation Administration
USAID   US Agency for International Development
USAID-L   USAID Library
USHA   United States Housing Authority
USOM   United States Operations Mission
VA   Veterans Administration
WBGA   World Bank Group Archives
WHI   Jean and Willard Garvey World Homes, Inc. Papers, Special Collec-
          tions and University Archives, Wichita State University Libraries
WHO   World Health Organisation Archives
ZOTO   Zone One Tondo Organization

Notes

INTRODUCTION

1. Raymond M. Foley, "Evolution of the United States Housing Programme," *UN Housing and Town and Country Planning Bulletin* 3 (February 1950): 11.

2. Nelson Lichtenstein, "Social Theory and Capitalist Reality in the American Century," in Lichtenstein, ed., *American Capitalism: Social Thought and Political Economy in the Twentieth Century* (Philadelphia: University of Pennsylvania Press, 2006), 1.

3. Harry S. Truman: "Statement by the President upon Signing the Housing Act of 1949," July 15, 1949; quoted in Gerhard Peters and John T. Woolley, The American Presidency Project, http://www.presidency.ucsb.edu/ws/?pid=13246.

4. Peter Saunders, "Beyond Housing Classes: The Sociological Significance of Private Property Rights in Means of Consumption," *International Journal of Urban and Regional Research* 18, no. 2 (1978): 202–227; Saunders, *A Nation of Homeowners* (London: Unwin Hyman, 1990); Edward Scanlon, "Low-Income Homeownership Policy as a Community Development Strategy," *Journal of Community Practice* 5, no. 2 (1998): 137–154.

5. For more on the divergence approach, see Jim Kemeny, *Housing and Social Theory* (New York: Routledge, 2013).

6. Letter written March 8, 1954. H. Peter Oberlander and Eva Newbrun, *Houser: The Life and Work of Catherine Bauer* (Vancouver: University of British Columbia Press, 1999), 268.

7. Foley, 10.

8. N. J. Demerath and Richard N. Kuhlman, *Toward a Housing Programme for the Philippines* (Washington, DC: National

Housing Agency, 1945); Jacob Crane, "Notes on Advisory Housing Mission to the Philippines," December 1945, folder 1945–48, box 12, accession 71A3534, RG 207, NARA.

9. Report of the US Advisory Housing Mission to the Commonwealth of the Philippines, June 1946, v; International Labour Organisation, Asian Regional Conference Report, "Workers' Housing Problems in Asian Countries," Tokyo, September 1953 (Geneva: ILO, 1953), 59, folder ILO Asian Advisory Committee, 1953 Asian Regional Conference, box 13, accession 69A5149, NARA.

10. Letter from Harold Robinson, Deputy Director for Plans and Programs in the Housing and Urban Development Division of USAID, Department of State, to Robert J. Crooks, Director, Centre for Housing, Building and Planning at the United Nations, February 14, 1969, folder SO 144 (2–5), RG 3/9, box 34, UNA.

11. Richard Harris and Godwin Arku, "Housing and Economic Development: The Evolution of an Idea since 1945," *Habitat International* 30 (2006): 1007–1017.

12. John Archer, *Architecture and Suburbia: From English Villa to American Dream House, 1690–2000* (Minneapolis: University of Minnesota Press, 2005), 261, 263–264; William M. Rohe and Harry L. Watson, eds., *Chasing the American Dream: New Perspectives on Affordable Homeownership* (Ithaca, NY: Cornell University Press, 2007).

13. John P. Dean, *Home Ownership: Is It Sound?* (New York: Harper & Brothers, 1945); Rosalyn Baxandall and Elizabeth Ewen, *Picture Windows: How the Suburbs Happened* (New York: Basic Books, 2000), 109–110.

14. United Nations Human Settlements Programme, *Financing Urban Shelter: Global Report on Human Settlements* (London: Earthscan, 2005), xxv.

15. Hernando de Soto, *The Mystery of Capital: Why Capitalism Triumphs in the West and Fails Everywhere Else* (New York: Basic Books, 2000), 4, 6.

16. Robert M. Buckley and Jerry Kalarickal, eds., *Thirty Years of World Bank Shelter Lending: What Have We Learned?* (Washington, DC: World Bank, 2006), 31, 77.

17. For just a few examples, see Dean; Jim Kemeny, *The Myth of Home-Ownership: Private versus Public Choices in Housing Tenure* (London: Routledge & Kegan Paul, 1981); Alan Gilbert, "Promoting Rental Housing: An International Agenda," in J. D. Hulchanski and M. Shapcott, eds., *Finding Room: Policy Options for a Canadian Housing Strategy* (Toronto: University of Toronto Centre for Urban and Community Studies, 2004), 389–399; Peter Marcuse and W. Dennis Keating, "The Permanent Housing Crisis: The Failures of Conservatism and the Limitations of Liberalism," in Rachel G. Bratt, Michael E. Stone, and Chester W. Hartman, eds., *A Right to Housing: Foundation for a New Social Agenda* (Philadelphia: Temple University Press, 2006), 139–162.

18. Buckley and Kalarickal, 91.

19. Raquel Rolnik, "Statement of the Special Rapporteur on Adequate Housing as a Component of the Right to an Adequate Standard of Living, and on the Right to Non-Discrimination in This Context," 10th session of the Council on Human Rights, March 9, 2008, http://www.ohchr.org/en/issues /housing/pages/housingindex.aspx.

20. Memo from Harold Robinson, Regional Housing Advisor, Bureau for Latin America Agency for International Development, to Carl Coan, n.d., but most likely 1962, folder 16, box 1, CCC.

21. John A. Hannah, Administrator, USAID, testimony before the Senate Foreign Relations Committee, June 11, 1971, p. 3, folder 49, box 1, CCC.

CHAPTER ONE

1. US 81st Cong., HR 4009, Hearings before the Committee on Banking and Currency, April and May 1949, 422.

2. For discussion of the longstanding American desire for homeownership, see Lawrence Vale, "Ideological Origins of Affordable Homeownership Efforts," in William M. Rohe and Harry L. Watson, eds., *Chasing the American Dream: New Perspectives on Affordable Homeownership* (Ithaca, NY: Cornell University Press, 2007).

3. Creed for Women Realtors (1950), as quoted in Jeffrey M. Hornstein, *A Nation of Realtors: A Cultural History of the Twentieth-Century American Middle Class* (Durham, NC: Duke University Press, 2005), 185.

4. The Octavia Hill Society constituted one of the most long-lasting, important transatlantic voluntary organizations in the mid- to late nineteenth century. The Octavia Hill system of integrated management was eventually used in Hong Kong, Tanzania, Australia, and South Africa, and other British colonies as well. For discussion of American reliance on British models, see E. L. Birch and D. Gardner, "The Seven-Percent Solution: A Review of Philanthropic Housing, 1870–1910," *Journal of Urban History* 7 (August 1981): 403–438. For a history of the expansion into the colonies, see Jennifer Robinson, "Power as Friendship: Spatiality, Femininity, and 'Noisy' Surveillance," in Joanne Sharp, Paul Routledge, Chris Philo, and Ronan Paddison, eds., *Entanglements of Power: Geographies of Domination/Resistance* (London: Routledge, 2000).

5. Robert B. Fairbanks, "From Better Dwellings to Better Neighborhoods: The Rise and Fall of the First National Housing Movement," in John F. Bauman, Roger Biles, and Kristin M. Szylvian, eds., *From Tenements to the Taylor Homes: In Search of an Urban Housing Policy in Twentieth-Century America* (University Park, PA: Penn State University Press, 2000).

6. Peter Marcuse, "Housing Policy and the Myth of the Benevolent State," in Rachel G. Bratt, Chester Hartman, and Ann Meyerson, eds., *Critical Perspectives on Housing* (Philadelphia: Temple University Press, 1986), 248–258; Daniel T. Rodgers, *Atlantic Crossings: Social Politics in a Progressive Age*

(Cambridge, MA: Harvard University Press, 1998), 463; John F. Bauman, "The Eternal War on the Slums," in Bauman, Biles, and Szylvian, 10. For more on Lawrence Veiller's National Housing Association (1910–36), see also Fairbanks, 26.

7. Quote from Edith Elmer Wood, *Housing Progress in Western Europe* (New York, 1923), 1–4, 64. Gerald Daly offers a fascinating critique of the housers' love affair with Britain, highlighting the errors and misperceptions of observations by Wood, Catherine Bauer, and others. In only viewing "showpiece estates" in London, not seeking out resident views, and ignoring other domestic criticisms of evolving British housing policies, Daly argues, "the American housing program was influenced and misled by the British paradigm" and consequently replicated many of the problems of British interwar housing estates. Gerald Daly, "The British Roots of American Public Housing," *Journal of Urban History* 15, no. 4 (August 1989): 399–434.

8. A. Scott Henderson, *Housing and the Democratic Ideal: The Life and Thought of Charles Abrams* (New York: Columbia University Press, 2000).

9. Eugenie Ladner Birch, "Woman-Made America: The Case of Early Public Housing Policy," *Journal of the American Institute of Planners* 44, no. 2 (April 1978): 130–144; D. Bradford Hunt, "Was the 1937 US Housing Act a Pyrrhic Victory?" *Journal of Planning History* 4, no. 3 (August 2005): 197–198.

10. Alexander von Hoffman, "A Study in Contradictions: The Origins and Legacy of the Housing Act of 1949," *Housing Policy Debate* 11, no. 2 (2000): 301.

11. Gail Radford, *Modern Housing for America: Policy Struggles in the New Deal Era* (Chicago: University of Chicago Press, 1996), 66–67.

12. Rodgers, 287–289; quote, 288. Rodgers notes Wood "exaggerated Ackermans' role but not the force of the British precedent."

13. PWA reports were made available to interested individuals through the Housing Study Guild, a lending library of sorts begun by Henry Wright, Lewis Mumford, and Albert Mayer in 1933; box 1, folder 22, US Central Housing Committee, Housing Study Guild records, CU. Quote from Rodgers, 477.

14. Radford; Henderson; Peter Oberlander and Eva Newbrun, *Houser: The Life and Work of Catherine Bauer* (Vancouver: University of British Columbia Press, 1999).

15. Hunt, 214.

16. Michael R. Hughes, *The Letters of Lewis Mumford and Frederic J. Osborn* (Bath: Adams & Dart, 1971), 143–144. Hunt makes a similar observation about the lack of a new generation of housing experts in "How Did Public Housing Survive the 1950s?" *Journal of Policy History* 17, no. 2 (Spring 2005): 196.

17. James Ford, *Slums and Housing*, vol. 2 (Greenwood, CT: Negro University Press, 1972), 772; as cited in Gwendolyn Wright, *Building the Dream: A*

Social History of Housing in America (Cambridge, MA: MIT Press, 1981), 234–235.

18. Quoted in Oberlander and Newbrun, 269–270.

19. Ibid.

20. Peter Hall, "Urban and Regional Planning in Britain and America: Ends and Means," *US Department of Housing and Urban Development International Review* 1, no.1 (November 1978): 91.

21. John Bacher, *Keeping to the Marketplace: The Evolution of Canadian Housing Policy* (Montreal: McGill-Queen's University Press, 1993); Richard Harris, *Building a Market: The Rise of the Home Improvement Industry, 1914–1960* (Chicago: University of Chicago Press, 2012), 202–205.

22. Letter from Jacob Crane to Herbert Nelson, March 20, 1944, folder NAREB 1942, box 2, accession 69A5149, RG 207, NARA.

23. Jacob Crane and Hugh R. Pomeroy, "A Post-War Housing Program for the United States—Draft for Committee Discussion," October 1943, page 2, folder NAHO Committee, box 2, accession 69A5149, NARA.

24. Crane and Pomeroy did not dismiss the need for rentals and for decent public housing, nor did they encourage homeownership as a sound financial choice for all families. Still, they argued homeownership worked for the majority if it was made less vulnerable to changing macroeconomic conditions. Crane and Pomeroy, 6–7, 10–11.

25. Matthew Lasner, *High Life: Condo Living in the Suburban Century* (New Haven: Yale University Press, 2012), 98–99, 136.

26. Michael Foot, *Aneurin Bevan, A Biography*, vol. 2, *1945–1960* (New York: Atheneum, 1974), 64–65.

27. The LCC governed the entire county of twenty-eight metropolitan boroughs and the City of London, taking charge of welfare and social services (health, education, housing), protective services (fire, ambulances), and amenities services (town planning, public works like sewerage, parks, museums). The City of London was (and still is) a one-square-mile borough in the center of London with unique administrative status. The other twenty-eight boroughs were Battersea, Bermondsey, Bethnal Green, Camberwell, Chelsea, Deptford, Finsbury, Fulham, Greenwich, Hackney, Hammersmith, Hampstead, Holborn, Islington, Kensington, Lambeth, Lewisham, Paddington, Poplar, St. Marylebone, St. Pancras, Shoreditch, Southwark, Stepney, Stoke Newington, Wandsworth, Westminster, and Woolwich. London County Council, *London Statistics*, vol. 1, *1945–1954*, 1.

28. J. Yelling, *Slums and Redevelopment: Policy and Practice in England, 1918–1945* (New York: St. Martin's Press, 1992); M. Swenarton, *Homes Fit for Heroes: The Politics and Architecture of Early State Housing in Britain* (London: Heinemann Educational Books, 1981).

29. Foot, 64–65.

30. Director-General of the Ministry of Information Frank Pick, "Britain Must Rebuild: A Pattern for Planning," and July 3, 1942, Document B produced

by Clerk of the Council, Comptroller of the Council, Chief Engineer, Architect, and Valuer, "Housing after the War—General Policy and Preparations"; Meeting Minutes, September 23, 1941, LCC/CL/HSG/1/12, LMA.

31. T. G. Randall, Chairman's November 18, 1941, report notes, LCC/CL/HSG/1/12, LMA.

32. Michael Hebbert, *London: More by Fortune Than Design* (Chichester, West Sussex: John Wiley & Sons, 1998), 63.

33. Richard M. Titmuss, *Problems of Social Policy* (London: HMSO and Longmans, Green, 1950), 330; quoted in Foley, 22–23.

34. Letter from Carl Feiss, architectural professor at Columbia University, to Charles Abrams, December 5, 1940, reel 50, Charles Abrams Papers, CU.

35. Ibid.

36. "Four Million Houses in 10 or 12 Years," *Evening Standard*, September 30, 1943. Bossom later became one of the founders of the Anglo-Texan Society in London in 1953; oil interests continued to bring Texans to London throughout the 1950s and thereafter. Ivan Roots, "Bossom, Alfred Charles, Baron Bossom (1881–1965)," *Oxford Dictionary of National Biography* (Oxford: Oxford University Press, 2004), accessed December 9, 2005, http://www.oxforddnb.com/view/article/40778. Many thanks to Annie Pinder at the PA/HLA for sending me this information.

37. Mardges Bacon, *Le Corbusier in America: Travels in the Land of the Timid* (Cambridge, MA: MIT Press, 2001).

38. Michael Hebbert, "A Hertfordshire Solution to London's Problems? Sir Frederic Osborn's Axioms Re-Considered," in *Garden Cities and New Towns, Five Lectures* (Hertfordshire: Hertfordshire Publications, 1990), 40.

39. After such a "radical" statement, Abercrombie went on to demur, "This does not mean, of course, that popular wishes can always be gratified; but that the expert is brought into touch with human realities." These comments can be found in Patrick Abercrombie's foreword to Arnold Whittick's research on the types of homes British citizens preferred. Arnold Whittick, *Civic Design and the Home*, Rebuilding Britain Series 10 (London: Faber and Faber, 1943), 5–6.

40. Frederick J. Osborn, *Overture to Planning*, Rebuilding Britain Series 1 (London: Faber and Faber, 1941), 9, 26–27. For a fuller biography of Osborn, see Gordon Cherry, ed., *Pioneers in British Planning* (London: Architectural Press, 1981).

41. Osborn, introduction to Lewis Mumford, *The Social Foundations of Post-War Building* (London: Faber and Faber, 1943), 5–6.

42. Ibid.

43. Nuffield College Social Reconstruction Survey, *Britain's Town and Country Pattern: A Summary of the Barlow, Scott, and Uthwatt Reports*, Rebuilding Britain Series 2 (London: Faber and Faber, 1943), 13–14. The 1940 Royal Commission on the Distribution of the Industrial Population, (commonly known as the Barlow Commission after its chair, Sir Montague Barlow), was

part of a triumvirate of studies emphasizing regional planning. The Barlow Commission concentrated on the distribution of industry and population. The Expert Committee on Compensation and Betterment (the Uthwatt Report, 1941) and the Report of the Committee on Land Utilisation in Rural Areas (the Scott Report, 1943) built on the recommendations of the Barlow Report to issue recommendations tailored to the problems of land values (Uthwatt) and rural areas (Scott). All three urged decentralization, rural preservation, and the power of eminent domain for a nationalized planning body.

44. Frank Mort and Miles Ogborn, "Transforming Metropolitan London, 1750–1960," *Journal of British Studies* 43 (January 2004): 1–14.

45. Pepler succeeded prominent town planner Thomas Adams as planning inspector to the Ministry of Health in 1919. He also helped found and served as a secretary, treasurer, and erstwhile examiner to the Town Planning Institute from 1913 to 1959 (an institute inspired by Ebenezer Howard's garden cities). Pepler's twenty-eight-year chairmanship of the Joint Planning Examination Board, along with his mentorship of such rising stars as Patrick Abercrombie and Stanley Adshead, added to his repute. He would later become the leading advisor to Singapore and other British colonies. Myles Wright, *Lord Leverhulme's Unknown Adventure: The Lever Chair and the Beginnings of Town and Regional Planning 1908–48* (London: Hutchinson Benham, 1982), 8, 113–116.

46. Sir Montague Barlow, Royal Commission on the Distribution of the Industrial Population Report: Presented to Parliament by Command of His Majesty, January 1940, Cmnd. 6153 (London: HM Stationery Office, 1940; reprinted 1942), Appendix IV and Addendum to Memorandum, 288–316; references to Robert Moses, 295–296.

47. Ibid.

48. Hughes, 143–144; Charles Abrams, *The Future of Housing* (New York: Harper & Brothers, 1946).

49. Letter written January 1, 1947, quoted in Eric Mumford, "The 'Tower in a Park' in America: Theory and Practice, 1920–1960," *Planning Perspectives* 10 (1995): 29.

50. "A Conversation with Robert Moses," oral history, 1973, CUOH.

51. Letter from Moses to George F. Man, American Car and Foundry Co. on Church St. in NY, June 20, 1944, reel 15 MN#22815, NYC Dept. of Parks, Gen'l Files, Administration, Housing 1942–44, NYMA.

52. Letter from Moses to Arthur Hodgkiss, September 12, 1945, reel 16 MN#22816, NYC Parks, Gen'l Files, Administration, Housing 1944–45, NYMA.

53. Mumford, 10–11; Kermit Carlyle Parsons, ed., *The Writings of Clarence S. Stein: Architect of the Planned Community* (Baltimore: Johns Hopkins University Press, 1998), 112, 180, 446, 447n. For examples of Osborn's use of Mumford's critiques, see LCC Architect's Department Town Planning,

Wandsworth Borough Council, County of London Plan, Scheme 19, LCC/AR/TP/2/158, LMA.

54. Donald Leslie Johnson, "Origin of the Neighbourhood Unit," *Planning Perspectives* 17 (2002): 227–245.

55. Eleanor Smith Morris argues the British made two unfortunate alterations to the American neighborhood scheme (shops were placed in the center of the neighborhood next to the community center, and they employed a two-stream primary school), but that the neighborhood principle was still "used extensively by all local authorities and New Towns throughout the 1950s and 1960s." Conversely, Andrew Homer believes British plans departed dramatically from the American model in their attempt to integrate social classes through neighborhood units before falling out of favor entirely in the mid-1950s because of sociological studies demonstrating that "living in neighbourhoods did not make people more neighbourly." Eleanor Smith Morris, *British Town Planning and Urban Design: Principles and Policies* (Essex: Longman, 1997), 138–142; Andrew Homer, "Creating New Communities: The Role of the Neighbourhood Unit in Post-War British Planning," *Contemporary British History* 14, no.1 (Spring 2000): 63–80; quote, 71.

56. The US provided an astronomical $50 billion through Lend-Lease, a program set up in March 1941 to facilitate American export of war material to "aid in resisting aggression." See Christine Macy, "The Architect's Office of the Tennessee Valley Authority," in Christine Macy, Jane Wolff, Barry M. Katz, and Steven Heller, eds., *The Tennessee Valley Authority: Design and Persuasion* (Princeton: Princeton Architectural Press, 2007), 40.

57. Unsigned memo, March 22, 1945, CO/537/5130, PRO.

58. Ibid.

59. Memo from Barman for Sir Hugh Beaver, Controller General, Ministry of Works, November 29, 1944, CO/537/5130, PRO. There was a high level of British interest in the TVA in the 1930s, especially as a potential model for development programs in Scotland and Wales. See Anthony Badger, "State Capacity in Britain and America in the 1930s," from David Englander, ed., *Britain and America: Studies in Comparative History, 1760–1970* (New Haven: Yale University Press, 1997), 299. For more on the global reach of the TVA, see David Ekbladh, *The Great American Mission: Modernization and the Construction of an American World Order* (Princeton: Princeton University Press, 2010).

60. Actually, most American and British temporary housing came in bungalow form. The protest should have focused on temporary housing generally, but this was lost in nationalist rhetoric. See CO/537/5130, PRO.

61. "Unfavourable Publicity to Lend-Lease Houses," no date or label, but most likely Ministry of Works document, CO/537/5130, PRO.

62. Ibid.

63. Highest allocations in 1945 were as follows: Croydon (1,500), Willesden (900), Ealing (700), Walthamstow (700), Tottenham (600), West Ham (600), Harrow (500), Hendon (500), Mitcham (450), East Ham (407). Temporary Houses, Allocation of American Houses, List A. No date is stamped on this document, but given those that precede and follow it, it is most likely from early 1945, CO/537/5130, PRO.

64. Untitled news clipping, *News Chronicle*, April 27, 1945, CO/537/5130, PRO.

65. Unsigned memo, HLG 101/814, PRO.

66. USA House statistic from handwritten memo, Miss Close to Mr. Whiting, February 5, 1947, HLG 101/814, PRO.

67. Ernest W. Pavey claimed to have written this report based on fifteen to seventeen years of research, including not only the USA Houses but also a study of prefabrication efforts in the British Colonies Supply Mission. Pavey memo, October 24, 1945, reel 16 MN#22816, NYMA.

68. Robert Moses response to Pavey memo, reel 16 MN#22816, NYMA.

69. Wright, 220.

70. The 500,000 units were supposed to be constructed over a fourteen-year period. In the actual Housing Act of 1949, that number rose to 810,000 units over six years.

71. Rosalyn Baxandall and Elizabeth Ewen, *Picture Windows: How the Suburbs Happened* (New York: Basic Books, 2000), 90.

72. Ibid., 93.

73. Don Parson, "The Decline of Public Housing and the Politics of the Red Scare," *Journal of Urban History* 33 (2007): 405.

74. Jim Kemeny, *The Myth of Home-Ownership: Private versus Public Choices in Housing Tenure* (London: Routledge & Kegan Paul, 1981), 6; Baxandall and Ewen, 106.

75. "Prime Minister in South London: Lively Reception," *Times*, July 5, 1945, 4.

76. Ibid.

77. Labour Party Manifesto, "Let Us Face the Future: A Declaration of Labour Policy for the Consideration of the Nation," 1945.

78. Quoted in Foot, 63.

79. Osborn and Whittick, 1977, 53, as cited in Dennis Hardy, *From Garden Cities to New Towns: Campaigning for Town and Country. Planning, 1899–1946* (New York: Routledge, 1991) 278.

80. My italics. Gordon Cherry, *Town Planning in Britain since 1900* (Oxford: Blackwell Publishers, 1996), 122–123.

81. Radford, 32.

82. The fourteen new towns were Stevenage (1946), Harlow (1947), Hemel Hempstead (1947), Crawley (1947), East Kilbride (1947), Aycliffe (1947), Glenrothes (1948), Welwyn (Garden City, 1920; New Town, 1948), Hatfield (1948), Peterlee (1948), Basildon (1949), Bracknell (1949), Cwmbran (1949), and Corby (1950). Cherry, *Town Planning*, 124. Abercrombie only chose

two of the fourteen sites (Stevenage and Harlow), but all generally adhered to his community principles in 1950. By 1974, however, population size had increased from Abercrombie's ideal 50,000 per town, to in some cases over 100,000. John M. Hall, *London: Metropolis and Region* (Oxford: Oxford University Press, 1976), 20. The LCC took responsibility for securing new sites through the 1950s. New Town site search, LCC/AR/CB/1/155 passim, LMA.

83. Rodgers, 493–494.

84. While the Labour Party promised "fair compensation" and betterment in their 1945 election manifesto, and while they made clear the 1947 act was part of their larger move to nationalize land, this legislation would not have been possible without the previous efforts of Conservatives in the Uthwatt Report, for instance, nor would it have been possible without some degree of interparty consensus about postwar planning.

85. Planning Appeals and Decisions, LCC/AR/TP/1/72, LMA. In the US, by contrast, plan-making was completely separate from development control; according to geographer Peter Hall, "The planning system is therefore, a local one administered by local zoning boards and, very importantly, it derives not from any nationalization of development rights but from 'police power' under which compensation is not payable. . . . In practice it is a great deal more flexible than the British system." Hall, "Urban and Regional Planning," 86.

86. Hebbert, *London: More by Fortune than Design*, 72. As geographer Peter Hall notes, the 1947 act was modified slightly but not substantively by the 1968 Planning Act and the 1972 Local Government Act in Britain. Hall, "Urban and Regional Planning," 85.

87. Keith C. Clark, "The British Labor Government's Town and Country Planning Act: A Study in Conflicting Liberalisms," *Political Science Quarterly* 66, no. 1 (March 1951): 92–93.

88. Cherry, *Town Planning in Britain since 1900*, 124–125.

89. Foot, 50–52.

90. Memo to the Director of Housing and Valuer, March 31, 1950, LCC/HSG/GEN/1/15/002, LMA.

91. Michael Harloe, *The People's Home: Social Rented Housing in Europe and America* (John Wiley & Sons, Aug 15, 2011).

92. Report of the Director of Housing and Valuer, March 1948, Housing Committee Papers, March-April 1948, LCC/MIN/7630, LMA. Quote from a Mass Observation in Hull Archive interview in 1948, quoted in Nick Tiratsoo, "The Reconstruction of Blitzed British Cities, 1945–55: Myths and Reality," *Contemporary British History* 14, no. 1 (Spring 2000): 42.

93. Paul Foot, "Sale of the Century," *Guardian*, January 8, 2003.

94. Alistair Horne, *Harold Macmillan*, vol. 1, *1894–1956* (New York: Viking, 1989), 330.

95. John A. Davenport, "Socialism by Default," *Fortune* 39 (March 1949).

96. Bourne also included a particularly outrageous reference to the "lessons" of the American Indian: "In conclusion, our people will not benefit from this paternalism. You need look no further than the American Indian to see how his self-reliance, individual initiative, and producing power were drained from him by Government control over his life." US 81st Cong., HR 4009, Hearings before the Committee on Banking and Currency, April and May 1949, 368–369.

97. Eisenhower speech at Columbia Forum of Democracy, as quoted in US 81st Cong., HR 4009, Hearings before the Committee on Banking and Currency, April and May 1949, 464; Holden testimony, 463; Snyder, 569; Whitlock, 599–600, 606–607.

98. Ibid., 551–561.

99. Ibid., 413–451.

100. Letter from Herbert U. Nelson, Executive Vice President of NAREB, to Walter Reuther, February 2, 1949, US Congress, House Committee on Banking and Currency, Cooperative Housing Abroad, February 10, 1950, 271.

101. Walter Reuther, *Homes for People, Jobs for Prosperity, Plans for Peace: A Program to Meet the Inner and Outer Threats to Democracy's Survival*, Pamphlets in American History, Butler Microforms, Columbia University.

102. The emphasis on these countries makes perfect sense, since in 1948, 20% of Sweden's dwelling units were coops, Holland, 33%, Denmark, 35%, and Switzerland, 24%. US Congress, House Committee on Banking and Currency, Cooperative Housing Abroad, February 10, 1950, 3.

103. Slogan on the ECA's letterhead, LCC/HSG/GEN/1/15, LMA.

104. United States Congress, Senate Banking and Currency Subcommittee investigating and studying European housing programs, *Cooperative Housing in Europe: A Report* (Washington, DC: 1950), 3.

105. Ibid., 2.

106. LCC memo, November 22, 1949, LCC/HSG/GEN/1/15, LMA.

107. In London, the LCC toured the visitors around South Lambeth and Howard Hill Estates, two of the most successful suburban relocation sites for London dwellers. Ibid., 2–5.

108. *Wall Street Journal*, April 4, 1950.

109. Letter from the Ministry of Health to I. Ungar, LCC, November 21, 1949, LCC-HSG-GEN-1-15, LMA; US Congress, Banking and Currency Committee, Hearings before the Committee on Banking and Currency, 81st Cong., 2nd sess. on HR 8276 (Washington, DC: 1950), ii.

110. Ibid., 2.

111. US Congress, Banking and Currency Committee, Extension of Rent Control, 1950 Hearings, HR 8276, May 8–17, 1950, 372–373.

112. Letter from Clarence Stein to Cyril Walker, Director of Housing and Valuer for the LCC, May 15, 1950, LCC/HSG/GEN/1/16, LMA.

113. In 1951, over $700 million of the Bowery Bank's assets were in FHA modernization loans and mortgage loans to veterans. See Bowery Bank

statement, January 1, 1951. References to American visitors in letter from the Workers Travel Association Ltd. to the LCC Housing Department, May 16, 1952; and LCC Programme for Visit of 25 Americans, July 4, 1951, LCC-HSG-GEN-1–17, LMA.

114. Cedric Bolz, "Zero Hour Has Come and Gone: Allied Efforts to Alleviate the Ruhr Housing Shortage from 1945 To 1949" (Master's thesis, Simon Fraser University, 1991), 70, 74, 94.

115. "Historical Census of Housing Tables—Homeownership," US Census Bureau, Housing and Household Economic Statistics Division, accessed December 2, 2004, http://www.census.gov/hhes/www/housing/census /historic/owner.html.

116. Characteristics of 1-Family Home Transactions, sec. 203, HHFA press release May 13, 1960, folder UN-ECE Correspondence, box 4, RG 207, NARA.

117. Kenneth T. Jackson, *Crabgrass Frontier: The Suburbanization of the United States* (Oxford: Oxford University Press, 1985); Robert Beauregard, *When America Became Suburban* (Minneapolis: University of Minnesota Press, 2006).

118. International Cooperation Administration Manual, "Use of Local Currencies in Construction of Housing," April 10, 1959, folder ICA General 1957– 59, box 4, RG 207, NARA.

119. Letter from Herbert Nelson to Roy J. Burroughs, HHFA, April 1, 1955, folder NAREB 1942, box 2, accession 69A5149, RG 207, NARA.

120. Letter from B. Douglas Stone, Acting Assistant to the Administrator, HHFA, to Herbert U. Nelson, NAREB, March 18, 1954, folder NAREB 1942, box 2, accession 69A5149, RG 207, NARA.

121. Stanley Baruch, Chief, Latin America—Europe Branch, Housing Division, memo to Douglas Stone, Acting Assistant to the Administrator, HHFA, March 18, 1955, folder FOA General-1955, box 4, RG 207, NARA.

122. ECA, "Marshall Plan Helps European Housing," 1950, folder Denmark, box 1, RG 286-C, NARA.

123. George L. Reed, memo, January 14, 1955, folder FOA General-1955, box 4, RG 207, NARA.

124. Ibid.

125. Dispatch 576, American Consulate General, Bombay, India, January 7, 1952, accession 71A3534, box 6, RG 207, NARA.

CHAPTER TWO

1. "The Opening Ceremony of Miners' Housing in Yingko," *Central Daily News*, April 12, 1955, translated by T. K. Djang, folder 1955, box 4, RG 207, NARA.

2. Samuel Hale Butterfield, *US Development Aid: An Historic First* (Westport, CT: Praeger, 2004), 2.

3. Quote from President Truman's counsel, Clark Clifford, in Butterfield, 2.

4. Benjamin Hardy was also a press officer in Nelson Rockefeller's Inter-American Affairs program in Brazil prior to joining the State Department. Quotes are from Christine Hardy Little's memories of her discussions with her husband in 1946. Transcript of Christine Hardy Little Oral History, Truman Library, 1973, 10–12.

5. Inaugural Address of Harry S. Truman, January 20, 1949, the Avalon Project at the Lillian Goldman Law Library, accessed February 27, 2009, http://avalon.law.yale.edu/20th_century/truman.asp.

6. Gilbert Rist, *The History of Development: From Western Origins to Global Faith* (London: Zed Books, 1997), 71.

7. Crane, "Housing, City Planning, and the 'Point Four' Program."

8. Jacob L. Crane and Ellery Foster, "Housing in International Economic Development," paper for the Bemis Foundation Conference, MIT, April 30, 1953, p. 7, box 1, Entry 810, RG 469, NARA; Richard Harris and Ceinwen Giles, "A Mixed Message: The Agents and Forms of International Housing Policy, 1945–1973," *Habitat International* 27 (2003): 171.

9. Jeffrey W. Cody, *Exporting American Architecture, 1870–2000* (London: Routledge, 2003), 23.

10. Ibid.

11. C. Tyler Wood, handwritten speech notes, n.d., but most likely between November 1949 and January 1950, Reports and testimony folder, box 4, C. Tyler Wood Papers, ML.

12. The "dollar gap" denoted a trade relationship where Europeans imported more from the US than they could afford. Europeans and the US dealt with this deficiency through a liquidiation of gold and dollar reserves ($18 billion), remittances and private capital ($11 billion), US aid to ECA countries ($17 billion), and US aid to non-ECA countries ($6 billion) from 1914 to 1948. Total dollar gap during that same timeframe was approximately $52 billion, not including wartime purchases. C. Tyler Wood speech before Annual Conference of the Production and Marketing Administration, December 5, 1949, Tyler Wood Speeches: 1948–50 folder, box 4, Tyler Wood Papers, ML.

13. Ibid.

14. "After the Marshall Plan, What?" transcript of American Forum of the Air, May 13, 1950, Tyler Wood Speeches: 1948–50 folder, box 4, Tyler Wood Papers, ML.

15. C. Tyler Wood speech to Conference of Tobacco Growers, Dealers and Warehousemen, January 18, 1950, folder Speeches, 1948–50, box 4, Tyler Wood Papers, ML.

16. Greg Castillo, "Domesticating the Cold War: Household Consumption as Propaganda in Marshall Plan Germany," *Journal of Contemporary History* 40, no. 2 (April 2005): 261–288. See also Castillo, *Cold War on the Home Front: The Soft Power of Midcentury Design* (Minneapolis: University of Minnesota Press, 2010); Ruth Oldenziel and Karin Zachmann, eds., *Cold War Kitchen:*

Americanization, Technology, and European Users (Cambridge, MA: MIT Press, 2011); Laura Belmonte, *Selling the American Way: US Propaganda and the Cold War* (Philadelphia: University of Pennsylvania Press, 2010); Jack Masey and Conway Lloyd Morgan, *Cold War Confrontations: US Exhibitions and Their Role in the Cultural Cold War* (Baden, Switzerland: Lars Müller, 2008); David Crowley and Jane Pavitt, eds., *Cold War Modern: Design 1945–1970* (New York: Harry N. Abrams, 2008); Beatriz Colomina, *Domesticity at War* (Cambridge, MA: MIT Press, 2007).

17. Gilbert Rist discusses the rise of the developed-underdeveloped dichotomy in the context of American hegemony and argues, "This new way of dividing up the world was remarkably attuned to North American interests." Rist, *The History of Development: From Western Origins to Global Faith* (New York: Zed Books, 1997), 75.

18. For discussion of European postwar slums and shantytowns, see Anne Power, *Hovels to High Rise: State Housing in Europe since 1850* (London: Routledge, 1993), 42 (France), 171–72 (UK), 289–90 (Denmark).

19. Crane and Foster; Crane, "Housing, City Planning, and the 'Point Four' Program."

20. Dan R. Hamady, Assistant to the Administrator, International Housing Activities Staff, "HHFA International Responsibilities," to William F. Russell, Deputy Director for Technical Services, Foreign Operations Administration, June 24, 1955, file FOA General 1955, box 4, RG 207, NARA.

21. Ibid.

22. Eleanor Roosevelt, *India and the Awakening East* (New York: Harper & Bros., 1953), xi–xvi.

23. Charles Abrams, *Man's Struggle for Shelter in an Urbanizing World* (Cambridge, MA: MIT Press, 1964), 89–104.

24. Richard Lacayo, "Suburban Legend: William Levitt," *Time*, July 3, 1950.

25. Richard Harris, "Slipping through the Cracks: The Origins of Aided Self-Help Housing, 1918–53," *Housing Studies* 14, no. 3 (1999): 282; Harris, "A Burp in Church: Jacob L. Crane's Vision of Aided Self-Help Housing," *Planning History Studies* 11, no. 1 (1997): 3–16.

26. Jacob Crane's draft article for Administrator Foley, March 3, 1952, p. 4, folder NAHRO 1947, box 2, RG 207, NARA.

27. Ellery Foster, letter to George L. Reed, Associate Director of the National Housing Board of Burma, January 29, 1952, folder FOA Burma 1952, box 1, RG 207, NARA.

28. Dan R. Hamady, Assistant to the Administrator, International Housing Service, HHFA, text of talk to be given at the International Program of the National Association of Housing and Redevelopment Officials Annual Conference, October 21, 1956, folder NAHRO 1947, box 2, RG 207, NARA.

29. Henry Luce, "The American Century," *Life Magazine*, February 17, 1941.

30. Letter from Roy J. Burroughs to George L. Reed, FOA, November 18, 1954, box 4, RG 207, NARA.

31. Hamady.
32. Report by Catherine Bauer, Delegate of the US Federal Public Housing Authority to the International Congress for Housing and Town Planning meeting held in Hastings, UK, November 6, 1946, folder UNESCO 1946–56, box 12, RG 207, NARA.
33. UNRRA concluded its activities in Europe in 1947, and in China in 1949.
34. "A Brooklyn Man Chosen by Chiang," *New York Times*, January 21, 1946, 32.
35. Ibid.
36. Chang Kia-ngan, "Home Loans in China," informal report to Meng Ling Chang, April 7, 1945, box 4, RG 207, NARA.
37. Letter from Norman Gordon to Jacob Crane, November 5, 1946. box 4, RG 207, NARA.
38. George Marshall had his own connection to China, having served as the American ambassador from 1945 to 1947. "Walter Henry Judd: An Inventory of His Papers," Manuscript Collections, Minnesota Historical Society; Hearings before the Committee on Foreign Affairs, House of Representatives, 80th Cong., 1st sess., November 1947, US Government Printing Office, Washington, DC: 1947, Digital Collection of Congressional Debates, MFA.
39. Hearings before the Committee on Foreign Affairs, November 1947.
40. Ibid.
41. Statement of the Secretary of State [George Marshall] before the Joint Session of the Senate Committee on Foreign Relations and the House Committee on Foreign Affairs, Monday, November 10, 1947, 10 a.m., folder 13 "Speeches by Others: 1948–50," box 4, C. Tyler Tyler Wood Papers, ML.
42. Of that sum, $510 million was allocated to essentials like food, fuel, and clothing. Marshall Testimony to the House of Representatives Committee on Foreign Affairs, February 20, 1948, Digital Collection of Congressional Debates, MFA.
43. Memo from O. Edmund Clubb, American Consul General, to the Secretary of State, September 24, 1947, box 4, RG 207, NARA.
44. Economic Cooperation Administration, "Far East Programs: Fiscal 1952 Budget, Formosa, $65,000,000," Confidential Report, February 20, 1951, box 4, RG 207, NARA.
45. Ibid.
46. Advisory services continued during the war. Roughly $800,000 of ECA's financing for fiscal 1952 paid for White's ongoing recommendations on all manner of issues, including but not limited to all forms of modern transport, refineries, and electric power, with the ultimate objective of creating a self-supporting industrial economy. ECA Far East Programs: Fiscal 1952 Budget, $65 million, February 20, 1951, box 4, RG 207, NARA.
47. Confidential letter from Raymond T. Moyer, JCRR, to John B. Nason, Deputy Director, ECA Program in China, September 9, 1949, China (JCRR) subject files, 1948–56, box 38, RG 469, NARA.

48. Stages 2 and 3 began in 1951 and 1953. JCRR memo, June 24, 1949, China (JCRR) subject files, 1948–56, box 38, RG 469, NARA.

49. Letter from John B. Nason, Deputy Director, China Program, to Raymond T. Moyer, JCRR, September 30, 1949, China (JCRR) subject files, 1948–56, box 38, RG 469, NARA.

50. Melvin Gurtov, "Recent Developments on Formosa," *China Quarterly* 31 (July–September 1967): 77.

51. Samuel P. S. Ho, "Economics, Economic Bureaucracy, and Taiwan's Economic Development," *Pacific Affairs* 60, no. 2 (Summer, 1987): 233–236.

52. The JCRR's land reforms also had an unplanned consequence: JCRR members witnessed "the adverse consequences of population pressure on arable land" in the course of their travels, and these experiences galvanized JCRR members—Jiang Menglin in particular—to lead the family planning movement in Taiwan. Ralph W. Huenemann, "Family Planning in Taiwan: The Conflict between Ideologues and Technocrats," *Modern China* 16, no. 2 (April 1990): 181–182.

53. "Strategy on Orient Shifts," *New York Times*, January 1, 1950.

54. Robert H. Deans notes that "anti-grant feelings in Congress" grew all the way into the mid-1950s. Deans, "Potential Effects of US Commodity Grants to Other Countries," *American Journal of Agricultural Economies* 50, no. 4 (November 1968): 1012.

55. The four stated goals of the Mutual Security Mission were: (1) "defense support and military assistance," (2) "economic stability," (3) "progress toward self-support," and (4) the "strengthen[ing of] the government—assist[ing the] Chinese Government in economic and technical fields so that by its own efforts it can attract growing support from Chinese communities (world-wide) and greater prestige throughout the world." FOA Taipei memo, October 21, 1954, box 4, RG 207, NARA. Stanton H. Burnett, *Investing in Security: Economic Aid for Noneconomic Purposes* (Washington, DC: Center for Strategic and International Studies, 1992), pt. 2, chap. 1. Quote from Ngaire Woods, *The Globalizers: The IMF, the World Bank and Their Borrowers* (Ithaca: Cornell University Press, 2006), 34.

56. The two harbors were in far better shape than land transportation networks like railroads and highways, and the ECA devoted more money toward the latter—only about one in seven transportation aid dollars went to the docks. Unlike workers on railroads or highways, however, dockworkers lived next to ports long after construction was completed. Economic Cooperation Administration, "Far East Programs: Fiscal 1952 Budget; Formosa, $65,000,000," Confidential Report, February 20, 1951, box 4, RG 207, NARA.

57. *Report of Labour Statistics* 2 (1954), as quoted in T. K. Djang, "Aided Self-Help Housing Programmes for Workers in Formosa," [June 1955?], box 4, RG 207, NARA.

58. Fraleigh arrived in Taiwan in November 1952. Letter to George Reed, FOA, July 10, 1954, box 4, RG 207, NARA.

59. The home would be owned by the union until all amortization payments were made, at which point the laborer would become the homeowner.

60. Roy J. Burroughs, "More and Better Houses: A Radio Talk for Housing," November 11, 1954; and "Better Housing for Free China: A Foreigner's Comment," draft for review, November 1, 1954, box 4, RG 207, NARA.

61. Mutual Security Agency memo, December 17, 1953, box 4, RG 207, NARA.

62. Djang.

63. ICA Project Proposal and Approval Summary, May 1954–June 30, 1956, folder 1955, box 4, RG 207, NARA.

64. "Tachen Evacuees to Build Own Houses with NT$20M. Disbursed by US Gov't.," *China Post*, June 9, 1955, folder 1955, box 4, NARA.

65. Letter exchange between T. R. Bowden, Deputy Director of the Mutual Security Mission to China, FOA, with Mr. B. Douglas Stone, Acting Assistant to the Administrator, HHFA, December 1954–January 1955, box 4, RG 207, NARA.

66. ICA Project Proposal and Approval in China (Formosa), "Public Housing Program," July 1954–June 1957, p. 2, box 4, RG 207, NARA.

67. "Auspicious Occasion for Kaohsiung Laborers Who Move into Their New Quarters," *Hsin Shing Pao*, Taipei, April 3, 1955, box 4, RG 207, NARA.

68. US Technical Assistance to Housing in Free China Report, November 1954, prepared by Albert Fraleigh, Office of Assistant Director of Operations and Information Office, Foreign Operations Administration, Mutual Security Mission to China, box 4, RG 207, NARA.

69. *Housing through Non-Profit Organizations: Seminar Sponsored by the UN and the Government of Denmark in Collaboration with the Organization of American States, Copenhagen, September–October 1954* (New York, UN Department of Economic and Social Affairs, 1956), 49.

70. Ibid., 12, 32.

71. Ibid., 13, 49–50.

72. Ibid., 63.

73. Djang, 2.

74. David Allen Baldwin, *Economic Development and American Foreign Policy, 1943–1962* (Chicago: University of Chicago Press, 1966), 83.

75. The official exchange rate in 1954 was NT$15.65 to one US dollar, but according to Albert Fraleigh, was more realistically about NT$27 to one US dollar. Letter to George Reed, FOA, July 10, 1954; and memo from T. K. Djang, Technical Assistant, to Roy J. Burroughs, International Housing Finance Advisor, HHFA, December 3, 1954, box 4, RG 207, NARA.

76. National Housing Program Working Group minutes, December 7, 1954, box 4, RG 207, NARA.

77. Memo from Roy J. Burroughs, HHFA, to George L. Reed, FOA, December 8, 1954, box 4, RG 207, NARA.

78. Ibid.

79. My italics. Report of the National Housing Program Working Group, December 7, 1954, box 4, RG 207, NARA.
80. Ibid.
81. Letter from Hugo Prucha, Housing Advisor in the ICA's MSA Mission to China, to Roy J. Burroughs of the HHFA, November 4, 1955, box 4, RG 207, NARA.
82. T. R. Bowden, National Housing Exhibition Report, November 14, 1955, folder 1955, box 4, RG 207, NARA.
83. Ibid.
84. Osborne T. Boyd, "Review of International Cooperation Administration's World-Wide Housing Programs," *Land Economics* 35, no. 1 (February, 1959): 78.
85. For just one example among many, see ICA Project Proposal and Approval in China (Formosa).
86. Minutes, 24th Weekly Meeting of the National Housing Program Working Group, December 14, 1954, box 4, RG 207, NARA.
87. FOA memorandum, "Recent Lowcost Housing Activities in Taiwan," August 19, 1954, folder 1951–54; Djang, "Aided Self-Help Housing Programmes for Workers in Formosa."
88. Letter from Roy J. Burroughs to George L. Reed, FOA, November 18, 1954, box 4, RG 207, NARA.
89. Ibid.; Letter from Roy J. Burroughs to Hugo Prucha, December 28, 1955, folder 1955, box 4, RG 207, NARA.
90. Letter from Roy J. Burroughs to George L. Reed, November 18, 1954.
91. FOA report, "Housing Program for Free China," January 30, 1954, box 4, RG 207, NARA.
92. See, for example, T. R. Bowden's memo to C. T. Meng, Minister of the National Housing Commission, on November 22, 1955. In this memo, Bowden included the precise text for a proposed amendment to section 877. Box 4, RG 207, NARA.
93. FOA report, "Housing Program for Free China."
94. ICA Project Proposal and Approval in China (Formosa).
95. Ibid. This report is repeated almost verbatim by an ICA report, "Progress Report: Tachen Selfhelp Housing Resettlement Program," November 16, 1955, folder 1955, box 4, RG 207, NARA.
96. Attachment to letter from Fraleigh to George L. Reed, Acting Chief of the Housing Division, FOA, April 18, 1955, folder 1955, box 4, RG 207, NARA.
97. ICA report, "Progress Report: Tachen Selfhelp Housing Resettlement Program."
98. Interestingly, UN experts like Donald Monson would recommend the further development of the Taipei-Keelung metropolitan area along British post–World War II planning principles, with greenbelts restricting central city growth and new towns or satellite cities accommodating growth. Letter

from Donald Monson to Ricardo Luna, UN, September 4, 1964, folder 6, box 309, series 175, UNA.

99. V. Antolic, *Greater Rangoon Plan* (New York: United Nations Programme of Technical Assistance, Department of Economic and Social Affairs, January 12, 1961), 5–6, folder UN Technical Assistance Mission in Burma, Town Planning (Kachin State), box S-0175-0218, UNA. Antolic prepared these observations from August 8, 1953, to December 31, 1958.

100. Memo from George Reed to Jacob Crane, May 29, 1952, folder FOA Burma 1952, box 1, RG 207, NARA.

101. Housing meeting notes, ECA, March 6, 1951, folder FOA Burma 1950–51, box 1, RG 207, NARA.

102. Ibid.

103. Press release, ECA Office of Information, February 12, 1951, folder FOA Burma 1950–51, box 1, RG 207, NARA.

104. Housing meeting notes, ECA, March 6, 1961, folder FOA Burma 1950–51, box 1, RG 207, NARA.

105. Abbott Low Moffat, Chief of the US Special Technical and Economic Mission to Burma, Report, October 31, 1950, folder FOA Burma 1948–57, box 1, RG 207, NARA.

106. Letter from Ellery A. Foster to Jacob Crane, November 13, 1950, folder FOA Burma, 1948–57, box 1, RG 207, NARA.

107. The villages of Thayagon, Htaukkya, Htaiktugan, and Dayebo bought 100,000 square feet in February 11, 1953, but Prome was the first large urban purchase.

108. Hugo Prucha report to the National Housing and Town and Country Development Board, Report of visits to Chauk, Yenangyaung, and Prome, September 16–21, 1954, folder FOA Burma 1948–57, box 1, RG 207, NARA.

109. Unsigned memo, January 16, 1962, folder Burma 1962, box 1, RG 207, NARA.

110. US Embassy report to the State Department, April 6, 1960, p. 6, folder Burma 1960–61, box 1, RG 207, NARA.

111. Even though significantly higher than the UK's Ministry of Housing and Local Government's standard of between 14.3 to 57.2 persons per acre, these densities "seem[ed] practical and reasonable, taking social, economic, and climatic conditions into account." Antolic, 56–58. UN advisors failed to enact these grand plans because of basic obstructions by the Burmese national government (including the refusal to permit aerial planning photographs) and because of UN advisors' own shortcomings. The Swedish advisor I. Ditlef-Nielsen confessed that his inability to speak Burmese and Kachin seriously hampered his ability to carry out basic planning surveys. Letter from I. Ditlef-Nielsen to J. M. Saunders, Chief of the Office for Asia and Far East, Bureau of Technical Assistance Operations, Department of Economic and Social Affairs, UN, August 3, 1962, folder UN Technical

Assistance Mission in Burma, Town Planning (Kachin State), box S-0175-0218, UNA.

112. Chŏn Nam-il, *Han'guk chugŏ ŭi sahoesa* (Kyŏnggi-do P'aju-si: Tobegae, 2008), 375n1.

113. Ibid., 152–153.

114. Chŏn; "Korean Rebuilding," *Time Magazine*, October 26, 1953; Ch'a Chong-ch'ŏn, Yu Hong-jun, and Yi Chŏng-hwan, *Sŏul-si kyech'ŭngbyŏl chugŏ chiyŏk punp'o ŭi yŏksajŏk pyŏnch'ŏn* (Seoul: Paeksan Sŏdang, 2004).

115. Kim Mahn-Je, "The Republic of Korea's Successful Economic Development and the World Bank," in Devesh Kapur, John Prior Lewis, and Richard Charles Webb, eds., *The World Bank: Its First Half Century* (Washington, DC: Brookings Institution Press, 1997), 18.

116. There are some discrepancies in the records about exactly how much money was involved for CRIK. For instance, Mahn-Je Kim argues CRIK sent a total of US$218 million to the ROK between 1950 and 1956, while Collins and Park put the number at US$397.8 million. The US contribution to UNKRA was $162.5 million out of a total budget of $250 million. Fifty million dollars of the American contribution came out of leftover funds from ECA's Korea program. "UN Plans Rebuilding of Korea," *Washington Post,* July 22, 1951.

117. W. Macmahon Ball, "Review: Gene M. Lyons, *Military Policy and Economic Aid—The Korean Case, 1950–1953*," *Journal of Asian Studies* 21, no. 4 (August 1962): 561.

118. Woo Jung-en, *Race to the Swift: State and Finance in the Industrialization of Korea* (New York: Columbia University Press, 1991).

119. The Ministry of Social Affairs and the Ministry of Finance directed all housing-related activities in the Republic of Korea at this time.

120. Different standards resulted in different assessments of need: the US figure for housing need came to nearly 900,000 houses in 1952, while the Korean government estimated need at 500,000.

121. "Korean Rebuilding," *Time Magazine,* October 26, 1953.

122. Burton P. Jenks, *Korean Housing Survey* (1952), a report used to write UNKRA's five-year program. No folder, box 65, NARA.

123. Tasca had previously served as an assistant in the ECA's Office of the United States SpecialRepresentative in Europe. See Records of US Foreign Assistance Agencies, 1948–61, RG 469, NARA. Tasca's first two recommendations come from Steven Hugh Lee, *Outposts of Empire: Korea, Vietnam, and the Origins of the Cold War in Asia, 1949–1954* (Montreal: McGill-Queen's University Press, 1995), 189–190. Tasca's third recommendation can be found in Kapur et al., 19n3.

124. The FOA handled all US aid except loans. The $200 million was left over because of the suspension of military conflict.

125. KCAC was defunct by the end of 1956. Report of the Washington Unified Command Team (Defense-State-ICA-USIA) on the Inter-Agency Relationships Involved in Providing the Office of the Economic Coordinator,

American Embassy, and US Information Service, Seoul, Korea with Continued Administrative and Logistic Support, September 19, 1955, box 9, NARA. C. Tyler Wood's biography is available in the Collection Summary Sheet, C. Tyler Tyler Wood Papers, ML.

126. The FOA was a short-lived independent agency outside the State Department that consolidated overseas economic and technical aid from 1953–54 before being absorbed into the new ICA.

127. C. Tyler Wood, memo, November 18, 1955, folder Housing, box 36, RG 469, NARA.

128. Letter from Bert Fraleigh, Supply Operations Advisor, to Richard C. Knight, Far East Housing Advisor of the Housing Division, ICA, January 9, 1956. box 65, RG 207, NARA.

129. Approval of both parties indicated in an FOA cablegram, April 8, 1955, folder Housing, box 36, RG 469, NARA.

130. William Zeckendorf notes in his autobiography that he also recruited many Korean architects to be trained at Webb and Knapp after his tour of the peninsula in 1953. He remembered proudly that "in 1967, when I flew out to Korea . . . I found my trainees had become the leading architects in Korea." William Zeckendorf with Edward McCreary, *The Autobiography of William Zeckendorf, 1905–1976* (New York: Holt, Rinehart and Winston, 1970), 243. Quote in text from *Homes for Korea*, pamphlet, n.d., box 65, RG 207, NARA.

131. *Homes for Korea* pamphlet.

132. "NAHB Official Sees 'Steady' '56 Market," *Washington Post,* July 22, 1955.

133. "Private Industry's Point Four," *Washington Post and Times-Herald,* August 21, 1955.

134. Report from Guido Nadzo, Chief of the Housing Division of ICA, to Grant Whitman, Deputy UNC Economic Coordinator, June 19, 1956, box 65, RG 207, NARA.

135. Stellan C. Wollmar, Community Development Division, ICA, Highlight Report August 1957, pp. 7, 1957 folder, box 65, RG 207, NARA.

136. ICA memo, December 11, 1957, 1957 folder, box 65, RG 207, NARA.

137. USAID memo to John Sparkman, n.d., but definitely 1962, AID 1962–63 folder, box 15, RG 207, NARA.

138. ICA memo, December 11, 1957, 1957 folder, box 65, RG 207, NARA.

139. Guido Nadzo, Housing Advisor, USOM/Korea, End of Tour Report, October 26, 1963, 1963 folder, box 65, RG 207, NARA.

140. FOA Project Proposal and Approval Summary, Republic of Korea, FY 1957, p. 5, 1957 folder, box 65, RG 207, NARA.

141. ICA memo, December 11, 1957.

142. Wollmar, 3–4.

143. Ibid.

144. Han'guk Sahoe Kwahak Yŏn'guwŏn, *Kijon chut'aek saŏp e kwanhan pip'anjŏk punsŏk pogo: Tosi kaebal ŭl wihan yebi yŏn'gu* (Seoul: 1965), 39.

145. Nadzo, 1963.

146. June Manning Thomas and Hee-Yun Hwang, "Social Equity in Redevelopment and Housing: United States and Korea," *Journal of Planning Education and Research* 23, no. 8 (2003): 11.

147. USAID Office of Housing, *A Case Study of the Korean Housing Investment Guaranty Program, 1971–1977* (Washington, DC: PADCO, 1977).

148. Valérie Gelézeau, "Korean Modernism, Modern Korean Cityscapes, and Mass Housing Development: Charting the Rise of Ap'atu Tanji since the 1960s," in Rüdiger Frank, James E. Hoare, Patrick Köllner, and Susan Pares, eds., *Korea Yearbook 2007: Politics, Economy, and Society* (Leiden, Holland: Brill, 2008), 165–191.

149. Confidential memo, TCA, September 29, 1952, South and Southeast Asia folder, box 3, entry 911, RG 469, NARA.

150. Ibid.

151. Dean Rusk, memo, November 9, 1963, 1963 folder, box 65, RG 207, NARA.

152. Nina Shafran, "US-USSR Cooperation in Housing and Other Construction," *HUD International Review* 1, no. 2 (May 1979): 67–71.

153. For more on Soviet housing efforts, see "Special Issue: Cold War Transfer: Architecture and Planning from Socialist Countries in the 'Third World,' " *Journal of Architecture* 17, no. 3 (2012); and in particular, Łukasz Stanek's introduction, "The 'Second World's' Architecture and Planning in the 'Third World.' "

154. Castillo, xiv.

CHAPTER THREE

1. John F. Kennedy, inaugural address, January 20, 1961; quoted at Gerhard Peters and John T. Woolley, The American Presidency Project, http://www.presidency.ucsb.edu/ws/?pid=8032.

2. Gilbert Rist, *The History of Development: From Western Origins to Global Faith* (London: Zed Books, 1997), 73–76.

3. Gwendolyn Wright, *The Politics of Design in French Colonial Urbanism* (Chicago: University of Chicago Press, 1991); Colin Clarke, *Decolonizing the Colonial City: Urbanization and Stratification in Kingston, Jamaica* (Oxford: Oxford University Press, 2006); Carl H. Nightingale, *Segregation: A Global History of Divided Cities* (Chicago: University of Chicago Press, 2012); Freek Colombijn, *Under Construction: The Politics of Urban Space and Housing during the Decolonization of Indonesia, 1930–1960* (Leiden: KITLV Press, 2013).

4. Felix Driver and Brenda Yeoh, "Constructing the Tropics: An Introduction," *Singapore Journal of Tropical Geography* 21, no. 1 (March 2000): 1–5; Stephen Frenkel, "Jungle Stories: North American Representations of Tropical Panama," *Geographical Review* 86, no. 3 (July 1996): 317–333; David Arnold, " 'Illusory Riches': Representations of the Tropical World, 1840–1950," *Singapore Journal of Tropical Geography* 21, no. 1 (March 2000): 6–18; Victor

Savage, "Tropicality Imagined and Experienced," *Singapore Journal of Tropical Geography* 25, no. 1 (March 2004), 26–31; Nancy Leys Stepan, *Picturing Tropical Nature* (Chicago: University of Chicago Press, 2001); Michel Bruneau and Georges Courade, "Existe-t-il une géographie humaine tropicale? A la recherché du paradigme de Pierre Gourou," *L'espace géographique* 13, no. 4 (1984): 306–316; Hervé Théry, "Tropiques et tiers monde: Un débat toujours actuel pour les géographes," *Tiers-Monde* 28, no. 112 (1987): 813–822; Felix Driver and Luciana Martins, eds., *Tropical Visions in an Age of Empire* (Chicago: University of Chicago Press, 2005); Jean Gallais, "L'évolution de la pensée géographique de Pierre Gourou sur les pays tropicaux (1935–1970)," *Annales de Géographie* 90, no. 498 (1981): 129–150; Bernard Smith, *European Vision and the South Pacific*, 2nd ed. (New Haven: Yale University Press, 1989); Anthony D. King, *The Bungalow: The Production of a Global Culture* (New York: Oxford University Press, 1995), 47; Anthony D. King, *Colonial Urban Development: Culture, Social Power, and Environment* (London: Routledge and Kegan Paul, 1976).

5. David Arnold, "Inventing Tropicality," in *The Problem of Nature: Environment, Culture and European Expansion* (Cambridge, MA: Blackwell Publishers, 1996), 142–143.

6. Fidel Tavárez, " 'The Moral Miasma of the Tropics': American Imperialism and the Failed Annexation of the Dominican Republic, 1869–1871," *Nuevo Mundo Mundos Nuevos* website, July 13, 2011, consulted 13 February 2014; http://nuevomundo.revues.org/61771.

7. G. Anthony Atkinson, "Building in the Tropics: Research into Housing in Tropical Countries, Especially in the Commonwealth," RIBA Architectural Science Board, April 18, 1950, HDB 1094, NAS.

8. *UN Housing and Town and Country Planning Bulletin* 6 (May 1952).

9. Anatole Solow (Housing Director of the Washington, DC–based Pan-American Union), "Housing in Tropical Areas," *UN Housing and Town and Country Planning Bulletin* 2 (April 1949): 11.

10. Dr. Curt R. Schneider, "Brief Summary of Status and Plans of the 'Tropical Medicine Survey,' " in *Proceedings of the Fourth Conference, Industrial Council for Tropical Health, Sponsored by the Harvard School of Public Health, July 20–22, 1960, in Boston* (Boston: Harvard School of Public Health, 1961), 35–37.

11. Catherine Bauer Wurster, "The Current Change in Civic Hopes and Attitudes," *UN Housing and Town and Country Planning Bulletin* 1 (November 1948): 37; Solow, 17. Otto Koenigsberger's *Manual of Tropical Housing and Building* perhaps came closest to offering this sort of guidebook in 1974; it was translated into many languages, including Bahasa. Otto Koenigsberger, *Manual perumahan dan bangunan tropika*, trans. Abdul Majid Ismail (Pulau Pinang: Penerbit Universiti Sains Malaysia, 1994).

12. Catherine Bauer Wurster, "Housing Aid for Underdeveloped Countries," Study of International Housing by the Subcommittee on Housing,

Committee on Banking and Currency, US Senate, 88th Cong., 1st sess., March 1963, 53.

13. Philip D. Curtin, "Medical Knowledge and Urban Planning in Tropical Africa," *American Historical Review*, 90 (3): 600.

14. My translation. J. H. Calsat, "Afrique française: L'habitat en climat tropical," in Congrès International de l'Habitation et de l'Urbanisme, *L'Habitation dans les pays tropicaux* (Lisbon: 1952), 14.

15. Atkinson also mentioned the uplands as a third type of tropical climate in a later conference paper. The uplands were hot during the day and cool at night. Atkinson, "Tropical Architecture and Building Standards," Conference on Tropical Architecture held at University College, London, March 24, 1953.

16. Jean Royer, ed., *L'Urbanisme aux colonies et dans les pays tropicaux*, 2 vols. (La Charité-sur-Loire, 1932–35); see especially 2:37–74. The original International Federation for Housing and Town Planning (London), the International Housing Association (Frankfort am Main), and the Congrès International des Habitations à Bon Marché joined forces to form the new International Federation for Housing and Town Planning (Brussels) in 1938. IFHTP Papers, HDB 1051, NAS. UK Contributions to International Organisations, Department of Scientific and Industrial Research, Overseas Activities of DSIR, DSIR/17/416, PRO.

17. Royal Tropical Institute homepage, February 13, 2014, http://www.kit.nl /kit/History.

18. George Anthony Atkinson, "British Architects in the Tropics," *Architectural Association Journal* 69 (June 1953): 7–21.

19. Coffee plantations were important in Indonesia, while rubber dominated the Malayan peninsula. Top Secret Second Draft memo Joint Logistics Planning Committee (45), 10/1: Development of Singapore and South Malaya as an advance base, WO 203/5490, PRO. For more on the importance of Southeast Asia to Britain, see Tilman Remme, "Britain, the 1947 Asian Relations Conference, and Regional Co-Operation in South-East Asia," in Anthony Gorst, Lewis Johnman, and W. Scott Lucas, eds., *Post-War Britain, 1945–64* (London: Pinter, 1989), 126–127; quote from Richard Tucker, *Insatiable Appetite: The United States and the Ecological Degradation of the Tropical World* (Berkeley: University of California Press, 2000), 265–66. The US Rubber Company briefly owned 22,000 acres of plantations on the Malayan peninsula in the 1920s, but most Americans fled during the anti-colonial communist war for independence (the British "Emergency," 1948–60). Synthetic rubber did not surpass natural production until 1962. Gary R. Hess, *The United States' Emergence as a Southeast Asian Power, 1940– 1950* (New York: Columbia University Press, 1987), 271.

20. J. M. Fraser, *The Work of the Singapore Improvement Trust, 1950* (Singapore: Malaya Publishing House, 1950), 1.

NOTES TO PAGES 95-97

21. Donarld S. Burke, "American Society of Tropical Medicine and Hygiene Centennial Celebration Address," draft MS (Philadelphia, 2003), 12, https://www.astmh.org/AM/Template.cfm?Section=Meeting_Archives &Template=/CM/ContentDisplay.cfm&ContentID=1500.

22. For one example, see "The International Labour Organisation and Housing," *UN Housing and Town and Country Planning Bulletin* 3 (February 1950): 48–51.

23. For detailed reports of the council conferences, see *Industry and Tropical Health* 1–7 (1950–70). Eli Chernin, *Tropical Medicine at Harvard: The Weller Years, 1954–1981; A Personal Memoir* (Boston: Harvard School of Public Health, 1985), 30–31. For pre-1954 history of Harvard's School of Public Health, see G. C. Shattuck, *Tropical Medicine at Harvard* (Boston: Harvard School of Public Health, 1954).

24. The conference series petered out through benign neglect during the 1960s, but Harvard renewed its international tropical health efforts in a fresh venture in 1970. Eventually known as the Harvard-Wellcome Project, the London-based Wellcome Trust offered a "reverse lend-lease" of £1 million to support American research in tropical medicine. Harvard's School of Public Health and the London School of Hygiene and Tropical Medicine would co-operate for a ten-year period; the purpose of the project was to help young scientists "embark on long-term careers of research in the tropics" and to "strengthen collaborative relationships already existing between the schools in Boston and London." The dean's report proudly declared, "The grant will be of great importance to the development of international activities in the tropics over the next decade." *Industry and Tropical Health* 4 (1961): index.

25. Jacob Crane letter to Roy Borroughs, February 1, 1951, accession 69A5149, box 13, NARA.

26. Adam Rome, *The Bulldozer in the Countryside: Suburban Sprawl and the Rise of American Environmentalism* (Cambridge: Cambridge University Press, 2001), 60.

27. Ibid., 58–64; Bernard Wagner, "Design for Livability: A Discussion of Livability Problems Arising from Proper Orientation in Regard to Sunlight," *Technical Bulletin* 15 (1950): 1–10.

28. UN Report of Mission of Experts, "Low Cost Housing in South and South-East Asia," November 20, 1950–January 23, 1951 (New York: UN Department of Social Affairs, 1951).

29. Kayanan worked as the chief planner of the National Urban Planning Commission in the Philippines, and Thijsse played a similarly important role in Indonesian planning. Pauline K. M. van Roosmalen, "Expanding Grounds: The Roots of Spatial Planning in Indonesia," in Freek Colombijn and Martine Barwegen, *Kota lama, kota baru: Sejarah kota-kota di Indonesia sebelum dan setelah kemerdekaan / The History of the Indonesian City before and after Independence* (Ombak, Yogyakarta, 2005), 75–117.

30. Ibid.
31. Jacob Crane, "Huts and Houses in the Tropics," Unasylva 3, no. 3 (May–June 1949), 99–105.
32. UN Report of Mission of Experts; "Housing in the Tropics," UN Housing and Town and Country Planning Bulletin 6 (May 1952): 2.
33. UN Report of Mission of Experts, 34–36.
34. Crane, "Huts and Houses in the Tropics."
35. UN Report of Mission of Experts, 134.
36. Richard Harris, "Silence of the Experts: Aided Self-Help Housing, 1939–1954," Habitat International 22, no. 2 (1998): 166.
37. Richard Harris and Ceinwen Giles, "A Mixed Message: The Agents and Forms of International Housing Policy, 1945–1973," Habitat International 27 (2003): 176–177.
38. Solow, 12.
39. Crane, "Huts and Houses in the Tropics."
40. Howard T. Fisher, "Developmental Design: An Approach to the Production of Better Buildings and Structures at Lower Cost," n.d., but most likely 1957, folder SO 144/8, RG 3/9, box 47, UNA.
41. Douglas H. K. Lee, Physiological Objectives in Hot Weather Housing: An Introduction to Hot Weather Housing Design for Use of United States Aid Missions rev. ed. (1953; Washington, DC: Housing and Home Finance Agency, 1969), iii.
42. For contemporaneous discussion of other aided self-help programs, see Jacob L. Crane and Robert E. McCabe, "Programmes in Aid of Family Housebuilding: Aided Self-Help Housing," International Labour Review 61, no. 4 (April 1950). For a historic overview, see Richard Harris, "Slipping through the Cracks: the Origins of Aided Self-Help Housing, 1918–53," Housing Studies 14, no. 3 (1999): 281–309.
43. The Tuskegee program targeted impoverished, rural African American families with little federal aid beyond limited Farmers Home Administration loans and HHFA sponsorship—the latter, mostly to produce a handbook of best practices for "rehabilitating housing in war-torn areas" and building "modern design houses" abroad. "Preliminary suggestions regarding a low-cost housing program in Alabama for rural Negroes," Tuskegee Institute, August 20, 1940; Ernest E. Neal, "Low Cash-Cost Housing: A Progress Report on Experimentation at Tuskegee Institute," Rural Life Information Series Bulletin [Tuskegee Institute] 2 (1950): 6, 26. William A. Russell, "Building Self-Help Homes," Housing Research (Fall 1951): 27, 34.
44. Luis Rivera Santos, Executive Director of the Social Programs Administration of the Department of Agriculture and Commerce, "An Analysis of Existing Housing Programs in the Commonwealth of Puerto Rico with Special Emphasis on Aided Self-Help Activities," 1955, folder Aided Self-Help 1955, box 15, accession 69A5149, RG 207, NARA.

45. Unfortunately, no data is available for homeownership rates in 1939. Roughly 65% of all shanty dwellers owned their units by 1955, but the quality of the house discounted the value of this high rate for planners. César Cordero Dávila, Executive Director of the Puerto Rico Housing Authority, memorandum to the Staff Director of the House Banking and Currency Committee regarding Housing Problems and Policies of the Commonwealth of Puerto Rico, December 16, 1955, box 2, Jacob Crane Collection, CU, 3.
46. Crane and McCabe, 8–9.
47. Letter from Pieter Pauw, Director of Planning, Puerto Rico Housing Authority to Jacob Crane, HHFA, December 14, 1949, folder Aided Self-Help 1952–53, box 15, accession 69A5149, RG 207, NARA.
48. The Land Law of 1941 addressed longstanding issues of inequity between sugar companies and landless laborers by creating the Puerto Rico Land Authority, which in turn expropriated land from large corporations in violation of the 500-Acre Limitation Act and redistributed property to landless *agregados*. The 500-Acre Limitation Act had its origins in the 1900 Organic Act; it would later be embedded in the Constitution of the Commonwealth of Puerto Rico. Ismael García-Colón, *Land Reform in Puerto Rico: Modernizing the Colonial State, 1941–1969* (Gainesville: University Press of Florida, 2009).
49. Puerto Rico Housing Research Board, *Aided Self-Help and Mutual Aid: A New Approach to Low Cost Housing in Puerto Rico* (Río Piedras, Puerto Rico: 1959), 15.
50. Zaire Dinzey-Flores points to Rubén Nazario Velasco's article as a useful discussion of the individualization of landownership. See Velasco, "Pan, casa, libertad: De la Reforma agrarian a la especulación inmobilaria," in Fernando Picó, ed., *Luis Muñoz Marín: Perfiles de su gobernación, 1948–1964* (San Juan, Puerto Rico: Fundación Luis Muñoz Marín, 2003), 144–64.
51. Douglas Rosenbaum, head of the Puerto Rico field station of the Division of Slum Clearance and Urban Redevelopment, explains these two problems in greater detail in Rosenbaum, "Palms, Poverty, Progress: That's Puerto Rico's Slum Clearance Story," *Journal of Housing* 1–7 (July 1954): 234–237.
52. Dávila, 9.
53. Ibid.
54. Ibid., 3.
55. Tyrwhitt was the director of the seminar and an advisor to the Indian government. Letters by Eleanor M. Hinder, Chief, Office for Asia and the Far East Programme Division, Technical Assistance Administration, UN, to Jacob Crane, October 12–13, 1953, folder 1–5, box 1, Jacob Crane Collection, CU.
56. The US and Guatemalan governments worked together through an autonomous agency called the Instituto Cooperativo Interamericano de la

Vivienda (1956–62). For a full report of the agency's activities to 1960, see *El programa del Instituto Cooperativo Interamericano de la Vivienda: De barracas a hogares modernos* (Washington, DC: USAID, 1963); "The Development of an Urban Aided Self-Help Housing Program in Guatemala City, Guatemala," *Ideas and Methods Exchange* 50 (1961). For Nicaragua, see " 'Colonia Managua': An Aided Self-Help Housing Project in Nicaragua," *Ideas and Methods Exchange* 58 (1962). After American housing advisors left in 1962, the Guatemalan government moved to a split public-private system with low-income housing dominating the former, and credit-based private ownership for the latter. USAID would play a role in bolstering home credit institutions.

57. Letter from Jacob Crane to Ernest Weissmann, August 28, 1953, folder 1–5, box 1, Jacob Crane Collection, CU.

58. Laura Briggs, *Reproducing Empire: Race, Sex, Science, and US Imperialism in Puerto Rico* (Berkeley: University of California Press, 2002), 118.

59. Ibid.; A. W. Maldonado, *Teodoro Moscoso and Puerto Rico's Operation Bootstrap* (Gainesville: University Press of Florida, 1997).

60. Dávila, 6.

61. Memo by Carl C. Taylor, November 13, 1951, folder Aided Self-Help 1952–53, box 15, accession 69A5149, RG 207, NARA.

62. Letter from Pieter Pauw to Jacob Crane, December 14, 1949.

63. Jacob Crane, "Workers' Housing in Puerto Rico," *International Labour Review* 49, no. 6 (1944): 629.

64. For sample floor plans, see *Departamento de Hacienda, planos modelos: Boletin de informacion* (Santurce: Puerto Rico, 1955), index, folder 2–11, box 2, Jacob Crane Collection, CU. Quote from HHFA, Office of the Administrator, "International Exchange of Experience in Housing and Community Development: Aided Self-Help Housing in Tropical Puerto Rico," August 1950, 5–6, box 41, RG 469, NARA.

65. Letter from William E. Warne to Douglas Stone, December 4, 1954, folder Aided Self-Help 1954, box 15, accession 69A5149, NARA.

66. Ibid.

67. Although unsigned, this memo was probably written by Jacob Crane. HHFA, Office of the Administrator, "International Exchange of Experience in Housing and Community Development: Experience in Greece under the American Mission for Aid to Greece and the Economic Cooperation Administration," June 1950, box 41, RG 469, NARA.

68. Zaire Dinzey-Flores, "Temporary Housing, Permanent Communities: Public Housing Policy and Design in Puerto Rico," *Journal of Urban History* 33, no. 3 (March 2007): 476.

69. Census of Housing, 1940, 1950, and 1960, Puerto Rico, accessed March 14, 2011, http://www.census.gov/prod/www/abs/decennial/.

70. William K. Divers, President, Savings and Loan Foundation, Washington, DC, statement, "Thrift Institutions," Study of International Housing by

the Subcommittee on Housing, Committee on Banking and Currency, US Senate, 88th Cong., 1st sess., March 1963, 293–294.

71. Dinzey-Flores, 478.

72. Dinzey-Flores brilliantly demonstrates the ways in which public housing residents undermined these visions of temporary, transitional housing by establishing multigenerational communities. The survival techniques of displaced persons represented more the power of community in the face of adverse socioeconomic circumstances than a widespread Puerto Rican desire for permanent public housing neighborhoods, however.

73. Dávila, 8.

74. Dávila, caption to fig. 11.

75. Memo from Luis Rivera Santos, Housing Research Board, to Jacob Crane, February 21, 1957, and Crane's reply, February 6, 1957, folder 2–4, box 2, Jacob Crane Collection, CU.

76. Letter from George L. Reed to Jacob Crane, August 9, 1960, folder 2–5, box 2, Jacob Crane Collection, CU.

77. Jacob Crane, "Puerto Rico State Housing Programs and Commonwealth Programs," July 30, 1960, pp. 1–2, folder 2–5, box 2, Jacob Crane Collection, CU.

78. Letter from Jacob Crane to George L. Reed, August 2, 1960, folder 2–5, box 2, Jacob Crane Collection, CU.

79. Crane, "Puerto Rico State Housing Programs and Commonwealth Programs," 10.

80. George Reed, "Here Comes the Housing Bank," September 28, 1961, folder 2–8, box 2, Jacob Crane Collection, CU.

81. George Reed, "Do We Need a New Kind of Land Reform?" January 25, 1961, p. 5, folder 2–8, box 2, Jacob Crane Collection, CU.

82. Ervan Bueneman, *Special Report on Techniques of Aided Self-Help Housing: Some Examples of US and Overseas Experience* (Washington, DC: HUD Office of International Affairs, 1973), 5.

83. Thomas S. Hines, *The Imperial Façade: Daniel Burnham and American Architectural Planning in the Philippines* (Berkeley: University of California Press, 1972); Hines, "American Modernism in the Philippines: The Forgotten Architecture of William E. Parsons," *Journal of the Society of Architectural Historians* 32, no. 4 (December, 1973): 316–326.

84. Manuel Roxas, "Message of the President of the Philippines," *Philippine Congressional Record, House of Representatives* 1, no. 5 (June 3, 1946): 117, NLP.

85. Paulo Alcazaren, Luis Ferrer, Benvenuto Icamina, and Neal Oshima (photographer), *Lungsod Iskwater: The Evolution of Informality as a Dominant Pattern in Philippine Cities* (Pasig City: Anvil Publishing, 2010), 61.

86. Jacob Crane, "Notes on Advisory Housing Mission to the Philippines," December 1945, folder 1945–48, box 12, accession 71A3534, RG 207, NARA.

87. Report of the US Advisory Mission to the Philippines, June 1946, box 12, accession 71A3534, NARA.

88. Letter from John Tierney, PHA, to Jacob Crane, HHFA, July 28, 1948, folder 1945–48, box 12, accession 71A3534, NARA.

89. Cesar Lorenzo trained as housing economist and statistician for the National Housing Commission of the Philippines after working as a statistician with the Food and Agriculture Organisation of the United Nations. Lorenzo, Comments on the Note to Jacob Crane prepared by John Tierney, July 30, 1948, folder 1945–48, box 12, accession 71A3534, NARA.

90. Jacob Crane, "Summary of Recommendations—Advisory Housing Mission to the Philippines," August 29, 1946, folder 1945–48, box 12, accession 71A3534, NARA.

91. "Former District Resident Plays L'Enfant Role in Design of New Philippine Capital City," *Washington Post*, August 14, 1948; Letter from Jacob Crane to Governor Jesús Piñero, July 14, 1948, folder 1945–48, box 12, accession 71A3534, NARA.

92. Romeo B. Ocampo, "Historical Development of Philippine Housing Policy, Part I: Prewar Housing Policy," Occasional Paper 6, November 1976, 21.

93. In 1958, the RFC was replaced by the Development Bank of the Philippines, an agency that in 1960 finally addressed the needs of lower-income clients by issuing loans with ten- to fifteen-year amortization periods at 8% interest. *Report and Recommendations of the Joint Philippine-American Finance Commission* (Washington, DC: Government Printing Office, 1947), 60–61.

94. John L. Tierney, Roy J. Burrough, and Earl V. Gauger, *Report of the US Advisory Housing Mission to the Commonwealth of the Philippines* (Manila: June 1946), 24–26, folder 1945–48, box 12, accession 71A3534, NARA.

95. The cost of these resettlement schemes was high, with the NLSA clearing all lands, building basic infrastructure and housing, and then awaiting resident repayment over the successive ten years; in the end, the government could only relocate 11,000 families—a minuscule fraction of the roughly 2 million residing in Manila in 1960. Paul Monk, *Truth and Power: Robert S. Hardie and Land Reform Debates in the Philippines, 1950–1987* (Clayton, Victoria: Monash University, Centre of Southeast Asian Studies, 1990); International Cooperation Administration, "The Housing Phase of Land Resettlement," March 21, 1956, 1946–54 folder, box 11, RG 207, NARA.

96. My italics. Fred Ruiz Castro, Executive Secretary of President Ramon Magsaysay, memo to the Chairman of the National Economic Council, December 1, 1954, folder 1946–54, box 11, accession 71A3534, RG 207, NARA.

97. Andrada also had a direct link to the US, having attended the Naval Academy before becoming first commodore of the Philippine Navy. "Housing Plan Merits Cited," *Manila Times*, July 28, 1956, 11, 1946–54 folder, box 11, RG 207, NARA.

NOTES TO PAGES 114–116

98. The HFC did not actually begin insuring mortgages until 1957. Romeo B. Ocampo, "Historical Development of Philippine Housing Policy, Part II: Postwar Housing Policy and Administration, 1945–59," Occasional Paper 7, January 1977, 2; Minutes of the inaugural meeting of the National Housing Council, Manila, October 18, 1956, p. 1, folder 1946–54, box 11, accession 71A3534, NARA; Republic Act 580, 2nd Cong. of the Republic of the Philippines, 2nd sess., September 15, 1950, NLP.

99. The PHHC had the legal right to insure mortgages, but it never acted on this right. Frank Cordner, "Housing Challenge to the Philippines," US Foreign Operations Mission to the Philippines, September 11, 1953, 10; Wagner, 5.

100. Wagner.

101. Ocampo, "Historical Development of Philippine Housing Policy, Part II," 2.

102. Address delivered by Commissioner J. V. Andrada, Chairman-General Manager, HFC, at Batangas Rotary Club, October 1, 1956, p. 7, folder 1946–54, box 11, accession 71A3534, NARA.

103. For a concise summary of all work up to 1962, see Morris Juppenlatz, "Preliminary Report: UN Low Cost Housing Assignment, Philippines," November 20, 1962, appendix 2, folder part A, box 1720, ser. 175, UNA. For advisory work from 1962–68, see Bernard Wagner, *Housing and Urban Development in the Philippines* (Manila: USAID/Manila, January 1968).

104. Charles Abrams and Otto Koenigsberger, "A Housing Program for the Philippine Islands," UN Technical Assistance Administration, January 14, 1959, 74, 77–78.

105. Reports include the 1961 and 1964 UN self-help housing studies, the 1962 World Bank report, the 1962–66 study by UN housing and planning expert Morris Juppenlatz, the 1966 Savings and Loan technical assistance study by Raymond P. Harold, and the USAID-funded report by HUD, among others. William Levitt visited the Philippines once and then declined further invitations, writing, "I've been there." Unsigned note from *New York Herald Tribune* staff member to Jacob Crane, September 29, 1948, folder 1945–48, box 12, accession 71A3534, NARA; Barbara M. Kelly, "Expanding the American Dream: Building and Rebuilding Levittown," *International Journal of Urban and Regional Research* 18, no. 1 (1994): 158.

106. World Bank, *Philippines Staff Project Report: Manila Urban Development Project* (Washington, DC: World Bank, 1976), iv.

107. Wagner, *Housing and Urban Development in the Philippines*, 50.

108. Singapore and Hong Kong housing histories have some fascinating parallels, including both governments' use of large squatter fires as justification for massive public housing schemes. Hong Kong's large Shek Kip Mei fire of 1953 preceded the Bukit Ho Swee Fire of 1961, so it is natural to suspect that the PAP referred to the Colonial Office's work in developing its Resettlement Programme in Hong Kong. I have not found any evidence of PAP leaders deliberately imitating Hong Kong practices in the PRO or NAS,

however. Undoubtedly, the free movement of British planners and shared institutional culture helped leaders on both islands understand and keep abreast of each others' work. See Alan Smart, *The Shek Mei Myth: Squatters, Fires, and Colonial Rule in Hong Kong, 1950–1963* (Hong Kong: Hong Kong University Press, 2006); and Nancy H. Kwak, "The Politics of Singapore's Fire Narrative," in Greg Bankoff, Uwe Lübken, and Jordan Sand, eds., *Flammable Cities: Urban Conflagration and the Making of the Modern World* (Madison: University of Wisconsin Press, 2012), 295–313.

109. The FMS included the Negeri Sembilan (Nine States), Perak, Selangor, and Pahang; Singapore became the capital of the Straits Settlements in 1832.

110. Unsigned minutes, SIT 951/50, HDB 1090, NAS.

111. Letter to C. W. A. Sennett, Chairman of the Sing Housing Committee, from K. Kiramathypathy J., Medical Practitioner, Singapore, June 26, 1947, HDB 1084; SIT minutes, HDB 1090, NAS.

112. Remme, 126–127.

113. Municipal Health Officer to Director of Building Research in England, July 8, 1947, HDB 1223, NAS.

114. Memo from Canton to Rae, February 25, 1948, HDB 1223, NAS.

115. Comments to Anthony Atkinson's talk, "Building in the Tropics."

116. Letter from J. M. Fraser, Chairman, to Town Treasurer, Mumbasa, Kenya, June 11, 1956 in reply to a request for help in setting up a Trust in Kenya, HDB 1057, NAS.

117. Jacob Crane, in Summary of Remarks at the Singapore Rotary Club, January 10, 1951; Letter from J. M. Fraser to Andrew Gilmour, Secretary for Economic Affairs, Singapore, February 9, 1951, HDB 1278, NAS.

118. "Asia" in this case denotes India, Pakistan, Federation of Malaya and Singapore, Thailand, Republic of Indonesia, and the Philippines. United Nations Report of Mission of Experts.

119. Fraser most likely penned these unsigned SIT documents, as the style and timing match his previous writings. Unfortunately, none of the files in this series indicate which US cities Stanley Woolmer went to, or whom he worked and studied with. Letter from Stanley Woolmer, Chief Architect of SIT, to M.I.T., February 9, 1953, HDB 1086, NAS.

120. *International Conference on Regional Planning and Development: An Interim Report* (London, 1955), HDB 1238, NAS.

121. The organization changed its name to the American Society of Heating and Air-Conditioning Engineers in 1954, and then merged in 1959 with the American Society of Refrigerating Engineers and become the American Society of Heating, Refrigeration, and Air-Conditioning Engineers. G. Anthony Atkinson, "Building in the Tropics."

122. Jacob Crane, Summary of Remarks at the Singapore Rotary Club, January 10, 1951, HDB 1278, NAS.

123. Woolmer to M.I.T., 44, 54, 55, 71.

124. Architects Maxwell Fry and Morton Shand, among others, began MARS as the British arm of the Congrès Internationaux d'Architecture Moderne (CIAM). For more on the conference itself, see reel 24, Charles Abrams Papers, CU.

125. Letter from Howe Yoon Chong, CEO of HDB to G. F. Penny, Head of Tropical Building Section, Department of Scientific and Industrial Research, Building Research Station, November 11, 1960; memo by Teh Cheang Wan, Chief Architect of HDB re: visit by Mr. P. Whiteley, Tropical Paint Research Fellow, from Building Research Station, October 31, 1960, HDB 1223, NAS.

126. Jacqueline Tyrwhitt, comments in "Standards of Housing Accommodation," in United Nations, *International Action in Asia and the Far East*, Housing, Building, and Planning 9 (New York: United Nations, 1955), 65.

127. Letter from Chief Architect of HDB to Secretary, CEO, Chairman, October 23, 1961, HDB 1223, NAS.

128. Memo by Henry S. Richmond, March 16, 1965, Urban Development Training Program, HHFA folder, box P246, Asia Foundation Papers, HIA.

129. Various letters and reports from folder Social and Economic: Urban Development Training Program, HHFA, box P246, Asia Foundation Papers, HIA.

130. Oral history of Alan Choe, interviewed August 1, August 29, 1997, by Cheong Eng Khim, reel 4, NAS.

131. Ibid.

132. Like Singapore's fund, the Chinese forced savings program required set contributions—in this case, to the China Construction Bank—from both employees and employers in exchange for low-interest mortgage loans. Lan Deng, Qingyun Shen, and Lin Wang, "Housing Policy and Finance in China: A Literature Review," Report for HUD, November 2009, 12; Mark Duda, Xiulan Zhang, and Mingzhu Dong, "China's Homeownership-Oriented Housing Policy: An Examination of Two Programs Using Survey Data from Beijing," Working Paper 05–7 for the Joint Center for Housing Studies of Harvard University, July 2005.

133. Duda, Zhang, and Dong, 74.

134. Robert Powell, *Line, Edge, and Shade: The Search for a Design Language in Tropical Asia; Tay Kheng Soon and Akitek Tenggara* (Singapore: Page One, 1997), 10.

135. Ibid., 13.

136. Ellen Shoshkes, "Jaqueline Tyrwhitt: A Founding Mother of Modern Urban Design," *Planning Perspectives* 21 (April 2006): 194.

137. Tay Kheng Soon, *Mega-Cities in the Tropics: Towards an Architectural Agenda for the Future* (Singapore: Institute of Southeast Asian Studies, 1989); Robert Powell, Andrew Lee Siew Ming, Leong Teng Wui, Lee Kah Wee, Lena Lim U. Wen, *No Limits: Articulating William Lim* (Singapore: Select, 2002), 138.

CHAPTER FOUR

1. Paul G. Hoffman, *World without Want* (New York: Harper and Row, 1962), 20.
2. Willard Garvey interview, 1993, tape 1, box 100, WHI; "Foreign News: Peasant against Famine," *Time Magazine*, May 16, 1960.
3. "Agriculture: Garvey's Gravy," *Time Magazine*, June 8, 1959.
4. Jean and Willard Garvey letter to Mr. and Mrs. Edward Maynard, Hother Trading and Steamship, Hong Kong, October 21, 1959, file folder 7, box 1, WHI.
5. William Graham, Robert Martin, and Willard Garvey talk to the Committee on Foreign Economic Practices of the Business Advisory Committee in Washington, DC, August 28, 1958, folder 7, box 1, WHI.
6. Under Title I, host governments could repay the loans slowly at favorable rates. Title II provided food for famine relief as a government-to-government grant. General Accounting Office, "Compilation of Information on the Operation and Administration of the Agricultural Trade Development and Assistance Act of 1954, commonly known as Public Law 480," vols. 1–3, December 1960.
7. USAID, "Food for Freedom: New Emphasis on Self-Help," *1967 Annual Report on Public Law 480*, 1969, 28, USAID-L.
8. Willard Garvey interview, WHI.
9. Donald Monson, Chief Advisor, United Nations Development Program Project, report on Future Urban and Housing Development in Taiwan, July 1966, from folder 136, box 3, CCC.
10. Christopher Amadeus Leu, "Congress and the Role of Private Enterprise in the United States Foreign Assistance Programs" (PhD diss., University of California, Los Angeles, 1973), 208–209.
11. Even within the Big Six, the American company Cargill dominated the market, pulling in nearly $2 billion according to its first annual report in 1964. "A Summary of Cargill's History," Cargill, 2010, accessed July 21, 2010, http://www.cargill.com/company/history/index.jsp.
12. Transcript of telephone conversation between C. Robert Bell and Willard Garvey, June 4, 1960, file folder 19, box 7, WHI.
13. Gail Radford, *Modern Housing for America: Policy Struggles in the New Deal Era* (Chicago: University of Chicago Press, 1996), 197–198.
14. Inter-American Development Bank, *40 Years: More Than a Bank* (Washington, DC: IADB, 2001), 8–9.
15. Arbenz had instituted an agrarian reform program that redistributed uncultivated lands to the masses. This decision earned him the loyalty of poor Guatemalans and the enmity of landowners like the American United Fruit Company, who protested compensation rates for expropriated lands being set according to the United Fruit Company's own underassessed values on prior tax returns. Peter H. Smith, *Talons of the Eagle: Latin America, the United States, and the World* (Oxford: Oxford University Press, 2008), 149–

152. Quote from Charles D. Brockett, "An Illusion of Omnipotence: US Policy toward Guatemala, 1954–1960," *Latin American Politics and Society* 44, no. 1 (Spring 2002): 111.

16. Mutual Security Administration Housing Policy Circular, January 14, 1955, folder FOA General-1955, box 4, RG 207, NARA.

17. *Foreign Economic Policy for the Twentieth Century: Report of the Rockefeller Brothers Fund Special Studies Project III* (Garden City, NY: Rockefeller Brothers Fund, 1958), 20–21.

18. R. Douglas Stone letter to Dan Hamady, HHFA, June 9, 1955, folder FOA General-1955, box 4, RG 207, NARA.

19. Charles Abrams, *Man's Struggle for Shelter in an Urbanizing World* (Cambridge, MA: MIT Press, 1964), 142–143; Draft notes for the US delegation to the Eleventh Inter-American Conference, Quito, Ecuador, February 1, 1960, folder 212, box 5, CCC.

20. By 1957, exports from Latin America were valued at $4.7 billion. *Foreign Economic Policy for the Twentieth Century*, 21.

21. Report to Congress on the Mutual Security Program, 85th Cong., 2d sess., HR 451, June 30, 1958, folder ICA General 1957–59, box 4, RG 207, NARA.

22. "Housing in Latin America," *Peruvian Times*, October 13, 1961, file folder 12, box 61, WHI.

23. These first savings and loans also differed significantly from their US counterparts in that they had no FHA or savings deposit insurance. USAID, "Report on Housing and Urban Development as of December 31, 1962," AID 1962–63 folder, box 15, RG 207, NARA.

24. Roy J. Burroughs, HHFA, letter to Stanley Baruch, Chief of Latin American division of ICA, April 11, 1957; Morton Bodfish letter to John Hollister, ICA, March 21, 1957, folder ICA General 1957–59, box 4, RG 207, NARA.

25. Soft loans were made in foreign exchange or in goods and services with longer repayment periods, lower interest rates, or repayment in inconvertible currency. David Allen Baldwin, *Economic Development and American Foreign Policy, 1943–1962* (Chicago: University of Chicago Press, 1966), 7.

26. Thomas Zoumaras, "Containing Castro: Promoting Homeownership in Peru, 1956–61," *Diplomatic History* 10, no. 2 (Spring 1986): 170.

27. Lee Thayer, *Hogares Peruanos S.A.: A Study of Private US Enterprise in Foreign Housing* (Wichita, KS: Wichita State University, 1964), 9–10.

28. Smith, 139.

29. Owens-Corning Fiberglas, *Annual Report—1959*, 20–21.

30. Zoumaras, 174.

31. Senator Sparkman, "Revised Legislation to Create an International Home Loan Bank," Senate Congressional Record, vol. 108, no. 181, 87th Cong., October 4, 1962, folder 14, box 1, CCC.

32. AID-IDB Housing Loans, August 1, 1962, AID Loans 1962 folder, box 14, RG 207, NARA.

33. Public Law 86-472, 86th Cong., HR 11510, May 14, 1960, 2, AID Loans 1962 folder, box 14, RG 207, NARA.

34. "Aided Self-Help Housing: Its History and Potential," Office of International Affairs, HUD, May 1976, 17; "Aided Self Help Housing in Africa," *Ideas and Methods Exchange* 65 (c. 1962): iii.

35. A. A. Carney, Regional Advisor, Report on the Mission to the Ministry of Health and Housing to the Kenya Government, Nairobi, November 19– December 4, 1965," Addis Ababa, UN EC-Afr, 1965, folder part B, box 79, ser. 175, UNA.

36. F. H. J. Nierstrasz, "Report on Housing Policy to the Government of Ghana," November 1967, p. 9, folder 1, box 80, ser. 175, UNA.

37. Nierstrasz, 6.

38. Memo from R. E. Fitchett, Regional Advisor, Housing and Industrial Development, ECA, to B. Nomvete, Head, Industry Division, "Housing Policy in African Countries and ECA Collaboration Therewith," August 24, 1965, folder part B, box 79, ser. 175, UNA.

39. Diana Tussie, *The Inter-American Development Bank*, vol. 4 (Boulder, CO: Lynne Rienner, 1995), 79.

40. "ECA Proposal for Follow-up Work in Aided Self-Help Housing," n.d., but most likely July 1965, folder part B, box 79, ser. 175, UNA.

41. "Aided Self Help Housing in Africa," 25.

42. "Housing in Latin America," *Peruvian Times*, October 13, 1961, file folder 12, box 61, WHI.

43. Ibid.; Philip Shabecoff, "The Housing Problem in Latin America: Views of Rodman Rockefeller," *New York Times*, October 21, 1962, as reprinted in *Peruvian Times*, November 16, 1962, p. 18, file folder 32, box 63, WHI.

44. Janice Perlman, *Favela: Four Decades of Living on the Edge in Rio de Janeiro* (Oxford: Oxford University Press, 2010), 71; Leandro Benmergui, "The Alliance for Progress and Housing Policy in Rio de Janeiro and Buenos Aires in the 1960s," *Urban History* 36, no. 2 (2009): 304, 321–22.

45. Speech on behalf of the Cuban Government to the Ministerial Meeting of the Inter-American Economic and Social Council (CIES), sponsored by the Organization of American States (OAS) at Punta del Este, Uruguay, on August 8, 1961.

46. Thayer, 1.

47. Hogares Peruanos, S. A., "Application to the Export-Import Bank of Washington for a Loan of the PL 480 Counterpart Funds for Use in Peru," September 1, 1960, p. 7, file folder 19, box 63, WHI.

48. Myrmarie A. González, *Puerto Rico y el "Sueño Americano": Un acercamiento a los sub urbano; caso de Levittown en Toa Baja, Puerto Rico* (Thesis, University of Puerto Rico Programa Graduado de Historia, 2013).

49. Diane E. Davis, *Discipline and Development: Middle Classes and Prosperity in East Asia and Latin America* (Cambridge: Cambridge University Press, 2004), 1–5.

50. F. Belaunde-Terry, "Casas para o povo (Houses for the people)," *Américas* 2, no. 12 (December 1950): 19–22.

51. Inter-American Development Bank Act Amendments of 1967, Hearings before the Committee on Banking and Currency and the Sub-Committee on International Finance, House of Representatives, 90th Cong., 1st sess., May 3, 4, 9, 1967, 64–65.

52. Unsigned, undated memo, most likely written by Dan McLellan or a member of the Mutual El Pueblo, July 1962, file folder 23, box 13, WHI.

53. Ibid.

54. "Missionary Builds Credit Network," *Washington Post*, May 8, 1966, K1.

55. The Development Loan Fund and American businesses located in Peru provided credit for the mutuals. Both faltered because of bad management. "Report on the Status of the Long-Term Home Loan Financing Programs in Peru through Savings and Loan Institutions," July 18, 1961, unsigned report, probably written by US government agency, file folder 8, box 58, WHI.

56. Inter-American Development Bank Act Amendments of 1967.

57. Memo from Floyd Baird to Howard Wenzel, June 6, 1962, file folder 23, box 13, WHI.

58. David S. Parker, "Middle-Class Mobilization and the Language of Orders in Urban Latin America: From Caste to Category in Early Twentieth-Century Lima," *Journal of Urban History* 31, no. 3 (March 2005): 371–72.

59. Unfortunately, none of the available sources about Hogares Peruanos indicate whether these families had single- or dual-income households.

60. "Application to the Export-Import Bank of Washington," 7, WHI.

61. Converted from US dollars to Peruvian soles at 1:8.928, the exchange rate listed in "Blossoming Credit Activity Brings Peruvian to Wichita," *Wichita Eagle*, February 11, 1967, file folder 32, box 63, WHI; FHA Analysis and Recommendations for Housing Guaranty Proposal Case Number 527-HG-002, December 6, 1962, AID Investment Guarantees 1962 folder, box 14, accession 69A5149, RG 207, NARA.

62. "Application to the Export-Import Bank of Washington" 5, WHI.

63. "Blossoming Credit Activity Brings Peruvian to Wichita."

64. "Application to the Export-Import Bank of Washington," 7, 10, WHI.

65. Report by Francis Violich, Department of City and Regional Planning, UC Berkeley, October 25–26, 1957, 4, Accredited Schools of Planning folder, box 14, accession 69A5149, RG 207, NARA.

66. Howard Wenzel, "Random Comments on My Experience in Peru," memo to Lee Thayer, February 25, 1963, file folder 2, box 1, WHI.

67. For more on John F. C. Turner, see Ray Bromley, "Peru 1957–1977: How Time and Place Influenced John Turner's Ideas on Housing Policy," and Richard Harris, "A Double Irony: The Originality and Influence of John F. C. Turner," *Habitat International* 27, no. 2 (June 2003).

68. Amendment 'A,' Cooley Loan Application Attachment 1, October 11, 1963, file folder 8, box 42, WHI.

69. Status Report, December 1, 1963, Project 3, file folder 20, box 94, WHI.

70. "Abunda la tierra par a resolver la crisis de vivienda," *La Prensa*, August 19, 1956, file folder 19, box 63, WHI.

71. In Hong Kong, roughly 80% of the 1,096 square kilometers is uninhabitable hilly terrain, resulting in some of the highest residential densities in the world. The entire city-state of Singapore was less than 700 square kilometers in the 1960s. James Lee, *Housing, Home Ownership and Social Change in Hong Kong* (Aldershot, Hampshire: Ashgate, 1999), 46–47.

72. Memo from G. Desmond to Ernest Weissmann, November 12, 1964, folder 6, box 967, ser. 0175, UNA.

73. Letter from Nils Goran Astrom to Carlos Dabezíes, Chief, Latin American Section, Bureau of Technical Assistance Operations, UN, September 22, 1966, folder 6, box 0967, ser. 0175, UNA.

74. Application to AID for Housing Investment Guaranty, May 11, 1964, file folder 19, box 63, WHI.

75. "US-Style Homes Put Up in Mexico," *New York Times*, September 18, 1960, R14.

76. Alan Carnoy, memo, April 7, 1975, folder 111, box 3, CCC; "Housing Project Sell-Out in Tunis," *New York Times*, January 22, 1967; income figure from Keith Owen Fuglie, "The Demand for Potatoes in Tunisia: Are They a Cereal Substitute?" *European Review of Agricultural Economics* 21 (1994): 283. Dollars recalculated for inflation using http://www.dollartimes.com/calculators/inflation.htm.

77. All dollar amounts are listed in actual, not adjusted values. AID-IDB Housing Loans, August 1, 1962, AID Loans 1962 folder, box 14; USAID, "Report on Housing and Urban Development as of December 31, 1962," AID 1962–63 folder, box 15, RG 207, NARA.

78. Clifton B. Luttrell, "Good Intentions, Cheap Food and Counterpart Funds," *Federal Bank Reserve of St. Louis Review* (November 1982): 12.

79. Richard Bilillich, *The Protection of Foreign Investment: Six Procedural Studies* (Syracuse: Syracuse University Press, 1990), 147–150.

80. Daniel Marx, Jr., "The United States Enters Export Credit Guarantee Competition," *Political Science Quarterly* 78, no. 2 (June 1963): 258.

81. Ibid., 259.

82. US Agencies Engaged in Overseas Financing Operations, October 6, 1960, AID Loans 1962 folder, box 14, RG 207, NARA.

83. Edmund Jan Osmanczyk and Anthony Mango, *Encyclopedia of the United Nations and International Agreements*, 3rd ed., vol. 4 (New York: Routledge, 2004), 2547.

84. My italics. Dean Rusk, Department of State, memo to All Diplomatic Posts, November 6, 1961, AID Investment Guaranties 1960–61 folder; Dan R. Hamady, HHFA, to Joe Walton, October 17, 1962, AID Investment Guarantees 1962 folder, box 14, RG 207, NARA.

85. Hamady, HHFA, to Walton, October 17, 1962.

86. Ibid.
87. Memo from Richard Metcalf, Special Assistant, to James Moore, Assistant Administrator, OIH, HHFA, June 7, 1963, AID Investment Guaranties 1962 folder, box 14, RG 207, NARA.
88. Ibid.
89. The Senate prevailed over the NAHB in setting the assumption of risk at 75% in the first iteration of HIG. That percentage would later go up to 100 for some projects. "Secondary Mortgage Market," n.d., from folder 212, box 5, CCC.
90. Memo from Dick Metcalf, HFFA, to James A. Moore, HHFA, October 11, 1963, AID Investment Guarantees 1963 folder, box 14, RG 207, NARA.
91. Unclassified AID circular, December 16, 1967, folder 1, box 42, WHI.
92. Stanley Baruch, "Report of Acting Inspector General re Housing Investment Guaranty Program in Latin America," March 23, 1972, folder 284, box 7, CCC.
93. Memo from Metcalf to Moore, October 11, 1963.
94. Statement of Paul L. Burkhard made before the Committee on Foreign Relations regarding the Act for International Development of 1961, June 20, 1961, folder 213, box 5, CCC.
95. Draft notes for the US delegation to the Eleventh Inter-American Conference, Quito, Ecuador, February 1, 1960, folder 212, box 5, CCC.
96. Leo Goodman, housing consultant for the UAW, press release, April 20, 1961; and Boris Shishkin, Secretary of the AFL-CIO Housing Committee, letter to John Sparkman, May 12, 1961, folder 87, box 2, CCC.
97. Remarks of Harold Robinson, Deputy Director for Plans and Programming, HUD, Bureau for Latin America, USAID, at University of California, April 29–30, 1966, 13.
98. "Loeb-Rhoades Unit to Finance Homes in Cali, Colombia," *Wall Street Journal*, September 7, 1962.
99. USAID Alliance for Progress, press release, August 30, 1962, AID Investment Guarantees 1962 folder, box 14, RG 207, NARA.
100. FHA Analysis and Recommendations for Housing Guaranty Proposal Case Number 527-HG-002, December 6, 1962, AID Investment Guarantees 1962 folder, box 14, RG 207, NARA.
101. FHA Latin American Division, Application Case Number 527-HG-002, January 27, 1964, AID 1962–63 folder, box 15, RG 207, NARA.
102. Department of State press release, "Loan to Aid Mexico Ease Housing Shortage," September 5, 1963, file folder 5, box 46, WHI.
103. Remarks of Harold Robinson, Regional Housing Advisor, Latin America, AID, before Senior Executives Conference of Mortgage Bankers Association of America, Dallas, TX, January 21, 1963, folder 212, box 5, CCC.
104. HHFA, "Establishing Savings and Loan Associations in Less Industrialized Countries: For Use of USAID Missions," *Ideas and Methods Exchange* 38 (March 1948, revised June 1963).

105. Both Weaver and McMurray were ex-officio members. USAID press release, "Bell Names Committee to Advise AID on Housing," May 16, 1963, AID Housing and Urban Development Advisory Committee, 1963 folder, box 14, accession 69A5149, RG 207, NARA.

106. Memo from James A. Moore to Robert C. Weaver, October 23, 1963, AID Housing and Urban Development Advisory Committee, 1963 folder, box 14, RG 207, NARA.

107. Morton J. Schussheim, Assistant Administrator for Program Policy, HHFA, memo to James A. Morton, Assistant Administrator, Office of International Housing, HHFA, September 23, 1963, AID Housing and Urban Development Advisory Committee, 1963 folder, box 14, RG 207, NARA.

108. Memo from Dean Rusk, State Department, to Stanley Baruch, HUD, March 30, 1966, folder 281, box 7, CCC.

109. "Peace Corps Branches into Finance to Boost Foreign Buying Power," *Wall Street Journal,* August 21, 1961, 1.

110. USAID records show $780 million in guaranty authority, but Senator Proxmire rounded that number down to $700 million. Seven hundred million dollars divided by 800 million individuals yielded 87.5 cents per person. Hearings before the Subcommittee on Housing and Urban Affairs of the Committee on Banking, Housing and Urban Affairs, US Senate, 92nd Cong., 2nd sess., May 24–25, 1972, 16.

111. Ibid., 19, 177–178.

112. Dean Rusk, USAID circular, December 5, 1963, AID Investment Guarantees 1963 folder, box 14, RG 207, NARA.

113. Joint release, State Department–HHFA, FHA-AID Latin American Housing Agreement Reached, December 2, 1963, AID Investment Guarantees 1963 folder, box 14, RG 207, NARA.

114. Operating Principles for Provision of HHFA Support in Carrying Out the AID Housing Investment Guaranty Program, August 23, 1963, AID Investment Guarantees 1963 folder, box 14, RG 207, NARA.

115. Memo from Rusk to Baruch, March 30, 1966.

116. Congressional Record-House, March 8, 1972, H1882, n.p., folder 281, box 7, CCC; Foreign Assistance Act of 1967, PL 90–137, part I, chap. 1, sec. 102.

117. Stanley Baruch, Secretary-General, VIII Inter-American Savings and Loan Conference, Report on VIII Inter-American Savings and Loan Conference in Managua, Nicaragua, February 4, 1970, box 11, folder 502, CCC.

118. Hearings before the Subcommittee on Housing and Urban Affairs, May 24–25, 1972, 19.

119. "Manila Workshop Newsette," October 30, 1968, box 3, folder 135, CCC.

120. Charles LeMenager, California Department of Housing and Community Development, "Demonstration in Low-Cost Housing Techniques," HUD Project California LIHD 3, Contract H650, June 1970, 24–25.

121. Continental Homes, Inc., "Application to the Agency for International Development for a Cooley Loan in Ceylon," [1967?]; "Low-Cost Housing," pamphlet produced by Lockheed, n.d.; HUD and FHA Insuring Office Directors, memo on Precast Concrete Panel Construction, February 2, 1967, file folder 13, box 84, WHI.

122. Richard C. Knight, vice president, International Operations, "Foreign Aid and the Congress: An Editorial," *National Savings and Loan League Journal* (December 1971): 24–25, folder 107, box 2, CCC.

123. Peter Marcuse and Ronald van Kempen, eds., *Globalizing Cities: A New Spatial Order?* (Oxford: Blackwell Publishers, 2000).

124. Memo from Metcalf to Moore, June 7, 1963.

125. Italics mine. Legislation on Foreign Relations through 2008, Joint Committee Print, Senate Committee on Foreign Relations and House Committee on International Relations 1A, March 2010, 98.

126. Department of State circular, August 30, 1962, AID Investment Guarantees 1962 folder, box 14, RG 207, NARA.

127. Letter from Robert Weaver to A. Willis Robertson, Chairman of the Senate Committee on Banking and Currency, c. 1962, folder 13, box 1, CCC.

128. These were Senator Proxmire's words describing the group neglected by American housing assistance. Hearings before the Subcommittee on Housing and Urban Affair, May 24–25, 1972, 16–17.

129. General Accounting Office report to Senate Committee on Foreign Relations, *Interim Report on the Agency for International Development's Housing Investment Guaranty Program* (Washington, DC: 1973), 14–15.

130. Ibid., 10–11.

131. Statement of Stanley Baruch, Director of the Office of Housing, Agency for International Development, Department of State, in Hearings before the Subcommittee on Housing and Urban Affairs, May 24–25, 1972, 68–69.

132. Report of the Staff Survey Team of the Subcommittee for Review of the Mutual Security Programs on the Housing Investment Guaranty Program and the Economic Aid Program in Panama, 88th Cong., 1st sess., November 19, 1963, 6–7.

133. Ibid., 10.

134. "Housing Investment Guaranty Program," unsigned memo, 1974, box 1, folder 64, CCC.

135. Ibid., 29–35.

136. US Office of Management and Budget, *Budget of the United States Government* (Doc. ed.), appendix (Washington, DC: US GPO, 1998), 96.

137. Ibid., 97; US Office of Management and Budget, *Budget of the United States Government* (Doc. ed.). Appendix (Washington, DC: US GPO, 2010), 858.

138. USAID, *History of the Agency for International Development's Housing and Urban Development Program* (Washington, DC: Community Consulting Group, International, 1987), 22.

139. Ibid., 28–29.
140. Overseas Private Investment Corporation, *Bridging the Housing Gap in Emerging Markets* (Washington, DC: OPIC, 2000), 4; Jane R. Zavisca, *Housing the New Russia* (Ithaca: Cornell University Press, 2012), 49–50, 64.
141. Interview with Willard Garvey, WHI.

CHAPTER FIVE

1. Angelo R. Mozilo, "The American Dream of Homeownership: From Cliché to Mission," transcript, John T. Dunlop Lecture, Joint Center for Housing Studies of Harvard University, February 4, 2003, 20.
2. Peter Ward discusses at length American policymakers' resistance to acknowledging—must less aiding—domestic self-help housing. This chapter does not contradict Ward's point so much as it supplements it, as I argue policymakers viewed Native American and inner-city programs as a sort of "Third World at home." Meanwhile, self-construction for "average" Americans followed the do-it-yourself model rather than the self-help one. Peter M. Ward, "Self-Help Housing Ideas and Practice in the Americas," in Bishwapriya Sanyal, Lawrence J. Vale, and Christina D. Rosan, eds., *Planning Ideas that Matter: Livability, Territoriality, Governance, and Reflective Practice* (Cambridge, MA: MIT Press, 2012), 283–310; Richard Harris, *Building a Market: The Rise of the Home Improvement Industry, 1914–1960* (Chicago: University of Chicago Press, 2012).
3. *New York City Housing Authority v. Muller*, 270 N.Y. 333 (March 17, 1936), 342–343; Congressional Record, April 21, 1949, 4943, reel 50, Charles Abrams Papers, CU.
4. "An Act to Amend the Real Property Law by Adding a New Section 294-b," recommendations by Charles Abrams to the Association of the Bar of the City of New York, February 27, 1947, 6, reel 50, Charles Abrams Papers, CU.
5. Abrams made some piercing observations about homeownership in this broader tract, including that "the phenomenal uptrend in mortgage debt tends to undermine the security of ownership." Abrams, *Revolution in Land* (New York: Harper & Brothers, 1939), 275; A. Scott Henderson, *Housing and the Democratic Ideal: The Life and Thought of Charles Abrams* (New York: Columbia University Press, 2000), 175. For the UN report, see Charles Abrams, "Urban Land Problems and Policies: Preliminary Analysis," in *Current information on urban land policies* (New York: United Nations, 1952) 5–92.
6. "Final Draft for Consideration by Seminar Drafting Committee," reel 24, Charles Abrams Papers, CU.
7. *New York Times*, April 24, 1956.
8. Alan Carnoy, *Democracia Si! A Way to Win the Cold War* (New York: Vantage Press, 1962); Carnoy, *The Greatest Failure of American Foreign Aid* (San Francisco: Larum Publishing, 1972).

9. Memo, Alan Carnoy, April 7, 1975, folder 111, box 3, CCC.

10. Ibid.

11. The first quote was by Cole in 1953, and the second by Mason in 1959. Robert Frederick Burk, *The Eisenhower Administration and Black Civil Rights* (Knoxville: University of Tennessee Press, 1984), 113, 116.

12. Ibid., 117.

13. Ibid., 121.

14. Mary L. Dudziak, *Cold War, Civil Rights: Race and the Image of American Democracy* (Princeton: Princeton University Press, 2000), 91-92.

15. Ibid., 54; Laura A. Belmonte, *Selling the American Way: US Propaganda and the Cold War* (Philadelphia: University of Pennsylvania Press, 2010).

16. Greg Castillo, *Cold War on the Home Front: The Soft Power of Midcentury Design* (Minneapolis: University of Minnesota Press, 2010), 147; Elaine Tyler May, *Homeward Bound: American Families in the Cold War Era* (New York: Basic Books, 1990), 17.

17. Stanley Woolmer, *Housing in the United States: A Study of Its Background, Problems, and Achievements with a Consideration of the Applicability of Its Technical Methods to Tropical Countries* (Cambridge, MA: Harvard University Research Fellow Report, 1952), 25.

18. Ibid., 26-27.

19. I put the commonly used term *guest* in quotes, as the word deliberately positioned nonwhite residents as impermanent visitors. Extract from Minutes of a Meeting of the Colonial Information Policy Committee, July 21, 1949; Minutes of the Working Party for the Colonial Information Policy Committee Meeting, September 8, 1949, CO 537/5130, PRO.

20. Mervyn Jones, "A Question of Colour," *New Statesman and Nation* 42, no. 1066 (August 11, 1951): 148-149. Examples of "Little Harlem" references abound; for one example, see "Coloured Immigrants," letter to the editor, *Times* (London), October 25, 1955, 7.

21. Quote from Theodore S. Repplier, as found in Castillo, 128.

22. Carol Anderson, *Eyes off the Prize: The United Nations and the African American Struggle for Human Rights, 1944–1955* (Cambridge: Cambridge University Press, 2003), 204.

23. Letter from Bernard E. Loshbough, Advisor on Housing and Community Development, TCA–New Delhi, to Jacob Crane, HHFA, January 22, 1952, accession 71A3534, box 6, RG 207, NARA.

24. Jacob Crane, reply, January 30, 1952, accession 71A3534, box 6, RG 207, NARA.

25. Penny M. Von Eschen, *Race against Empire: Black Americans and Anticolonialism, 1937–1957* (Ithaca, NY: Cornell University Press, 1997), 44, 149.

26. These ideas were first published as a book in 1960. W. W. Rostow, *The Stages of Economic Growth: A Non-Communist Manifesto* (Cambridge: Cambridge University Press, 1990).

27. David Ekbladh, *The Great American Mission: Modernization and the Construction of an American World Order* (Princeton: Princeton University Press, 2010), 228.

28. Quoted in Michael S. Carliner, "Development of Federal Homeownership 'Policy,'" *Housing Policy Debate* 9, no. 2 (Fannie Mae Foundation, 1998): 311.

29. Rachel G. Bratt, "Homeownership for Low-Income Households: A Comparison of the Section 235, Nehemiah, and Habitat for Humanity Programs," in William M. Rohe and Harry L. Watson, eds., *Chasing the American Dream: New Perspectives on Affordable Homeownership* (Ithaca: Cornell University Press, 2006), 42.

30. Quoted in Carliner, 311.

31. The Housing and Urban Development Act of 1968 created section 235. The Housing and Community Development Act of 1987 terminated the program in 1989 because of scandals and mismanagement. Bratt, 45. See also Andrew Highsmith, "Prelude to the Subprime Crash: Beecher, Michigan, and the Origins of the Suburban Crisis," *Journal of Policy History* 24, no. 4 (2012): 572–611.

32. *Home: Fannie Mae; Fifty Years of Opening Doors for American Home Buyers* (Washington, DC: Fannie Mae, 1988), 25.

33. "Poverty of American Indians Called Mirror of US Problem," *Washington Post and Times-Herald,* May 10, 1964, A12.

34. Quote from David M. P. Freund, *Colored Property: State Policy and White Racial Politics in Suburban America* (Chicago: University of Chicago Press, 2007), 13. Matt Lassiter also discusses the "color-blind" discourse of the property rights movement in *The Silent Majority: Suburban Politics in the Sunbelt South* (Princeton: Princeton University Press, 2006), as does Liz Cohen in *A Consumers' Republic: The Politics of Mass Consumption in Postwar America* (New York: Vintage, 2003), 213; Robert Self, *American Babylon: Race and the Struggle for Postwar Oakland* (Princeton: Princeton University Press, 2003), 272; and Mark Brilliant, *The Color of America Has Changed: How Racial Diversity Shaped Civil Rights Reform in California, 1941–1978* (Oxford: Oxford University Press, 2010), 204. Kevin Kruse analyzes the urban origins of suburban conservatism in *White Flight: Atlanta and the Making of Modern Conservatism* (Princeton: Princeton University Press, 2005).

35. Becky Nicolaides, *My Blue Heaven: Life and Politics in the Working-Class Suburbs of Los Angeles, 1920–1965* (Chicago: University of Chicago Press, 2002), 308.

36. Daniel Martinez HoSang, *Racial Propositions: Ballot Initiatives and the Making of Postwar California* (Berkeley: University of California Press, 2010), 61–86.

37. Ekbladh, 230.

38. There is a massive body of literature explaining the failures of American public housing. See Lawrence Vale, *From the Puritans to the Projects: Public Housing and Public Neighbors* (Cambridge, MA: Harvard University Press,

2000); John F. Bauman, Roger Biles, and Kristin M. Szylvian, eds., *From Tenements to the Taylor Homes: In Search of an Urban Housing Policy in Twentieth-Century America* (University Park, PA: Penn State University Press, 2000); and D. Bradford Hunt, *Blueprint for Disaster: The Unraveling of Chicago Public Housing* (Chicago: University of Chicago Press, 2009), for concise summaries. Nicholas Dagen Bloom tells a fascinating counterstory in his account of New York City Housing Authority's anomalous, highly successful public housing program in *Public Housing That Worked: New York in the Twentieth Century* (Philadelphia: University of Pennsylvania Press, 2009). Lawrence Vale's *Purging the Poorest: Public Housing and the Design Politics of Twice-Cleared Communities* (Chicago: University of Chicago Press, 2013) explains not only the original placement of public housing but the more recent trend of reclearing public housing communities.

39. Kenneth T. Jackson, *Crabgrass Frontier: The Suburbanization of the United States* (New York: Oxford University Press, 1985), 294.
40. Vale, *From the Puritans to the Projects*, 6–7.
41. Guy Stuart, *Discriminating Risk: The US Mortgage Lending Industry in the Twentieth Century* (Ithaca: Cornell University Press, 2003), 10; Calvin Bradford, "Financing Home Ownership: The Federal Role in Neighborhood Decline," *Urban Affairs Quarterly* 14, no. 3 (March 1979): 325–326.
42. Douglas S. Massey and Nancy A. Denton, *American Apartheid: Segregation and the Making of the Underclass* (Cambridge, MA: Harvard University Press, 1993), 206.
43. Massey and Denton, "Trends in the Residential Segregation of Blacks, Hispanics, and Asians: 1970–1980," *American Sociological Review* 52, no. 6 (December 1987): 802, 823, 813–814.
44. Massey and Denton, "Hypersegregation in US Metropolitan Areas: Black and Hispanic Segregation along Five Dimensions," *Demography* 26 (1989): 373–392; Reynolds Farley and William H. Frey, "Changes in the Segregation of Whites from Blacks during the 1980s: Small Steps toward a More Integrated Society," *American Sociological Review* 59 (February 1994): 23–45.
45. Massey and Denton, *American Apartheid*, 196.
46. Bradford, 329.
47. Exec. Order 12892, 59 Fed. Reg. 2939 (1994).
48. From the late 1980s until 2003, community groups regularly negotiated agreements with banks whereby lenders would make mortgage commitments targeted at low-income and minority households in exchange for the community groups' promise to not challenge proposed mergers, acquisitions, new branch openings, and other standard actions. The Office of Thrift Supervision sharply reduced the number of lenders regulated by the Community Reinvestment Act in 2003. The Home Ownership and Equity Protection Act (1994) attempted to check predatory lending, with limited successes. Alex F. Schwartz, *Housing Policy in the United States: An Introduction* (New York: Routledge, 2006), 242–246.

49. Daniel Immergluck, *Credit to the Community: Community Reinvestment and Fair Lending Policy in the United States* (Armonk, NY: ME Sharpe, 2004), chap. 5.

50. Peter Marcuse, "Homeownership for Low-Income Families: Financial Implications," *Land Economics* 48, no. 20 (May 1972): 134.

51. Louis Hyman, *Debtor Nation: The History of America in Red Ink* (Princeton: Princeton University Press, 2011), 232.

52. Barry Bluestone and Mary Huff Stevenson, *The Boston Renaissance: Race, Space, and Economic Change in an American Metropolis* (New York: Russell Sage Foundation, 2000), 89–91; Lawrence Vale, *Reclaiming Public Housing: A Half Century of Struggle in Three Public Neighborhoods* (Cambridge, MA: Harvard University Press, 2003), 176.

53. Ervan Bueneman, *Special Report on Techniques of Aided Self-Help Housing: Some Examples of US and Overseas Experience* (Washington, DC: HUD Office of International Affairs, 1973), 16.

54. Harold Robinson, "Aided Self-Help Housing: Its History and Potential," HUD Office of International Affairs, May 1976, 38.

55. Bueneman, 21.

56. For a more thorough history of this aspect, see Harris.

57. Rafael Corrada, Chairman, "Self-Help and Mutual Aid Housing," General Report for the World Planning and Housing Congress in San Juan, Puerto Rico, May 28–June 3, 1960, 15–16.

58. Ibid., 13.

59. Paul A. Argenti and Thea Haley, "Fannie Mae Case-GS," *Fannie Mae News*, 2003, accessed May 31, 2012, http://fanniemaenews.com/what-is-fannie-mae.

60. Remarks delivered by Franklin D. Raines at the Securities Industry Association, Boca Raton, FL, November 8, 2002, as cited in Argenti and Haley, 11.

61. *HUD: International—Meeting the Global Challenge*, HUD Office of Policy Development and Research, December 2000, 56–57, folder Re-called Publications Issued by Sec. A. Cuomo, box 4, Regional Administrator Program subject files, 1965–2003 (ARC 7787131), HUD–Region IX (San Francisco), NARA–San Bruno.

62. The Urban Institute, *Assessment of American Indian Housing Needs and Programs: Final Report* (Washington, DC: HUD Office of Policy Development and Research, 1996), 21.

63. David Listokin with Robin Leichenko and Juliet King, *Housing and Economic Development in Indian Country: Challenge and Opportunity* (New Brunswick, NJ: Center for Urban Policy Research Press at Rutgers University and Fannie Mae Foundation, 2006), 52.

64. Letter from Roy Nash, Superintendent, Sacramento Indian Agency, to FHA, October 7, 1938; Letter from Jay Keegan, Deputy Administrator, FHA, to Roy Nash, October 13, 1938; Letter from Roy Nash to Charles McKean, Jr.,

Chairman of the Council at Wilton Rancheria, October 19, 1938, folder 790, Federal Housing Administration, box 231, coded subject files, 1900, 1956, BIA–Sacramento Area Office, RG 75, NARA–San Bruno.

65. The Urban Institute, xii.

66. Prepared Statement of the Office of Public and Indian Housing, HUD, in Joint Hearing before the Committee on Indian Affairs, US Senate and the Committee on Banking, Housing and Urban Affairs, US Senate, 105th Cong., 1st sess., March 12, 1997, 58–61.

67. Memo from Commissioner of Indian Affairs John O. Crow to Area Director, Sacramento, November 5, 1971, folder Rancheria Act Information 1958–72, box 1, Tribal Group Files, 1970–85, ARC 6002244, BIA Central CA Agency, NARA–San Bruno.

68. Nicolas G. Rosenthal, *Reimagining Indian Country: Native American Migration and Identity in Twentieth-Century Los Angeles* (Charlotte: University of North Carolina Press, 2012), 2.

69. The legal process occurred in stages, as select reservations were chosen for termination. California's Termination Act of August 18, 1958, was amended in 1964. Memo from Leonard M. Hill, Area Director, BIA Sacramento Area Office, August 19, 1958, folder Rancheria Act Information 1958–72, box 1, Tribal Group Files, 1970–85, ARC 6002244, BIA Central California Agency, NARA–San Bruno.

70. Letter from Jon L. Adams to Richard H. Burcell, Superintendent, August 12, 1975, folder Auburn Rancheria—Termination 1963–[77], box 1, Tribal Group Files 1970–85, ARC 6002244, BIA Central California Agency, NARA–San Bruno.

71. Richard Metcalf, "The Demand for Low-Rent Public Housing on the Pine Ridge Indian Reservation, South Dakota, as of July 1961," PHA Economics Branch, 4490, box 1, Richard Metcalf Collection, CU.

72. Metcalf, 15.

73. Memo exchange between Richard Metcalf, Roy J. Burroughs (HHFA), and Richard T. Knight (State Department), December 10–18, 1962, folder AID-General 1962, box 15, RG 207, NARA.

74. Ibid.

75. Leland S. Burns, *Housing: Symbol and Shelter—International Housing Productivity Study*, A Report Prepared for and Submitted to AID, US Department of State, Los Angeles: Graduate School of Business Administration, UCLA, February 1970, 47, xiii, USAID Library.

76. Talk by Richard Metcalf before Governors' Interstate Indian Council, Missoula, Montana, August 15, 1961, 4490, box 1, Richard Metcalf Collection, CU.

77. The BIA supervised construction, the HAA financed and provided housing authority guidance, and the PHS supplied water and sanitation facilities. Letter from M. G. Ripke, Acting Director, BIA–Area IX, to John Crabtree, May 7, 1968, folder 005-Chron Copies, Housing Dvlp. 1968, box 1, Area

Mission Correspondence 1964–72 (Accn. 75-00-004), BIA–Sacramento Area Office, RG 75, NARA–San Bruno; Bueneman, 17.

78. In the installment contract system, families would pay monthly installments on their loan but not receive title until the full amount had been deposited. Many contracts gave families no equity over time, and properties could be seized with one missed payment. Charles Abrams, *Forbidden Neighbors: A Study of Prejudice in Housing* (New York: Harper & Brothers, 1955), 138.

79. Annual Report of the Commissioner of Indian Affairs, 1966, 16.

80. US Department of Housing and Urban Development and US Department of the Treasury, *One-Stop Mortgage Center Initiative in Indian Country: A Report to the President* (Washington, DC: Treasury Department, 2000), 7, as cited in Listokin, 194.

81. Address by Joseph Burstein before the Second National Housing Workshop of the National Association of Housing and Redevelopment Officials, Detroit, Michigan, October 28, 1964, folder 344, box 8, CCC.

82. Summary, Housing Conference, Billings Area Office, August 2–3, 1966, folder 396-Housing Development-General-1966, box 1, Area Mission Correspondence 1964–72 (Accn. 75–00–004), BIA–Sacramento Area Office, RG 75, NARA–San Bruno.

83. Ibid.

84. "Mutual Help Housing Evaluation Case Studies," HUD Region IX Program Planning and Evaluation, August 1981, 3, folder Studies/Evaluations of Indian Programs, box 12, Regional Administrator Program subject files 1965–2003 (ARC 7787131), HUD Region IX (San Francisco), NARA–San Bruno.

85. Indian Housing tab, folder/Binder HUD Region IX, Orientation (February 1988), box 3, Regional Administrator Program subject files, 1965–2003 (ARC 7787131), HUD–Region IX (San Francisco), NARA–San Bruno.

86. "Mutual Help Housing Evaluation Case Studies"; Bueneman, 20.

87. Although Burstein did not say so explicitly, it can be inferred that he meant Congress and housing officials exhibited less enthusiasm.

88. Annual Report of the Commissioner of Indian Affairs, 1964, 11–12.

89. These units had no running water or electricity. Annual Report of the Commissioner of Indian Affairs, 1966, 16.

90. Alaska State Housing Authority Remote Housing Report no. 2, "Low-Income Housing Demonstration Program: Grayling, Metlakatla, and Bethel, Alaska," December 1968, 6.

91. Ibid., 5.

92. Letter from Marie McGuire to Rodman C. Rockefeller, July 11, 1968, folder Mutual Help Housing Gen. 3, box 23, RG 75, NARA–DC.

93. Ervan Bueneman, *Special Report on Techniques of Aided Self-Help Housing: Some Examples of Overseas and US Experience* (Washington, DC: HUD Office of International Affairs, 1973), 21.

NOTES TO PAGES 186-190

94. Thomas B. Williams, *Indian Housing in the United States: A Staff Report on the Indian Housing Effort in the United States*, 94th Cong., 1st sess., Senate Committee on Interior and Insular Affairs, February 1975, 7. For a full account of the Homeownership Improvement Program, including the various funding mechanisms, see Bureau of Indian Affairs records at RG 75, boxes 21–27, NARA-DC.

95. Letter from Stuart C. Edmonds, acting Deputy Chief, Branch of Plant Management, to Chief, October 6, 1964, folder Housing Improvement, box 23, RG 75, NARA-DC.

96. In the Central California Agency of the BIA, for example, only 2% of all housing applicants received funding in 1977. Letter from Elmer R. Pankey, Housing Development Officer of the Central California Agency, BIA, to Glen Villa, June 3, 1977, folder HIP 551-79-102 (Villa, Glen), box 2, Housing Improvement Grant Files 1968–74, Central California Agency, RG 75, BIA, NARA-San Bruno.

97. Letter from Area Director William E. Finale, BIA-Area IX, to Wallace Seal, County Coordinator, Community Action Agency, Inc., August 8, 1968, folder 005-Chron Copies, Housing Dvlp. 1968, box 1, Area Mission Correspondence 1964–72 (Accn. 75-00-004), BIA-Sacramento Area Office, RG 75, NARA-San Bruno.

98. Only about 25,000 units were actually built out of the projected 40,000. The Urban Institute report, 102.

99. "A Study of Urban Indian Problems," report requisitioned by Robert L. Bennett, Commissioner of Indian Affairs, December 31, 1968, folder Urban Indian Report-2/3/69, box 2, Area Mission Correspondence 1950–71, BIA-Sacramento Area Office; Report on Accomplishments of the Bureau of Indian Affairs, 1953–59, June 11, 1959, folder 344.2 Accomplishment Reports, Annually [1955–67], box 2, Area Mission Correspondence 1948–70, BIA-Sacramento Area Office, NARA-San Bruno.

100. "Evaluation Report: Indian Housing Study," Program Planning and Evaluation Branch, HUD-Region IX, August 1972, 13, folder Indian Programs, box 12, Regional Administrator Program subject files 1965–2003 (ARC 7787131), HUD-Region IX (San Francisco), NARA-San Bruno.

101. Marshall Kaplan, Gans, and Kahn, *Oglala Sioux Model Reservation Program: The Development Potential of the Pine Ridge Indian Reservation*, Planning Phase Report, May 16, 1968.

102. National Savings and Loan League Community Development Divisions, "Proposal for Technical Services—Housing Planning, Design and Construction," January 9, 1976, folder 520, box 11, CCC.

103. "S-L Group Aids Housing Abroad and Now in US Too," *Washington Post*, June 1, 1974.

104. Statement of Paul G. Reilly on behalf of the National Savings and Loan League before the US Senate Committee on Interior and Insular Affairs,

Indian Affairs Subcommittee on Indian Housing Problem, May 1, 1975, folder 518, box 11, CCC.

105. June 1, 1974.

106. Statement of Paul G. Reilly, May 1, 1975.

107. "Savings and Loan Feasibility on Indian Reservations, February 22, 1973," Contract between National League of Insured Savings Associations and the US Department of the Interior—Bureau of Indian Affairs, folder 518, box 11, CCC.

108. Ibid.

109. Richard Nixon: "Statement about Signing the Indian Financing Act of 1974," April 13, 1974, Gerhard Peters and John T. Woolley, The American Presidency Project, accessed January 1, 2012, http://www.presidency.ucsb.edu/ws/?pid=4174.

110. Statement of Paul G. Reilly, May 1, 1975.

111. Letter from G. Ronald Peake, Chief, Division of Housing Assistance, BIA, to Richard Knight, vice president, International Division, National Savings and Loan League, Washington, DC, October 2, 1974, folder 509.5, box 11, CCC.

112. The two major exceptions to the trust system were Alaskan Natives and Pueblo Indians. The Alaska Natives Claims Settlement Act of 1971 (along with amendments in 1987) removed all aboriginal rights to lands in Alaska and replaced them with village and regional corporations; Natives held corporate stock and enjoyed protection against alienation through a system of bylaws. New Mexico Pueblos communally owned land with fee simple title (not in trust by the US government).

113. "American Indians Betrayed Again," *Chicago Tribune*, May 19, 1982, A21.

114. "Federal Budget Blade Falls on Aid to Indians," *Chicago Tribune*, November 8, 1981, B12.

115. "Reagan Vows to Aid Indians, but Runs into Skepticism," *Washington Post*, January 18, 1983, A9; "Economy Carves New Trail of Tears for Tribe," *New York Times*, January 31, 1983, A1.

116. "Story of American Indian Still a 'Trail of Tears,'" *Chicago Tribune*, February 27, 1983, 1.

117. Briefing Book 1987, 8–9, folder Region IX–Briefing Books, box 3, Regional Administrator Program subject files, 1965–2003 (ARC7787131), HUD–Region IX (San Francisco), NARA–San Bruno.

118. Prepared statement by W. Ron Allen, president of the National Congress of American Indians, March 12, 1997, Joint Hearing before the Committee on Indian Affairs, US Senate and the Committee on Banking, Housing and Urban Affairs, US Senate, 105th Cong., 1st sess., March 12, 1997, 108–114.

119. Urban American Indians and Alaska Natives had significantly different housing experiences from the Native populations discussed here, with roughly 51% of the former owning in 1996, despite a majority of such

households being above 95% of area media income. Urban AIAN dwellers more closely followed the pattern of African American homeownership, with high aspiration and low achievement of the so-called American dream. Three-fourths of all AIANs claimed to prefer ownership over rentals, for instance, and two-thirds of one interview pool indicated they preferred single-family homes over all other types. The Urban Institute, 148–149.

120. Listokin, 195.

121. Interestingly, section 184 permitted the alienation of tribal trust and allotted trust land in default, although ownership would need to be transferred to another Native American buyer. This legal change made land a security for more liquid assets, as opposed to a resource to be conserved. Washington State also included section-184 insurance for non-Native American properties off reservation trust land for tribal members such as former and current BIA workers starting June 2005. *Our Home: Section 184 Indian Home Loan Guarantee Program Final Guidebook,* Our Home series (Washington, DC: HUD, 1996), introductory letter, 1–3, 2–5; "For Native Americans, Buying Has Become Easier," *New York Times,* September 18, 2005, K10.

122. HUD Office of Native American Programs, *Our Home: Achieving the Native American Dream of Homeownership,* Our Home series (Washington, DC: HUD,1995), 4.

123. Ibid., 5.

124. Ibid., 15.

125. An "Indian area" is defined as the space within which an IHA or tribe provides housing through its authority as a sovereign nation, and includes any land held in trust by the federal government and fee simple land, so long as they are within the jurisdiction of the IHA or tribe. *Our Home: Section 184 Indian Home Loan Guarantee Program Final Guidebook,* 1–1, 1–4.

126. Ibid.

127. Elem Pomo site problems came to HUD's attention when a newspaper article claimed violent disputes over casino profits might stem from health issues and exposure to contaminants. "Clear Lake Pomo Indians Blame Mercury," *San Francisco Chronicle,* n.d.; memo from Robert G. Barth at SFCPOST to C. Raphael Mecham at PHXPOST, November 3, 1995, folder Gaming Dispute Elem Indians, box 12, Regional Administrator Program subject files 1965–2003 (ARC 7787131), HUD–Region IX (San Francisco), NARA–San Bruno.

128. The Urban Institute, 179. Section 502 of the Housing Act of 1949 was amended in 1990 to emphasize the priority given to first-time buyers and to provide government loan guaranties for private lenders rather than a direct home loan to the prospective owner. General Accounting Office, *Native American Housing: VA Could Address Some Barriers to Participation in Direct Loan Program* (Washington, DC, 2002), 19.

129. Listokin, 229.

130. National Indian Justice Center, *Our Home: Providing the Legal Infrastructure Necessary for Private Financing,* Our Home series (Washington, DC: HUD, 1996).

131. Richard Harris and Godwin Arku, "Housing and Economic Development: The Evolution of an Idea since 1945," *Habitat International* 30 (2006), 1013.

132. Michele Alacevich, *The Political Economy of the World Bank: The Early Years* (Palo Alto, CA, and Washington, DC: Stanford University Press and the World Bank, 2007).

133. Bueneman, 23.

134. Richard J. Margolis, *Something to Build On: The Future of Self-Help Housing in the Struggle against Poverty* (Washington, DC: International Self-Help Housing Associates, 1967), 66.

135. Peter M. Ward cites Hans Harms in this quote. Ward, 286.

136. The Housing Assistance Council dates this program to 1933, whereas John F. C. Turner claims it happened in 1931–32, with Eleanor Roosevelt's assistance. Housing Assistance Council, *A Brief and Selective Historical Outline of Rural Mutual Self-Help Housing in the United States* (Washington, DC: Housing Assistance Council, 2004), 2; John F. C. Turner, "Self-Help Housing," in Willem Van Vliet, ed., *The Encyclopedia of Housing* (Thousand Oaks, CA: Sage Publications, 1998), 528.

137. The program eventually transitioned in 1962 to integrated housing projects, but only African Americans were eligible the first twelve years. "Amateurs Work in Homes Project—Do-It-Yourself Group Finds Building Can Be Success," *New York Times*, May 20, 1962, R16.

138. Quote from newspaper article, not directly from Blackburn. "Undereducated's Plight Spurs System for Success," *Chicago Daily Defender,* June 28, 1969, 32; "Amateurs Work in Homes Project," R16.

139. "Slum Therapy: Indianapolis Negroes Build Their Own Homes with 'Assembly Line'; 'Sweat Equity' Takes Place of Cash down Payments by Low-Income Residents," *Wall Street Journal*, November 13, 1967, 1.

140. Ibid.

141. "Self-Help Home Ownership Program Brings New Life to Slum Dwellers," *Chicago Daily Defender*, August 23, 1967, 8.

142. "Romney Praises Homes for Poor," *New York Times*, September 19, 1967, 30.

143. Art Collings, *A Brief and Selective Historical Outline of Rural Mutual Self-Help Housing in the United States*, 8th ed. (Washington, DC: Housing Assistance Council, 2004), 2–6.

144. Report of the First National Conference on Self Help Housing, December 6–9, 1965, Warrenton, Virginia, appendix B, AFSC.

145. Margolis.

146. Joseph Burstein, "New Techniques in Public Housing: Part 2: The Federal Role," *Law and Contemporary Problems* 32, no. 3 (Summer, 1967): 538–539.

147. This exchange eventually came full circle when the Turnkey III Homeownership Program was made applicable to Indian housing programs.

Mark K. Ulmer, "The Legal Origins and Nature of Indian Housing Author-ities and the HUD Indian Housing Programs," *American Indian Law Review* 13, no. 2 (1987/1988): 111. For a full directory of Turnkey Programs, see *Special Report: Turnkey Programs, Housing Act of 1949 Development Progress Directory* (Washington, DC: Department of Housing and Urban Develop-ment, Housing Production and Mortgage Credit, FHA Division of Research and Statistics, December 31, 1972).

148. "Buying from Developers: A New Approach to Public Housing; How the 'Turnkey' Method Works—a Guide to Developers and Builders," HUD, Public Housing Administration, Washington, DC, April 15, 1966, folder Turnkey Indian Housing, box 22, RG 75, NARA-DC.

149. "Turnkey III Homeownership Opportunities for Indian Families," HUD website, http://portal.hud.gov/hudportal/HUD?src=/programdescription /turnkey3, accessed February 1, 2014.

150. Irving H. Welfeld, "Section 235: Home Mortgage Interest Reduction," in Willem van Vliet, ed., *The Encyclopedia of Housing* (Thousand Oaks, CA: Sage Publications, 1998), 514–515.

151. "Urban Homesteading: A Guide for Local Officials," US Department of Housing and Urban Development, Office of Community Planning and Development, 1987.

152. *The Urban Homesteading Catalogue*, vol. 1 (Washington, DC: US Department of Housing and Urban Development, Office of Policy Development and Research, 1977), i–vi, 14–15.

153. *Housing Affairs Letter*, June 2, 1995, 7, folder HUD "Scandals," 1989–99, box 4, Regional Administrator Program subject files, 1965–2003 (ARC 7787131), HUD–Region IX (San Francisco), NARA–San Bruno.

154. William C. Apgar and Matthew Franklin, "Creating a New Federal Housing Corporation: A Summary of Eight Public Forums on the Future of FHA," US Department of Housing and Urban Development and the Joint Center for Housing Studies at Harvard University, 1995, 18.

155. Ingrid Gould Ellen, John Napier Tye, and Mark A. Willis, "The Secondary Market for Housing Finance in the United States: A Brief Overview," in Susan M. Wachter and Marvin M. Smith, eds., *The American Mortgage System: Crisis and Reform* (Philadelphia: University of Pennsylvania Press, 2011), 12.

156. Richard Ronald, *The Ideology of Homeownership: Homeowner Societies and the Role of Housing* (New York: Palgrave Macmillan, 2008), 148.

157. Matthew Lasner, *High Life: Condo Living in the Suburban Century* (New Haven: Yale University Press, 2012).

158. *A Special Letter from the Secretary: 30th Anniversary*, Washington, DC, HUD, October 1995, p. 2, folder HUD Secretaries S. Pierce, Jack Kemp, Andrew Cuomo, box 4, box 4, Regional Administrator Program subject files, 1965–2003 (ARC 7787131), HUD–Region IX (San Francisco), NARA–San Bruno.

159. "The National Homeownership Strategy: Partners in the American Dream," HUD, May 1995.

160. "Greenspan Attacks Bad Underwriting," and "Agency, Greenspan Disagree on Risk," *Housing Affairs Letter*, October 24, 1997, p. 7, folder HUD "Scandals" 1989–99, box 4, Regional Administrator Program subject files, 1965–2003 (ARC 7787131), HUD–Region IX (San Francisco), NARA–San Bruno.

161. Ibid.

162. Local Partnership Event Planning Guide, *National Homeownership Week: Making the American Dream a Reality*, June 5–12, 1999, sponsored by the National Partners in Homeownership, 18.

163. *Vision for Change: The Story of HUD's Transformation*, HUD, 2000, 64, folder Re-called Publications Issued by Sec. A. Cuomo, box 4, Regional Administrator Program subject files, 1965–2003 (ARC 7787131), HUD–Region IX (San Francisco), NARA–San Bruno.

164. Violet Law, "Section 8 Homeownership Program: Is the Push for Homeownership Helping or Hurting?" *Shelterforce* 136 (July/August 2004), accessed June 2, 2012, http://www.shelterforce.com/online/issues/136/section8.html.

165. Peter M. Ward, "Informality of Housing Production at the Urban-Rural Interface: The 'Not So Strange Case' of the Texas *Colonias*," in Ananya Roy and Nezar AlSayyad, eds., *Urban Informality: Transnational Perspectives from the Middle East, Latin America, and South Asia* (Lanham, MD: Lexington Books, 2004), 247.

166. The Money Smart Financial Education Curriculum also targeted farm workers and public housing residents.

167. "Delivering Results to Colonias and Farmworker Communities," HUD, 2004, 13.

168. *Economic Benefits of Increasing Minority Homeownership*, HUD Report summary in "Minority Homeownership on Stage," *Housing Affairs Letter*, October 18, 2002, 2, folder December 2001–February 2002 Regional Director Richard Mallory, box 4, Regional Administrator Program subject files, 1965–2003 (ARC 7787131), HUD–Region IX (San Francisco), NARA–San Bruno.

169. Chris Warren, "American Dream Builder," *New York Stock Exchange Magazine*, May 2005, 32–36.

170. The quote is from the commission's summary of Mozilo's testimony. *The Financial Crisis Inquiry Report: Final Report of the National Commission on the Causes of the Financial and Economic Crisis in the United States* (Washington, DC: Government Printing Office, 2011), 105.

CHAPTER SIX

1. John Williamson, "What Should the World Bank Think about the Washington Consensus?" Peterson Institute for International Economics, July

1999; accessed May 13, 2013, http://www.iie.com/publications/papers/paper.cfm?researchid=351.

2. Ibid.

3. Gilbert, "Promoting Rental Housing: An International Agenda," in J. D. Hulchanski and M. Shapcott, eds., *Finding Room: Policy Options for a Canadian Housing Strategy* (Toronto: University of Toronto Centre for Urban and Community Studies, 2004), 212.

4. Cecilia Zanetta, *The Influence of the World Bank on National Housing and Urban Policies: The Case of Mexico and Argentina during the 1990s* (Aldershot, Hampshire: Ashgate, 2004), 3; Joseph Stiglitz, "Scan Globally, Reinvent Locally: Knowledge Infrastructure and the Localization of Knowledge," Keynote address, First Global Development Network Conference, Bonn, December 1999, 8, as cited in Alan Gilbert, "Learning from Others: The Spread of Capital Housing Subsidies," *International Planning Studies 9*, nos. 2–3 (2004): 200; last quote, 212.

5. See World Bank/IFC Archives, Oral History Program, transcript of interview with Burke Knapp (New York: Columbia University Oral History Research Office, July 1961), 36. Quote from United States, *Foreign Relations of the United States, 1951*, vol. 2, *The United Nations; The Western Hemisphere* (Washington, DC: Government Printing Office, 1952), 35ff.

6. Devesh Kapur, John Prior Lewis, and Richard Charles Webb, eds., *The World Bank: Its First Half Century* (Washington, DC: Brookings Institution Press, 1997), 169.

7. Ibid., 169–170.

8. Ibid., 171.

9. Interview with Burke Knapp, 34.

10. Knapp, 40.

11. Many Bank officials—Knapp included—worked in the State Department prior to their time at the Bank. Ibid.

12. Michael Cohen, *Learning by Doing: World Bank Lending for Urban Development, 1972–82* (Washington, DC: World Bank, 1983), 1.

13. Kapur et al., 317.

14. From 1972 to 1981, 51% of all urban development projects were for housing (or 46% of all urban development lending). Ibid.

15. Edward Ramsamy, *The World Bank and Urban Development: From Projects to Policy* (New York: Routledge, 2006) 79–82. For a longer history of evolving expert ideas about housing as economic development, see Richard Harris and Godwin Arku, "Housing and Economic Development: The Evolution of an Idea since 1945," *Habitat International 30* (2006): 1007–1017.

16. Michael Cohen, "Aid, Density, and Urban Form: Anticipating Dakar," *Built Environment 33*, no. 2 (May 31, 2007): 145.

17. World Bank, *Senegal: Sites and Services Project* (Washington, DC: World Bank, 1983), http://documents.worldbank.org/curated/en/1983/10/1560198/senegal-sites-services-project, 57, 69.

18. Ibid., 7.
19. This is not to say that such negotiations precluded violent conflicts over landownership. See Mohamadou Abdoul, "Urban Development and Urban Informalities: Pikine, Senegal," in Abdoumaliq Simone and Abdelghani Abouhani, eds., *Urban Africa: Changing Contours of Survival in the City* (Dakar: CODESRIA, 2005), 241. For more on the evolution of Cap Vert, see Roger Navarro, "'Irrégularité urbaine' et genèse de l'africanité urbaine au Cap Vert (Sénégal)," in Catherine Coquery-Vidrovitch and Serge Nedelec, eds., *Tiers-mondes: L'informel en question?* (Paris: L'Harmattan, 1991).
20. World Bank, *Senegal: Sites and Services Project*, 71.
21. Ibid., 65, 73.
22. Ibid., 6.
23. International Bank for Reconstruction and Development, *Senegal: Tradition, Diversification, and Economic Development* (Washington, DC: IBRD, 1974), 121.
24. World Bank, *Senegal: Sites and Services Project*, 72–73.
25. Dates are project approval years. Alongside projects devoted to sites and services specifically, the World Bank also had numerous urban development projects that incorporated sites-and-services techniques. Later projects are not included in this list. Projects and Operations database, World Bank, 1947–current, http://www.worldbank.org/projects, August 15, 2013; Ramsamy, 93; Robert M. Buckley and Jerry Kalarickal, eds., *Thirty Years of World Bank Shelter Lending: What Have We Learned?* (Washington, DC: World Bank, 2006), 18. Dollars in 2013 currency using the US inflation calculator available at http://www.usinflationcalculator.com/.
26. Harris and Arku, 908–909. Urban lending only made up 4.1% of all Bank lending in fiscal 1981, for example. Cohen, *Learning by Doing*, 2.
27. Kapur et al., 263–264.
28. World Bank, Project Completion Report, *Botswana: Francistown Urban Project* (Credit 471-BT), February 25, 1983, 10.
29. Ibid., iv.
30. R. S. DeVoy, USAID, *Botswana Shelter Sector Assessment*, June 1979; CDM and Associates report for USAID, *Economic and Affordability Analysis of Sanitation Alternatives for Self-Help Housing Areas in Botswana*, WASH Field Report 148, January 1986, Development Experience Clearinghouse, USAID.
31. The certificate of right was a special government title given to low-income households specifically to denote security of tenure. This was different from the renewable residential lease of ninety-nine years for higher income groups, called a fixed term grant and modeled after the former colonial British system.
32. World Bank, Project Completion Report, *Tanzania—First National Sites and Services Project* (Credit 495-TA), February 15, 1984, 11.
33. World Bank, Project Completion Report, *Zambia: Lusaka Squatter Upgrading and Site and Services Project* (Loan 1057-ZA), June 30, 1983, 14–15.

34. Dollar amount converted to 2013 dollars. Original costs were $28.5 million in 1975 and $69.4 million in 1978. World Bank Operations Evaluation Department, *Kenya Impact Evaluation Report: Development of Housing, Water Supply, and Sanitation in Nairobi* (Washington, DC: April 25, 1996), 9–11, 16.

35. Ibid., 42.

36. World Bank, *Indonesia Impact Evaluation Report: Enhancing the Quality of Life in Urban Indonesia—The Legacy of Kampung Improvement Program* (Washington, DC: Operations Evaluation Department of the World Bank, June 29, 1995), 58. See also *Report and Recommendation of the President of the IBRD to the Executive Directors on a Proposed Loan to the Republic of Indonesia for a Second Urban Development Project* (Washington, DC: World Bank, October 7, 1976).

37. World Bank, *Indonesia Impact Evaluation Report*, 54.

38. Ibid., 71.

39. Memo, K. A. Bohr and D. Strombom, Philippines: Tondo Project, Manila, Back-to-Office Report, March 11, 1974, Manila Urban Development Project, Philippines, P004445, Loan 1272 / Loan 1282-Correspondence, vol. 1, World Bank Group Archives (hereafter WBGA).

40. Zone One Tondo Organization, *ZOTO Is People's Power* (Manila, 1973). This collection of writings has no named author but is rather the first in a series of bound collections of ZOTO reports intended to teach others about radical squatter organization.

41. Greg Bankoff, "Constructing Vulnerability: The Historical, Natural and Social Generation of Flooding in Metropolitan Manila," *Disasters* 27, no. 3 (2003): 103.

42. Ibid.

43. Responses to questions posed by the World Bank, October 31, 1973, Manila Urban Development Project, Philippines, P004445, Loan 1272 / Loan 1282-Correspondence, vol. 1, WBGA.

44. Quote from Finance Minister Cesar Virata's records of annual meeting with Robert McNamara on September 29, 1972. Kapur et al., 558.

45. Kapur et al., 558.

46. These agencies were the People's Homesite and Housing Corporation, the Presidential Assistant on Housing and Resettlement Agency, the Tondo Foreshore Development Authority, the Central Institute for the Training and Relocation of Urban Squatters, the Presidential Committee for Housing and Urban Resettlement, the Sapang Palay Development Committee, and the Inter-Agency Task Force to Undertake the Relocation of Families in Barrio Nabacaan, Villanueva, Misamis Oriental. *National Housing Authority Primer* (Quezon City: NHA Information Division, 2010), 15, Records of the National Housing Authority.

47. Later administrations tried to expand these sorts of government-backed private operations to low- and middle-income mass housing projects, mostly through the operation of credit insurance and mortgage guaranties for

private developers (Home Guaranty Corporation, 2000– and its predecessors, the Home Financing Commission, 1950– and the Home Insurance and Guaranty Corporation, 1986–). Corazon Aquino's administration also nurtured social housing programs for low-income families, including the provision of amortization support and development financing (Social Housing Finance Corporation, 2004–), later managed centrally by a new agency, the HUD Coordinating Council (1986–). Republic of the Philippines Office of the President, *Key Shelter Agencies* (Quezon City: NHA Information Division, 2011), NHA.

48. Quoted in Richard P. Claude and Thomas B. Jabine, "Exploring Human Rights Issues with Statistics," from Jabine and Claude, eds., *Human Rights and Statistics: Getting the Record Straight* (Philadelphia: University of Pennsylvania Press, 1992), 9.

49. "Report and Recommendation of the President of the International Bank for Reconstruction and Development to the Executive Directors on a Proposed Loan to the Republic of the Philippines for a Second Urban Development Project," December 7, 1978, World Bank Online Project Archives.

50. Philippines Second Urban Development Project Staff Appraisal Report, World Bank, December 1, 1978, 42, World Bank Online Project Archives.

51. Ibid., 3.

52. Ibid., in order, 42, 7.

53. *Kenya Impact Evaluation Report*, 44.

54. World Bank, *Housing: Enabling Markets to Work* (Washington, DC: International Bank for Reconstruction and Development, 1993), 5–6.

55. Ibid., 34.

56. Bertrand Renaud, "Another Look at Housing Finance in Developing Countries," *Cities* 4, no. 1 (February 1987): 28–34.

57. Robert Buckley, Loïc Chiquier, and Michael J. Lea, "Housing Finance and the Economy," in Chiquier and Lea, eds., *Housing Finance Policy in Emerging Markets* (Washington, DC: World Bank, 2009), 10.

58. Finance and Private Sector Development Unit, South Asia, World Bank, *Project Appraisal Document on a Proposed Credit in the Amount of SDR 66.1 Million [US $100 million] to the Republic of India for a Low Income Housing Finance Project*, April 18, 2013, n.p. See also United Nations Centre for Human Settlements, *The Global Strategy for Shelter to the Year 2000* (Nairobi: UN-HABITAT, 1990); United Nations Human Settlements Programme, *The Challenge of Slums: Global Report on Human Settlements, 2003* (Sterling, VA: Earthscan, 2003).

59. First statistic from Harris and Arku, 908. Second from World Bank, *Housing*, 6.

60. Robert M. Buckley and Jerry Kalarickal, eds., *Thirty Years of World Bank Shelter Lending: What Have We Learned?* (Washington, DC: World Bank, 2006), xii.

61. Ira Gary Peppercorn and Claude Taffin, *Rental Housing: Lessons from International Experience and Policies for Emerging Markets* (Washington, DC: World Bank, 2013), ix.
62. Ibid.
63. USAID Office of Private Resources, "An Introduction to the Overseas Private Investment Corporation," March 1970.
64. Overseas Private Investment Corporation, *Bridging the Housing Gap in Emerging Markets*, 1–2.
65. Ibid.
66. Overseas Private Investment Corporation, "Housing and Mortgage Financing," n.d., accessed October 1, 2010, http://www.opic.gov/financing/loan -structures/housing-mortgage-financing.
67. Ibid., 4–6.
68. European organizations like the British Royal Institute of Chartered Surveyors, the German Pfandbrief Association, and the European Group of Valuers Associations all participated, and they carried with them nineteenth-century systems of titling like the British-Australian Torrens system. Growth market economies like South Korea, meanwhile, brought traces of older Japanese land laws into debate. (These laws were themselves rooted in Meiji-era international exchanges with Prussians in particular); http://www.appraisalinstitute.org/about/history.aspx.
69. Broad Cove Partners, home page, accessed October 1, 2010, http://www .broadcove.com.
70. Overseas Private Investment Corporation, "Highlights," March 2007, 2.
71. *HUD: International—Meeting the Global Challenge*, HUD Office of Policy Development and Research, December 2000, 50–51, folder Re-called Publications Issued by Sec. A. Cuomo, box 4, Regional Administrator Program subject files, 1965–2003 (ARC 7787131), HUD–Region IX (San Francisco), NARA–San Bruno.
72. Ibid., 34–36.
73. Ibid., ii.
74. Quoted in Financial Crisis Inquiry Commission, *The Financial Crisis Inquiry Report: Final Report of the National Commission on the Causes of the Financial and Economic Crisis in the United States* (Washington, DC: US Government Printing Office, 2011), 104. See also Ashok Bardhan and Dwight Jaffee, "The Impact of Capital Flows and Foreign Financing on US Mortgage and Treasury Interest Rates," *Research Institute for Housing America*, 2007 report; and James Barth, *The Rise and Fall of the US Mortgage and Credit Markets: A Comprehensive Analysis of the Market Meltdown* (Indianapolis: Wiley, 2009).
75. Richard Harris, "International Policy for Urban Housing Markets in the Global South since 1945," in Faranak Miraftab and Neema Kudva, eds., *Cities of the Global South Reader* (New York: Routledge, in press). Many thanks to Richard Harris for sharing this article prepublication.

76. Anonymous interviewee, Northville V in Batia, Bocaue, Bulacan, Philippines, January 8, 2013.

CONCLUSION

1. Hearings before a Subcommittee of the Committee on Banking and Currency, US Senate, 88th Cong., 1st sess., April 22, 23, 24, 25, 1963, 24.
2. Lynn M. Fisher and Austin J. Jaffe, "Determinants of International Home Ownership Rates," and Soula Proxenos, "Homeownership Rates: A Global Perspective," in *Housing Finance International* (September 2003); Carl R. Gwin and Seow-Eng Ong, "Do We Really Understand Home Ownership Rates? An International Study," Working Paper Series, Baylor University, 2004; Steven C. Bourassa, Donald R. Haurin, Patric H. Hendershott, and Martin Hoesli, "Determinants of the Homeownership Rate: A Survey of Recent Contributions," February 11, 2013, Swiss Finance Institute Research Paper no. 11-49, available at SSRN: http://ssrn.com/abstract=1953196 or http://dx.doi.org/10.2139/ssrn.1953196.
3. Kristopher S. Gerardi, Christopher L. Foote, and Paul S. Willen, "Reasonable People Did Disagree: Optimism and Pessimism about the US Housing Market before the Crash," in Susan M. Wachter and Marvin M. Smith, eds., *The American Mortgage System: Crisis and Reform* (Philadelphia: University of Pennsylvania Press, 2011), 26–59.

Index

Page numbers in italics indicate figures.

Abercrombie, Patrick, 19, 21, 24–25, 32, 250n39, 253n82
Abrams, Charles: federal government's link with business interests and, 132, 155–56; global middle-class homeownership and, 156; homeownership and, 168, 286n5; on housing and community development, 168–69; housing program expertise and, 233; human rights and, 235; property rights and, 168; transnational exchanges on homeownership and, 168; tropical housing research and, 115, 119; US advisors and, 51, 96; US overseas housing programs and, 4–5, 214
Ackerman, Frederick L., 15, 248n12
Adams, Frederick J., 119
Adams, Jon L., 182
ADB (Asian Development Bank), 210
Africa: aided self-help overseas housing programs in, *136*, 136–38, *137*; fair housing and, 179–80; federal aid for overseas homeownership and, 169; federal government's link with business interests and, 149; homeownership models and, 247n4; housing-productivity relationship research and, 182; "incremental housing model"

and, 218–19, 301n34; international dimension of racial inequalities in US homeownership and, 171–72; low-income urban housing programs and, 214–16; mass homeownership and, 215; overseas S&L programs and, 156; property rights and housing and, 215, 218, 300n19, 300n31; South Africa and, 92, 139, 179–80, 247n4; sub-Saharan Africa and, 10, 211; suburbanization and, 149, 169; transnational exchanges and, 183; tropical housing research and, 94; "tropical region" concept and, 92; upgrading projects and, 215, 217–19; US advisors and, 4–5, 96; US business interests overseas and, 139, 149, 164; US overseas housing programs and, *136*, 136–38, *137*; World Bank sites-and-services projects and, 11–12, 214–16, 218–19, 301n34. *See also specific countries*
African Americans: aided self-help housing programs and, 195; homeownership rates and, 177; inner-city communities of color homeownership programs, 195; international dimension of racial inequalities in US homeownership and, 91, 123, 170–73; loan denial rates and, 194;

305

homeowners and, 178; self-help housing programs and, 177–78, 178–79, 199;
self-help modernization program and,
186–87, *187*, *188*; self-help project assessment and, 185–86; self-sufficiency
and, 180, 186, 192, 200; S&L assistance
and, 43, 189–91; spatial integration and,
167, 175–80; split public-private system
and, 17, 132, 172–74, 178; termination
policy and, 181–82, 291n69; third world
and, 286n2; transnational exchanges
and, 168–69, 172, 177–80, 183–84,
189–90, 195, 199–200, 230; USAID and,
186; VA and, 6, 16, 173; white middle-
class and, 6, 9, 100, 171, 173–75, 190;
World Bank and, 186. *See also* inner-city
communities of color, and homeownership programs; Native Americans,
and homeownership; public housing
programs, US
United States homeownership model (mass
homeownership). *See* mass homeownership (US homeownership model)
United States Housing Authority (USHA),
6–7, 16
United States International Housing
Service, 3–4
United States Operations Mission (USOM),
65–66, 73, 106
UNKRA (United Nations Korea Reconstruction Agency), 75–80, *77*, *78*, *79*, 84,
264n116
UNRRA (United Nations Rehabilitation
and Relief Administration), 42, 54, *55*,
259n33
upgrading projects (modernization discourse): Africa and, 215, 217–19; decolonization era overseas homeownership
and, 100, 106, 112, 120, *121*, *122*; Latin
America and, 106; relocation programs
and, 211–12; self-help overseas housing
programs and, 186–87, *187*, *188*; South/
Southeast Asia and, 112, 116, 120, *121*,
122, 124, 213, 215, 217–21, 224–25;
World Bank and, 7, 164, 208, 213, 215,
217–19, 225
Urban and Environmental Credit Program
of 1998, 163–64
Urban Homesteading Demonstration, 201
Urban Renewal Administration, 3
Uruguay, 135–36

USAID (United States Agency for International Development): aided self-help
overseas housing programs and, 195;
American dream of homeownership
and, 228; consensus and, 207–8, 211;
decolonization era homeownership
and, 96–97; development programs and,
172; fact-gathering missions and, 122;
federal insurance for US businesses in
overseas homeownership programs and,
151–53, 155–57, 162, 283n89, 284n110;
housing-productivity relationship research and, 182; insurance overseas
homeownership programs and, 227–29;
low-income overseas homeownership
and, 161–64, 210, 217, 227–29; mass
homeownership and, 164–65, 230–31;
mortgage aid for overseas homeownership and, 148–50, 214; OPIC and, 208,
227–30; overseas S&L programs and,
158; South Korean housing programs
and, 82–83, 85; transnational exchanges
and, 189; tropical housing research and,
275n105; US domestic homeownership
and, 186; US overseas housing programs
and, 3–4, 5–6, 70, 96, 136–38, *137*, 157,
164–65
USHA (United States Housing Authority),
6–7, 16
USOM (United States Operations Mission),
65–66, 73, 106
US Steel company, 171
US-USSR Agreement on Cooperation in the
Field of Housing and Other Construction in 1974, 86
Uthwatt Report (GB), 33, 250n43, 254n84

Vale, Lawrence J., 174, 239
Veiller, Lawrence, 14–15
Venezuela, 97, 135–36, 150, 155, 183
Vereeniging Koloniaal Institute (Dutch
Colonial Institute), 94
Veterans Administration (VA): aided self-
help housing programs and, 195; domestic homeownership and, 6, 16, 173;
inner-city communities of color homeownership programs, 195; investment
guaranties and, 191; mortgage assistance and, 201; mortgage insurance
and, 6
Vietnam, 149, 169, 228

HISTORICAL STUDIES OF URBAN AMERICA
Edited by Lilia Fernández, Timothy J. Gilfoyle, Becky M. Nicolaides, and Amanda Seligman
James R. Grossman, editor emeritus

The Creative Destruction of Manhattan, 1900–1940
By Max Page

Streets, Railroads, and the Great Strike of 1877
By David O. Stowell

Faces along the Bar: Lore and Order in the Workingman's Saloon,
1870–1920
By Madelon Powers

Making the Second Ghetto: Race and Housing in Chicago, 1940–1960
By Arnold R. Hirsch

Smoldering City: Chicagoans and the Great Fire, 1871–1874
By Karen Sawislak

Modern Housing for America: Policy Struggles in the New Deal Era
By Gail Radford

Parish Boundaries: The Catholic Encounter with Race in the
Twentieth-Century Urban North
By John T. McGreevy